PATHS TOWARD A CLEARING

African Systems of Thought

General Editors
Charles S. Bird
Ivan Karp

Contributing Editors
Thomas O. Beidelman
James W. Fernandez
Luc de Heusch
John Middleton
Roy Willis

PATHS TOWARD A CLEARING

Radical Empiricism and Ethnographic Inquiry

MICHAEL JACKSON

INDIANA UNIVERSITY PRESS
Bloomington and Indianapolis

Manufactured in the United States of America

Library of Congress Cataloging-in-Publication Data
Jackson, Michael
Paths toward a clearing : radical empiricism and ethnographic
inquiry / Michael Jackson.
p. cm. — (African systems of thought)
Bibliography: p.
Includes index.
ISBN 0–253–33190–0. — ISBN 0–253–20534–4 (pbk.)
1. Kuranko (African people) 2. Ethnology—Philosophy.
3. Ethnophilosophy. 4. Knowledge, Theory of. I. Title.
II. Series.
DT516.45.K85J3 1989
306'.089963—dc19

88–46021
CIP

2   3   4   5   93   92

It is difficult not to notice a curious unrest in the philosophic atmosphere of the time, a loosening of old landmarks, a softening of oppositions, a mutual borrowing from one another on the part of systems anciently closed, and an interest in new suggestions, however vague, as if the one thing sure were the inadequacy of the extant school-solutions. The dissatisfaction with these seems due for the most part to a feeling that they are too abstract and academic. Life is confused and superabundant, and what the younger generation appears to crave is more of the temperament of life in its philosophy, even tho it were at some cost of logical rigor and of formal purity.

—William James (1976:21, originally published 1904)

CONTENTS

Preface

Although I studied anthropology as an undergraduate, many years passed and I traveled a long way before my interest in the subject came fully into focus. The turning point was 1964, when I was a volunteer community development worker with the United Nations Operation in the Congo (now Zaire). The country was in the throes of a widespread rebellion, and one of the few untroubled places I knew was a coffee plantation on the Lulua River in Kasai. The plantation had been abandoned by its Belgian owners two years before and brought back into production by a group of Franciscans, working with young Congolese men, many of whom had lost their homes and families in the fighting that had brought the secession of Kasai to an end.

Sometimes at night I would go down to the river to watch the hippos come ashore to browse. The grassland glittered with the light of fireflies, as if entire galaxies had disintegrated and fallen from the sky. Other evenings I listened with growing fascination to a Bena Lulua boy who explained to me the meaning of his initiation scars, the purpose of the statuettes I'd seen among the manioc, or the kaolin with which mourning women covered their faces. Or I read a dog-eared copy of *Les structures élémentaires de la parenté* I'd found in a bookcase in the main house, my imagination captured by the idea that beneath the empirical diversity of social life lay universal structuring principles of reciprocity and exchange. In this seemingly closed universe of elementary structures there was, however, Lévi-Strauss observed, "always some freedom of choice" (1969a:xxiii).

It was in this dual quest for universal "laws of the mind" and "the exigencies of social life," this dialectic of givenness and choice, that I rediscovered the allure and paradox of anthropology. For, as the anthropologist struggles to transcend his or her particular cultural background and field experiences in order to arrive at general truths, he or she is caught in a bind which is both epistemological and political because the assumption of a detached or universal view entails the presumption of cultural and intellectual privilege (Herzfeld 1987:3). It is the same dilemma which oppresses Western intellectuals who, while pursuing the humanist aim of establishing the equality of all people, are themselves living proof that all people are not equal, since their knowledge, abilities, and backgrounds are always particular and privileged (Sartre 1983:239–40).

The burden of this book is how one might adopt a universalistic standpoint without implying special claims either for the "truth" of one's view or the status of oneself.

As in the work of Vico, Tylor, Morgan, Bastian, Mauss, and Durkheim, the search for universal cultural patterns has always been constitutive of the anthropological project, and protests such as that of Boas against closed designs and invariant patterns have been followed by periods of renewed interest in what Wolf calls "the enduring features of the human psyche and sociality" (1964:20). Notions of

universal linguistic forms, biogenetic structures, basic needs, moral and develop-
mental patterns have all enjoyed their vogue. But many anthropologists have gone
about their task of totalizing cross-cultural comparison as though it were un-
problematic. Methodologically, it is often implied that anthropology grants us
a means of transcending our own cultural circumstances and entering empathically
into the lives of others. If there are obstacles to attaining this goal they are, one
gathers, technical rather than temperamental, matters of language and logistics
rather than of epistemology. With some notable exceptions (Devereux 1967, Fabian 1983, Herzfeld 1987, Said 1978), few anthropologists reflect deeply on the
contradiction between the presumed coevalness that permits an ethnographer to
have an understanding of the people he or she lives with and the images of radical
otherness that pervade much ethnographic writing, where "shame" cultures are
contrasted with "guilt" cultures (Herzfeld 1987:1–27), "mortuary rituals" are semantically segregated from "funerals" (Danforth 1982:5–7), and exotic labels such
as "witchcraft," "sorcery," and "totemism" create an impression that *they* are utterly
unlike *us* (Lévi-Strauss 1969b). To what extent do anthropologists unwittingly abet
the distorting tendencies of the popular media, where Third World peoples are
typecast as political refugees and famine victims, defined in terms of the *absence*
of freedom, as *lacking* in economic rationality, *wanting* in resources, illiterate, im-
poverished, undernourished (Freire 1972:21–29)? Seen as historically peripheral,
they become for us negations of ourselves and needful of what we have. Specters
of the not-self or objects of our compassion, it makes little difference. Their voices
go unheard, their customs derided, their experiences masked, so that "humanity"
itself seems to belong only to the powerful and rich.

In this book I focus on experiences which ethnographers have in common with
the people they study, and I try to see how the anthropological project may be
more than the inadvertent or uncritical projection of "our" concerns and needs
onto "them." Accordingly, I emphasize the participatory side of fieldwork, the reflective dimension in theorizing, and the dialectic between the knowledge we construct of others and the knowledge they construct of themselves and of us.

The theoretical ideas which inform this work are drawn from the existentialist
and pragmatist traditions. But while my interest lies in the kind of metacultural
understanding that Sartre and Merleau-Ponty sought, this should not be construed
as a search for the *essence* of human Being but for ways of opening up dialogue
between people from different cultures or traditions, ways of *bringing into being*
modes of understanding which effectively go beyond the intellectual conventions
and political ideologies that circumscribe us all.[1]

Twenty-one years separate the red roads of Zaire, where I first chose my intellectual path, and the laterite roads of northeast Sierra Leone to which I returned
in 1985 for my fifth stint of fieldwork among the Kuranko. I wish to acknowledge
my gratitude to the Wenner-Gren Foundation for Anthropological Research and
the Australian Research Grants Committee for funding my 1985 research and to
Professor Roger Keesing and his colleagues in the Anthropology Department at the
Australian National University for granting me two summer fellowships (1986–87,

1987–88), intervals of comparative security during a three-year period of unemployment.

I dedicate this book to friends and family—Tom Beidelman, Wojciech Dabrowski, René Devisch, Kathy Golski, Ranajit and Mechtilde Guha, Christine Helliwell, Michael Herzfeld, Emily and D'arcy Jackson, Heidi Jackson, Ivan Karp, Douglas Lewis, Francine Lorimer, Judith Loveridge, Sewa and Rose Marah, Jadran Mimica, Brian Moeran, Keith Ridler, Tim Strong, Bob and Myrna Tonkinson, Anita Jacobson-Widding, Michael Young—"so that the path does not die" (*kile ka na faga*).

PATHS TOWARD A
CLEARING

ONE

Introduction

This book is a break in a journey—to take stock, to get my bearings, to survey the ground I have covered and the ground I have yet to cross. My ancestors, the Kuranko would say, have "gone ahead": Adorno, Devereux, Dewey, Foucault, Heidegger, Merleau-Ponty, Sartre, Turner. They have blazed trails. But we all must find our own way across the broken landscape, and by trial and error find the paths for ourselves.

My novel *Barawa, and the Ways Birds Fly in the Sky* (1986) was a point of no return, and of disenchantment. It ends at the edge of the sea: an ethnographer, unsure of his direction and identity, walking along the tide-line, looking down at a film of water that reflects "pale gray clouds in a cocoa-coloured sky." The image was meant to echo the close of Michel Foucault's *The Order of Things*, an image of man returned "to that serene non-existence in which he was formerly maintained by the imperious unity of Discourse," erased "like a face drawn in sand at the edge of the sea" (Foucault 1970:386,387). By grounding my narrative in the history of a place rather than the life of any one person, I also hoped to echo a view which the Kuranko might easily hold, of the subject as a "singularity" in the sense in which astronomers use the term: a point in space and time where experience is had, where the world happens upon itself, a place of intersection (Lévi-Strauss 1981:625–26).

But while I agree with both Foucault and Lévi-Strauss in eschewing any notion of the individual subject as the primary source and final arbiter of our understanding, I do not want to risk dissolving the lived *experience* of the subject into the anonymous field of discourse, allowing Episteme or Language or Mind to take on the epistemological privileges denied to consciousness and subjectivity.[1] In my view, notions such as Culture, Nature, Language, and Mind are to be regarded as instrumentalities, not finalities. Together with tools, physical skills, and practical knowledge, they belong to a world whose horizons are open, the quotidian world in which we live, adjusting our needs to the needs of others, testing our ideas against the exigencies of life. Concepts do not transcend this life-world, mirroring its essence or revealing its underlying laws. They cannot get us above or outside experience, only move us from one domain to another, making connections. Thought is like a path, says Heidegger, a way into and through the world, a movement toward a clearing. Thought is not a way out, and a philosophy which abstracts, "which seeks to elevate itself above the everydayness of the everyday, is empty" (Steiner 1978:81).

In this kind of *Lebensphilosophie*, the subject must figure, even if only as a necessary moment in the passage of objectivity toward objectivity, the point where
preexistent worlds enter our experience and are made over by us to others (Sartre
1968:97). But we have to go further, because human praxis does more than con-
serve the situation from whence it arises; *it surpasses it.* "For us," Sartre observes,
"man is characterized above all by his going beyond a situation, and by what he
succeeds in making of what he has been made—even if he never recognizes himself
in his objectification" (91). Adorno makes a similar point. Praxis, he notes, "is
characterized above all by the fact that the qualitatively new appears in it . . . it
is a movement which does not run its course in pure identity, the pure reproduction
of such as already was there" (Buck-Morss 1977:54).

It is because lived experience is never identical with the concepts we use to
grasp and represent it that I want to insist, along with Sartre and Adorno, on its
dialectical irreducibility.[2] Making lived experience the starting point in this book
should not, however, be taken to mean that I am according any epistemological
privileges or any particular ontological status to the experiencing *subject.* It is the
character of lived experience I want to explore, not the nature of man.

LIVED EXPERIENCE AND RADICAL EMPIRICISM

Lived experience overflows the boundaries of any one concept, any one person,
or any one society. As such, it brings us to a dialectical view of life which emphasizes the interplay rather than the identity of things, which denies any sure steading
to thought by placing it always within the precarious and destabilizing fields of history, biography, and time. Indeed, by forcing upon our attention the unrepeat-
ability of events, dialectical thought entails what Walter Benjamin called "a stubborn subversive protest against the typical, the classifiable" (Arendt 1968:45). It
remains skeptical of all efforts to reduce the diversity of experience to timeless categories and determinate theorems, to force life to be at the disposal of ideas.[3]

Dialectic philosophy, however, runs the risk of fetishizing thought as an act
of resistance to identity, conclusiveness, and closure. For this reason, I want to
stress that lived experience encompasses *both* the "rage for order" *and* the impulse
that drives us to unsettle or confound the fixed order of things. Lived experience
accommodates our shifting sense of ourselves as subjects and as objects, as acting
upon and being acted upon by the world, of living with and without certainty,
of belonging and being estranged, *yet resists arresting any one of these modes of experience in order to make it foundational to a theory of knowledge.*

Such an all-encompassing conception of experience avoids narrowing down
the field of experience to *either* the subject *or* the object, theory *or* practice, the
social *or* the individual, thought *or* feeling, form *or* flux. Phrased in this way, however, such a conception of experience is too general to be useful. Clearly, it must
be grounded somehow in the actual events, objects, and interpersonal relationships
that make up the quotidian world. But this requires apposite metaphors, particular
ground rules, and discursive techniques. I want to call this rather ad hoc methodol-

ogy and discursive style *radical empiricism,* a term William James coined to emphasize that experience includes "transitive" as well as "substantive" elements, conjunctions as well as disjunctions, and to encourage us to recover a lost sense of
the immediate, active, ambiguous "plenum of existence" in which all ideas and
intellectual constructions are grounded (James 1976; Edie 1965).

THE EXPERIENCE OF SELF AND OTHER

Radical empiricism is first and foremost "a philosophy of the *experience* of objects
and actions *in which the subject itself is a participant*" (Edie 1965:119).[4] This implies
that there is no constant, substantive "self" which can address constant, substantive "others" as objects of knowledge. We are continually being changed by as well
as changing the experience of others. "Our fields of experience," writes James,
"have no more definite boundaries than have our fields of view. Both are fringed
forever by a *more* that continuously develops, and that continuously supersedes
them as life proceeds" (James 1976:35). The "self" cannot, therefore, be treated
as a thing among things; it is a function of our involvement with others in a world
of diverse and ever-altering interests and situations.

The importance of this view for anthropology is that it stresses the ethnographer's *interactions* with those he or she lives with and studies, while urging us to
clarify the ways in which our knowledge is grounded in our practical, personal,
and participatory experience in the field as much as our detached observations.
Unlike traditional empiricism, which draws a definite boundary between observer
and observed, between method and object, radical empiricism denies the validity
of such cuts and makes the *interplay* between these domains the focus of its interest.
This is the same focus as in quantum mechanics. It is the *interaction* of observer
and observed which is crucial. The physicist participates in the reality under investigation; his or her methods alter and even constitute it. As Werner Heisenberg
puts it, "We can no longer speak of the behaviour of the particle independently
of the process of observation. As a final consequence, the natural laws formulated
mathematically in quantum theory no longer deal with the elementary particles
themselves *but with our knowledge of them*" (Heisenberg 1958:29, emphasis added).

While observation in physical science is one-way, and the relationship between observer and observed asymmetrical, anthropology involves *reciprocal* activity and *interexperience* (Devereux 1967:18–31). This makes the relationship between knower and known infinitely more complicated. Indeed, given the arduous
conditions of fieldwork, the ambiguity of conversations in a foreign tongue, differences of temperament, age, and gender between ourselves and our informants, and
the changing theoretical models we are heir to, it is likely that "objectivity" serves
more as a magical token, bolstering our sense of self in disorienting situations, than
as a scientific method for describing those situations as they really are. The orderly
systems and determinate structures we describe are not mirror images of social reality so much as defenses we build against the unsystematic, unstructured nature of
our *experiences* within that reality.[5] Theoretical schemes and the neutral, impersonal idioms we use in talking about them give us respite from the unmanageable

flux of lived experience, helping us create illusory word-worlds which we can more easily manage because they are cut off from the stream of life. In this sense, objectivity becomes a synonym for estrangement and neutrality a euphemism for indifference.

Our habit of excluding the lived experience of the observer from the field of the observed on the grounds that it is a "regettable disturbance" is, as George Devereux shows, a stratagem for alleviating anxiety, not a rule of scientific method. A radically empirical method *includes* the experience of the observer and defines the experimental field as one of interactions and intersubjectivity. Accordingly, we make ourselves experimental subjects and treat our experiences as primary data. Experience, in this sense, becomes a mode of experimentation, of testing and exploring the ways in which our experiences conjoin or connect us with others, rather than the ways they set us apart.[6] In this process we put ourselves on the line; we run the risk of having our sense of ourselves as different and distanced from the people we study dissolve, and with it all our pretensions to a supraempirical position, a knowledge that gets us above and beyond the temporality of human existence. As for our comparative method, it becomes less a matter of finding "objective" similarities and differences between other cultures than of exploring similarities and differences between our own experience and the experience of others. This, of course, demands the presence, not the absence, of the ethnographer.

A remarkable example of this approach is Renato Rosaldo's essay on Illongot headhunting. It is worth quoting at length:

> If you ask an older Illongot man of northern Luzon, Philippines, why he cuts off human heads, his answer is a one-liner on which no anthropologist can really elaborate: he says that rage, born of grief, impels him to kill his fellow human beings. The act of severing and tossing away the victim's head enables him, he says, to vent and hopefully throw away the anger of his bereavement. The job of cultural analysis, then, is to make this man's statement plausible and comprehensible. Yet further questioning reveals that he has little more to say about the connections between bereavement, rage, and headhunting, connections that seem so powerful to him as to be self-evident beyond explication. Either you understand it or you don't. And, in fact, for the longest time I simply did not.
>
> It was not until some 14 years after first recording this simple statement about grief and a headhunter's rage that I began to grasp its overwhelming force. For years I had thought that more verbal elaboration (which was not forthcoming) or another analytical level (which remained elusive) could better explain the kinds of things these older men, when enraged by grief, can do to their fellow human beings. *It was not until I was repositioned through lived experience* that I became better able to grasp that Illongot older men mean precisely what they say when they describe the anger in bereavement as the source of their desire to cut off human heads. (Rosaldo 1984:178–79, emphasis added)

The "lived experience" to which Rosaldo refers was his wife's death in northern Luzon in 1981. Through his own experience of bereavement he came to understand "the rage that can come with devastating loss" (180). Before this crisis, Rosaldo had tended to dismiss Illongot accounts of why they hunted heads "as too simple, thin, opaque, implausible, stereotypic, or otherwise unsatisfying" (179). His attempts at analysis emphasized notions of retribution, payback, exchange, and balancing a ledger, metaphors derived from his own culture which widened rather than closed the gap between his experience and the experience of the Illongot. After living through bereavement himself, Rosaldo saw things in a new light and began to perceive connections between Illongot experience and his own—the grounds of a common humanity.

Such a phenomenological perspective is not, however, without its risks. "Unsympathetic readers," Rosaldo notes, "could reduce [my] paper to an act of mourning or to a report on a personal discovery of the anger possible in bereavement" (185). But Rosaldo's essay does far more than this. It demonstrates the value of studying affect and will as well as thought and shows how our understanding always emerges out of our interactions and experiences with others in the everyday world: "most anthropologists write about death as if they were positioned as uninvolved spectators who have no lived experience that could provide knowledge about the cultural force of emotions" (193).

This approach to social life, beginning not with external social patternings but with the "personal and affective life" and how it is "actualized in and orders the shapes of social action over time" also characterizes Michelle Rosaldo's renowned study of the Illongot (1980:20). Michelle Rosaldo, however, emphasizes the ways in which the Illongot notion of anger (*liget*) "belongs to a unique semantic field" which does not parallel the English word *angry* in every respect (1980:22, 221–22). Nonetheless, it is acknowledged that *liget* and *anger*, though connoting culturally divergent meanings and contexts of use, overlap at certain points, allowing the European ethnographer purchase on the Illongot world. The point is that the term *liget* is used in many kinds of situations, some of which we would find strange, others of which we could readily identify with (27–28, 45–47 for examples).

Renato Rosaldo's essay reminds us of the continuity of experience across cultures and through time, the psychic unity of our species, the force of what William James called "conjunctive relations," which make it possible for us to reach into experiences as seemingly alien as headhunting. This emphasis on connectedness goes against the grain of traditional empiricism, which assumes that the knower and the known inhabit disconnected worlds and regards experience as something passively received rather than actively made, something that impresses itself upon our blank minds or overcomes us like sleep (James 1976:21–27; Dewey 1960:80; Schrag 1969:8). Rosaldo's essay also brings home to us the extent to which our thought is metaphorical and our choices of metaphor partly determinative of the kind of understanding we reach.

SENSES OF UNDERSTANDING

Radical empiricism seeks to grasp the ways in which ideas and words are wedded to the world in which we live, how they are grounded in the mundane events and experiences of everyday life. It follows the dictum of William Carlos Williams: "No ideas / but in things." It is not only the ideas and words of others that we subject to this scrutiny, but also our own. It is thus fascinating and pertinent to note how the separation of subject and object in traditional empiricism is in large measure a function of the sensory mode and metaphor it privileges: vision.

In formulating the empiricist canons of modern social science, John Locke wrote: "The perception of the mind is most aptly explained by words relating to the sight" (quoted in Fabian 1983:108).[7] Thus the plethora of terms in our Western epistemological vocabulary which evoke the notion of knowledge as seeing (eidos, eidetic, idea, ideation, intuition, theory, theorize) or refer to optics as a metaphor of understanding (reflect, speculate, focus, view, inspect, insight, outlook, perspective) (Edie 1963:552, 1976:174).[8]

This visualist bias has the effect of distancing the subject from the object, of seeing them as discontinuous entities. John Dewey explains the process:

> The theory of knowing is modeled after what was supposed to take place in the act of vision. The object refracts light to the eye and is seen; it makes a difference to the eye and to the person having an optical apparatus, but none to the thing seen. The real object is the object so fixed in its regal aloofness that it is a king to any beholding mind that may gaze upon it. A spectator theory of knowledge is the inevitable outcome. (1980:23)

"Visualism," to use Fabian's term, also implies a *spatialization* of consciousness in which knower and known are located at several removes from one another and regarded as essentially unalike, the one an impartial spectator, the other subject to his gaze (Bourdieu 1977:1; Turner 1985:178). For this reason, "visualism" is dehumanizing; it denies coevalness (Fabian 1983:108). It runs counter to Terence's great maxim *Homo sum: humani nil a me alienum puto* (I am human, and nothing human is alien to me).

The alienating effects of visualism can also be related to the impact of perspective and literacy upon our consciousness. As Sigfried Giedion shows, perspective (literally, "clear-seeing") becomes the principal Western conception of space from the early fifteenth century and has the immediate effect of privileging the way things appear from a fixed, detached point of view—that of the observer. "With the invention of perspective the modern notion of individualism found its artistic counterpart. Every element in a perspective representation is related to the unique point of view of the individual spectator" (Giedion 1941:31). Perspective, however, is not the space-conception of either the pre-Renaissance world or the preliterate world. Consider Christine Helliwell's vivid evocation of life in a Dayak longhouse in Kalimantan Barat (West Borneo). The "flow of sound and light is crucial," she writes; "the longhouse community as a whole is defined and encircled more by these two things than by anything else." Whereas previous ethnographers had compared Dayak longhouses to *lines* of privately owned, semidetached houses along a street, Helliwell concentrates her attention on "lived space," drawing on her own field experiences and emphasizing what is heard and felt as much as what is seen:

I recall, while living in the Gerai longhouse, writing letters back to Australia in which I constantly referred to the longhouse as a "community of voices," for I could think of no more apt way to describe the largely invisible group of which I found myself to be a part. Voices flow in a longhouse in a most extraordinary fashion; moving up and down its length in seeming monologue, they are in fact in continual dialogue with listeners who may be unseen but are always present. As such they create, more than does any other facet of longhouse life, a sense of community. Through the sounds of their voices neighbours two, three, four, or five apartments apart are tied into each other's world, into each other's company, as intimately as if they were in the same room. During my first two months in the longhouse, sharing the apartment of a Dayak household, I could not understand why my hostess was constantly engaged in talk with no one. She would give long descriptions of things that had happened to her during the day, of work she had to do, of the state of her feelings and so on, all the while standing or working alone in her longhouse apartment. To a Westerner, used to the idea that one's home stops at its walls, and that interaction beyond these involves a projection of the voice or of the self which makes impossible the continuation of normal domestic chores, her behaviour seemed eccentric to say the least. It was only much later, on my second fieldtrip, that I came to realise that the woman's apparent monologues *always* had an audience, and that they were a way of affirming and recreating the ties across apartments that made her a part of the longhouse as a whole rather than a member of an isolated household. In addition, I recognised with time that she was almost certainly responding to questions floating across apartment partitions that I, still bewildered and overwhelmed by the cacophony of sound that characterises longhouse life, was unable to distinguish. Eventually I too came to be able to separate out the distinct strands that were individual voices, which wove together magically in the air and flowed through the spaces of separate apartments. These were never raised as the dialogue moved through four or even five partitions, but their very muteness reinforced the sense of intimacy, of membership in a private, privileged world. Such conversations were to be taken up at will and put down again according to the demands of work or sleep: never forced, never demanding participation, but always gentle, generous in their reminder of a companionship constantly at hand. For me, even in memory they remain utterly compelling: the one aspect of longhouse life that distinguishes it most clearly from the Western world to which I have since returned. (Helliwell 1988)

My experience of living in a Kuranko village is very similar. Kuranko conceive of a community as a cluster of common centers connected by paths, a conception grounded in the physical layout of the village itself. A Kuranko village is made up of a number of open spaces called *luiye* around which are grouped circular thatched houses. The *luiye* are interconnected by a labyrinth of narrow lanes and dusty paths along which people move in the day-to-day round of village life.

In a Kuranko village, there is no one main path leading to a privileged vantage point where one can take up the position of spectator or observer. On the contrary, the structure of the village enforces participation. Even from a hammock on a veranda, looking out into a *luiye*, half-hidden by the low eaves of the house, one is part of the goings on in the village, immersed in its sights and smells and sounds: the feel of a cracked mud wall against the palm of one's hand, the pungent odor of cassava leaf and dried fish sauce, the fetid smell of bodies, the cries of children, the rhythmic thud of mortars pounding rice, the crowing of a rooster, the raised voices of men debating some vexed issue in the court *gbare*.

Not long after beginning fieldwork in Firawa in 1969, I, a creature of a deeply ingrained cultural habit, climbed the hill overlooking the village *to get things into perspective* by distancing myself from them. From the hilltop, I surveyed the village, took panoramic photographs, and achieved my bird's-eye view, believing that my superior position would help me gain *insights* into the organization of the village when, in fact, it was making me lose *touch* with it.

Ten years later I was living in Firawa with my wife and daughter, Heidi. One evening Heidi and I climbed the hill above the village. No one else ever did. There were no paths, only tall brakes of elephant grass, granite boulders, and acacias. At the crest of the hill I found the gnarled and charred lophira tree where I had taken my photographs of Firawa in 1969. I asked Heidi what she thought of the view. "It's all right," she said, "except you can't see anyone in the village from here." And indeed, there was no human movement visible; only the smoke from cooking fires.

Those ten years had seen me cease to be a detached observer and become a part of Firawa. I recognized the village as a second home. The transition was, I sometimes thought, like the transition that occurs in a friendship. At the time of first meeting someone you like, you are somewhat guarded; you try to get to know the other person through conversation, an exchange of views and experiences. But then, to live with the other person, even for a while, gives rise to a different kind of understanding, one which suspends the sense of separateness between self and other and evokes the primordial meaning of knowledge as a mode of being-together-with.[9]

My sketch of the Kuranko village as *lived space* entails replacing the space conception of perspective with that of cubism.[10] It suggests a topoanalysis which emphasizes the sense of living in a place, of experiencing it from all sides, moving and participating in it instead of remaining on the margins like a voyeur (Bachelard 1964:8). Eschewing the supervisory perspective of traditional empiricism (which, as Foucault observes, privileges gaze as an instrument of both knowledge and control[11]), the radical empiricist tries to avoid fixed viewpoints by dispersing authorship, working through all five senses, and reflecting inwardly as well as observing outwardly.

But striving for these goals, as I discovered when writing *Barawa*, brings one hard up against the limitations of literacy. Marshall McLuhan argues that perspective derives unconsciously from print technology (1967:68). Like perspective, literacy privileges vision over the other senses, abstracts thought from social context, and isolates the reader or writer from the world (McLuhan 1962). "If oral communication keeps people together," notes David Riesman, "print is the isolating medium *par excellence*" (1970:114). Similar perils attend what Richard Rorty calls "textualism," the idea that there is nothing outside of texts, that all lived experience can be reduced to intertextuality: "stimulus to the intellectual's private moral imagination provided by his strong misreadings, by his search for sacred wisdom, is purchased at the price of his separation from his fellow-humans" (1982:158).

Ethnographic knowledge that is constructed out of verbal statements or likens experience to a text which can be "read," deciphered, or translated, is severely restricted, if for no other reason than that the people with whom anthropologists live and work are usually *nonliterate*. To desist from taking notes, to listen, watch, smell, touch, dance, learn to cook, make mats, light a fire, farm—such practical and social skills should be as constitutive of our understanding as verbal statements and espoused beliefs. Knowledge belongs to the world of our social existence, not just to the world of academe. We must come to it through participation as well as observation and not dismiss lived experience—the actual relationships that mediate our understanding of, and sustain us in, another culture, the oppression of illness or solitude, the frustrations of a foreign language, the tedium of unpalatable food—as "interference" or "noise" to be filtered out in the process of creating an objective report for our profession (Fabian 1983:108).

Consider one example of how the abstract and undeclared context of an ethnographer's work conflicted with the immediate social context of the village in which he sojourned. When Paul Stoller started fieldwork among the Songhay of Niger, he set himself the task of completing a language-attitude "survey." (Again, the motif of the disinterested overview.) After a month's hard work, a casual remark by an informant named Mahamane suggested to the ethnographer that a previous informant, Abdou, had exaggerated the number of languages he spoke. Stoller double-checked. Abdou readily admitted that he spoke only two languages, not four. Stoller asked him why he had lied.

> Abdou shrugged his shoulders and smiled. "What difference does it make?" He looked skyward for a moment. "Tell me, Monsieur Paul, how many languages did Mahamane tell you that he spoke?"
> "Mahamane told me that he speaks three languages."
> "Hah! I know for a fact that Mahamane speaks only one language. He can speak Songhay and that is all."
> "What!"
> I stomped back to Mahamane's shop.
> "Abdou tells me that you speak only one language. But you just told me that you speak three languages. What is the truth?"
> "Ah, Monsieur Paul, Abdou is telling you the truth."
> "But how could you lie to me?"
> "What difference does it make, Monsieur Paul?" (Stoller 1987:9)

Clearly, knowledge is never neutral or disinterested, at least not for the Songhay. The intellectualist assumption that knowledge can be gathered without reference to context of use or the personality of the informant and the ethnographer is shown up as a sham. Without a context in which knowledge can be placed, a goal against which its usefulness can be gauged, the questions of the ethnographer are seen as pointless. Any answer will do. What difference does it make?

Following this episode, Stoller rejected the notion of impartial observation and decided for participation—to resist taking notes and simply sit with the Songhay and listen. "You must learn the meaning of the Songhay adage 'One kills something thin in appearance only to discover that inside it is fat,'" an old marabout tells him (11). For Stoller, this shift from the arcane, other-worldly goals of academe to the immediate, mundane, and practical field of Songhay existence meant, quite literally, apprenticing himself to Songhay teachers, accepting their knowledge in their terms, and exploring the contexts in which that knowledge was used.

But what becomes of ethnography when it locates knowledge in the world of everyday existence and gives up the quest for some supraempirical point of view?

Let us return briefly to the question of literacy. Literacy has the effect of isolating us and our ideas from the lived world of social experience. But it also predisposes us to think of social experience in sequential, lineal terms (Lee 1970). Consider the notion of lineage or lineal descent. Applied to most African societies, the term *lineage* is a misnomer. Even when one finds an indigenous word that is nearly identical to our word *lineage*, there may be an indefinite relationship between the word and what it appears to designate. For example, among the Tiv of Nigeria, the word *nongo* means literally "line" or "queue," though it "refers primarily to the living representatives of a lineage," a grouping without any real genealogical depth (Bohannan 1970:37). A more inclusive term, *itŷo* ("patrilineage"), which one might expect to suggest a descent "line," conjures up for the Tiv an image of "the father's path" or way of doing things rather than a "line" of succession and ancestry (38). This is reminiscent of the way the Kuranko speak of their relationships with both contemporary kin and forebears as networks of paths or ropes (Jackson 1982a:16–17). When ancestors are named at a sacrifice, they are called at random as they come to mind and asked to "pass on the sacrifice to everybody, named and unnamed" (Jackson 1977a:132). Similarly, when sharing genealogical information with me, Kuranko villagers would not list the names of forebears in strict lineal sequences but rather cluster them as belonging to the father's or mother's "place" (*fa ware* or *na ware*) or as "paternal ones" and "maternal ones" (*fa keli meenu* and *na keli meenu*), suggesting images of place and parentage, not long lines of descent (Jackson 1977b:68).[12]

Meyer Fortes's Tallensi ethnography provides a superb example of how relationships are conceptualized spatially and temporally in terms of images of a house and a begetting. First Fortes notes, rather surprisingly, that "the Tallensi have no term for the lineage" (1949:10). He then goes on to assimilate their metaphors to his own:

A lineage of any order is designated the "house" (*yir*) or the children (*biis*) of the founding ancestor. . . . In contexts where the emphasis is on the lineage considered as a segment of a more inclusive lineage, it is commonly described as a "room" (*dug*) of the more inclusive "house" (*yir*). . . . As this nomenclature shows, the internal constitution of the lineage is modelled on that of the polygynous joint family. (10–11).

What Fortes calls a lineage is thus a house or household (*yidem*), a group of people who feel they share "one blood" or "one begetting."[13] Unfortunately, however, the concept "lineage" and the charts and diagrams that go with it impose an abstract linearity on this lived reality, something Evans-Pritchard comments on in his account of how the Nuer figure a lineage system: "When illustrating on the ground a number of related lineages they do not present them the way we figure them in this chapter as a series of bifurcations of descent, as a tree of descent, or as a series of triangles of ascent, but as a number of lines running at angles from a common point." Nuer see the "lineage system," Evans-Pritchard says, "primarily *as actual relations between groups of kinsmen within local communities rather than as a tree of descent,* for the persons after whom the lineages are called do not all proceed from a single individual" (1940:202, emphasis added).

But the problem with the concept of lineage is not only its bias toward linear perspective. It gives rise to *models* of segmentary organization and social order which take on a life of their own. One consequence is that the life-world of the people gets eclipsed and the anthropologist comes to compare societies not in terms of empirical realities but in terms of reified concepts, confusing map with territory, the structure of discourse with the structure of things (Dewey 1929:170; Korzybski 1941).[14] A second consequence is that the jargon of the anthropologist creates an illusion of difference and masks what he has in common with the people he studies: a sense of being in time and space, begotten by someone and belonging to some place. In this sense, it is worth remembering that the English *be* and the German *bin* are cognate with Indo-European words meaning to build, dwell, engender; being-in-the-world is always a kind of dwelling (Heidegger 1977:325–26; Bachelard 1964).

Now if it is true that linear perspective and literacy prevent coevalness, then there is a good case for trying to understand the world through bodily participation and through senses other than sight (Fabian 1983:108; Rorty 1979:39; Stoller 1984; Stoller and Olkes 1986). Let us not forget the taste of Proust's *petite madeleine,* nor music, nor dance, nor the sharing of food, the smell of bodies, the touch of hands.

In anthropology, such explorations are necessary if only because the people we study often privilege sensory modes other than sight as foundational to social knowledge. If we want to find common ground with them, we have to open ourselves to modes of sensory and bodily life which, while meaningful to us in our personal lives, tend to get suppressed in our academic discourse.

Let us briefly consider two societies where the five senses are given different emphases and meanings than in contemporary Western societies: the Suya of Central Brazil and the Northern Yaka of Zaire.

Among the Suya, seeing is not believing. Both vision and smell are "antisocial" faculties. "The eyes are literally the seat of antisocial power" and associated with witchcraft (Seeger 1981:87). Witches possess extraordinary vision but hear and speak badly. Hearing and speaking are the "eminently social faculties" and the ear and mouth are the most important organs. Thus, while the Suya decorate the ears and lips with disks, the eyes and nose are left unornamented. "Through the perforation of the mouth and the earlobe and the insertion of painted disks, the body itself is socialized. Ear disks and lip disks are related to fundamental concepts of person, morality, and the symbolism of body parts" (91).

Among the Yaka, quite different sensory emphases exist. Social interaction is construed as a kind of weaving or intertwining. One powerful expression of this is dancing, which lustfully celebrates the flow of vital force (*m-mooyi*) between human beings and between people and nature. Dancing is compared with sexual intercourse and commensality, which likewise create reciprocity through physical co-presence and intertwining (Devisch 1983, 1985a, 1985b). For the Yaka, social relations involve "exchanges of feeling," and in this process the senses of touch and smell are paramount.

> Eating, drinking, and procreating, which involve olfactory and tactile contact, are the acts that constitute the domestic zone and that generate symmetrical reciprocity. . . . As the Yaka say, "By its very nature, eating must be shared" (*-diisasana*). Eating circum-scribes a space of physical co-presence "where bodies intrude on one another" (*-dyaatasana*). Procreating is spoken of as "causing one another to intertwine legs" (*-biindasana maalu*). . . .
> *Olfactory contact* . . . "puts oneself beside oneself" and inserts the individual into the social and natural domains. Procreation, by which the sexes and generations are mediated and differentiated, is symbolized and concretized among the Yaka as "smelling one another": sexual partners "induce each other to secrete smell and to take in each other's smell" (*fyaasana, -nyuukisana*). In other words, smelling constructs a liminal process between the procreators: it provides a bodily matrix for a reciprocal interaction in which the poles (inner/outer, self/other, giver/receiver) are joined and set apart. (Devisch 1985a:597, 596)

Illness is felt to be a disturbance in this symbolic interweave of self, society, and cosmos—"a bad smell"—and therapy is a way of revitalizing social and cosmic con-nections, as well as giving rebirth to the sick individual, through bodily metaphors of hunting, weaving, and sexual regeneration (Devisch 1984).

CRISIS, CONTEXT, AND CONCERN

These allusions to illness and healing bring us to yet another way in which radical empiricism differs from traditional empiricism: its refusal to reduce lived experience to mathematical or mechanical models and then claim that these models are evidence or representations of the essential character of experience. As John Dewey puts it:

> When we view experientially this change, what occurs is the kind of thing that hap-pens in the useful arts when natural objects, like crude ores, are treated as materials for getting something else. Their character ceases to lie in their immediate qualities, in just what they are and as directly enjoyed. Their character is now representative; some pure metal, iron, copper, etc. is their essence, which may be extracted as their "true" nature, their "reality." To get at this reality many existent constituents have to be got rid of. From the standpoint of the object, pure metal, these things to be eliminated are "false," irrelevant and obstructive. They stand in the way, and in the existent thing those qualities are alone significant which indicate the ulterior objective and which offer means for attaining it. (1929:133)

To recover a sense of the qualities of experience we have to go further than the traditional empiricist's interest in predictable, regular patterns. First, we must recognize the temporality of experience. Experience is not reducible to timeless laws or essences; it is a boundless process. As such it includes things refractory to order, liminal events, crises and reversals, events uncanny and contingent (Turner 1985:179, 190–91, 210–11). In Dilthey's terms, experience embraces both the typical or customary *(Erfahrung)* and the idiosyncratic, or exceptional and fleeting *(Erlebnis)* (see Benjamin 1968:117). Second, we must recognize that direct, prereflective experience is no less significant than the experience that comes of reflection and ratiocination. Sensible and emotional experiences are not confused forms of cognition, to be dismissed, as Lévi-Strauss does, as epiphenomena simply because they do not have explanatory value (1969b:142, 1981:667–68). The smell of eucalypts after rain and biochemical explanations of this same experience should not be ranked in terms of a distinction between subjective appearance and objective reality, for the illumination is as meaningful as the analyses that result from our reflections on it. Dewey expresses it as follows:

> The features of objects reached by scientific or reflective experiencing are important, but so are all the phenomena of magic, myth, politics, painting, and penitentiaries. The phenomena of social life are as relevant to the problem of the relation of the individual and universal as are those of logic; the existence in political organization of boundaries and barriers, of expansion and absorption, will be quite as important for metaphysical theories of the discrete and the continuous as is anything derived from chemical analysis. The existence of ignorance as well as of wisdom, of error and even insanity as well as of truth will be taken into account.
> That is to say, nature is construed in such a way that all these things, since they are actual, are naturally possible; they are not explained away into mere "appearance" in contrast with reality. Illusions are illusions, but the occurrence of illusions is not an illusion, but a genuine reality. What is really "in" experience extends much further than that which at any time is *known*. . . . It is important for philosophical theory to be aware that the distinct and evident are prized and why they are. But it is equally important to note that the dark and twilight abound. (1929:20)

Third, we must recognize that conceptual orders are not so much "representations" of the inherent orderliness of the world as forms of wishful thinking—obligative truths or *post festum* rationalizations whose relationship to lived experience always remains indeterminate. Fourth, we must critically examine the ways in which a preoccupation with pattern and order is linked historically to a concern for controlling nature and other human beings, a form of instrumental rationality (Dewey 1929:126; Horkheimer and Adorno 1972). By turning from epistemology toward the everyday world of lived experience, the radical empiricist is inclined to judge the value of an idea, not just against antecedent experiences or the logical standards of scientific inquiry but also against the practical, ethical, emotional, and aesthetic demands of life (Dewey 1980:136–38; James 1978:30–40; Rorty 1982:203–8; Whitehead 1947:226). This means that the traditional empiricist's hankering after order and control is to be seen as just one of many consoling illusions, one stratagem for making sense of an unstable world, not as an "accurate representation of reality" or a privileged insight into the way the world "really" works (Rorty 1979:10, 1982:194).

It is sometimes thought that this instrumental theory of truth reduces all ideas to a matter of practical expediency or personal whim. But in going beyond the traditional empiricist's correspondence theory of truth, Dewey wanted to emphasize that ideas have to be tested against the *whole* of our experience—sense perceptions as well as moral values, scientific aims as well as communal goals. For Dewey, both the source and the consummation of ideas lie within the social world to which we inescapably belong. That is why the pragmatist regards open-ended, ongoing conversation *with* others as more "edifying" than the task of completing a systematic explanation *of* others (Rorty 1979:365–73). In ethnography, this means abandoning induction and *actively* debating and exchanging points of view with our informants. It means placing our ideas on a par with theirs, testing them not against predetermined standards of rationality but against the immediate exigencies of life.

Such engagement leads away from "the overarching universal of a strictly objective method" to what Merleau-Ponty calls "a sort of lateral universal," acquired through an "incessant testing of the self through the other person and the other person through the self. It is a question of constructing a general system of reference in which the point of view of the native, the point of view of the civilized man, and the mistaken views each has of the other can all find a place" (1964:119). It is an anthropology whose concern "is neither to prove that the primitive is wrong nor to side with him against us, but to set itself up on a ground where we shall both be intelligible without any reduction or rash transposition" (122).

Merleau-Ponty's allusion to universals brings us to a consideration of the existential leitmotifs which are explored throughout this book: thrownness, finitude, and uncertainty. In Heidegger's terms, our being-in-the-world is a "thrownness" (*Geworfenheit*); we are "thrown" (*geworfen*) into a world which has been made by others at other times and will outlast us. We choose neither the time nor the place of our birth, and our origins are not of our own making. Yet, this world we encounter as "simply there" is something we actively enter into and make over to ourselves. We realize its givenness as possibility. Even if nothing we do seems to change the world, it is disclosed in the very fact of our existence. Moreover, even if we go along with what is given, accepting our contingency and denying our freedom, we contribute to the way the world will be for those who follow us into it.

Most people, however, do more than fall back into the given world. They live it as a choice, celebrating necessity as a kind of freedom[15] or denying determinacy through revolt, fantasy, critique, or sheer perversity. Here is how Dostoyevsky expresses this idea:

> even if man was nothing but a piano key, even if this could be demonstrated mathematically—even then, he wouldn't come to his senses but would pull some trick out of sheer ingratitude, just to make his point. And if he didn't have them on hand, he would devise the means of destruction, chaos, and all kinds of suffering to get his way. . . .

I believe this is so and I'm prepared to vouch for it, because it seems to me that the meaning of man's life consists of proving to himself every minute that he's man and not a piano key. And man will keep proving it and paying for it with his own skin; he will turn into a troglodyte if need be. (1961:114–15)

Along with the sense of thrownness goes a sense of life as finite, an inevitable movement toward death. Against time and the decay of the body, we construct notions of ourselves as enduring and invincible—hero myths, beliefs in reincarnation, notions of an afterlife and ancestorhood, fantasies of living on in the memories of others and in immortal works—masks, really, which Ernest Becker (1973) interprets as defenses against the universal terror of death. Indeed, the quest of traditional philosophy for a stable, etherealized knowledge of the world may be one such attempt to "buy off" contingency, to get us above the world of materiality and change and magically bring us a kind of immortality (Dewey 1929:44–63).

Here we touch on the third leitmotif: the precarious and perilous character of existence. As Dewey observes, people everywhere seek security and stability in the face of the world's hazards. Making a home or establishing a set routine is, in this sense, on the same footing as constructing an intellectual system. But the problem with our intellectual endeavor to transcend the vicissitudes of lived experience is that it inclines us to believe there is a deep split within Being itself between a "higher" conceptual realm where certitude may be found and an "inferior" realm of the sensory, bodily, material, and practical life which is intrinsically unstable and uncertain. From this metaphysical split, other dualisms follow—between mind and matter, spirit and body, rational thought and sensuous appetite—but "all have their origin," argues Dewey, "in a fear of what life may bring forth. They are marks of contraction and withdrawal" (1958:22).

One such escape from lived experience is provided by the intellectualist notion that knowing is a kind of outside beholding rather than a matter of participation in the ongoing drama of the world (Dewey 1980:291). But if knowledge is not so much a systematic revelation of the inner logic of antecedent events as a way of dealing with life in the here and now, then the anthropologist's preoccupation with regularity, pattern, system, and structure has to be seen as less an objective reflection of social reality than a comment on his personal and professional need for certitude and order.

Consider an episode in my own fieldwork. In the first few months in the field I began research on Kuranko dream interpretation and quickly collected many stereotypical interpretations of dream images. To dream of hoeing a farm portended a kinsman's death, a fish with scales foretold the birth of a male child, a fish without scales foretold the birth of a female child, drowning or floundering in deep water indicated a conspiracy against the dreamer, people felling trees in deep forest indicated the failure of a conspiracy, climbing a mountain or flying like a bird presaged prosperity and happiness, and so on. Within a month I had recorded quite a repertoire of such interpretations and begun trying to discern in them some underlying system of meaning. But then I myself had a strange and perplexing dream, which I related to a diviner, curious to know what he would make of it.

·I was in a bare room, reminiscent of one of the classrooms in the District Council Primary School in Kabala where I had first met Noah Marah, my field assistant. Suddenly a corrugated iron door opened into the room and a book was passed through the doorway as if by an invisible hand. For several seconds the book hung in midair, and I made out on its cover in bold type the word ETHNOGRAPHY. I had a definite impression that the book contained only blank pages. Then the door swung open again and a tremendous presence swept into the room and lifted me up bodily. I was borne aloft, as if in the hands of a giant, and carried out of the room. The pressure of the giant's hold against my chest made it hard for me to breathe. I woke up, afraid (Jackson 1978b:120, 1986:97).

The diviner, Fore Kargbo, was puzzled by the dream and discussed it with other elders. I was asked if the giant flew up into the sky with me and whether or not he placed me back on the ground. When I had answered his questions, Fore said my dream foretold that I would become an important person, "like a chief." The book signified knowledge, the giant was a djinn who wished to help me,[16] flying like a bird was a sign of happiness, being high up was auspicious, and finding oneself in a strange place among strange people signaled imminent prosperity. The immediate effect of Fore's remarks was to alleviate some of my anxieties about filling my notebooks with data and gaining a systematic understanding of Kuranko society. But Fore's sympathetic response to my dream suggested a different approach to Kuranko dream interpretation than the one I had been pursuing. I now emphasized the use-value rather than the veracity of ideas associated with divination. There was no determinate system of meaning to be uncovered, since meanings are given anew in the context of each consultation and in relation to the concerns of each consulter. If there was any notion of objectivity in Kuranko dream interpretation its point was to foster confidence in the divinatory methods and help people face the hazards of life, not to underwrite an abstract commentary on antecedent social or mental events.

By broadening its empirical field to include participatory knowledge and subjective concerns, anthropology places the knower within the world of the known and gives incompleteness and precariousness the same footing as the finished and fixed. In other words, it urges us not to subjugate lived experience to the tyranny of reason or the consolation of order but to cultivate that quality which Keats called negative capability, the capability of "being in uncertainties, Mysteries, doubts, without any irritable reaching after fact & reason. . . ." (1958:193).

These last few pages will no doubt invite an inevitable criticism. Do notions such as "negative capability" and "negative dialectics" or existential a prioris such as thrownness, finitude, and uncertainty reflect universal experience or the particular concerns of a small group of twentieth-century European intellectuals? Can such notions give us a foundation for edifying cross-cultural comparison? How can one reconcile, for example, West African notions of prenatal choice with Heidegger's notion of thrownness? How does the Hindu doctrine of reincarnation jell with the existentialist's assumption of human finitude? And doesn't the recurring emphasis in existential and phenomenological writing on individual experience contradict the ontological priority in many non-Western societies on social *relationships*? One way of answering these questions is to ask whether we fare any better in beginning cross-cultural comparison with "belief systems" such as witchcraft and sorcery, systems of inheritance and succession, forms of economic production, modes of social control, or myth, since many of these frames of reference suggest radical *discontinuities* between "them" and "us," and fail to clarify on what grounds we can presume to reach an understanding of such "alien" beliefs and practices. Another answer is to recapitulate a point I have already made, that our understanding of others can *only* proceed from within our own experience, and this experience involves our personalities and histories as much as our field research. Accordingly, our task is to find some common ground with others and explore our differences from there. The existential a prioris I have outlined above seem to me as good a place as any to begin this task, since they situate human beings within the unified field of Being.

PARTS AND WHOLES

At a conference of Africanists held at the University of Uppsala in August 1987, Marie-Claude Dupré prefaced her paper on the *kiduma* masks of the Bateke with this memorable remark: "A fetishist is a man who cannot relate to a whole woman, but only to a part of her—her shoes, her bracelet, her perfume. An anthropologist is a fetishist too as long as he relates to only part of social reality because he cannot cope with the whole."

Our endeavor to enlarge the field of empiricism is a little like wanting to take all the African masks from their glass cases in European museums and return them to where they are worn and charged with life. Museum authorities will obstruct us, and even if we succeed in getting the masks back to Africa, the villages where they were originally made may no longer exist and new masks may have supplanted the old. Escaping the static and airtight categories of traditional empiricism, where life is divided into the legal, the political, the economic, the social, the historical, and so forth, is perhaps as impossible as returning our ancestor masks to Africa and to life. Our class upbringing commits us to classification, and the conventional forms of our discourse trap us in dualisms and dichotomies. Even if we do sometimes throw off our conceptual chains, we fear the loss of identity and authority that follows from our freedom. To break away from closed systems and completed structures is thus a test of our ability to live "without the consolation that truth cannot be lost" (Adorno 1973:34). It is like forfeiting the coherent and consoling structural universe of Lévi-Strauss and entering the splintered, provisional, and contradictory world of Adorno. Or, to use these thinkers' own analogies, it is like moving from Wagner's romanticism and chromaticism (Lévi-Strauss's inspiration) to Schönberg's atonality, with its rejection of classical harmony and its repudiation of eternal, formal laws (the model of Adorno's "atonal philosophy").[17]

But it is storytelling, not music, which is the basis of the discursive style I experimented with in *Barawa* and continue to make use of in this book. Stories, at least in the Kuranko tradition, cultivate a certain degree of impersonality so that the experiences of the author are made available to others who can discover in them meanings of their own. Eugenio Montale calls this "the second life of art."

A story is thus suggestive rather than definitive of meaning. It begins in the experience of one person, but others make it over to themselves and give it new uses and interpretations. But even more important to me than this hermeneutical openness of narratives, or even their ability to communicate the fullness and immediacy of life, is the way they reflect and embody one fundamental modality of lived experience: the journey.

This connection between narrative and journey is widely recognized. The classical Greek word *istorias* from which we derive our word *history* meant "trackings," and in modern Greek *istoria* means both "story" and "exciting event" (Herzfeld 1985:207). Heidegger speaks of the task of philosophy as bringing thought "on to a path" within a forest, a movement toward a clearing, and Walter Benjamin used the down-to-earth image of sauntering or idling (*flânerie*) to describe the importance of random detail and fortuitous encounters in his intellectual journeys of exploration.

These images disclose the intimate connection between our bodily experience in the everyday world and our conceptual life. Thus, the universal *form* of narrative as well as its recurring themes of exploration and pilgrimage, of initiatory journeys and heroic quests, and even of mundane sorties into city streets (as in Joyce's *Ulysses*) all give evidence of habitual bodily modes of interaction and experience— moving to and fro, back and forth in the world—*though there does not necessarily have to be any one point of departure, any fixed goal, or any particular denouement.*

To use narrative form in this way is to move away from excessive abstraction and ground one's discourse in the sentient life of individuals interacting with objects and with others in the quotidian world. It is also to acknowledge that discourse always belongs to a context of worldly interests and influences, that our theories are allegories of our lives, and our philosophy an inadvertent memoir born of the dialectic between what is given to us and what we make of it (Nietzsche 1973:19). To point out that the discursive style I have adopted in this book is grounded in narrative and makes use of metaphors taken from mundane existence is thus to place my thought in relation to my cultural background and to declare my personal affinities and aims.

TWO

Two Lives

I remember him now as he appears in the one photograph I managed to take of him. I had drawn back into the shadows of a doorway, surreptitiously focused my telephoto lens, and caught him as he looked away. His remnant teeth are kola-stained, his hair grizzled, his body stiffened by rheumatism. He is sitting on a raffia mat on the edge of our porch, supported by his stave, and he is grinning at something or someone outside the frame. Perhaps at Pauline, my wife—though that is a detail I cannot corroborate.

That I no longer know exactly what was happening outside the frame of the photograph on that particular day and cannot say for certain whether my memory of Saran Salia is now shaped by the photo or by the man himself is perhaps an object lesson for ethnographers like me, reluctant to see lived experience eclipsed by the generalizations and cliches of discourse.

He and Pauline died in the same year, 1983. In 1985 I returned to Firawa to find his house a charred ruin—the house he had given me and my family to use six years before for as long as we stayed in the village.

I passed my first evening alone there, fossicking among the debris. Some fragments of tortoise shell, a few broken porcupine quills, a handful of cowries, a couple of crumpled horns, a trace of mica in the ash and rubble: this was all that remained of the healing arts he practiced, which had, perhaps, died with him. I sat on the fire-blackened porch where we had spent so many hours talking together. Fire finches flickered like lost souls in the gutted rooms, tapping out—or so I imagined—some message from the afterlife that I was too dumb to decipher.[1] I strolled across the abandoned garden we had made together and found the bedraggled palm from which he had cut a bunch of bananas—a metaphor for kinship[2]—to give us against our journey the night of our departure from the village. I stood awhile in the darkness. Insects shrilled in the grass. I thought if I was patient enough, if I had faith, he would appear out of the shadows, leaning on his stave, a conspiratorial grin on his face, his hand outstretched. . . . *There are many ways that a bird can fly in the sky.*

In the difficult weeks that followed, I often pondered the way the old medicine-master had met and dealt with tribulation in his life. My ghost dialogues with him helped me objectify my situation and see that in adversity life may be affirmed more deeply than at any other time. Saran Salia often made Kuranko initiation exemplify Kuranko social life in general. Through the terrors and ordeals of initiation, one learned to face adversity alone, to withstand hardship, to live *through* it rather than hope to avoid it.[3]

In the following pages I recount the lives of two Kuranko men, leaving implicit the comparisons that may be made with my own life. For my aim is not to make *any* individual life a center of meaning but to emphasize the significance of crisis for a theory of culture. I wish to show that human life is never merely a matter of apathetic assent to givenness but an active relationship with the circumstances that befall a person. Our concept of culture must, I argue, be made to include those moments in social life when the customary, given, habitual, and normal is disrupted, flouted, suspended, and negated,[4] when crises transform the world from an apparently fixed and finished set of rules into a repertoire of possibilities, when a person stands out against the world and, to borrow Marx's vivid image, forces the frozen circumstances to dance by singing to them their own melody.[5]

Such a notion of culture may, at first sight, be difficult to sustain in traditional societies where the modern conception of possessive individualism and of the personal life as a project of self-making (*Bildung*) is not obviously constitutive of the *Weltanschauung*. In Kuranko, for example, there is no word for life-story, no genre of autobiography, and people do not ordinarily speak of their lives as lived *against* the cultural grain but rather as developed *within* the compass of ancestral values and decrees. As Walter Ong puts it, "You do not find climactic linear plots readyformed in people's lives" (1982:143). Nor do you find them in narrative performance, where digressions, false starts, and the absence of consistently chronological order or plot closure is often found (Jackson 1982a). In conventional discourse, one's personal experience of initiation, marriage, Islam, illness, and so on is assimilated to the experience of others; it is typical, not unique. The personal life is contingent upon one's place within a field of social relations; it is not set apart or defined by its transcendence.

Many anthropologists are wont to see such a traditional conceptualization of the personal life as a *description* of experiential reality. Prepared to accept the discursive idiom of "primitive" people at its face value, they rapidly reduce individual experience to the shared language that articulates it and dismiss subjectivity as merely epiphenomenal. The Gestalt notion of the self as a moment or aspect of *interaction* is, however, no more binding or determinative of actual experience than is the contrasted "modern" notion of the self as skin-encapsulated and autonomous. Both notions are best regarded as metaphors (Olney 1972:34–35). They do not so much describe the world as mediate the gap and resolve the tension between how, on reflection, individual experience inclines one to see the world and how, in its ideological constructs, one's culture makes it out to be.

A MEDICINE-MASTER'S STORY

In *Barawa* I recounted a little of my friendship with Saran Salia Sano and of my endeavors to record his life-story. Such a biography was, I knew, an artifice, and piecing it together was made even more difficult because one of Saran Salia's classificatory sons, a dogmatic Muslim on whom the old man depended for food and shelter, was opposed to any talk of traditional fetish medicines. My persistence was finally rewarded when, over a period of several weeks in early 1979, Saran Salia shared experiences and divulged information that both moved and astounded me.

As a young man he had served an apprenticeship with a teacher (*karamorgo*) in Siguiri, Guinea, and become master of a Kuranko cult named for the powerful bush spirit, *Kome*. In his old age, Saran Salia spoke of his twenty-eight years as medicine-master (*besetigi*) and *Kome*-master (*Kometigi*) with fulfillment and nostalgia:

> I was given money, cows, gowns, salt, rice—everything! Though I've given up now, people still give me things. But above all I have been given affection [*madiye*]. Even today, children follow me everywhere offering to do things for me. Yesterday a young man came and volunteered to clear my backyard, and young Salia here makes mats for me. You see why I've never regretted being *Kometigi*?

Salia, my neighbor's son, was sitting with us on the porch. I asked him what the old man had done for him.

"Many things. I cannot tell you all."

"Tell me some."

"Saran Salia's apprentice [*karandan*] took care of me in the *fafei* [initiation lodge]. Saran Salia is my teacher. After that he is my father [Salia's own father was dead]. I respect him as my father."

"Yes, but what do you do for him?

"I mend the fence around his yard."

"He makes mats for me," Saran Salia interjected, "finds me firewood, brings me fish he's caught. He gives me sweet food!"

I remembered how in previous years I'd often found several boys sleeping in Saran Salia's house, sent by their parents to be protected from witchcraft. And whenever the *bilakorenu* (uninitiated boys) quarreled and scrapped, Saran Salia would always be quickly on the scene, bawling the kids out, settling the dispute, a respected presence who used to remind me strongly of my own beloved grandfather.

It had, however, been many years since he had practiced medicine or been active in the *Kome* cult. Beholden to his Muslim "son" for his immediate livelihood (and ultimately for a decent burial), Saran Salia had been obliged to repudiate fetish medicines and renounce *Kome*. It had been a hard price to pay for security in his old age.

"Even now," he said, "when the xylophonists play *Kome* music and sing *Kome* songs, I hear it and want to dance. . . ."

A snatch of one of the *Kome* songs came to mind—*Sembe, sembe, sembe le, Kome la, eh Kome wo; n'de min i le nyonto ken yen* (Great power has *Kome*, eh *Kome*; I have not, have you, its equal seen)—and I wondered vaguely if the old man rued the loss of the power and prestige he had once enjoyed as *Kometigi*.

But Saran Salia tempered his regrets with gratitude toward his Muslim "sons":

This Alhadji and this Lahai [Abdulai], they built this house and said: "Father, live
here. Father, you're not going to farm any more; you're unable to work. Live here and
rest. Let us find your mouth [i.e., bring you food]. You are old. Live sweetly now."
Well, up to today, everything is sweet.

Saran Salia hesitated and looked earnestly into my face: "As you are, you love
me. As you are, I love you. You love my children and my children love you. Since
you have come and asked me to tell you all I know from my childhood up to now,
this is what I will tell you."

In the days that followed, sitting together on the mud-plaster porch of Saran
Salia's house, we talked at length about his childhood and youth and of the crises
in early life that shaped his destiny. But Saran Salia spoke of himself not as a free
agent but always as part of a kinship network.[6] His family was his *sabu*, the "agency"
or "means" whereby he existed and had identity:

> Ever since my birth, I am in my elders' hands. To make a farm . . . we made that
> farm until I donned the clothes of manhood [i.e., was initiated]. They favored me.
> I was eating sweetly [i.e., happy and well cared for at home]. In my elder brother's,
> Malfore Sano's hands, I was also eating sweetly.

As if unsure of what he might say next, Saran Salia paused.

"What did you fear as a child?" I asked.

"Djinn, witches, the masters of the *korte* medicine, the dead [*fure*]. I feared
them greatly. When I was a boy you did not dare go outside on the day a person
had died."

As Saran Salia talked on, recalling the trepidation he'd felt as a boy toward
the men's cults and cult sacra (*sumafannu*; literally, "secret things"), I began to
understand the significance of initiation in a Kuranko man's life: the moment when
one's childhood anxieties are finally allayed, when one is inducted into the cults,
when one sees into their mysteries and is introduced to the magical medicines
which give fortitude (*yuse gbele*; literally, "a hard heart"), bravery (*kerenteye*), self-
confidence (*kalai nyerela*; literally, "belief self in"), and new understanding (*hankili
kura*). But before we spoke further of initiation, I wanted to know more about his
childhood and his parents.

One morning, after we had taken up our usual positions—he in a hammock,
I sitting on a nearby chair—on the porch of his house, I asked him what had been
the unhappiest time in his boyhood.

His reply was immediate and abrupt: "The day my father died."

It had been ten farm seasons after his birth. His mother and his elder brother,
Malfore, died a few years later, not long after his initiation. But his memories of
them all were vague: "When those ones died, they passed from my mind [*an bo
ran n'kuma*]. I went and chased after *Kome*. I drew the *Kome* rope for twenty-eight
years."

As it turned out, Saran Salia had not gone in pursuit of *Kome* immediately
after his initiation or even after the deaths of his mother and elder brother. Cer-

tainly he was more than ordinarily fascinated by *Kome*. As a boy he had both feared it and felt it was "something extraordinary." During his initiation he was lured by the gifts the *Kome*-master received and the power he commanded. "When I first saw it I wanted to be it," he told me. "As *Kometigi*, everyone fears you, but you fear no one because you have been immunized against all the harmful medicines."

What actually decided Saran Salia to become a *Kome*-master was the breakup of his first marriage:

> The time I decided [*n'dun ta wati mi*] was when they took a certain woman away from me by force [i.e., another man ran away with his first wife with the connivance of the girl's father]. That man taunted me. "Show me that your iron can cut my iron!" he said to me. "If you are a man, then do what you will!" I said, "Me!" There and then I took up the *Kome* tether. You understand? Whoever sees *Kome*, dies!

Two things struck me about Saran Salia's account. First, I was impressed by the way he had mastered his fear of *Kome* by embracing and embodying the object of that fear, the bush spirit itself. (It reminded me of how I had learned to deal with nightmares as a child by cultivating an indifference to them, laying myself open to my worst fears, challenging the dark dream forces to do their damnedest.) Later, Saran Salia was to confide that the image of a fearsome bush spirit drawn on a tether by the *Kome*-master was a deliberate fiction, meant to intimidate noninitiates and women. *Kome* the bush spirit and the *Kome*-master were one and the same.

This identification is the key to understanding Saran Salia's *particular* attraction to *Kome*. By becoming *Kometigi* he entered into and overcame the dread which the figure of *Kome* inspired in him as a child. At the same time his powerful position as cult master enabled him to recover, under the aegis of *Kome*, his own impugned manhood and pride.

Saran Salia's project had three phases: the internalization of an objectivity (as a child he felt afraid of *Kome*), the externalization of a subjectivity (during his initiation he saw *Kome* to be a man-made object, a cultural artifact), and the self-conscious reinternalization of objectivity *in his own way, in his own terms, for his own use* (he became a *Kome*-master). Following Sartre, we might say that his project was "a mediation between two moments of objectivity" (Sartre 1968:99). The initial moment was when *Kome* appeared to him as facticity, an alien reality beyond his grasp or control. The final moment was when *Kome* became a thing of *his* making—a gown *he* wore, a mask *he* donned, a role *he* assumed. Other became self.

Though Saran Salia was conditioned by his childhood fears of *Kome* and obliged in adult life to maintain the given image and guard the traditional secrets of the *Kome* cult, it is in the last analysis *he who brings Kome into being*, not the other way around. A unique constellation of events—his childhood anxieties, the deaths of his parents and elder brother, his wife's desertion and her lover's jibes—shaped Saran Salia's interest in the *Kome* cult. But finally it is upon his decision to become *Kometigi*, his praxis, that the continuity of the cult *as a cultural institution* depends. From an objectivist point of view it often appears that the personal life is reducible to cultural forms and plays little part in the creation of these forms. The present case suggests otherwise.

The indeterminate relationship between personal experience and cultural form leads us to the second striking feature of Saran Salia's account: the implication that he may have used his position as *Kometigi* to prosecute a personal vendetta.

Not long after he became *Kometigi*, his errant wife, her lover, and her father died. Though I pressed him on the matter, Saran Salia would neither admit nor deny that he had deliberately used his power as *Kometigi* or his knowledge of magical medicines to kill them (Jackson 1986:182). Since killing by sorcery is tantamount to murder in Kuranko law, I thought his evasiveness might be a way of avoiding incriminating himself. But then I recalled what Saran Salia had told me on other occasions about his lifelong involvement with traditional medicines and I revised my views (173–77).

There are three branches of traditional Kuranko medicine: curative, prophylactic and protective, and lethal. Curative medicine (*dandan bese*) is mainly herbal, and the knowledge of leaves and the healing arts can be acquired by men or women without any special training. The other branches of medicine are male preserves and involve secret knowledge and specialist instruction. The first includes the making and dispensing of protective fetishes (*kandan li fannu*; literally, "enclosing things"), spells (*haye*), and antidotes (*yobe*) to the various lethal substances used in sorcery. The second includes the making and dispensing of four lethal medicines (*korte, koli, nyenkafori, gboye*) and the use of the curse (*gborle*). Every medicine-master (*besetigi*) is trained in all these branches of medicine and is able to treat the two kinds of illness distinguished in Kuranko nosology: *altala kiraiye* (arising from "natural causes"; literally, "God illnesses") and *morgofi'kiraiye* (arising from sorcery; literally, "black/evil person illnesses").

Saran Salia chose, however, to practice only the first two branches of medicine: curative and prophylactic/protective. In other words, he forswore using his knowledge of lethal medicine for personal ends and refused to put his skills at the disposal of others wishing to avenge slights or redress injustices by underhanded means. This is not to say that people haven't died as a consequence of his command of magical medicines. Once he confided that he had "never used medicines to kill, but those that tested me did not live long." But what this meant was that his mastery of antidotes and prophylactics made him immune to sorcery so that whenever someone tried to harm him the magical medicines *were turned back upon* the user, afflicting him in the same way an unprotected victim would have been afflicted.

From the outset, Saran Salia's command of powerful medicines, like his command of *Kome*, gave him fearlessness (*kilanbelteye*) and self-possession (*miran*). But, like the exponents of Eastern martial arts, he came to see that the proper exercise of power is not in using it to gain an advantage over others but in containing it, holding it under control. Self-mastery, in the Kuranko view, is the beginning of social adroitness (*hankili*). Yet Saran Salia's choice to practice only the healing arts and eschew the destructive arts of sorcery was by no means fortuitous. It was a matter of personal judgment, a decision *for* protecting the vulnerable and curing the sick rather than selling his services to the envious and aggrieved, a decision *for* helping his community rather than using his powers to prosecute private vendettas.

The germ of these decisions is contained in the word *bese* itself, which is the generic term for all medicines, therapeutic, prophylactic, and lethal. *Bese* is thus ambiguous, like the Greek word *pharmakon*. In his reading of Plato's *Phaedrus*, Derrida observes:

> This *pharmakon*, this "medicine," this philter, which acts as both remedy and poison . . . introduces itself into the body of the discourse with all its ambivalence. This charm, this spellbinding virtue, this power of fascination, can be—alternately or simultaneously—beneficent or maleficent." (1981:70).[7]

Derrida goes on to note the metaphorical use of the term *pharmakon* in the Socratic dialogue as signifying that which seduces, which leads one beyond the world of face-to-face relationships, beyond the "sheltered enclosure" of one's community. For Socrates this movement is thought of as one from speech to writing, a transgression in which openness gives way to the occult and sociability is eclipsed by sorcery. The Kuranko term *bese* suggests a similar set of tensions, summarized metaphorically in terms of the contrasted worlds of village and bush (the known versus the unknown, the moral versus the amoral, the communal versus the self-interested). I have explored this dialectic of village and bush elsewhere (Jackson 1982a). Here I am concerned only to place Saran Salia's project in its cultural context, to point out that his cultivation of *bese* in its therapeutic and socially constructive aspects entailed a choice which was at the same time a resolution of the perennial tension of Kuranko life between acting within the common grain or against it.[8]

In his declining years, Saran Salia remained faithful to his vision. Parents sent their children to him for protection against witchcraft. Men came to him for antidotes and prophylactics against sorcery. He sorted out the petty quarrels of the village boys. He spent hours in the heat of the day going on his rounds to see that the chief's ban on cooking fires was being observed. When I and my family visited Firawa in early 1979 he gave us his house. In his long life he married thrice and once inherited a wife. His wives died young; so too did three of his four children. Much of his life he had lived alone. He had become a kind of father to others, sheltering and protecting neighbors from the sinister designs of an inscrutable world and giving hospitality to a curious white stranger whose purposes never ceased to amuse him.

The Kuranko speak of initiation as the time a child is cleansed of its childish proclivities, tamed, made socially skilled, transformed into a self-contained, complete person. Saran Salia remembered his initiation as one of the happiest times in his life, when he cast off the clothes of a child and put on the gown of a man. But I cannot help thinking that his personhood was achieved not just by undergoing the ordeals of formal initiation (*biriye*), not just by passing through the set passage of a communal rite; his personhood was achieved through what he chose to make of the adventitious and traumatic events that overwhelmed him in his childhood and youth. It was the gown of *Kome*, a gown he often spoke of as an ally, a double, as much as the *gbangbale* gown of initiation that enabled him to come into his own. It was a gown he donned, a role he assumed in his own way, in his own style. And it is this style, now that he is dead, that I remember most.

A STORYTELLER'S STORY

I see him now—assured, risible, indefatigable—spellbinding us in a crowded, windowless room. In the penumbra of a hurricane lamp I scribble notes and adjust my tape recorder. The man behind me jerks to one side and orders a small boy to give me more space. The fetor of the room is suffocating. Before the night is out, Keti Ferenke Koroma will tell me he knows more stories than I have tapes to record them. He will challenge me to stay on after the others have drifted off. But weariness will defeat me and I too will wend my way home through the darkness of the village and fall asleep, dreaming already of the fantastic figures and images he has seeded in my mind.

At first meeting no one could have seemed more unlike the tentative, wry, and self-effacing Saran Salia. But Keti Ferenke attracted me just as the old medicine-master had. A born raconteur, he encouraged my interest in Kuranko oral narratives and was always willing to arrange a storytelling session in his Kondembaia house or, if necessary, travel twenty miles to my house in Kabala to record myths.

His intellectual adroitness and wit made him the perfect informant. Critique seemed second nature to him. He would never explain social usages away by saying simply that they were ancestrally given,[9] but would address them as matters to be expatiated on, dilemmas to be resolved. Oral narrative (*tilei*) was the perfect vehicle for his intellectual curiosity. Since the genre was ostensibly make-believe, a form of entertainment, he could cunningly conceal his serious and often provocative opinions in them. Moreover, he could create stories himself and pass them off as part of the traditional corpus. In Keti Ferenke I discovered a man with a critical and ironic sense of his own culture, someone whose creative bent accommodated orthodox views yet always remained subtly apart from them.

I suppose it was inevitable that sooner or later I would ask him to tell me the story of his life. But when he did recount his own story in February 1972 it was with such alacrity, and in such an unabashedly personal way, that I was taken aback. Something else surprised me too: certain uncanny parallelisms between the events which had deeply influenced the course of his life and the events which had figured so centrally in Saran Salia's life. Yet these lives could not by any stretch of the anthropological imagination be reduced to cultural determinants. Each man had addressed his experiences in his own way, and though both exemplified conventional values this was not a consequence of mindless conformity but a result of what they had self-consciously made of what they had suffered.

Here, then, is Keti Ferenke's story in his own words:

My mother hailed from Kamadugu Sukurela. My [maternal] great-grandfather,[10] Lai Bundo, came before[11] my [maternal] grandfather, Yerewa Bile. My grandfather Yerewa

Bile's mother, Yerewa, hailed from Sambaia Bendugu. Yerewa Fule and Samaia Fule—
my great-grandfathers shared them.[12]

They took Sama Fula and married her to my great-grandfather Kundembe Koroma.
She bore Sama Magba, and Sama Magba was the father of our present chief Seku.
Our great-grandmother Yerewa Fula was married to our great-grandfather Lai Bundo
of Kamadugu Sukurela. They had Yerewa Bile. Yerewa Bile married Sinkari Sira from
Farandugu. He brought her to Kamadugu Sukurela. Sinkari Sira's eldest daughter was
my own mother, Sira Keti. My other mother was Sira Sayon, Sinkari Sira's second
daughter. The third daughter was Banda Kuma. Banda Kuma came before Mantile
[Manti Lai]. Manti Lai came before Muru Lai, who was also called Mema Sira. Mema
Sira was the last daughter; she married Manti Tamba.

Now of my mother Keti. My grandfather Tina Ferenke went and found her. She
was to have been the old man's wife. At that time my grandfather Tina Ferenke was
Paramount Chief. He brought her to Kondembaia. But he was very old, and he said:
"Since I am so old I bequeath her to my children." He gave her to the erstwhile chief
Bala, though Bala was not chief at that time. Not long after, Tina Ferenke died. My
father, Samaran Bala, contested the chieftaincy. But he was advised to bide his time
and allow Sama Magba to become chief. So the chieftaincy was given to my grandfather Sama Magba. He had many children. Everyone was aware of what a tremendous
thing chieftaincy is.

Then my grandfather Sama Magba died. Once again my father, Samaran Bala, raised
his hand and declared his candidacy. He won the chieftaincy. But before he became
chief he said, "I have many wives but my younger brother has none. Therefore I will
give my brother the woman that my father gave to me." He took my mother Keti and
gave her to his younger brother, Kona Sumban. At that time no one knew about me.
I did not know about the world. I did not even know where I was.[13]

Our father, Samaran Bala, won the chieftaincy. Those whose eyes were open on
these events included the other sons of my grandfather Tina Ferenke—my fathers Tara
Kona, Samaran Sefile, and Kona Sumban. They were the ones that our eyes opened
upon. Our grandfather Tina Ferenke may have had many children, but we do not know
them; we only know of those that our eyes opened upon.[14]

When my mother married my father Kona Sumban they had their first child, my
elder sister [Tina]. My fathers sat down and said: "Eh, our father did not have any
daughters and so could not name one of his children after his own mother. Yet he
gave this woman in marriage to us. Now that she has given birth to her first-born
daughter, we should name the child after our father's mother, Tina." So my elder sister
was named after our grandfather's mother, Tina Sise. They called her Tina Sise because
our grandfather's mother, Tina, was of the Sise clan. Thus our grandfather was the
child of a Sise woman.

My elder sister Tina was weaned and my elder sister Kulako took the breast. When
she was weaned, I, Keti Ferenke, took the breast. Then I was weaned and my younger
brother Bile took the breast. But Kulako and Bile both died. I am the only one alive—I
and my elder sister Tina. Kulako and Bile have gone ahead of us. I live in Kondembaia
for no other reason than that I was born here.

Up to this point Keti Ferenke has spoken almost entirely in terms of genealogical time. His generation and birth are placed within the field of cognatic ties. His
identity is assimilated into a universe of givens: filiation, birth-order-position,

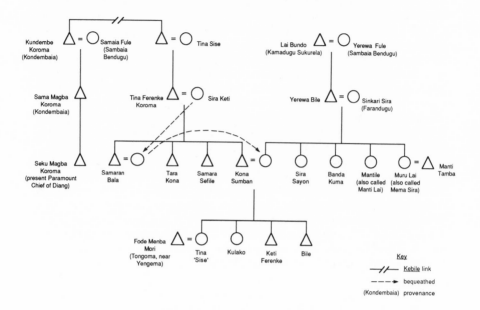

Genealogical Chart of Keti Ferenke Koroma

name. Now, however, he begins to speak of his life in terms of biographical time. He recounts personal experiences, tells of a singular destiny:

That is how I was born. My mother Keti and my father Kona Sumban were together until we were all born. Then I began to become aware of things around me. One of my first memories is of my elder father taking my elder sister and giving her in marriage to Fode Menba Mori. When she married Fode Menba Mori she moved from here and went and settled in Tongoma, near Yengema. . . .

Then my [maternal] grandmother died in Kamadugu Sukurela. We went there for the funeral.

On our way back to Kondembaia my mother said, "Now, Ferenke, we have come from your grandmother's funeral but your elder sister is not here. I want you to go and tell her what has happened. Tell her to come." But my mother had a severe head-ache. I said, "Heh, I'm not going. You're not well. I'll go when you are better. Now, with you unwell, I don't want to go." But my mother said, "Go," and I had to accept it. "Yeh," I said, "that is that."

I left Kondembaia on the twenty-ninth of the month before Ramadan.[15] I entered Alkalia on the first day of Ramadan.[16] I went on to Tongoma. When I reached Tongoma I told my elder sister Tina about the death. My brother-in-law [numorgo] said, "Now this is the fast month. You must wait here until the fast month ends, then you can go home. I will say goodbye to you when I've finished my prayers. You can go then." So I stayed.

I was totally unaware that the headache my mother was suffering from when I left had now become worse. In the middle of the fast month my mother Keti died. She died while I was away. I knew nothing of it. But my father was with her till the end.

On the last day of the fast month—it was a Friday—my father went to pray. The women had already cooked rice for the prayer-day. On his way to the prayer-ground (*selikenema*), he began to tremble. The Muslims were already at their prayers, sitting in rows. At that time my younger brother Bile was still alive. He went and supported my father and said, "Father, you cannot go and pray, you are trembling. Let us go back home." But my father said, "Leave me be, let us go, nothing will happen to me." As my younger brother let him go, he began trembling again. The prayers ceased. People said, "This man has a fever." They took my father home. But he died that day. It was a terrible thing. From Friday, through Saturday, until Sunday no one could bury him because his death had been so sudden and strange.[17]

At that time my father's elder brother was Paramount Chief, but the white men had summoned him to Freetown.[18] He was in Freetown when his brother died. He was told of his brother's death as he was on his way back home. He told the District Commissioner what had happened. The D. C. gave him his own *woro nani*.[19] Then my elder father came on here and met the burial party. Everyone was crying. They were crying for me because I was the eldest son. I had gone to my elder sister to tell her of our grandmother's death, and my mother had died. Then, on the last day of the same month, my father had died. Both of them had died while I was away. It was a terrible thing, a strange thing. Everyone was crying. They said, "Ferenke has not come yet, Ferenke has not come yet, Ferenke has not come yet, Ferenke has not come yet." I was still in Tongoma. My heart was beating loudly, loudly, loudly, loudly. Then I said, "Let me go home." My brother-in-law said goodbye and I started off.

From Tongoma, as far as Diang Sukurela, I heard nothing of the deaths. They kept the news from me. No one I met told me anything about the deaths. I arrived home and suddenly found myself in the middle of the funeral rites. There was nothing I could do. What Allah had destined had happened.

I knew that my father was the man who brought me into the world, but my elder father was the one who was now responsible for me. I knew he would take care of us. My father had gone, but the man who had been married to my mother before him—chief Bala—was still alive. So I was not broken-hearted. I have found no fault with my elder father. He has found wives for me, and I now have my own children. He sends me on errands, but he has never wronged me. I do what I want. Indeed, I feel my father never died. Even had he lived, both he and I would have been in chief Bala's hands. So my heart is at peace.

That is how I was born. I have explained it all—my father's side and my mother's side. I have explained it all to you. Some of it you will forget, some you will not forget. You asked me to tell you about my life. That is it.

Keti Ferenke was about ten or eleven years old when his parents died. Thirty years later, recounting those traumatic events to me in 1972, his attitude seemed resigned, almost fatalistic. It was a characteristic Kuranko way of talking: one's luck in life depended upon external circumstances and innate dispositions; one's fate (*sawura*) was fixed. Yet this is only a partial view, more typical of how Kuranko explain things in retrospect than how they actually live.

In conversation, Keti Ferenke often boasted to me of his intelligence. It was this faculty of insight and understanding (*hankilimaiye*) that enabled him to create and tell stories with such skill and verve. But his intelligence "came from Allah," and so too did the inspiration for his stories. However, in the Kuranko view one's moral worth is ultimately contingent upon the attitude one takes up toward such innate endowments, what one does with what one has. Thus, although Keti Ferenke attributes his creative genius and inspiration to Allah, he acknowledges that the development of the ideas he "receives" for stories is his responsibility, a matter of his own work. The composition of his narrative, "The Abuse of the Killing Word" (Jackson 1982a:164–67), is instructive. The germinal idea, of how the power of life and death came to be in Allah's hands, not human hands, simply, as he put it, came into his head. Subsequently, working on his farm, lounging in his hammock at home, he tried to come up with a plausible and familiar situation that would realize the idea. To be sure, many elements in this story are derived from the traditional repertoire, and the structure, like the moral conclusions, are fairly conventional. But the composition of the story, like the performance of it, is a matter of individual judgment, of self-conscious work.

A person is held responsible for managing the *relationship* between inner dispositions and outward behavior, between what, in Kuranko terms, is "found" or "encountered" and what is "made." This dialectic between given endowments, proclivities, and strictures *and* chosen attitudes and modes of comportment lies at the heart of Kuranko ethics (Jackson 1982a:21–31). Keti Ferenke alludes to it in this wry comment on his storytelling: "I could never stop thinking of stories, yet I could stop myself telling them. If I am asked to tell a story, I cannot stop thinking of one to tell, but I can stop myself telling it." In short, though it is predestined that he compose stories, he can deny or mask this inclination if social propriety demands it.

A kind of paradox arises here. Though the social order was created by Allah and the "first people" (*fol' morgonnu*) long ago, it is recapitulated only by dint of purposeful human activity in the here and now. The ancestral values upon which the Kuranko set such great store do not come into being, generation after generation, of their own accord. At the same time that it is necessary to play up the vital role of each individual in the construction of social reality (during initiation, for instance) it is also necessary to play down that role lest the omnipotence of Allah and the ancestors be called into question. The powers of individual initiative and praxis (associated with the bush) are thus regarded ambivalently because, though the social order (associated with the village) depends on such powers, they also contradict the ontological priority given to the collectivity. The very existence of the human subject as one who "stands out" or "emerges" must be eclipsed by a conception of the subject as one who is a part of, not apart from, the group.

Keti Ferenke resolves this paradox in three ways. First, though he is the author of his own stories he attributes their inspiration to a transcendent rather than a personal source. Second, he allows his stories to pass into tradition without any acknowledgment or commemoration of their origins in his experience as a singular individual. Third, in his stories he is careful to extol individual initiative and choice only in relation to communal values and conventional wisdom.

In these ways the stories become a kind of symbolic capital, a common fund, disguising their origins in personal experience and creative work. But the disguise often slips, as in Keti Ferenke's remarks revealing the dialectic between cultural forms and individual praxis:

> To start with, my great-great-grandfather was a chief. Down to my grandfather, they were all chiefs. Until my father, they were all chiefs. Now, when you are born into a ruling house you will be told many things. If you are a fool you'll be none the wiser, but if you are clever you will scrutinize everything. And when you lie down, you will think over certain things. If you do this, it is good. This is how I think of things. Though it is only Allah that gives thought to a person.
>
> When you are told something, it is good if it stays in your mind. What I have to say about the stories is this: I only think of them. They just come into my mind, just like that. I am not asleep. I am not in a dream. But when I think of them, I put them all together into a story.

In his life-story, Keti Ferenke conveyed a stoical, almost fatalistic attitude: one's destiny is in the hands of others. In his fictions and conversations, however, his attitude is quite different: one should take nothing for granted, accept nothing at its face value, be wary and aware of everything and everyone, scrutinize, reflect upon, see beyond the immediate appearance of things. Time and again he harks back to the notion of *hankilimaiye* (intelligence, insightfulness, adroitness, gumption, wit, nous) as the best safeguard against being deceived or fooled.

It is this preoccupation with intelligence that explains his active leadership of the *Due* (or *Doe*) lodge in Kondembaia, his hometown, a lodge he describes as "an association of intelligent people."

The leader of the lodge is called the *Do karamorgo* (*Do* teacher) or *Dobe*, and members are known as *Dodannu* (on an analogy with *Sisibe*, brooding hen, and *Sisidannu*, hatched chickens), and a special language of transposed syllables and muddled vowels enables initiates to communicate with each other in public without noninitiates knowing what they are saying. Code words, special handshakes and greetings also form part of the cabalistic lore of the lodge, and initiates are taught various verbal and interrogatory techniques for divining the hidden intentions of strangers. Initiates also amuse themselves with wire-puzzles and riddles, and Keti Ferenke took great delight in teasing me with such conundrums as "How many people are there in the world?" and "How many steps does a person take in the course of a day?"[20]

Keti Ferenke's preoccupation with the difference between reality and appearance was particularly evident in his attitude to women. Possibly his numerous cautionary tales against men being deceived by women's wiles reflect the crises in his own marriages.[21]

His first wife hailed from Kamadugu Sukurela, his mother's hometown. Keti Ferenke once described to me how, when his wife was four to six months pregnant with their first child, she pestered him to make love to her. They were living on their farm and Keti Ferenke was due to make a trip back to Kondembaia. His wife begged him not to go and tried to persuade him to stay and sleep with her. Keti Ferenke's refusal was in a sense justified; the Kuranko say that sexual intercourse during pregnancy endangers the life of the fetus. He made his trip to Kondembaia as planned, leaving his wife in good health. But later that month she fell ill and, during her illness, confessed to having tried to kill Keti Ferenke by witchcraft. She said she'd felt humiliated and shamed when Keti Ferenke had refused to sleep with her. She had enlisted the support of a coven of witches—"armies of the night"—and tried to harm him. When the coven failed to find him the witches turned upon her and beat her with blows upon her back. Keti Ferenke recalled that during her illness she had been unable to sit up straight and had suffered severe back pains. The evening after she had confessed to witchcraft she had a miscarriage (she had been pregnant with twins). Keti Ferenke's father, chief Samaran Bala, suggested they take her back to Kondembaia, but she died that night.

It is tempting to see Keti Ferenke's insistence on the need for vigilance and forethought in the light of these traumatic events. Appearances are misleading, relationships are fickle, and the truth is elusive and hidden: he develops these ideas in several narratives which stress the need to know the background to each and every event, to grasp the reality beneath and beyond the immediacy of things (Jackson 1982a: narratives 1 and 19).

Keti Ferenke relies upon two narrative stratagems to explore this view. The first is to privilege friendship (dienaye) over kinship (nakelinyorgoye) and so emphasize chosen over given ties. While kinship implies identifications and obligations that are immutable and incontrovertible, the bonds of friendship are ad hoc and negotiable (see Jackson 1982a:192–98). Thus, to discuss problems of mutuality, loyalty, trust, and integrity in terms of friendship rather than kinship is to stress the critical role of individual discernment and gumption in the construction of a viable social order. The second stratagem is to privilege mind over society, to stress a person's intelligence rather than his or her social position. Here too the focus on how one uses one's head rather than on one's socially determined identity helps to bring home the significance of individual praxis in the construction of the social order. In Keti Ferenke's case it is difficult not to see this bias as a reflection of his own peripheral position in a ruling lineage. He has used his wits—like his involvement in the Due lodge—as a kind of compensation for his marginality to positions of secular power. I think this is borne out in the following comments:

We say kina wo and kina wo [near homophones]. They are not one [the first means "beehive," the second "elder"]. If you hear kina [elder], he knows almost everything. But if you hear kina [beehive], it does not know anything. The elder could be found in the younger and the younger could be found in the elder.

Even if a person is a child, but behaves like an elder, then he is an elder. If he thinks like an elder, then he is an elder. Even if a person is old and senior, if he behaves like a child then he is a child. Therefore, this matter of seniority comes not only from the fact that one is born first, or from the fact that one is big and strong; it also concerns the manner in which a person behaves and does things. For example, you will see some old men who have nothing; they are not called "big men" [morgo ba, "elders"]. But some young men have wealth; because of that they are called morgo ba. Therefore, whatever Allah has put in your head, that will make you what you are. I am speaking now, but some of these words of wisdom [kuma kore] which I am explaining to you are not known by everyone. You may ask a man and he may know of them. But I have explained them. Therefore, am I not the elder? There are some elders who know of these things, but I have explained them. Therefore, if you hear the word *kina* you should know that it is *hankili* [intelligence] that really defines it.

In his narratives, Keti Ferenke exaggerates the importance of individual praxis over inherited position, not just as a way of rationalizing his own marginal situation but because he sees that though the foundations of the social order are given by ancestral fiat the *construction* of that order is problematic; it demands the active, intelligent engagement of individuals. This refusal to take social reality for granted, as something made by others or at other times, explains the scathing attacks in many of his stories on shortsightedness, stupidity, and dogmatism. A chief who uses his authority for selfish ends, a Muslim zealot who sees little beyond his beads and book, a father whose greed makes him negligent of his children, a woman obsessed with sex, a man whose avarice blinds him to the needs of his closest friend: these are the butts of his satire. It is neither the slavish adherence to given norms nor the unbridled expression of self-interest that makes for a viable social order, but considered acts informed by judgment and understanding.

FINAL REFLECTIONS

Keti Ferenke Koroma and Saran Salia Sano have much in common besides a shared culture: the tragic loss of their parents in childhood, troubled marriages, a marginality to secular power, and leadership of important Kuranko cults. Both men espouse traditional values yet regard the articulation of those values as problematic, something to be decided and done rather than simply assented to. To some extent this problematic arises from the ambiguity at the heart of all social existence: the indeterminate relationship between the eventfulness and flux of one's own life and the seemingly frozen forms of the ongoing cultural tradition.

The medicines used by Saran Salia and the intelligence vaunted by Keti Ferenke are ethically ambiguous, open to use for a personal advantage or for the commonweal. Each man has had to work to harmonize these disparate possibilities—something which is evident in the way they have played their roles in the *Kome* and *Due* associations as well as in the way Saran Salia has used his powers as *besetigi* to protect and care for the more vulnerable members of his community and the determination with which Keti Ferenke has used his skills as a storyteller to make people aware of the moral values upon which sociality depends. Though their social roles disguise the personal experiences and events which led them to take up those roles and play them in their own particular ways, their life-stories and their talk reveal those hidden elements. It is in this sense that praxis is always a vital and indeterminate relationship with givenness, a going beyond, a surpassing of one's situation, status, or role. The lives of Saran Salia and Keti Ferenke could not be deduced from, nor should they be reduced to, their social circumstances. This is not to say that we are free to make of our lives what we will; rather it is to suggest a pragmatist view of free will which, having noted what is singular about each human life, claims "the right to expect that in its deepest elements as well as in its surface phenomena, the future may not identically repeat and imitate the past" (James 1978:60), even when, as in most preliterate societies, social time is seen as an unchanging recapitulation of the ancestral past.

Clearly, cultural analysis must be dialectical. It must trace out the play and tension between the ideational order—the *Weltanschauung*—and the actual experience of individuals in the everyday world—the *Lebenswelt*.[22] Cultural anthropology tends to define its project in terms of the elucidation of necessary patterns and abiding structures; yet, equally significant is the lived world of contingent experience, of sickness and health, love and grief, mortality and crisis—the domain of the human project, of *Bildung*. Cultural reality is not just given; it must, in John Berger's words, be "continually sought out, held—I am tempted to say *salvaged*" (Berger 1979:72). If it is not it becomes "a screen of cliches" before which we are doomed to pass as mere shadows of our real selves.

Reflection on the *Lebenswelt* is equally important in grasping the dialectical character of ethnographical praxis itself. Our knowledge of the other is not just a product of our theoretical thought and research activity; it is a consequence of critical experiences, relationships, choices, and events both in the field and in the quotidian world of our professional and family lives. The dialectic between the immediate domains of sensible experience and the more abstract domains of anthropological discourse creates quite different modes of understanding for each one of us. Yet the synthetic character of our understanding is conventionally disguised in order to foster the impression that it is constructed through methods and models which, while revised by our empirical observations of others, remain unaffected by the empirical reality of our personal engagement with and attitude to those others.

Against this view it seems sounder and more honest to admit that our understanding is constituted dialectically out of the tensions and play between our intellectual tradition (*Weltanschauung*) and the adventitious circumstances of our particular lives. Doing so makes it more likely that we will hazard comparisons, not only between social structures and cultural forms *but also between our experiences of life.* Ethnography then becomes a form of *Verstehen*, a project of empathic and vicarious understanding in which the other is seen in the light of one's own experiences and the activity of trying to fathom the other in turn illuminates and alters one's sense of Self. To ignore these intersubjective grounds on which our understanding is constituted abandons us to the performance of banal comparisons between social *systems* or condemns us to the impasse of never being able to venture views about the experience of others. It is the impasse Kuranko speak of whenever they want to privilege doxa over opinion: *N'de sa bu'ro* (I am not inside them, i.e., I cannot read their thoughts), and *N'de ma konto lon*" (I do not know what is inside).

This phenomenological impasse can, however, be overcome by recognizing that we make ourselves, *in relation to others*, out of given and inherited circumstances we did not choose. Self and other share the same world, even though their projects differ. To fathom another is not, therefore, all projection and surmise, one insular subjectivity blindly reaching out to an alien other. To compare notes on experience with someone else presumes and creates a common ground, and the understanding arrived at takes its validity not from our detachment and objectivity but from the very possibility of our mutuality, the existence of the relationship itself. My interpretations of the lives of Saran Salia Sano and Keti Ferenke Koroma do not pretend objectivity. They reflect our shared experience, the fact of our friendship, which, by transcending linguistic and cultural differences, shows better than any argument that human being cannot be reduced to the fixed forms of cultural being without fundamental distortions.

THREE

Ajala's Heads

Thrownness and Free Will in
African Thought

The subject of this chapter is traditional African notions of free will and determinism. My approach will be to critically compare certain features of West African
thought with Sartrean existentialism and Freudian psychoanalysis. Two theoretical
issues are raised in doing this, both of which must be addressed if we are to arrive
at a viable method of cross-cultural comparison. The first concerns the often disguised and undeclared relationship between the ethnographer's personal background and the social analysis foregrounded in his or her writing. The second concerns the application of structuralist, existential, Marxist, or psychoanalytic models
drawn from the Western intellectual tradition to cultures whose modes of objectification are often atheoretical in character. My approach to these issues will be to
play up the similarities between how anthropologists and those we study organize
and interpret experience. In particular, I will focus on the way "our" models and
"their" beliefs share similar claims to objective truth and determinate principles.
I take the view that all such forms of objectification must be de-fetishized and de-
reified in order to reveal the grounds on which their very possibility rests. I will
argue that this kind of critique affords us a sound method for making cross-cultural
comparisons. I suggest that at the heart of all modes of understanding—theoretical
and atheoretical alike—lies a need to assure ourselves that the world out there is
coherent and built on a scale which is compatible with and manageable by us. Only
then can we enter into a relationship with it; only then can our sense of self be
stabilized. A "model" in science or a "belief system" in a preliterate society may
be compared with a nursery toy. As Lévi-Strauss observes in *La pensée sauvage*, they
offer us accessible homologues of the wider world which we can deploy, magically
as it were, to extend our power into that world and experience ourselves as subjects
(1966a:23–24).

Let us begin by noting that striking analogies often exist between Western and
non-Western world views. For instance, during the 1930s George Devereux was
engaged in the study of culture and personality among the Mohave. One of his
objectives was "to collect data on mental disorders in Mohave society and to interpret them in terms of Mohave culture and society" (Devereux 1969b:1). During
his first two field trips his bias was antianalytic and non-Freudian, but on his third

field trip in 1938 he realized there were many arresting affinities between Mohave folk models of psychopathology and the Freudian psychoanalytic model. These affinities persuaded him to undertake systematic psychoanalytic training (1969b:3; 1978a:372). As he puts it: "I remained an anti-Freudian until, in 1938, my Mohave informant taught me psychoanalysis, as Freud's patients had taught it to him" (1978b:366; cf. 1967:chap.10).

I underwent a similar intellectual conversion during my initial period of fieldwork among the Kuranko, not to psychoanalysis but to existentialism.

Throughout my first year of fieldwork I was struck by the ways in which Kuranko, particularly in their rituals and narratives, contrived to overthrow, place in abeyance, or controvert orthodox forms of thought and behavior. But such annulments of conventional forms were always a prelude to their reassertion. The dialectic intrigued me. I was not content to see it simply as a method of dramatically bringing into relief the ancestral values on which the social order was founded. Rather, it seemed to me evidence of an existential imperative: the need to address the given structure of one's social world not as a ready-made and preemptive body of rules to be passively and slavishly adhered to but as a set of possibilities to be realized through self-conscious purposeful activity. The Kuranko social order did not endure, generation after generation, through inertia; its creation and recreation depended on the decisive and concerted activity of each and every individual. In each generation anew, people had to enter into an active relationship with the world, struggling to make it their own and experience it as a product of their praxis, even though they were in fact recapitulating the very world they had been born into and were committed to the belief that the world ultimately reflected the primordial designs of the first people (*fol' morgonnu*) and of God, the *primum mobile*, the creator ruler (*dale mansa*).

When I began working on my Ph.D. I had hardly any familiarity with existential philosophy, but in my search for an interpretative framework compatible with what I understood to be the Kuranko conception of human existence I came upon the later work of Sartre. At once I was able to articulate some of the ideas that had remained inchoate during my period of fieldwork. In the following pages I summarize some of the apparent parallelisms between existential and West African conceptions of determinism and free will before turning to a more critical examination of them.

There is a Kuranko adage, *dunia toge ma dunia; a toge le a dununia*, which, translated literally, means "the name of the world is not world; its name is load." The adage exploits oxymoron and pun (*dunia*, "world," and *dununia*, "load," are near homophones) and implies that the world is like a head-load, the weight of which depends on the way one chooses to carry it. Such an attitude is suggestive of the existential view that man is never identical with the conditions that bear upon him; human existence is a vital relationship with such conditions, and it is the character of this *relationship* which it is our task to fathom.[1] This view is also implied by the Kuranko word which most closely translates our words *custom* and *tradition*: *namui*. The word is from *na* ("mother") and the verb *ka mui* ("to give birth," as in the term *muinyorgoye*; literally, "birth partnership," i.e., close agnatic kinship or "the bond between children of the same father"). Namui suggests that a person is born into a world of preestablished custom in the same way he or she is born into the father's kin group. But while one's social status and name are given through descent, one's temperament and destiny are shaped by one's mother's *influence,* hence the adage *ke l dan sia; musi don den; ke l dan wo bolo* ("a man has many children; a woman nurtures them; his children are in her hands") and the frequent attributions in Kuranko life of a person's fortunes to his mother's influence (Jackson 1977b:137–45). Because it is the *interplay* of formal determinants and informal influences which decides a person's destiny, we could say that "to be born is both to be born of the world and to be born into the world. The world is already constituted, but also never completely constituted; in the first case we are acted upon, in the second we are open to an infinite number of possibilities" (Merleau-Ponty 1962:453).

Sartre (1969) speaks of the "dialectic irreducibility" of lived experience (*le vécu*), by which he means that the special character of human existence cannot be dissolved into general forms or formulae without serious distortions.[2] Reductionism denies the perennially unique interplay of the given and the possible because it insists that man is determined *either* from within *or* from without. For Sartre, we are a synthetic unity of what we make out of what we are made (1963:49). Let us consider how this dialectic is expressed in various West African world views.

According to the Yoruba, each person is said to make a choice about his or her preferred destiny before he or she is born. A divinity called Ajala, "the potter who makes heads," molds heads from clay, fires them, and places them in a storehouse. Because Ajala is an incorrigible debtor whose mind is seldom on his work, many of the heads are badly thrown or overfired. *Ori,* the word for the physical head, also connotes the "internal head" (*ori-inú*), the inner personality "that rules, controls, and guides the life and activities of the person" (Idowu 1962:170), and the act of selecting one's *ori* is regarded as one of free will. But because of Ajala's irresponsible workmanship, many heads prove to be defective. Nevertheless, as soon as the choice of a head has been made, the person is free to travel to earth where his success or failure in life will depend largely on the *ori* he picked up in Ajala's storehouse.

Ori is, however, only one aspect of human being. *Emi,* which means both the physical heart and the spirit, is the imperishable aspect of the person which continues to be reincarnated. *Emi* is given by Olodumare, the supreme being, after Orinsanla, the creator god, has formed the physical body of a person out of clay. The third aspect of a person is called *ese* ("leg"). Abimbola notes that while a person's destiny derives from his *ori,* the realization of that destiny depends on *ese,* the legs (1973:85). A Yoruba tale nicely illustrates this complementarity of *ori* and *ese.* All the *ori* meet together to deliberate on a project they want to bring to fruition. But they fail to invite *ese.* Having made their resolutions, the heads find that without legs they do not have the means to carry out their designs. As Abimbola puts it, "the point of the story is that even if one is predestined to success by the choice of a good *ori,* one cannot actually achieve success without the use of one's *ese,* which is a symbol of power and activity" (86).[3] This "two-sided conception" of human destiny "is accepted by the Yoruba without question. It . . . means that in an inexplicable way, what happens to a person may be simultaneously the result of *Bi ó ti gbà a*—'As he received it (was destined),' and *A-f'-ọwọ̀-fà*—'that which he brings upon himself'" (Idowu 1962:183).

The significance which the Yoruba attached to *ese* is reminiscent of the way Sartre and Merleau-Ponty emphasize the importance of embodiment. Human intentionality is a bodily disposition as much as an inclination of the mind.[4] "Consciousness is in the first place not a matter of 'I think that' but of 'I can'" (Merleau-Ponty 1962:137). Different intentionalities may, however, coexist in a person and give rise to profound conflicts.

The notion that a declared prenatal choice influences the course of a person's destiny is widespread in West Africa (Fortes 1983). It is also widely held that a person may be ignorant of this choice and find his conscious aspirations in conflict with deeply ingrained dispositions.[5] Among the Igbo, *chi* is the incorporeal aspect of a person which presides over the prenatal choice of destiny. One's lot or portion on earth reflects a primordial bargain with one's *chi*. But once a person is thrown into the world, he and his *chi* may find themselves in disagreement. Thus, a person may fall victim to the demands of an intransigent *chi* or become locked into a struggle to revoke his prenatal choice (Achebe 1975). Similar views are held by the Tallensi. Before a person is born into the world his "soul" (*sii*) declares his choice of destiny before heaven (*Naawun*). This "spoken destiny" (*nuor-yin*) acts as an implacable force in a person's life, inclining him or her to renege on filial obligations and otherwise "reject ordinary human living" (Fortes 1983:17). However, as Fortes notes, "life—symbolized for the Tallensi in the breath (*ŋovor*)—is only the raw material for living. What one makes of it depends on other spiritual agencies" (15). The "prenatal destiny" must compete with a set of countervailing forces, signified by configurations of ancestors unique to each individual, which guide and assist a person toward the realization of his or her full social potential. The personal life is thus conceived of as a dynamic play between social and antisocial imperatives—in Fortes's terms, between Jobian fulfillment and Oedipal fate.

How are such opposed imperatives and competing intentionalities reconciled? In answering this question from the West African point of view we have to consider in more detail the kinds of complementary forces which may offset or countermand the prenatal destiny, providing room for intelligent purpose and conscious control in the actual working out of one's social destiny on earth. Edo ideas on this subject are particularly illuminating.

It is believed that before birth each individual predestines himself (*hi*) by making a declaration before Osanobua, the creator, setting out a life program and asking for everything needed to carry it through successfully. One's *ehi* ("destiny") acts as a kind of prompt at this time, and will remain in the spirit world as a guide and intermediary with Osanobua. Misfortune in life is explained as a failure to keep to the chosen life program, a result of having a "bad *ehi*," and a person may implore his *ehi* to intervene and improve his lot. Bradbury notes that *ehi* "represents the innate potentialities for social achievement with which each individual is believed to be endowed" (1973:263). But while *ehi* implies the absence of personal control over one's fortunes, the head (*uhumwu*) "admits a greater degree of responsibility." The head is the seat of thought, judgment, will, or character, of hearing, seeing, and speaking. It therefore complements *ehi* and, in the past, was the focus of a cult concerned with the headship of families and the rule of the state. The second force which complements *ehi* is the hand (*ikegobo*), which connotes manual skill and successful enterprise. Also the focus of a cult, the hand symbolizes a person's vigor and industry in farming, trading, craft work, and other undertakings. "It implies personal responsibility and self-reliance in a highly competitive and relatively individualistic society" (Bradbury 1973:265). The English saying "your fate is in your own hands" translates readily into Edo.[6]

The Edo conception of human destiny thus emphasizes the dialectical interplay of the prenatal dispositions and understanding (*communis sententia*) with the practical know-how acquired in the course of a person's *social* development. We must be careful, however, not to reduce the predeterminative domain of existence to the prenatal world and so give the impression that the social world is by contrast a domain of freedom and fulfillment. The established social order with its fixed traditions, conventions, and authority structures, into which a person is thrown at birth, can be just as oppressive, predeterminative, and problematic as the innate dispositions decided prenatally. Accordingly, the domain of a person's freedom does not lie over and above either the spirit world from whence he comes or the social world into which he is born but squarely between the two. Together they determine the parameters of a person's effective freedom. Praxis is thus a matter of negotiating a path between innate dispositions and social pressures, of harmonizing or reconciling the often opposed fields of nature and culture. Throughout Africa, this movement is allegorized as journeying between bush and village.

A common scenario in Kuranko oral narratives involves a young hero who hazards his life on a journey into the wilderness in search of an object, such as a musical instrument or a fetish, which will be of advantage to his community. In his confrontation with wild beings and in his struggles against the temptation to use his gains for selfish ends, the questing hero embodies recurring moral dilemmas in Kuranko social life, such as the competing claims of duty and desire, individuation and association. The resolution of these dilemmas depends upon the hero's powers of discernment and judgment, though he is sometimes aided by supernatural helpers or magical objects that occupy a position midway between the social world and the wilderness (Jackson 1982a).

Kuranko rites of initiation (*biriye*) plot a similar course between wildness and sociality, the crucial transformation from childhood to adulthood taking place in a "bush house," the *fafei*, which is burned to the ground when neophytes complete their initiation and return to their village. Initiation is sometimes spoken of as a "taming" (*kan kolo*) of the "wild" or "unripe" nature of the child. An uninitiated child "knows nothing," say the Kuranko; "a child is just as it was born; it has no social intelligence (*hankili sa la*)." Initiation provides "new understanding" (*hankili kura*); the child becomes a "new person" capable of assuming responsibility for his or her own thought and behavior. Central to this transition is the endurance of pain, *dime*, a word which connotes both emotional suffering and physical hurt. In the bush, cut off from emotional ties with the community, particularly with the mother, the pubescent child is subject to a series of ordeals which are said to simulate the crises which inevitably attend adult life. The neophyte is urged to control his or her *reaction* to suffering. Mastery of one's reaction to pain—standing stockstill, not blinking, not making a sound, not wincing when one is cut—is regarded as the paradigm of all self-mastery. In the Kuranko view it is only when a person learns to discriminate between the action of hurt and his or her reaction to it that he or she gains any measure of control or freedom.[7] *Yiri* (steadiness of body/mind) connotes this detached attitude to an inner state, whether pain, grief, anger, or love. *Kerenteye* (bravery) and *kilanbelteye* (fortitude) suggest moral fiber, an ability to withstand the tides of strong emotions. These virtues are all dependent upon the cultivation of an abstract attitude which produces consonance between intentions and actions. Various adages bring home the importance of this: *Morge kume mir' la i konto i wo l fo le* ("Whatever word a person thinks of, that will he speak," i.e., think before you speak lest you blurt out stupid ideas); *I mir' la koe mi ma, i wo l ke la* ("You thought of that, you do that," i.e., think before you act lest your actions belie your intentions).

In the Kuranko view, the way one comports oneself after leaving the initiation lodge, the *fafei*, is the way one will comport oneself for the rest of one's life.[8] A *ti wo bo l ka*, the Kuranko say; "one will not leave it." To fail the test of initiation is to remain a child, impetuous, thoughtless, and socially inept, just as one was born (*a danye le wo la*, "how one is made").[9] In such cases a person may become a butt of jokes and an object of pity, morally excused from responsibility for his or her incorrigible habits. *A ka tala, a soron ta la bole*, the Kuranko say; "he is blameless, he was born with it." Alternatively, the inscrutable designs of Allah may be invoked, since the Kuranko say that one's destiny (*sawura*) is ultimately a "gift of Allah," decided before one's birth and quite irreversible: *la tege saraka sa* ("no sacrifice can cut it"). However, whenever such fatalistic views are offered, whether in terms of prenatal choices as among the Tallensi and Edo or the irrevocable will of Allah as among the Kuranko, they are usually retrospective rationalizations of crises that have befallen people rather than prescriptions for practical conduct. Thus, while the Kuranko say that certain faculties such as self-possession (*miran*) and intelligence (*hankilimaiye*) or certain traits of temperament (*yugi*) are given by Allah, this does not mean that the mastery and use of such inborn dispositions are similarly given. On the contrary, they are to be regarded as "a field of instrumental possibilities," to use Sartre's phrase, which, though not infinitely malleable, may be opened up to scrutiny, subject to various interpretations, and experienced or reacted to in different ways. This, then, is the domain of choice and of human praxis.

Like rites of initiation, African curing rites involve an attempt to harmonize or reconcile the often competing imperatives of "town" and "bush." Among the BaKongo, agitation or "wildness" within a person must be counteracted by the "calming" or "cooling" effects of medicines culled from the domestic domain (Janzen 1978:203). This entails an adjustment of the relationship between internal and external fields of being, conceptualized in terms of the contrasts white/black (i.e., self/other) and town/bush. Similar ideas inform medical practice among the Songhay, who often conceptualize disease as an uncontrolled invasion of self or town by "the bush." As Jeanne Bisilliat shows, redressive action necessitates a comparable movement, but one which uses medicines from the "cultivated bush" and involves the controlled, conscious participation of the patient (1976:590).

According to these African models, "pathways" exist within the human body as well as between self and society and between society and the wilderness (Bisilliat 1976:555; Jackson 1982a:157–58; Willis 1978:143). The key to well-being lies in a person's ability to control traffic along these pathways. As the image suggests, physical and psychic health is intimately connected with the state of a person's relationship with others in his or her community[10]; it is a result of successfully harmonizing inner compulsion and external rules, of neither succumbing completely to one's "wild" dispositions nor becoming so rigidly rule-bound that one cannot see beyond one's own social position.[11]

In the modes of praxis considered thus far, a person always relies on an ally, mediator, or mentor who is able to tap and tame the wild energies of the bush: bush spirits in Kuranko oral narratives, cult masters associated with powerful bush spirits in Kuranko initiation, and medicine-masters with a command of medicines drawn from the wilderness in Kuranko curing rites. The wilderness is therefore not solely a domain of antisocial powers; it is the source of and a metaphor for the vital energies upon which the creation of a viable social order depends.[12] The harmonizing of innate compulsions and social imperatives does not mean overcoming, repressing, or expunging the "wild" but entering into a controlled relationship with it. As Riesman observes in his superb study of freedom in Fulani social life, "freedom in society is founded on the possibility of each person entering into a direct relation with the bush" (1977:257), a place of solitude where one may lose oneself but also find oneself by gaining in self-mastery and strength.

Perhaps the most important intermediaries between social and extrasocial domains are the diviners. In many West African societies they play the crucial role in helping a person redress the imbalance between innate and social imperatives. Among the Kalabari, for example, diviners are able to "diagnose the words" which a person's *teme* ("soul") spoke before coming to earth and, by confronting a person with the words, help him or her revoke them. In a ritual known as *bibi bari* ("calling back the mouth/speech") the bad words spoken by the *teme* before birth are exchanged for new and better ones (Horton 1962:205, 1983:56). Among the Tallensi, diviners are also able to help a person "exorcise" his or her evil prenatal destiny (*nuor-yin*) by revoking the bad words spoken before birth. But even more significant is the way a person establishes shrines to a unique configuration of "good destiny" ancestors—drawn from both patrilineal and matrilineal forebears—who assist him or her in leading a fulfilling social life. Again, diviners play crucial mediatory roles in communicating the wishes and inclinations of these ancestors to their wards and in advising appropriate sacrifices (Fortes 1983:23). In Dahomey it was believed that a person could tap the antinomian energies of Legba, the trickster, and so change the direction of the fate he or she chose before birth. Alternatively, diviners could help a person establish a shrine to Da, or luck (symbolized for the individual by the umbilicus and cosmologically by the snake and the rainbow), or act as intercessories between a person and his or her "guardian soul," so providing a means of averting predestined misfortune (Fortes 1983:8–9). Among the Edo the cult of the hand figured significantly in helping a person change his luck, and a man who consulted a diviner about his ill fortune might be advised to "serve his hand" by making offering at the cult shrine (Bradbury 1973:264).

The striking parallels that exist between existential and traditional West African conceptions of free will and determinism are nicely summarized by the Igbo adage "The world is a marketplace and it is subject to bargain" (Uchendu 1965:15) and this excerpt from an interview with Sartre:

> in the end one is always responsible for what is made of one. Even if one can do nothing else besides assume this responsibility. For I believe that a man can always make something out of what is made of him. That is the limit I would today accord to freedom: the small movement which makes a totally conditioned social being someone who does not render back completely what his conditioning has given him. (Sartre 1969:45)

But how far can we take these similarities, considering the differences between the aphoristic, implicit, and unsystematized character of traditional African thought and the abstract, systematic, and analytical character of Western philosophy? Given the fact that Sartre, in this passage, assumes authority for his own views while the Igbo adage takes its authority from tradition, are we not in danger of confusing analogy with homology, of exaggerating superficial resemblances and overlooking empirical differences? Is it perhaps fallacious, as one prominent African philosopher argues, to compare traditional African world views with modern scientific theories, elevating "folk world-views . . . to the status of a continental philosophy" (Wiredu 1980:chap. 3)?

I want to answer these questions by first looking at the way several notable studies of African thought have used the Freudian model of the unconscious. This critique will then lead back to a more searching consideration of the aptness of comparing existential and traditional West African world views.

In his essay "Oedipus and Job in West African Religion," first published in 1959, Meyer Fortes (1983) drew a fascinating analogy between Tallensi and Freudian conceptions of the person. The analogy is also explicit in the work of Victor Turner and Robin Horton in the 1960s and pervades the writing of many other Africanists.[13] A key concern in several of these seminal accounts of African thought is the nature of the unconscious, and it is in this regard that the Freudian model of the psyche has been found particularly illuminating. Turner, like Fortes, acknowledges his debt to Freud, and though he admits misgivings about basing analysis "directly on Freud's system" he enthusiastically uses "certain of his concepts analogously and metaphorically, as a means of gaining some initial purchase on a set of data hitherto unanalyzed in any depth and detail by [his] structuralist-functionalist colleagues." As Turner observes, "Freud's intellectual cutting tools were better honed to slice up the beast I was intent on carving" (1978:576). While

Horton is more critical of the possibility of *explaining* African thought in Freudian terms, he considers West African and Freudian models to be comparable enough to "provide inspiration for an exciting cross-cultural study of social psychologies" (1983:79) and in several important papers on the Kalabari (1961, 1962, 1967, 1983) has pursued such a study. My immediate concern, however, is with Horton's contention that a "Freudian-type framework of personality concepts is common in West Africa" (1961:115) and that to draw an analogy between Kalabari personality concepts and psychoanalytic ideas "is something more than a mere anthropologist's whim" (113).

Horton begins by rejecting Fortes's analogy between Oedipal fate and Tallensi notions of fate, since in the classical Greek texts Oedipus did not choose and could not change his fate, while in Tallensi thought a person's destiny is prenatally chosen and may be revoked. He then argues that Fortes

> would have done far better to have scrapped Oedipus and to have replaced him explic-
> itly with the Freudian idea of an Unconscious Self—a purposive agency whose desires
> are unknown to Consciousness and are frequently in conflict with it. For this idea paral-
> lels the Tallensi notion of a life-course chosen by a part of the personality before birth,
> a course both hidden from the post-natal consciousness and frequently opposed to the
> latter's aims. (112)

Next, Horton presents an account of the Kalabari conception of the personality in explicitly Freudian terms. "In Kalabari thought, the human personality is di-vided into two sections," the *biomgbo,* or "conscious mind," and the *teme,* "an im-material agency which is in existence before the individual is born and which sur-vives his death." The *teme* is a kind of "steersman of the personality" whose desires and wishes are inaccessible to the *biomgbo,* "both unconscious and in conflict with the contents of the consciousness" (113).

There are, however, serious empirical problems with Horton's Freudian gloss. First, as he himself notes, the source of personality conflicts among the Kalabari is status rivalry, not libidinous impulses and drives as in classical psychoanalytic theory (1961:114, 1967:57). It must also be stressed that while Freud contrasted the irrationality of the unconscious with the logical processes of the conscious mind (Fromm 1973:54), the Kalabari model of the personality is not built on such Eurocentric notions as reason and logic (cf. Hallen 1975:267–68). To draw an anal-ogy between Freudian and Kalabari models on the grounds that both recognize that much human behavior is not under conscious control is as spurious as conflating Freud's model of the mind with earlier spiritualistic or romantic models, which also postulated notions of the unconscious (Ellenberger 1970).[14] A second problem arises from the fact that the Kalabari tend to see the *teme* animistically, as a spirit-ual being rather than a mental process. In a paper on the Kalabari world view which appeared in *Africa* a year after his paper on destiny and the unconscious, Horton remarks that the word *teme* "can denote either a special mode of being, or an entity existing in that mode" (1962:199). He therefore translates *teme* as "spirit" in order to indicate that *teme* are sometimes ethereal and sometimes materi-alize as spirit beings. Moreover, he observes that not only are *teme* embodied, visible, and tangible under certain conditions; they are frequently located in certain places, objects, and shrines (199).

These ethnographic facts suggest a crucial difference between Kalabari and Freudian models. While *teme* are often social beings (who can associate with both people and *owuamapu* spirits), located in space and having bodily form (a sick person may "be worried by a bad *teme*"), the inner mental processes, drives, and repressed wishes that constitute the Freudian unconscious are not conceived anthropomorphically (Freud 1957:166–204).[15] Although Horton remarks this difference (1967:69, 1983:77) he downplays it as merely idiomatic. This is because his concern to show that the African model is "a system of theoretical discourse comparable to the systems of the natural sciences" (1983:77) is essentially *epistemological*, stressing the manner in which both traditional and scientific models seek unity underlying apparent diversity, trace causal connections, synthesize experience into abstract theories, and so on (1967:50–71). The trouble is that this mode of comparison tends to ignore the different sociohistorical conditions that govern the genesis of different world views as well as to overlook the different interests, applications, and practical consequences that different world views entail. Crudely put, an atomic model helps make atom bombs; the allegedly "comparable" African model of spirits, ancestors, and God does not.

This pragmatist critique can be developed further by considering the differences in the practical applications of Freudian and West African models of fate and free will. Freudian psychotherapy involves depth analysis of an individual's mind, of his or her dreams, memories, fantasies, and inhibitions. It involves a journey back through biographical time. In Africa, as we have seen, analysis of the hidden determinants of the personality involves divination, a method of looking not so much into a person's psyche as into his or circumstances. Bodily and social factors are just as significant as mental ones; the person is seen as part of a sociospatial force-field, and the diviner proceeds as a kind of "social analyst" who manipulates *external* objects such as cowrie shells and pebbles or communicates with *extrasocial* beings such as bush spirits in order to bring to light the hidden aspects of his client's situation (Jackson 1978b). The Freudian and African techniques for unmasking the hidden determinants of human fate imply quite different conceptual schemes.[16] While classical psychoanalytic thought tends to define the unconscious as a deep recess of *interior* being where external reality is "replaced" by psychical reality (Freud 1957:187), traditional African thought tends to construe the unconscious as a force-field *exterior* to a person's immediate awareness. It is not so much a region of the mind as a region in space, the inscrutable realm of night and of the wilderness, filled with bush spirits, witches, sorcerers, and enemies. In Kuranko, the word that most closely translates our word *unconscious* is *duworon*, which means covert, in hiding, or underhanded, by contrast with *kenema*, open to the public gaze. But like the word *duguro* (literally, "ground in") which also means "hidden," the stem of *duworon*, *dugu*, means "place" or "ground," and it is more consonant with Kuranko thought to speak of the *unknown* rather than of the *unconscious*, i.e., a sociospatial rather than an intrapsychic aspect of being-in-the-world.[17] In this connection it is interesting to note that Fortes, whose 1959 comparative essay on Tallensi religion is deeply influenced by psychoanalytic thought, observed ten years earlier that the Tallensi "do not conceive of the inner life of the individual as a distinct phenomenon apart from the external, material, and social facts of his life" (1949:227–28).

The African tendency to attribute bodily form and sociospatial identity to forces we tend to conceive of in the abstract as mental processes explains why, in traditional Africa, disturbed thought is often seen as evidence of spirit possession,[18] and prenatal dispositions—as among the Tallensi and Kalabari—are often anthropomorphized as ancestors or spirit beings. Such a way of conceptualizing what we would regard as inner psychic processes is not merely "idiomatic"; nor is it insignificant. On the contrary, it is profoundly related to the sociopolitical matrix of traditional African life, and a sound understanding of why African and Freudian models differ requires a consideration of the different implications these models have in the social worlds to which they belong.

First, though it is not necessary to explore here the relation between Freud's ideas and the social world in which he conceived them, the fact that the Freudian model of the unconscious has been so often revised since his time indicates not only changes in our understanding of the mind but changes in our sociopolitical environment. During the 1940s, Wilhelm Reich was arguing that consciousness was not ethereal but embodied (Reich 1949) and Sartre and Merleau-Ponty were insisting on the unity of conscious and bodily being (Sartre 1957; Merleau-Ponty 1962). At about the same time, Bion's work with battle-fatigued soldiers in World War II was leading to increasing emphasis on group dynamics in psychotherapy and, as a result, "the Freudian view of the psyche as a dark, hidden realm within the recesses of the individual lost some of its verisimilitude" (Poster 1978:110). Postwar research by Bateson and others on the relationship between mental disorder and communication breakdown in the family had a similar impact to critical theory, which also stressed the social rather than libidinous determinants of behavior (Fromm 1973). Others, such as R. D. Laing, were critical of the psychoanalytic model of intrapsychic defense mechanisms and endeavored to construct a systematic theory of "transpersonal defences" (Laing 1976:12), while Lacan defined the unconscious not in terms of an inner world of instinct and desire but in terms of the transpersonal world of intentions and projections that lies about us, "the discourse of the Other" (de Waelhens 1978:172–75; Jameson 1972:138). Such paradigm shifts toward a notion of the unconscious as embodied and socially embedded suggest that the Western model of the unconscious is coming to resemble the African one. However, as I have already argued, it is perhaps more instructive to study these models at the level of use rather than in the abstract.[19]

This brings me to my second point: although African and Western models of the unconscious sometimes seem to resemble each other epistemologically, they differ pragmatically, in both the interests they serve and the social values they imply. Consider, for instance, two influential Western models of the unconscious, those of Freud and Lévi-Strauss. While they may be contrasted on epistemological grounds (Rossi 1974), they tend to have similar sociopolitical consequences. Both the psychoanalyst and the structural anthropologist employ concepts and jargons that are seldom *as a matter of practical or moral necessity* made consonant with the ethos of the people they study.[20] African diviners and their clients, however, share a common world view. Moreover, the diviners assume no personal authority and accrue no social advantage from their skills; they act as transmitters of messages from the extrasocial world which their clients then act upon, usually by making a sacrifice (Jackson 1978b). Psychoanalysts and anthropologists, on the other hand, gain authority and prestige by using a fetishized notion of the unconscious to undermine the immediate self-understanding and praxis of others, insinuating into their consciousness a so-called "objective" understanding whose origins in the analyst's own personal and social situations are masked or scotomacized.[21] In other words, the division between conscious and unconscious corresponds to a *social* division between the knowing subject and the "objects" of knowledge: the "disturbed" patient or the "ignorant" savage.[22] To be sure, Africans also exploit restricted codes and the "unknown" to create social distinctions between initiates and noninitiates, elders and juniors, men and women, but the systematic manipulation of knowledge to maintain massive hierarchical structures of inequality is a singularly Western phenomenon.

My third point concerns the relation between African and Western models of the unconscious and social ideology. In his comparison of conscience in Fulani and Western societies, Paul Riesman assumes, albeit "provisionally," that the Fulani lack a strongly internalized superego. "The critical demands of conscience— the superego . . . have to rely more heavily on external representatives," i.e., "the actual presence of others *(aduna)*" (1977:165, 166).[23] Riesman's view corresponds to a view widely held among Africanists, that Africans tend to exteriorize and bestow social and bodily identity upon processes which Westerners tend to see as abstract and intrapsychic. Godfrey Lienhardt summarized the crucial difference:

> The Dinka have no conception which at all closely corresponds to our popular modern conception of the "mind" as mediating and, as it were, storing up the experiences of the self. There is for them no such interior entity to appear, on reflection, to stand between the experiencing self at any given moment and what is or has been an exterior influence upon the self. So it seems that what we would call in some cases the "memories" of experiences, and regard therefore as in some way intrinsic and interior to the remembering person and modified in their effect upon him by that interiority, appear to the Dinka as exteriorly acting upon him, as were the sources from which they derived. (1961:149)

A problem with this kind of account of African conceptions of the self, as Lienhardt himself points out (1985:143–47), is that one may be misled into thinking that empirical and epistemic levels of understanding are identical. However, the lack of emphasis on interiority in Dinka and Fulani thought does not necessarily reflect a modality of self-experience wholly different from our own; it may simply represent a different ideological *representation* of experience. My own view is that the relation between human experience of the world and ideological representations of the world is nonisomorphic and indeterminate. Let us return to the question of the supposed lack of a strongly internalized superego among the Fulani.

In the first place, empirically and logically, *some* Fulani must act out of inner moral compulsion since, as Melford Spiro has observed, "If norms were not internalized, parents would have none to transmit to their children because, *ex hypothesi*, they would not have internalized any in the course of their own socialization" (1961:118). In the second place, my own Kuranko research indicates that while people *explain* processes of moral retribution (*hake*) as a function of disturbed interpersonal relationships, i.e., in terms of exterior, nonpsychic mechanisms—cases of witchcraft confession show that inner moral qualms and guilt are just as much a part of Kuranko *experience* as they are of ours (see chapter 6). In any society, therefore, conventional modes of explaining phenomena should be seen not as descriptions of lived experience but as interpretations and rationalizations that reflect the exigencies of the sociopolitical order. Riesman himself makes this very point, showing that the Fulani emphasis on community makes it appropriate for them to see "psychic" phenomena as functions of social relationships. By contrast, the strongly individualistic ethos of the Western world entails a conception of the person as skin-encapsulated and autonomous, with a unique inner life that is not reducible to social processes (1977:73, 166–67).

If, as I have argued, the analogy between Freudian and African models of the unconscious is simplistic and misconceived, how viable is the existential analogy I have proposed between Sartrean and West African notions of free will and determinism?

Ifeanyi Menkiti claims that African and existential conceptions of the person are radically different, despite the fact that "on the face of things" existentialism seems a "natural ally" of African thought (1984:177–78). According to Menkiti, Sartre regards man as "a free unconditioned being, a being not constrained by social or historical circumstances" (178). Such a view is wholly incompatible with the ontological priority given in African world views to the social ground of human existence. However, this characterization of Sartre's views is based on Menkiti's reading of a 1946 lecture Sartre published but subsequently repudiated (Sartre 1973) and ignores Sartre's emphasis on the dialectic between the given sociohistorical conditions of existence and the human project which both reveals and surpasses them. In Sartre's own words, "men make their history on the basis of real, prior conditions . . . but it is *the men* who make it and not the prior conditions. Otherwise men would be merely the vehicles of inhuman forces which through them would govern the social world" (1968:87).

The philosopher Kwasi Wiredu argues that such a conception of freedom is fatuous. Citing the case of a confirmed drunkard, he observes: "It would surely be a poor assurance of free will to point out that it is still open to him whether he will drink 'akpeteshie' or beer, or that he can very well choose which bars to frequent" (1980:19). Wiredu then alleges that African traditional thought is predominantly fatalistic: "As the traditional saying goes, there is no avoiding the destiny appointed to a man by God (*Onyame nkrabea nni kwatibea*)" (19–20).[24] Wiredu fails, however, to distinguish between the retrospective rationalizations of misfortune (which tend, in all societies, to smack of fatalism and resignation) and the attitudes people adopt in the face of life, which, as we have seen, tend to emphasize personal responsibility. Research into other people's beliefs must always specify the context in which they are invoked and used; prescriptive values and post hoc rationalizations are seldom commensurate. If we are kept from seeing the context in which a belief is used then we are inclined, by default, to construe the belief in ways alien to the user, concerning ourselves with its epistemological status, its coherence, logicality, correspondence to reality, and so on. The contradictions between fatalistic and nonfatalistic attitudes to destiny in West African thought are thus more apparent than real. As Helaine Minkus observes in her study of Akwapim Akan notions of destiny (*nkrabea*), informants would commonly speak of their destinies as preordained and tied to the destinies of others (including divinities). But a person "is not thought to be a passive victim or object of forces external to him and totally beyond his influence." Much that happens to him "is regarded as justifiably and predictably proceeding . . . from his own precipitating acts" (1984:140).[25]

Another problem with existential theories is their diversity and cultural relativity, something which might seem to disqualify them from being used to establish universals in human experience. This argument has been forcefully put by Hallen (1976); but in characterizing Heidegger's and Sartre's thought in ways which heighten its contrast with African thought, Hallen, like Menkiti, fails to explore areas in which it is potentially most edifying. Moreover, by arguing that existential theories usually seek to establish universal essences, he seriously misrepresents Sartre and fails to understand that the possibility of interesting cross-cultural comparison afforded by *some* existential ideas does not imply any universal truth claims about human experience. Our search is for some common ground or vocabulary that will serve as a point of departure for comparison and dialogue across cultures; it is *not* a search for universal truths or essences.

A further difficulty in comparing existential and West African models of free will and determinism arises from the manner in which the models are articulated. Earlier, I remarked the close parallelism which Devereux discovered between Mohave and Freudian models of psychopathology. But, as Devereux himself notes, there are significant differences between these models. First, the Mohave do not systematize their psychiatric know-how into a single coherent etiological theory of mental disorder. Second, Mohave psychiatric beliefs are articulated in "supernaturalistic" rather than naturalistic terms (Devereux 1969b:9–16). Comparable differences exist between traditional African and Western cultural thought models, whether of Freud or of Sartre. While I have argued that such differences make the analogy between Freudian and West African notions of the unconscious untenable, I believe they are far less problematic in the case of the analogy I have drawn between Sartrean and West African notions of free will and determinism.

My justification for this position takes into account the special philosophical style of existentialism and the area of its concerns. For existentialism, as for traditional African thought, being is not fragmented and atomized but dispersed into the world in the form of human relationships, intentions, and projects. In seeking to understand the world we situate ourselves squarely within it rather than taking up a vantage point outside it (Sartre 1982:20, 51). This antipositivist stance implies that existentialism is skeptical about "systematic" philosophy and the whole project of mirroring the world in our thought (Rorty 1979). Existentialism does not seek to privilege its vocabulary as representing the "truth" or "essence" of things, and despite the arcane idiom of Sartre's major treatises there is no striving to disengage the world of his discourse from the world of others.[26] Rather than explain the world, Sartre offers us an "edifying" view of it by interrogating shared experiences from everyday life: queuing at a bus stop, reading a newspaper, being gazed upon in the street, confronting anti-Semitism.

When one considers the concerns rather than the style of existential and traditional African thought, there is again a striking consonance. Despite sociocultural differences there is a common preoccupation with our human struggle between yielding to the brute facticity of existence—the sense of being abandoned or thrown into a world made by others at other times—and the necessity of appropriating, addressing, and experiencing that world as something for which we are responsible, something we bring into being, something we choose. The manner in which a person lives this struggle cannot be explained wholly in terms of his or her social identity, for we are speaking here of an issue that arises from human existence itself before it is apprehended or elaborated in culture-specific terms. Thus, the anthropologist's struggle to be a part of another culture yet also a detached observer of it is but one instance of a universal struggle which in traditional West African societies finds expression in people's struggles to be creators of the very world that has created them.[27] In sum, existentialism places social facts within a universal ontological perspective. Accordingly, we neither presume "scientific" status for our world views in order to give them authority and legitimacy, nor deign to label the world views of other "folk" as a sign of their epistemological inadequacy. "Our" world views are placed on a par with "theirs" and seen not as "true" accounts of "external reality" but as ways of helping us cope with life, of making the world make sense.[28] If there is a context in which we can usefully compare the Freudian notion of the unconscious with traditional African notions of the unknown it is an existential one, the context of lived experience, in which there is always a sense of something alien, oppressive, predetermined, and peripheral to consciousness—the limits within which our praxis is confined (Ey 1978:296–99). But such a view rejects the scientific pretensions of psychoanalysis, seeing it simply as one instance of how human thought everywhere seeks to reconcile a sense of personal freedom with an equally strong sense of being conditioned and contingent.[29]

FOUR

How to Do Things with Stones

Most human beings find the aleatory, uncertain character of existence hard to accept. Uncertainty is met with anxiety and construed as a problem. It is a problem for both thought and action because most people seem to need the consolation of a world that is *in essence* as rationally ordered as their *thoughts about it* can be,[1] and they seem to be able to act in the world only when they are confident their actions will have a reasonable chance of achieving certain ends. Although many people accept, and even cultivate and enjoy, indeterminacy (as in games of chance and risky ventures), there is a threshold of tolerance beyond which chance ceases to be a matter of risks willingly taken and becomes an external tyranny to be desperately avoided.

This chapter is an exploration of what might be called the problem of the aleatory. I approach this problem through a detailed ethnographic account of divinatory practices among the Kuranko of Sierra Leone. Rather than consider Kuranko divination solely from the point of view of an outside observer, however, I extrapolate from and discuss my own experiences of consulting Kuranko diviners, thus complementing observation and native exegesis with insights gained as a participant.

Observation and participation have conventionally been conflated in social anthropology and the oxymoronic nature of the so-called participant-observation methodology overlooked. In practice one can observe and participate successively but not simultaneously. Moreover, since observation and participation yield different kinds of data, conventionally labeled objective and subjective, our research methodology in social anthropology *itself* brings us face to face with the problem of indeterminacy. Meaning is constituted through an *interplay* of procedures pretending to be inductive *and* a welter of interpretive preferences and prejudices (Popper 1969). Pure objectivity has, therefore, no "objective" status; it is as much a preformed, socially constituted attitude as the notion of pure subjectivity.

As Heisenberg has noted, this indeterminacy principle implies that "science alters and refashions the object of investigation. In other words, method and object can no longer be separated" (1958:16). The hermeneutical uncertainty we encounter in anthropological research can thus be linked in one direction to the problem of knowledge in quantum mechanics and, in another, to the problem of prediction in divination. When Einstein declared against the new physics, saying that God does not play dice with the universe,[2] he was in a sense admitting the same intolerance of the aleatory that, in a Kuranko village, leads a person to seek consolation in the predictive and systematizing powers of a diviner.

In divination, as in science, we seek to reduce ambiguity, to arrive at provisional certitudes which will offer us "something to go on" and help us cope with and act in an unpredictable world. My purpose in this chapter, then, is to argue an approach to Kuranko divination which does not pretend any epistemologically privileged or objective claims to knowledge. Accordingly, I hazard a view of Kuranko divination which draws on existential and pragmatist philosophies, which places Kuranko divinatory techniques on a par with our own anthropological methods and, by stressing the experiential grounds on which both are constituted, argues that any attempt to distinguish the former as superstition and the latter as science is misconceived.[3]

INDUCTIVE METHODS

The general Kuranko term for a diviner is *bolomafelne* (literally, hand-on-looker).[4] Although palmistry may have once been a divinatory technique among the Kuranko, the term probably refers to the fact that a diviner manipulates and "lays down" various objects (pebbles, cowries, kola nuts) in order to "see" what kind of sacrifice his client should offer. The commonest divinatory technique involves laying out river pebbles on the ground; thus an alternative term for a diviner is *beresigile* (one who sets down pebbles).[5] Less common divinatory techniques are sand-drawing and the casting of kola nuts or cowrie shells. Muslim diviners (called *morenu* or, in Krio, "moris" or "alphas") are reputedly able to predict a person's fortune or interfere with a person's destiny through such techniques as mirror-gazing, water-gazing, astrology, and oneiromancy. But consulting the Quran is the main means of Muslim divination.

Apart from pebble-divining, most techniques for bringing hidden things into the open are allegedly inductive, i.e., they presuppose a "determinative procedure, apparently free from mundane control, yielding unambiguous decisions or predictions"; they employ "nonhuman phenomena, either artificial or natural, as signs that can be unambiguously read. The prime condition is that the signs appear to be genuine, not manipulated" (*Encyclopaedia Britannica* 1974:917, 918). These techniques, familiar to us in positivist social science, are often used by persons who are not professed diviners, but only on specific social occasions. For example, after a man's death and burial, his widows are confined to the house for forty days (known as *labinane*, forty [days] lying down). At the end of this period the widows are led to the village streamside by the son of the sister of the deceased man; there, elderly women (not kinswomen) bathe and ritually purify them. As part of this purification rite a kola nut is split in half and the two cotyledons are thrown onto the ground. If the cotyledons fall facing in the same direction this signifies invariably that the husband's spirit harbors no grievance against his widow. If the cotyledons fall facing in opposite directions this signifies that the widow nurses a hidden grudge against her late husband or offended him while he was alive. The grudge or offense (*son yuguye*, bad behavior) must be confessed promptly; if no confession is made it is said that the woman will fall ill and die. Another example of unambiguous divination is the gun-firing rite performed by the prospective husbands of the female neophytes on the occasion of the latters' initiation (Jackson 1977b:193). If the gun fails to fire, this signifies that something is amiss with the forthcoming marriage; the girl may have a lover or be intending to elope. A diviner is consulted by the man's parents to find out what impediment there is to the marriage.

Divination through ordeal is unknown among the Kuranko, though the "swear" (*gborle*) is sometimes used in court cases. If a witness is a Muslim he may be required to swear on the Quran. Alternatively a calabash or basin containing gold, kola, salt, and water is brought. The witness swears in public that, should he lie, the gold, kola, and salt will "cut" his liver. Then he chews the kola and drinks the water.

Auguries play no more important a part in Kuranko society than they do in ours; the interpretations of many trivial events are so standardized and commonplace that diviners are seldom consulted about them. For example, if a person about to embark on some enterprise stubs his left foot against a stone this may be regarded as inauspicious; if he stubs his right foot this may be regarded as auspicious. However, the extent to which people take seriously or even notice such auguries is variable, often reflecting the degree of anxiety in their everyday life. This is also the case with dreams, although dream interpretation is taken more seriously than augury and a diviner is usually consulted (see Jackson 1978b:119–21 for details).

INTERPRETIVE DIVINATION

In larger Kuranko villages there are several diviners, each employing his own technique.[6] In the village of Kamadugu Sukurela (population about 550) there are five diviners: one is a mori, one uses cowrie shells, three use river pebbles. As we shall see, the choice of method reflects the particular manner in which the diviner first acquired his skills; people often remark, "It is in himself how he does it." Because the profession of divination is usually neither hereditary nor acquired through an apprenticeship, it is worthwhile noting some biographical details of individual diviners.

Kumba Wulan Bala Sise of Kamadugu Sukurela is a mori diviner. He studied the Quran under a *karamorgo* (Muslim teacher) in Guinea for seven years, then returned to his home village where, six years later, he became a practicing diviner. In 1972, when I first met Kumba Wulan, he had been in practice for four years. His faith in the Quran and in the truth of its prophecies give him confidence in his ability to divine. He continues to study the Quran and to deepen his understanding of it. It is his ultimate authority. When I asked him what he thought and how he reacted when one of his prognostications proved incorrect, he replied: "That concerns me and does not concern me: the Quran does not lie; whatever it says will come to pass unless I happen to misinterpret it." This reasoning is comparable to the way in which nonliterate Kuranko speak of books in general. Conversing once about our knowledge of the origins of life, one man told me: "*Altala* [God] gave life, no one knows when or how. You only know what is told to you or is in books. I cannot read or write so I only know what has been told to me, and no one has ever told me where life comes from; it is only through *Altala* that it is. You only know what is before you or in books. I was not there when *Altala* made life so I do not know. It might be in the books but I cannot read or write; in any case, books do not lie although the people who write them may lie."

It is characteristic of Kuranko diviners that any incorrect prognosis is not regarded as a challenge to the veracity of the system; the fault is found with the diviner himself. Although diviners sometimes grudgingly or obliquely admitted to me their own fallibility, a consulter who is convinced that a certain diviner is a liar or inept will be careful not to make public his attitude. Scandal or a libel suit could follow. Thus, the Kuranko seldom admit that a diviner or the divinatory system could be fallible. By contrast, in other African societies such as the Azande, doubt and skepticism are both common and openly expressed (Evans-Pritchard 1972:185).

We should also note here that Kumba Wulan has both Muslim and pagan clients. Moreover, he does not scorn other techniques or compete with other diviners to attract a larger clientele. In his own words, "They also tell the truth; they know their own way of doing it; God [*Ala*] instructs us all." In my experience, no *obvious* rivalries or jealousies exist among Kuranko diviners.

Other pagan diviners do not always receive their immediate inspiration and authority from God. Lai Mara, also of Kamadugu Sukurela, divines with river pebbles. Although born in Morfindugu (Mongo chiefdom), he has lived in Kamadugu Sukurela all his life. An elderly man, perhaps sixty-five years old, Lai did not become a diviner until about 1968. That year he fell ill with a serious stomach sickness, and one night, in a dream, a pale-complexioned female bush spirit appeared to him and gave him the notion of divining with river pebbles. The following morning he collected some river pebbles and they "told" him who could cure him of his sickness. He summoned this person, a kinsman, and was subsequently cured. Since then he has practiced divination.[7] Lai vowed that he never made an incorrect prognostication, saying, "If I were a liar then people would not come to me." As if to substantiate his claim he mentioned two cases, both of which concerned friends of mine in the village. He drew my attention to the fine embroidered shirt he was wearing and said that someone had given it to him as a token of gratitude when something he had foretold for him "came true." The person was Bundo Mansaray in whose house I lodged. Bundo had consulted Lai when he was about to leave the village some years previously to work in the diamond districts. Lai had divined that Bundo would make his fortune. Bundo went away and later returned a wealthy man by local standards. On another occasion Morowa's sister had asked Lai to tell her why she was unable to conceive a child. Lai told her not to worry, that she would have a child in the near future. Morowa's sister did in fact conceive soon afterward. Whether an incorrect prognosis would cause a consulter to go back and challenge the diviner or make him prefer thereafter to consult another diviner is a question to which I will turn later. But Lai's avowal that he was never wrong in his predictions may have been intended as a way of impressing me or it may mean that he never receives evidence of his errors.

Both Kumba Wulan and Lai insisted that it would be wrong for a diviner to make public his prognosis or diagnosis. The consultation is always private, and Kuranko diviners consider it wrong to discuss a client's affairs with others; such indiscretion, it is said, would lead people to lose trust and confidence in them.[8]

Bokari Wulare lives in Yataia, a small village with a mixed population of Limba, Mandinka, and Sankaran-Kuranko peoples situated in the Wara Wara hills behind Kabala. When he was a young man (he is now in his forties) he had a dream in which someone "gave him" the divining pebbles and told him to pick certain leaves and "wash" his face and eyes with them. In the morning he recollected the dream instructions and picked the leaves as directed, washing his face and eyes in a decoction of them. From that time he has been able to "see" messages in the stones. Bokari claims that God gave him the original dream instructions and that it is God's voice which speaks to him when he is divining. "I speak for God" was the phrase he used.

These three cases indicate that divinatory skills are acquired through ecstatic encounters and episodes. Lai's initiation is typical of other African societies, such as the Ndembu (Turner 1975:287–88) and the Nguni (Hammond-Tooke 1959:348), where illness followed by a visionary dream is the approved way of becoming a diviner. Bokari's case is reminiscent of the Jukun, whose diviners "have their eyes treated with a lotion of certain leaves in order to confer on them the necessary second sight" (Meek 1931b:329). The idea that diviners possess extraordinary powers of insight (they are said to have "four eyes") is common among the Kuranko. This "second sight" transcends ordinary vision. Often, while divining, a Kuranko diviner will close his eyes in order to "see" the message. In other African societies the figure of the blind seer (Tiresias is the great classical exemplar) is more completely elaborated. Among the Dinka, the word coor ("blind") is cognate with the word car ("to divine"), and blind people are often said to possess special powers of insight (Lienhardt 1961:68).

The Kuranko diviner clearly comes to regard himself as a humble transmitter of messages from the divinity to people. Lienhardt describes this attitude nicely, writing of a Dinka diviner: "he seems to see in that which has affected him the self-determining subject of activity and himself the object of it. People do not choose their divinities, they are chosen by them" (1961:151).[9] It should be noted that this traditional African attitude toward auctoritas also obtains in the case of storytelling, where individual authors disclaim their own roles in the creation of a story, attributing it to some external source of inspiration: divinity, fate, tradition, and so forth. It is my view that this mode of attribution is consistent with and entailed by an ethos which emphasizes community over individuality and assumes that the dynamic life of Being realizes itself in fields of relationship (involving persons, spirits, animals, ancestors, divinities, and even inanimate objects) rather than restricting itself to individual human beings in the form of fixed, intrinsic properties (Jackson 1982b). Storytellers and diviners alike ceremonially disengage their praxis from subjectivity to give recognition to this wider field of Being in which the individual practitioner plays a part as mediator, not maker. Positivist social science utilizes, in its arcane vocabularies and depersonalized style, comparable ceremonial forms of denying knowledge-constitutive subjectivity (Devereux 1967).

It is also noteworthy that the arbitrary and fortuitous events which lead a man to become a diviner are regarded by the diviners themselves as determined. In the same way they regard what they "see" in the random layout of the pebbles as determined. The diviner is allegedly passive and receptive, the technique allegedly objective, the procedure allegedly impersonal. Extrasocial powers, especially God, are said to determine and authorize the divinatory procedures; much as in positivist social science, subjective "interference," introjection, and projection are denied.

When Kuranko divination is compared with such sophisticated African systems as the Ifa divination of the Yoruba, it appears to be remarkably unsystematic. Even when compared with other divinatory systems in Sierra Leone, such as the *an-bere* of the Temne (Shaw 1985), Kuranko divination displays a lack of general consensus about the significance of particular pebble patterns and a paucity of interpretive rules or codes. When I brought this apparently idiosyncratic aspect to the attention of Bokari Wulare, he pointed out that different objects, techniques, and interpretations are used "because every person has a different destiny." He commented further that the individual stones signify nothing; it is only the pattern or arrangement of them which is meaningful. But this "structuralist" tenet was propounded in association with another idea: that when he utters the verses (*hayenu*) which include the name of the counsulter he receives a divine message. He could not himself explain what happened: "It is just a God-given thing." But clearly this divine inspiration enabled him to "see" a meaning in the stones; without this inspiration the pattern of the pebbles could *not* be read.[10] As for teaching his technique to others, Bokari remarked that he could only pass on his gift by having a pupil "wash" in the leaves as he had done; indeed, two of his sons have taken up divining in this way. Finally, like other diviners with whom I spoke on the matter, Bokari denied that diviners are ever charlatans: "None pretend; it is not like that." I know of no cases of deliberate fraudulence or malpractice from my Kuranko studies, but then the Kuranko are not preoccupied by questions of error and chicanery. As Lienhardt has pointed out with reference to the Dinka, "the experience of one false diviner, far from calling into doubt the abilities of all, reminded them of many others who really had the insight" (1961:69).

This was brought home to me in early 1979 when a friend, Abdulai Sano, consulted diviners at a time of material hardship and failing confidence. Although nominally a Muslim, Abdulai was in the habit of consulting both Quranic and pagan diviners. On this particular occasion his Muslim diviner saw in a dream that Abdulai should sacrifice a sheep; his pagan pebble-diviner directed the same sacrifice as a precondition for improving his fortunes. The following is excerpted from the conversation I had with Abdulai the evening following the sacrifice.

> "Have you ever gone to a diviner who told you something that did not eventuate?"
> "Yes. Once I went to a diviner [*bolomafelne*] when my child was ill. I asked him whether the child would live or die. The diviner told me the child would live, but the child died."

"Whose error was that?"

"The diviner used cowrie shells and threw them on a mat. He told me the child would live, yet it died. The child died through the will of Allah. But the diviner told me a lie [*funye*]."

"Why should he lie?"

"I went to a pebble-diviner [*beresigile*] about the same matter. He said that, though miracles happen, my child would die. Therefore he is superior to the other diviner, and I have consulted with him and taken his advice since that time."

A CONSULTATION

To illustrate the characteristic method of pebble-divining, I will describe a consultation in which I asked Lai Mara to comment upon a troubling dream I had had the previous night.

As is customary, we repaired to a quiet room and closed the door so that we would not be disturbed. Lai spread his mat on the floor, sat down, and took out his bag of divining stones. I paid him the usual consultation fee of twenty cents. Lai then gave me four pebbles and told me to think about whatever it was I wished to know. I did so, then returned the pebbles to him. He proceeded to chant his verses in a low voice, including my first name. Characteristically, the verses tend to be garbled, idiosyncratic, and meaningless to an outsider; this may be a dramatic device intended to impress the consulter or, more likely, a dissociative technique for the diviner himself. As he murmured his verses he gently and repeatedly knocked the back of his hand, in which he held some of the pebbles, against the floor. Many diviners put the coins of the fee with the pebbles. Having completed the verses after about thirty seconds, Lai began to lay out the pebbles on the floor, one by one. The four patterns on the following pages show the various layouts during this consultation; Lai's comments and interpretations are also noted. As is typical, dialogue between the diviner and the consulter is minimal.

With the first pattern, I am enjoined not to worry about my dream; I am well and have a prosperous future. The dream signifies good fortune. Upon concluding my work in Kamadugu Sukurela I will enjoy great happiness.

Lai then asks the pebbles: "Is there anything to be sacrificed?"

With the second pattern I am instructed to prepare a sacrifice of white kola nuts and, after consecrating them, to give them to a pale-complexioned girl (connotation: a virgin). This kind of sacrifice is characteristic of sacrifices meant to confirm a good prognostication. The symbols of whiteness and purity are regarded as means of "keeping the path open" or of purifying relationships between a person and his ancestors (see Jackson 1977a).

With the third pattern Lai comments: "We are safe; we are being protected/enclosed by God; there is no trouble pending." Two pebbles (8) are moved in after the others have been laid out. Lai explains that pebble clusters 1 and 7 are "gates" or "barriers."

Lai repeats the good prognosis: "Your dream is a sign of prosperity, you need not be afraid; for as long as you remain in the village there will be no trouble."

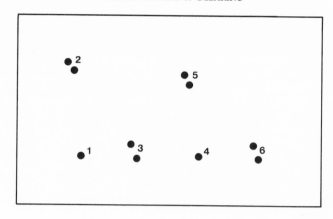

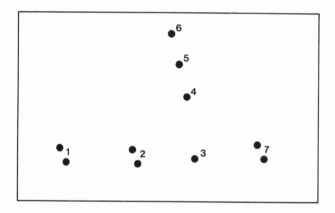

Lai reiterates instructions for the sacrifice I must offer. Indeed, it is typical for diviners to cast the stones two or more times to confirm the prognosis and finalize
details of the sacrifice.

At this point I decide to interrogate Lai about his methods. The consultation
becomes more relaxed and I recount the dream which brought me to him. Lai lays
out the pebbles once more in the fourth pattern and concludes: "This is the sacrifice
I have shown you; it signifies that your family are pleased with what you are doing
and often speak well of you. I have seen that and therefore I have told you to give
the sacrifice to an innocent girl so that when you return home your family will
be pleased with you."

Lai later asserted that neither the pebbles nor the patterns had any intrinsic
meaning. But, as he put it, "they speak"; he simply repeated or transmitted the
message which "came from" the pebbles. He also disavowed being influenced by
or taking into account his knowledge of people and events in the community. If
this is entirely true, then the Kuranko diviner is quite unlike the Zande witch doctor whose "revelations and prophecies are based on a knowledge of local scandal"
(Evans-Pritchard 1972:170) or the Ndembu diviner who utilizes his knowledge of

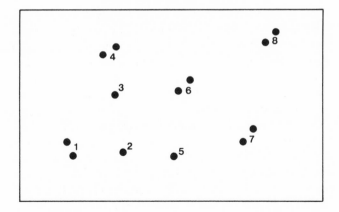

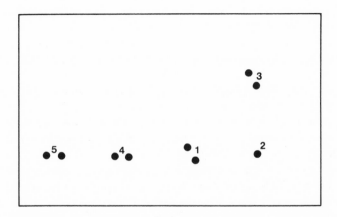

divisions, rivalries, and personalities in the community in order to arrive at an appropriate diagnosis (Turner 1972:47–48). Certainly the Kuranko diviner does not interrogate the consulter very much; rather, he "interrogates" the stones. But in the case of the consultation recorded above there is evidence that Lai's personal understanding of my research goals and my likely anxieties as a stranger in the village influenced his remarks.[11] That he should not be aware of his own introjections is simply a consequence of his conviction that he is merely a vehicle for passing on messages from divinity to man. Furthermore, if divination is not regarded as an aspect of subjectivity and consciousness, then dialogue between the diviner and the consulter is unnecessary. The absence of any extended dialogue during a consultation may also be explained in terms of the fact that Kuranko divination tends to be concerned with prospective rather than prior conditions. The Kuranko diviner is less interested in the cause and diagnosis of a consulter's condition than in discovering what course of action is required to reassure a troubled mind, avoid some misfortune, secure prosperity, clarify some confusion. The diviner characteristically defines his task as one of "seeing a sacrifice"; this does not involve a searching analysis of the individual and social situation in which the consulter finds him-

self. There is no "social analysis" such as Turner lucidly describes in his studies of
Ndembu divination (1972, 1975). For the Kuranko consulter the emphasis is thus
upon anticipatory knowledge which facilitates activity: making a sacrifice according to the precise instructions given by the diviner. This activity enables an abreac-
tion of anxiety. More generally, the future, which Kuranko associate with uncertainty and anxiety, is "annulled"; it becomes like the past, which is the source of
knowledge and the domain of certitude.

For both diviner and consulter it would seem that it is only when the prognosis
is associated with objective and external elements (i.e., is disengaged from subjectivity) that activity is facilitated. If external powers and agencies such as God and
the bush spirits have any functional importance in Kuranko society it is therefore
in the manner in which they enable individuals actively to determine their own
situation *or behave as if they could do so.* Such divine categories do not constitute
a rationale for the abnegation of the will or for collective acquiescence in a belief
in external causation. The paradox here (and one which is implied wherever we
find a cultural commitment to beliefs in categories of external causation) is that
a "belief" in external independent agencies or powers seems often to be a necessary
precondition for people to assume responsibility for their own situations and destinies.

The process of distancing or disengaging from subjectivity no matter how illusory may constitute, for our purposes, an adequate definition of magic (cf. Róheim
1970; Lévi-Strauss 1963:182, 197–98). Objects or words are invested with the emotions and events they stand for. It is perhaps worthwhile pointing out that magical
activity differs from the apparently identical behavior of the insane insofar as the
former does not involve a failure to distinguish between the objects or words and
the things they are made to stand for. I will return to this point when discussing
the relationship between belief and experience.

Divination entails a commitment by both diviner and consulter to the particular magical devices that allow externalization, objectification, and systematization.
The outcome of the consultation is a negotiated synthesis of the diviner's and the
consulter's perceptions and persuasions. The implicit collusion here makes it possible for the individual consulter to do something about his particular situation
(make a sacrifice as directed) and it also makes it possible for others to act with
him (in making the sacrifice), since his particular problem has been defined in
terms of collectively recognized categories. The latter process is similar to what
Park calls the establishment of "effective consensus" (1963:199) or the legitimizing,
certifying functions of divination. But the process of externalization involves two
parallel transitions: the consulter surpasses the chaotic and inchoate state in which
he finds himself and, through social action, is enabled to assume responsibility for
and determine his own situation; and the consulter's situation is classified according
to collective dogmas of causation and, as a consequence, the group (family, subclan, or village) is enabled to act decisively and systematically to determine its
situation. The diviner's role can thus be understood as one which ceremonializes
the transition from inertia to activity, a transition upon which both individual and

group existence depends. Some of the psychological and existential implications of this shift from passivity to activity will now be considered.

QUESTIONS OF VERIFICATION

Many writers have sought to explain how it is possible for diviners to maintain credibility and protect the authority of the system when there is such a great deal of inevitable error in prognoses and diagnoses (Firth 1956:160–61; Lévi-Strauss 1963:169; Fortes 1966:414; Park 1963:199; Horton 1967:244–48). Indeed, the study of purely formal properties and problems of belief *systems* has, to some extent, eclipsed the study of how beliefs are used and manipulated in actual situations. But before taking up the crucial issue of praxis, let me summarize the many ways in which anthropologists have shown how the credibility of divinatory systems is protected.

Sometimes, as among the Ndembu, the oracular element is absent from the system: "Diviners disclose what has happened, and do not foretell events" (Turner 1972:27). Frequently, prognostications are imprecise, impersonal, or conditional and thus difficult to challenge confidently in retrospect (Evans-Pritchard 1972:175; Turner 1972:50). And a diviner's pronouncements are usually held to be inspired by divine agencies; the veracity of the divine word is not called into question, only the mediatory skills of the diviner. Some exceptions to this rule are known. Among the Limba, "if a prediction or diagnosis turns out to be false, then this is interpreted as being because the spirit on that occasion told him (the diviner) a lie; it is not the man that is to blame" (Finnegan 1965:115). Meek reports that among the Jukun "a limit is set to the power of the divining apparatus by the belief that deities and ancestral spirits may use the apparatus in order to give lying messages for their own purposes" (1931b:327).

A diviner usually directs a sacrifice and specifies exact rules and procedures which the consulter must follow if the sacrifice is to be efficacious. This increases the likelihood or probability of an error being made by the consulter. Should the sacrifice not lead to the expected advantages, then blame may be attributed to the consulter rather than the diviner. Alternatively, intrusive countermagic may be found to be the cause of the failure. The Kuranko sometimes account for the ineffectiveness of a sacrifice by claiming that witches interfered with it or by suggesting that some of the men attending the sacrifice and receiving meat from it had been involved in love affairs with each others' wives. Such blanket rationalizations cannot, of course, be substantiated. It also happens that some consulters derive sufficient comfort from a diviner's advice to neglect making a confirmatory sacrifice. This is often the case when a prognosis is good; if it is bad a person will be less inclined to risk neglecting the sacrifice which will avert the anticipated disaster. I know this to be sometimes the case with the Kuranko, and the neglect of sacrifices, particularly those directed by a diviner, is often cited as a cause of a person's misfortune.

"Converging sequence" theory may provide a defense mechanism for the system. Here several possible causes may be referred to in explaining any single effect. An initial diagnosis may indicate one cause (ancestors, bush spirits, God) but action then cites another factor or perceives other elements which bear on the consulter's situation. The system itself is thus never subject to doubt (Horton 1967: 244–48).

Trickery and deliberate deception may be employed by the diviner, as among the Azande (Evans-Pritchard 1972:pt. 2, chap. 2). In some cases the consulter may unconsciously fulfill a certain prophecy or "create" evidence that corroborates a diagnosis. And, of course, many diagnoses are correct and many prognostications prove to be true (see, for example, Moore 1957 on the efficacy of scapulimancy among the Naskapi). Only corroborative evidence is noticed and it is "easy to obtain confirmations, or verifications, for nearly every theory—if we look for confirmations" (Popper 1969:36). Or we could say that there is no interest shown in the falsification or refutation of the system (something for which only one counterexample is required). The reason for this lack of interest in discrediting the diviner or challenging the truth of the divinatory system may be explained by the following discussion.

Let me emphasize once more the problem of the aleatory. A person goes to a diviner when he or she is troubled and confused, unable to make a definite decision or choose between alternative courses of action. The following dilemmas are those most often mentioned by the Kuranko as reasons for seeking the advice of a diviner. In each instance, a "liminal" situation presents itself—temporally and spatially "betwixt and between" (Turner 1970), characterized by choices that cannot easily be made and open to adventitious influences.

A woman cannot conceive a child. This situation admits two kinds of explanation: either the husband is infertile—a possibility that is usually rationalized away (see Jackson 1977b:87)—or the wife is barren. The uncertainty of the situation arises from the difficulty of knowing whether the woman will *ever* conceive a child (temporary barrenness is not uncommon).

A woman has a long and difficult labor. A diviner may be consulted to find out whether the cause is a bush spirit or not. If a bush spirit is involved the woman will be taken to another house for the delivery.

A man is about to marry. A diviner may be consulted to find out whether the wife will bear him children or not, whether or not the marriage will bring blessedness and good fortune, and so forth.

A man is about to brush his farm. A diviner may be consulted to find out whether or not there are bush spirits in the vicinity so that propitiatory sacrifices can be made to them.

A person is about to embark upon a journey. A diviner may be consulted to find out whether or not one will return safely or accomplish one's mission.

A person is troubled by a dream. A diviner will be able to say whether or not it is auspicious.

A kinsman is ill. A diviner may be consulted to find out whether the sickness is "natural" (*altala kiraiye,* sickness caused by God) or "human" (*morgo kiraiye,* sickness caused by human agency—witchcraft or sorcery).

A sickness or disease does not respond to treatment suggested by a besetigi *(medicine-master)*. Unlike the Mende diviners, who are sometimes healing doctors (Harris and Sawyerr 1958:56), the Kuranko besetigi is never a diviner and a diviner never practices therapeutic medicine. Medical knowledge is acquired through a long apprenticeship, not through revelation or vision.

A kinsman (particularly a child) dies suddenly. Witchcraft may be suspected in such cases and the men's witch-detecting cult, Gbangbe, will be called out. However, an ordinary diviner is usually consulted first.

A man is about to have his son or daughter initiated. A diviner's analysis of the child's situation will enable him to direct appropriate sacrifices to maximize the contestant's chances of success. Often he will be advised to keep the company of a pale-complexioned virgin girl.

A man is about to build a house. The diviner will direct appropriate sacrifices for the house site (usually a white flag is hung from a pole on the site); he will also judge whether or not the site is "clear" of the influences of the spirits of previous settlers.

In all of the above situations, divination works, in Meyer Fortes's words, as "a ritual means of making a choice" (1966:413). The diviner makes an unequivocal decision concerning his client; quite simply, a diagnosis or prognosis is given which is either auspicious or inauspicious. The diviner then concentrates on "seeing" a sacrifice and instructing his client in the precise procedures for making it. Almost every sacrifice will include at least one directive peculiar to it. Sacrifices are generally of two kinds: piacular, to avert disaster or ward off evil; or confirmatory, to assist the realization of an auspicious forecast. Failure to offer the sacrifice or to follow the exact instructions given for it increases one's chances of being struck down by ill fortune. Such a failure could also be used as a ready explanation if and when misfortune fell.

Kuranko divination has, to use Parsonian terms, an expressive and an instrumental aspect (cf. Beattie 1964:61). Yet, by being instrumental in assisting a person get back into relation with his or her situation *and act upon it*, divination mediates an expression of a universal human need for autonomy and understanding. The diviner's analysis transforms uncertainty into a provisional certainty, and his instructions for an appropriate sacrifice enable the consulter to move from inertia to purposeful activity (praxis). Quite simply, one regains one's autonomy; one acts upon the conditions which are acting upon one. And this autonomy precludes anxiety.

My own consultations with Kuranko diviners were prompted by anxieties about my work, about troubling dreams, about my wife's health during her pregnancy. On every occasion, despite the fact that I did not accept intellectually the assumptions underlying Kuranko divination, the consultations helped alleviate anxiety and I diligently made the sacrifices I was told were necessary. It is on the strength of such firsthand experiences of Kuranko divination that I argue that the psychological and existential changes effected by consulting a diviner are so immediate and positive that *the ultimate outcome of any prognostication or sacrifice does not necessarily inspire retrospective interest in the truth or falsity of the diviner's original propositions.*

This implies, of course, that studies of divination which are intellectualistic in their bias and thus focus on the problem of the credibility of the system reflect an objec- tivist methodology which plays down subjective experience. By relying on partici- patory experiences rather than disinterested observations I hope to have shown that one's methodology constitutes both the object under study and one's interpre- tation of it. Extrapolating from my own experience of Kuranko divination leads naturally to an emphasis on issues of uncertainty and crisis. It leads indeed to a pragmatist viewpoint, which does not reduce Kuranko divination to an object of intellectual knowledge but sees it rather in a wider frame of experience as an object of use. Unlike the intellectualistic viewpoint, the pragmatist viewpoint has the merit of being consistent with the Kuranko ethos itself. This point can be briefly elaborated by comparing Kuranko divinatory and storytelling arts.

Although divination addresses adventitious uncertainties and stories actually *create* uncertainties and dilemmas, the resolution of ambiguity is crucial in both cases:

> randomness is maximized before it is shown to be a kind of disguised order. In both the divinatory rite and the storytelling session people actively manipulate simulacra of the real world in order to grasp it more clearly and transform their experience of it. The pebbles in the diviner's hands are like the figures and images (*gestalten*) with which the narrator creates new interpretations, and both the diviner and the narrator make possible a transition from confusion to clarity, and an adjustment of individual freedom to its limiting conditions. (Jackson 1982a:235)

In these transformations, the "objective" consistency or truth of narrative events and divinatory techniques is not an issue. What is important to the Kuranko is whether the storytelling sessions and divinatory consultations enable worthwhile things to happen and help people act decisively and responsibly in their everyday social existence. In William James's terms, truth is what "*happens* to an idea. It *becomes* true, is *made* true by events. Its verity *is* in fact an event, a process" (1978:97).

ASPECTS OF BELIEF AND METHOD

It is now possible to consider in greater depth the probable status of the beliefs associated with Kuranko divination.

The most significant beliefs are phrased as unquestioned assumptions: the art of divining is acquired from extrasocial sources through some ecstatic episode; God communicates messages to the diviner via the river pebbles; ancestors influence the destinies and fortunes of people but people can influence the ancestors through sacrifices addressed to them.

One must remember, however, that such doctrinaire ways of phrasing beliefs are usually an artifact of the anthropological *interview*; in the context of *practical* activity a more provisional and opportunistic picture emerges. Partly on the basis of my own participation in rites of divination and sacrifice, partly on the basis of

discussions with diviners and other informants, I have advanced the view that beliefs are best regarded as tokens which are manipulated inventively in critical situations to achieve personal and collective goals simultaneously. The assertion that
beliefs are absolute and objectively given is rhetorically significant rather than empirically realized.

In support of this view the following points can be made. First, as we have
seen, Kuranko diviners admit there is a variety of techniques or sources of inspiration, *all of which* may mediate true understanding. This is consistent with a more
general anthropological observation: there is always a great variety of reasons or
motives (conscious and unconscious) for espousing a particular belief, and no two
individuals—whether from the same culture or from different cultures—will sub-
scribe to the same belief for identical reasons. *Si bis faciunt idem, non est idem* (see
Devereux 1961a:235). That is why I could use Kuranko divination *as if it were true*,
calling upon it as an "extra truth" (James 1978:98), an idea which one stores in
one's mind until such time as one sees a use for it and realizes its truth. But once
it has served its purpose, the idea is set aside, its truth again quiescent.[12] I maintain
that Kuranko beliefs in divination are of the same order: quiescent most of the
time, activated in crisis, but having no stable or intrinsic truth values that can
be defined outside of contexts of use. Second, beliefs are in most cultures often
simulated or feigned, and the strength of commitment is highly variable,[13] yet this
does not necessarily undermine the utility and efficacy of the beliefs in practice.
In other words, the relationship between the espoused or manifest belief (dogma)
and individual experience is indeterminate. We cannot infer the experience from
the belief or vice versa with complete certainty. Third, to investigate beliefs or
"belief systems" apart from actual human activity is absurd.

When anthropologists write as if beliefs were fixed, external facts which determine experience and activity, this is tantamount to saying that the "believers" are
mad. Let us consider the following remarks of Sylvano Arieti on the experience
of the schizophrenic:

> If we ask severely ill schizophrenics to explain why they believe their strange ideas
> in spite of all the evidence, they do not attempt to demonstrate the validity of the
> ideas. . . . Almost invariably they give this answer: "I know," meaning, "I know that
> it is so." The patient's belief is more than a strong conviction; it is a certitude . . .
> the patient is unable to lie about his delusions. . . . The delusions are absolute reality
> for him, and he cannot deny them. (1974:278)

It is not uncommon for anthropologists to write about people in other cultures
in just this way: as if they were unable to distinguish words and things, as if the
beliefs mastered and manipulated them (like projective delusions), as if, in a word,
they were autistic. It is of course quite true that Kuranko diviners never openly
question the ultimate authority of God. Nor do they consciously lie or cheat.
Among ordinary people, the authority of the "words of the ancestors" never seems
to be challenged, and the "way the ancestors did things" sanctifies and justifies all
of the customs inherited from them (Jackson 1977b:17–18). But the lack of evi-

dence *on the rhetorical plane* of a skeptical attitude does not justify a priori assumptions that the Kuranko are incapable of suspending disbelief or experiencing what George Steiner calls "alternity" (1973:224–27). Verbal responses are poor indices of inner states, and beliefs are more like metaphors than many dare imagine.

The Kuranko verb for "to know" is *a lon* (thence knowledge, *lonei*). "Known" things are said to be things learned. The noun *lanaiye* may be translated as "belief," its connotations being "confidence" or "trust" in another person or "conviction" about some idea. Thus the phrases *i la ra la?* (do you believe?) and *i la ra wo la?* (do you believe that?) carry the connotation "do you have a firm conviction that such and such is true?" I have never known a Kuranko to express doubt or uncertainty about divinatory methods but, as we have seen, individuals will have greater confidence or "belief" in one diviner than in others.

That the Kuranko regard the beliefs which sustain the divinatory process as externally factitious, independent of human subjectivity, and immune to human interference or governance should not lead us to conclude either that the beliefs have ontological corollaries or that they are never subject to manipulation, open to change, or held with variable conviction and for a variety of reasons. Working to grasp the native's point of view does not entail sharing his false consciousness. Nevertheless, trying to understand empathically the native's view of the world by using a participatory methodology, as I have done, implies an interest in dissolving the boundary which in anthropological discourse contrasts them and us in terms of a distinction between magic and science. It also implies an eagerness to put our anthropological texts on a par with the "texts" we collect in the field, critically examining *in both cases* the pretensions of those who author the "texts" to an intellectually or morally privileged position from which the other can be judged or a "true" understanding of him presumed.

In this chapter I have tried to work in terms of an existential issue—the problem of the aleatory—that is of concern to all human beings. When we examine the great variety of ways in which science and divination alike introduce a semblance of order and system into an uncertain universe, it begins to look as if establishing the "truth" of science or of divination in terms of some notion that the systems *correspond to* external reality is not necessary in order for these systems to help us cope with life and make it meaningful (cf. Rorty 1982:xvii). The lesson I take from my experience of consulting Kuranko diviners is that one does not have to believe in the truth claims of the system for it to work in a practical and psychological sense.

Why then, in science and divination alike, do practitioners concern themselves so much with the epistemological legitimacy of their systems? The answer is surely to be found in the common human need for subjectivity to distance itself from itself, to objectify itself in order to be manageable and meaningful—a process we see behind the use of stones and other objects in divination and in the dispassionate impersonal language of science. Yet, in neither case does the objectivist mode of discourse mirror or even determine the realities of practical existence.

FIVE

The Identity of the Dead

The person who suffers bereavement and loss is often plunged into an intense and oppressive solitude, pervaded by a sense of anger and victimage and by a sense that the tragedy is unique to oneself and cannot be shared or understood by others. Recovery is a matter of reforging ties with others, of realizing that one is not alone, that one's experience is not unique, that one is not doomed to mourn forever. This recovery of one's *social* existence entails *emotional* detachment. But my own experience of this process has taught me the importance of two observations Devereux makes. First, patterns of behavior and experience are not infinite in their variety, and those which are acknowledged and implemented as "normal" in one society will be found, albeit repressed, in others (Devereux 1978a:76–77). Second, it is in situations of crisis that this psychic unity of humankind is most dramatically revealed (75).

In the weeks after my wife's death, so strongly did I feel her presence that I lived my life among phantoms and feared for my sanity. Gradually I learned that this reaction to loss was not unusual. I also began to see how my own experience might be compared to the experience of Kuranko people, who speak of the dead not as remote abstractions but as living presences. Their addresses and food offerings to ancestors suddenly made sense to me, and their concern for the identity of the dead was, I realized, inseparable from a concern for the welfare of the living.

This ethnographic objectification of my feelings also brought home to me the extent to which Kuranko rituals of death and burial play down the emotions of the bereaved. Indeed, for the Kuranko, uncontrolled emotionality is inimical to the *social* transformations funerals are meant to effect. The reasoning here is similar to that used to explain why Kuranko narratives suppress idiosyncratic detail and individual identity: a neutral scenario enables each person to find his or her meaning in it without destroying the facade of conventionality and consensus. It is somewhat like the argument of those anthropologists who hold that subjectivism reduces discourse to solipsism and relativism, so precluding the possibility of general social analysis. In each case—funerals, narratives, discourse—sociality demands the suppression of that which most dramatically sets the individual subject apart from others: extraordinarily intense or private feelings.

To some extent my way of writing this chapter echoes this view. Rather than focus on the personal experiences of the bereaved, I want to emphasize the dialectic that exists in Kuranko funerals between emotional and ritual processes, between the feelings of the bereaved and conventional ideas concerning the identity of the dead.

Since Darwin (1872) and Freud (1950) first drew attention to the adaptive value of mourning, the evolved behavioral patterns of mourning and grieving have been studied in detail among both human and infrahuman groups (Pollock 1974). Some of the most compelling accounts of the bereavement reaction (Bowlby 1961, 1971, 1975; Krupp 1962; Parkes 1975) suggest that it is a special form of separation anxiety and that the universal patterns of grief, defense, mourning, and reaction to object loss are fundamentally phylogenetic adaptations. But neither individual experiences of bereavement nor social practices and beliefs associated with death can be *simply* reduced to these biogenetic givens.

Two of the most striking characteristics of funerals in all human societies are the manner in which the ubiquitous and probably innate patternings of the bereavement reaction are *assumed or simulated*[1] by persons other than the immediate bereaved (i.e., by persons who experience no direct personal loss),[2] and the manner in which the expression of grief is *delayed and socially managed.*[3] These psychological mechanisms of simulation and deferral[4] enable us to understand the social phenomenon of the double or second funeral (Hertz 1960) and the distinction which is commonly made between physical and social death; it is rare that these are conceived to take place simultaneously (Parkes 1975:183). The conscious management of grief and the social control of affect make it possible to coalesce and resolve together both personal problems of bereavement and community or family problems of social reintegration. From a sociological point of view, a funeral enables a great variety of individual emotions to find catharsis in the same collective activity (Devereux 1961a:236; Goldschmidt 1979:38). From a psychological point of view, a funeral enables the bereaved to work through the three phases of separation trauma—protest, despair, detachment[5]—and, after a period of social exclusion, to return to the community. From an existential point of view, a funeral enables people to transmute a situation in which death is visited upon them as an oppressive given into one in which they define the character of dying and decide the moment of death.

In the following ethnographic account of death and burial among the Kuranko I am interested primarily in the social management or manipulation of affect and in the ways bereavement patterns coalesce with ritual forms, the purpose of which is to resolve problems of concern to everyone in the community, not simply the bereaved. These problems, which constitute a kind of set, are: the contradiction between the continuity of society and the discontinuity of human life; the problem of separating one's feelings toward the corpse from one's memories of the deceased; and the problem of separating physical, idiosyncratic aspects of the dead person's identity from spiritual, cultural aspects.

DEATH

The Kuranko make a clear distinction between the deaths of animals and the deaths of people; in the first case death is a termination of existence, in the second case death is a transformation of existence. Of animals one uses the verb *ara faga*, "to die," and the same verb is used to describe homicide (*fagale*; a murderer is known as *morgo fagale*, "person killer").[6] Thus, if Tamba kills Yira one says *Tamba ara Yira faga*, but when referring retrospectively to Yira one would say *Yira ara sa*. The verb *ara sa*, "to die," is used in human cases. Most significantly it connotes the continuing influence of the spirit (*nie*) of the dead person in the lives of the living. Apart from these terms we should also note the verb *ara ban*, used to refer to cessation of activity, as when a piece of work is finished, a woman can no longer bear children, or a lineage "dies out." Further, there are numerous circumlocutory ways of speaking about death, e.g., *a nie ara ta*, "his life has gone," or *ara ta lakiraia ro*, "he has gone to *lakira* (to the realm of the ancestors)."

Some Kuranko believe in certain portents of death. For example, there are said to be as many stars as there are people in the world. When a person dies his star falls from the sky. Upon observing a falling star one should say *n'kel'miye*, "Mine are not the only eyes which have seen you," several times. In Barawa there is an immense granite inselberg known as *Sinikonke*. It is associated with the ruling Mara lineage of Barawa and some say that the ancestral rulers dwell there. At times one will hear xylophonists playing and singing praise-songs on the mountain and perhaps too the creaking of a great stone door as it swings open; these are omens that a man of the ruling lineage will soon die.

When a man is seriously ill or at the point of death his wives and daughters must leave him. Sometimes a dying man is removed from the house to a lean-to in the backyard. He is attended by a male friend, his eldest son, and by a senior wife (if she is past menopause) or an uninitiated daughter or sororal niece (who are considered to be sexually innocent). As in sickness, a man will avoid men who may have been sexually intimate with his wives, and he will avoid his wives lest one of them happen to be involved in an adulterous affair; such liaisons are regarded as polluting (*ka tinye*, "to despoil," "to ruin," "to pollute") and would exacerbate the invalid's condition. A woman is nursed by her eldest daughter for similar reasons.

The death is announced by the loud and high-pitched wailing, crying, and lamenting of the wives, daughters, sisters, nieces, and other close female kin. As the keening is taken up by other village women, men of the dead man's family go to notify the village chief and elders. A gun is fired to alert other villagers, some of whom may be at work on their farms some distance from the village. Special drum messages are also used. Finally, messengers are dispatched to other hamlets and villages in the chiefdom to notify kinsmen and friends of the death. Kola is tied with the stalks of the wrapping-leaves upward to signify a death. In the village, subclan (*kebile*) elders make preparations to send representatives and sympathy gifts (*sakondole*; literally, "death gifts") to the funeral.

Within two hours of the death, most of the men of the village, led by the village chief and his council of elders, will have assembled in the compound (*luiye*) outside the house where the man has died. Friends of the deceased, assisted by granddaughters of the deceased (*mamanianenu*), wash the corpse in fresh water, anoint it with palm oil, then place it on a new mat wrapped in a shroud of white satin or country-cloth. While the corpse is being prepared for burial in the house, village elders or the *keminetigi* ("master of the young men") send young men to cut grave logs from the *ture* tree, and dig the grave. Latecomers continue to arrive as the formal presentation of sympathy gifts begins. Women will often fall to the ground, wailing and lamenting, their cries taken up by the bereaved women inside the house. Men present their gifts (money, kola) to the dead man's sister's son, who passes the gifts on to the eldest son and brothers of the deceased. If the dead man was a member of a ruling lineage, then the gifts will be conveyed by a senior *jeliba* (xylophonist and praise-singer) to the dead man's brothers.[7] At the funeral of a man of rank, *jelibas* also play their xylophones and sing the favorite songs of the deceased as well as standard laments:

> This year oh, a gold cotton-tree has fallen, oh sorrow, a great cotton-tree has fallen this year oh (*Nyina oh, seni banda buira, oh yala, banda be buira nyina oh*).

> A great cotton tree—that reached to heaven—has fallen. Where shall we find support and shade again?

> Lie down, lie down Mara [name of a ruling clan], the war chief has gone. (Sayers 1925:22)

Up to this time the sound of women wailing has not ceased. But now the lamentation and keening stop suddenly as, from the house of the dead man, emerges a group of women: the *mamanianenu*. Slowly and dolefully they move around in a tight circle, singing dirges. After a while a few of the women approach the porch where the chief and elders are sitting. They maintain their morose performance, the quiet dirge, the shuffling, the deadpan faces, while the men throw money or kola on the ground at their feet. Without any change of expression, one *mamane* (or *mamaniane*, singular of *mamanianenu*; literally, "little grandmother") stoops and picks up the gifts. The group then disbands.

In the context of mortuary ritual the *mamanianenu* include all those who call the deceased *m'bimba* "my grandfather," i.e., sons' daughters, younger sons' wives, grandsons' wives. In ordinary life a joking relationship exists between grandparents and grandchildren; this is known as the *mamania tolon*. Discussion of the role played by the *mamanianenu* at their grandfather's funeral will be postponed until I have given further details of burial, sacrifices, widow quarantine, succession, and inheritance.

BURIAL

When the grave is dug, the topsoil is heaped on one side, separated from the bottom clay. The lower section of the grave is a six-foot trench, just large enough to accommodate the body. Exact measurements, using a measuring stick, are made by the gravediggers. The upper section of the grave is longer and wider and forms a kind of step which enables the burial party to place the body more easily and, subsequently, to "seal off" the lower section with mats, leaves, and logs. Graves are dug on the perimeter of the village among the trees, scrub, and rubbish. No formal marking of the grave site occurs and all that indicates the place of burial after a few months have passed is the earth mound overgrown with grass.

As soon as all sympathy gifts have been conveyed, the cortege moves toward the burial area. The corpse is shrouded and wrapped in a mat. Elders, representing all the subclans in the community, carry the body to the graveside, where it is immediately lowered into the bottom trench. Kamara (1932:94) records that the deceased's wives are allowed one final opportunity to gaze upon him, "but they must quit the spot before the body is actually lowered into the grave." He also notes (95) that the dead man's debtors and creditors should declare their claims or discharge their debts at this time; it is thought imperative that the dead man's eldest son clear his father's debts before the inhumation.

The mat enclosing the body is fixed to the sides of the grave with small wooden pegs. Then the heavy logs of *ture* wood are placed athwart the lower trench. Two more mats are placed over the logs and the mats covered with leaves which men of the burial party pick from trees in the vicinity. It is said that there may be one special leaf "for *lakira*" which will take the dead man's spirit to the realm of the ancestors. The earth is now returned to the grave, first the topsoil, then the bottom clay. In some instances, heavy stones are placed around the edges of the earth mound. These interment procedures are regarded as means of preventing the body from being exhumed (by animals) or the spirit from reentering it. The Kuranko quote an adage to emphasize the gravity and finality of death (in this case the separation of body and spirit): *ture tu tintu*, "the *ture* is very heavy," i.e., death is all-powerful; the *ture* logs are an impenetrable barrier.

When the burial is done, the men squat around the earth mound and then, tamping the clay with their hands, lean forward and murmur once in unison, "Come." This summoning of the spirit from the grave site is necessitated by the spirit's unwillingness to depart. Feeling abandoned and desolate, it will remain near the grave pining and calling, "You have left me alone, you have left me alone." It is tempting to see this belief as a projection of the pining, searching, and calling reactions of the bereaved (Parkes 1975); at least the belief "simulates" the feeling of loss experienced by the mourners.

The men who have attended the burial now wash their hands in water brought for the purpose. Those who entered the grave wash their feet (shoes are never worn), and tools used in digging the grave are also washed thoroughly. This cleanses people of the grave "dirt," which is polluting. The washing done, the men quickly quit the grave site. Kamara (1932:95) describes what is probably a Muslim custom, the eating of the "last rice" when friends and kin of the deceased share rice cakes known as *keme-de* ("grave-bread") or *de-kuna* ("bitter bread"), prepared by virgin girls.

SACRIFICES

As soon as the men return from the grave site, the sacrifices are offered. The first and major sacrifice (*ninki sarake*, "cow sacrifice") is of a cow or cows provided by sons or brothers of the deceased. It is offered to God (*Ala* or *Altala*). The cow is tethered to a sacrificial post in the middle of the *luiye*. Men of the village, representing every subclan (*kebile*), family (*dembaiye*), and category of persons, surround the beast in a circle, stretching their right arms and hands out toward it. Quranic verses (*haye*) are recited as the cow is consecrated to Allah. The animal is then forced to the ground by young men and oriented with its head toward the east. A Muslim officiant (*karamorgo*) quickly cuts its throat. With another knife or machete the *karamorgo* supervises the butchering of the carcass. Meat is distributed in the customary way: a portion for representative elders from all the village subclans, and portions for other people representing other categories, the anthropologist as a representative of the *tubabunu* ("Europeans"), a visitor from another village as a representative of his village, and so on.[8]

Other sacrifices may be made by the bereaved kin. These sacrifices are seldom of cattle, but of sheep, goats, chickens, and hens and, most usually, rice flour (*dege*). The sacrifices are this time consecrated to the lineage ancestors, the ritual congregation comprising only lineage members and a few matrikin. Numerous sympathy gifts such as kola, money, rice, and oil are brought by visitors and mourners, who continue to arrive in the village from far afield during the days following the inhumation. But for everyone except the immediate family of the dead man, the mortuary rites are effectively over once the main sacrifice has been offered.

QUARANTINE

Labinane (from *la*, "lying down," and *binane*, "forty") is the Kuranko term for the forty-day quarantine period which follows the burial; during this time, the widows are isolated from the ordinary life of the community.[9] While other bereaved kin observe mourning by binding threads of raffia around their necks for a seven-day period, the wives must remain inside their late husband's house for forty days. They let their hair hang loose (it is usually plaited), a conventional expression of the apathy or loss of interest in personal appearance which often characterizes mourning (Parkes 1975:65). Through an association which the Kuranko make between expression of grief and sentimental attachment to the deceased, it is argued that the widows participate in the death. They are in a state of ritual impurity, and their isolation may reflect a common tendency of people to stigmatize the bereaved (22–23). During their seclusion they are ministered to and protected by one of the dead man's sister's sons (*berinne*), and it is the sister's son who, drumming dolefully, leads the widows (who are dressed in white country-cloth gowns, the senior wife walking before) to the streamside for ceremonial purification when *labinane* is over. Anyone who has never lost a relative must not see this procession but remain indoors until it has passed. For such persons, even visual contact with the widows is polluting.

At the streamside, confessions are made. The purpose of the confession is to ascertain whether or not any of the widows nurse some grievance against the dead man, whose spirit attends the ceremony,[10] and whether or not the dead man's spirit has forgiven the wives for any misdemeanors, particularly sexual infidelities, which may have hurt his reputation during his life. The usual technique for deciding if a confession is required consists in splitting a two-cotyledon kola nut and throwing the cotyledons on the ground; if they fall facing each other ("even") then no confession is required, but if they fall in any other combination ("odd") then confession and absolution must follow or else the woman will fall ill and die, accursed by the vengeful ghost of her late husband. When the confessions are over the widows are bathed in the stream, either by a sister of the deceased or by elderly village women (past child-bearing age). The sister's son remains in attendance, playing his drum to warn people away from the area.

The widows now return to the village to a large meal prepared by close kin. This signifies the end of quarantine and the widows' forthcoming reincorporation into the ordinary life of the community.

CHEFARE

Within a few days of the ending of the period of seclusion for the widows, the distribution of the heritable property (*che*) takes place under the supervision of the eldest surviving brother of the deceased. The occasion is known as *chefare*.

Succession is by primogeniture, and the eldest son's assumption of his father's role as family head (*dembaiyetigi*) is signified by the inheritance of his late father's cap and gown. A man's property includes his wives (inherited widows are known as *che musu*), his children (inherited children are known as *che dan*), livestock, clothes, personal possessions, gardens and other land in cultivation, and food in store. The house is "joint owned" (*serefan*) and usufructory rights to land cannot be inherited. According to the levirate, the oldest surviving brother of the deceased inherits the widows, their children, and the bulk of the material property. If a widow chooses, she may marry another "brother" of her late husband. This is often the case when the relations between the inheriting brother and the widow's late husband were strained or hostile. A woman may fear the vengeance of her late husband's spirit if she marries a man he disliked, and she will also be mindful of the disadvantages her children may suffer in the household of an indifferent "father." The curse of the dead is known as *furekoe*, and it may be regarded as sanction against a widow's betraying her late husband's trust or ignoring his expectations.

Small items of heritable property such as articles of clothing are distributed among subclan "brothers" to signify the solidarity of the subclan and amity among its members. According to Kuranko folk etymology, *kebile* (subclan) means "inheritance-sharers"; theoretically, a man has claims upon and rights in the property of his subclan "brothers."

With the distribution of the heritable property done and the widows remarried, the sequence of mortuary rites comes to a close. Ideally the community has made the various adjustments necessary to accommodate the loss of a kinsman or neighbor, and the bereaved have reconciled themselves to a new life in which the deceased, now transformed into an ancestor, will play a very different role.

SOCIAL STATUS AND MORTUARY CUSTOMS

Hertz has contrasted the panic and concern at the death of an important person with the death of a stranger, a slave, or a child. Such a death, he writes, "will go almost unnoticed; it will arouse no emotion, occasion no ritual. It is thus not as the extinction of an animal life that death occasions social beliefs, sentiments and rites" (1960:76). This general tendency is true of Kuranko funerals, and an investigation of the way in which differences in the scale and character of the rites are correlated with differences in the social status of the dead person is of crucial importance in our endeavor to understand the relation between individual *affect* and customary patterns of social *behavior*. The relationships between social status and place of burial, composition of ritual congregation, and fate of the soul are shown in table 1.

TABLE 1.
Kuranko Social Status and Mortuary Customs

Social Status	Place of Burial	Ritual Congregation	Fate of the Soul
Paramount chief	Chief's *luiye*	Representatives of all villages in the chiefdom and from other "allied" or "related" chiefdoms	Becomes ancestor, influencing the well-being of the inhabitants of the chiefdom
Founder of a *luiye*	*Luiye*	As for any other male elder	Becomes ancestor, influencing the well-being of those living in the *luiye*
Adult man	Village perimeter	Immediate family (agnates), affines, matrikin, sororal nephew, representatives of all other subclans in the village	Becomes ancestor, influencing the lives of agnatic descendants and, to a lesser degree, the lives of sister's children
Married woman	Village perimeter	Husband's family	Becomes "nominal" ancestress; no real influence
Infant	*Sundu kunye ma*	Immediate family	Possible reincarnation
Accursed person or witch	"Bush" beyond village perimeter	Immediate family	Spiritual extinction

WOMEN

Because women have no politicojural status in the community, a woman's burial is simply a "family affair." And it is always the husband's family which organizes the burial. The Kuranko often point out (and it forms part of the formal speech when a bride is "given away") that "a woman belongs to her husband's group [kebile] while she is alive and even after she is dead." Marriage involves a transfer to the husband of all rights: in personam, in uxorem, in genetricem. Kamara writes: "A woman, not a virgin, but dying husbandless, may not be buried until some man is found who will stand in loco mariti. If she had a lover that lover will find himself obliged to pay 'dowry' for her—a cow or two—in order that she may be buried, duly a married woman" (1932:96). In the case of an elderly woman, long a widow, her grandson may represent and stand as her husband.

At the burial of a woman, it is the husband who leads the cortege to the grave site. If a woman dies while her husband is away from the village, burial is postponed up to one day while he is summoned. A woman's natal kin attend the burial but play no central part in the rites. As for the actual inhumation, it is noteworthy that a man is buried with his head to the east and lying on his right side; a woman is buried with her head to the east and lying on her left side. The "left" (maran) is associated with feminine, weak, polluting attributes; the "right" (bolieme) with masculine, strong, clear/clean attributes. The jurally minor status of a woman (a dependent of and "owned" by her husband) is indicated by the customs described above. A woman can only be buried by her husband or by a symbolic or proxy husband; if a man is unable to attend his wife's funeral he will delegate to a brother or friend the role of "husband." The personality traits which are attributed to women, partly on the basis of their jurally minor status, are weakness of will, temperamentality, capriciousness, sexual infidelity.

A person who dies a confessed witch or as a result of cursing does not receive ordinary burial. Those who die accursed are avoided by all except their immediate kin, who are contaminated by the curse anyway. People not only shun the bereaved family; they also avoid tears and expressions of sympathy for fear of being associated with the dead person and kin and thereby contaminated. Sympathy gifts are not given, and the inhumation is conducted unceremoniously, quickly, and covertly by the dead person's immediate family.

CHILDREN

Children who die in early infancy, before weaning, are buried with cotton pods around the body; it is said that a cloth shroud would bruise it. People are enjoined not to express grief or mourn at an infant's death since "tears burn the child's skin and cause it pain." The actual burial of a child is a perfunctory affair involving only the immediate family. Some consolation may be offered in the belief that the infant once dead may be reborn, the only instance of reincarnation beliefs among the Kuranko. A mother, disconsolate and grief-stricken over the loss of a child, may cut off its little finger, slip a sliver of wood under its fingernail, or tightly bind a finger with thread before it is buried. When she bears her next child she will examine its fingers for a mark which will indicate reincarnation. Yet, it is pointed out that prolonged grief over the loss of an infant is futile; even if the child is reborn it will die at the same age as its predecessor.

Infant dead are buried at the back of the house, in the domestic area known as the *sundu kunye ma* (literally, "behind/rear head on") where women prepare food and cook, where domestic refuse is discarded, and where lies the boundary between one compound and another. The front of the house (which, incidentally, is associated with the "male domain," *ke dugu*) opens onto the *luiye:* the compound area common to several agnatically interrelated households, which form a circle around it.

A child is, to use a phrase of Meyer Fortes's, only an "incipient person" (1973:309). Among the Kuranko, only initiation at puberty can create a "whole" person, a completely socialized adult. Until initiation, children are considered to be "impure" and incompletely born; physical birth must be complemented by the ceremonial "birth" undergone during initiation. The Kuranko emphasis upon the transient and unstable character of infant life may be a rationalization of the high infant mortality rate (in one village I surveyed it was 54 percent, birth to three years of age). But this emphasis is also a logical outcome of Kuranko conceptualizations of social positions.

Just as women are marginal to the politicojural domain, so infant children are marginal to the domestic domain. The custom of burying a dead infant among domestic refuse or under the hearthstones in the *sundu kunye ma* gives objective expression to its marginality. The rubbish comprises material which is also part way between life and death: groundnut husks (no kernel), husks of winnowed grain, ash from cooking hearths, sweepings from the house, discarded scraps of food, human excreta.[11] Moreover, an infant that is reincarnated will be named Sundu. The spirit of a dead infant does not leave the world of the living altogether, and while awaiting its new incarnation it resides in the body of the Senegalese fire finch (*tintinburuwe*), a tame townbird which nests in the eaves of houses and feeds on leavings and scraps in the *sundu kunye ma*. Hertz, commenting upon the Dayak and Papuan customs of placing the infant dead in trees, summarizes beliefs pertaining to the deaths of children:

> since the children have not yet entered the visible society, there is no reason to exclude them from it slowly and painfully. As they have not really been separated from the world of spirits, they return there directly, without any sacred energies needing to be called upon, and without a period of painful transition appearing necessary. The death of a new-born child is, at most, an infra-social event; since society has not yet given anything of itself to the child, it is not affected by its disappearance and remains indifferent. (1960:84)

The small-scale, perfunctory, and unceremonious character of infant burial rites has been noted in other African societies.[12] It seems that the key factors are the *minimal personality* and *marginal status* of children.

RULERS

In the mortuary rites for a ruler, *central status* (a chief/ruler is known as *suetigi*, "townowner/master"; or, if paramount, *nyeman'tigi*, "master/owner of the country," or *tontigi*, "law owner/master") is associated with *maximal personality* (*miran*, "charisma/dignity/bearing/oratorical prowess/warrior strength").

The funerals for rulers or men of ruling lineages are more elaborate, further prolonged, and larger in scale than for other categories of persons. The rites have been studied by Kamara (1932, 1933) and Sayers (1925); I will therefore briefly summarize those aspects of the rites which are pertinent, referring as well to field observations of my own.

The actual burial of a chief follows the pattern already described, except that mourners come from throughout the chiefdom. At the burial a sword is carried hilt downward to signify the death of a warrior and chief. After the burial, a "friendly" chief is called upon to fix the date for a special sacrifice known as *korfe*; the day is customarily the first Thursday after the new moon. Chiefs from other chiefdoms throughout Kuranko country are invited to attend this politically significant event. Visiting chiefs bring salt and cows to be sacrificed.[13] At the *korfe* for Fa Bolo Karifa Dialo of Sambaia, which Sayers observed in 1921, thirty cows were brought, though only twelve were actually slaughtered. Kamara notes that as many as one hundred cows are slaughtered on some occasions and both Kamara and Sayers suggest that there is a "potlatching" element in the *korfe:* "everyone tried to outdo his neighbour in generosity" (Sayers 1925:28); "every visiting chief bringing as many as he can get" (Kamara 1933:156). Comparatively few cows are slaughtered at a *korfe* today, and with the decline of chiefly powers and political alliances, mortuary rites for rulers are now comparatively low key.

Some indication of the former political significance of a *korfe* is given in Sayers's account. Three paramount chiefs attended: Bafara of Kalian, a member of the same clan and a political ally of the deceased; Bamba Fara of Nieni, neighbors to the east ruled by the Koroma clan; and the Borowa (Barawa?) chief, Karifa Dumari (Mara?), who attended briefly, "held himself ostentatiously aloof . . . and went home" (Sayers 1925:20). Barawa, situated to the northeast, beyond the "buffer" chiefdom of Kalian and ruled by the Mara, still retains a tradition of chauvinistic condescension toward the Sambaia Dialo (or Jallo) who are of foreign (Fula) extraction, Muslims, and erstwhile dependents upon Mara patronage.

On the Wednesday before the *korfe*, the *finas* (genealogists and "remembrancers" to the rulers) meet to appoint one of their members to announce the death on the following day. This does not mean that people are just now aware that the chief is dead, simply that the "social" death (the funeral) and the "physical" death (the burial) are regarded as quite different events.

On Thursday the death is formally announced, followed by a warrior's dance and accompanied by the weeping and lamenting of the bereaved kinswomen. In the afternoon, a bonfire is prepared. Kamara writes that a man "collects as much wood as will enable every man, woman and child attending the funeral to bring one log each" (1933:155). Sayers (1925:26–27) records that a *Koli* dancer leads the villagers (men, women, and children) into the bush and fells a tree with a double-bladed ax; everyone must take a sprig and avoid other people's sprigs touching their own.[14] Together with as much wood as they can carry, the villagers bring the sprigs back to town for the bonfire. It is lit that night, and clothes belonging to the deceased and salt are thrown onto the flames as a sacrifice and absolution.

On Friday the cows are sacrificed. Some are brought by visiting chiefs, others are contributed by sons, brothers, and affines of the dead man. Saturday (Simbire) is, through Islamic influence, considered a day of rest. Visitors are obliged to prepare and cook their own food.

Sunday is given over to dancing. To the sound of xylophones, harps, and flutes and in festive mood, first the dead man's sisters' sons, then male affines, then the visiting chiefs join in the dancing. All give further gifts to the brothers of the deceased, the chiefs to "show how big and rich they are" (Kamara 1933:156). The dancing continues throughout the day, punctuated by gift giving, commensality, and various mimetic performances. This marks the close of the ritual sequence.

ROLE REVERSALS AND MIMETIC RITES

From the preceding summary account of the sequence of events in Kuranko funerals one gains little insight into the emotions, motives, and reactions of individual participants. Indeed, while observing people's behavior during the various rites, there is often little to betray to the outsider the actual feelings of individuals. This is partly because emotions are constrained, organized, and expressed according to ritual prescriptions.

In the Kuranko view, spontaneous, private, or uncontrolled expressions of grief are not simply inappropriate; they are dangerous. Hiding one's true feelings (which requires the same kind of conscious control as simulating or feigning certain emotions) is related to the need to prevent recognition by the ghost of the dead person (cf. Goody 1962:89–90 on LoDagaa "mourning disguises"). The Kuranko explain that pining after the lost one is both futile and wrong. Too much weeping and lamenting at a funeral will make it difficult for the dead person's spirit to be accepted into lakira; the ancestors in lakira allegedly say, "The spirit is not with us until those on earth have kept quiet." Many Kuranko point out that the dead person's spirit will be loath to leave grief-stricken kin, a belief which possibly follows from an attribution of subjective grief to the lost "object." The manner in which subjective states such as pining, searching, guilt, and anger are projected onto the dead person was noted by Hertz (1960:50) long before psychological research enabled us to understand the mechanisms and processes involved (Parkes 1975). Grieving, pining, and uncontrolled weeping signify, in the Kuranko view, unduly prolonged attachment and oversympathetic identification with the dead person. As we shall see, grieving and weeping must cease before the spirit of the dead person will detach and dissociate itself from the world of the living and become transformed into an ancestor.

The dislocation, confusion, and consternation caused by a death must, according to the Kuranko, be signified by prescribed (i.e., socially determined) patterns of behavior, not by spontaneous and idiosyncratic expressions. For example, when a *jeliba* is buried the *jelimusu* (the "*jeli* women") play the xylophone (*balanje*), an instrument which they are normally prohibited from playing, and *jeli* men play the *karinya*, the metal bar which the *jelimusu* normally play. On some occasions, even men of the ruling lineage play the xylophone of a deceased *jeliba*. The Kuranko are quite explicit in relating these usages to the prevailing condition of social disorder.

SANAKU

It is noteworthy that the categories of persons involved in these prescribed patterns of disorderly and anomalous behavior are never the immediate bereaved. They are "joking partners." When a man has died, members of his *sanaku*-linked clan (*sanakuiye*, "interclan joking partnership") will often come to the house where the body lies and bind the hands, feet, and body of the corpse with rope. Holding one end of the rope, a *sanaku* will declare, "This rope will be untied when you people have given us something," or "You cannot bury this man; he is our slave," or, as the women are weeping, "Keep quiet, keep quiet, we're going to wake him up now." Again, as the cortege moves from the *luiye* to the place of burial, a *sanaku* may protest with such words as "He's not going, he's my slave," and as the sacrifice begins a *sanaku* may appear in the *luiye* with a pariah dog on a makeshift leash and announce, "I have brought my cow for sacrifice." These privileged modes of disparaging and abusing the person and lineage of the deceased are usually regarded by the Kuranko as indications of the prevailing confusion. Some informants say that the levity of the *sanakuiye tolon* (*tolon*, "joking play") is a way of deflecting people's attention from the gravity and sorrow of the occasion. Sayers (1925:24) describes one performance:

> There runs about the town, meanwhile, in and out amongst the people, a girl, clothed in filthy cast off male attire, ragged, with blackened face and arms, as though with the cinders and ashes of a burnt farm, and on her head is a symbolic bundle of faggots, as though to say—a slave fulfilling her household duties.

Sayers notes that the girl is a member of a *sanaku*-linked clan; the clansmen "as faithful servants . . . have a symbolic right to the body of the dead chief, to redeem which, his family and all the people must make presents." Although I have never observed this particular performance, I have had it described to me by informants who explain that the *sanaku*'s self-abasing behavior is a way of exaggerating the high status position of the deceased ruler.[15]

MAMANIANENU

Closely resembling the behavior of the *sanaku* jokers and prompting similar explanations is the behavior of a category of women known as *mamanianenu*. I described earlier the *mamane*'s doleful circular "dance" for gifts; the *mamanianenu* also help wash and dress the corpse for burial and mimic various idiosyncrasies of their late grandfather—his manner of walking, dancing, and speaking. As with the *sanaku*, the mimetic performers desist only when they are given gifts by those attending the funeral.

> One of the deceased's sons' wives dresses in the Chief's clothes and tries to imitate his walk and speech, for doing which she receives presents. Another puts on big trousers, goes to the bathing place and falls into the water. She comes out with the trousers full of water and then walks from Chief to Chief with a pestle which she uses to throw water on people. Anybody disliking dirty water buys her off with a present as soon as she tries to come near him. (Kamara 1933:156)

Sayers describes the "*mamani*" at a funeral, running about with a pestle and mortar looking for rice to pound. The behavior is interpreted as "feigning madness" (1925:24). Sayers also describes "*mamusa*" (literally, "our related woman," i.e., sister) who is *not*, as Sayers says, "one of the wives of the dead man"; she rolls a makeshift fishing net across the ground recollecting how sisters fish for their brother the chief when he is alive. The *mamanianenu* also perform a dance on the Thursday of a chief's funeral during which they fold and unfold their *lapa*, thus exposing themselves "obscenely" to the crowd. Again, gifts are given by the men who also enjoy with "quips and gibes" and salacious glances the momentary divestment of each of the late chief's sons' wives (26–27).

SOCIAL VERSUS PERSONAL

These "mimetic," "obscene," "mad," and transvestite performances by the *sanaku* jokers and the *mamanianenu* are far more characteristic of the funeral of a chief than of a commoner, and they do not occur at the funeral of a woman. Clearly, these usages somehow reflect the status of a person in life and after life. It is my view that the performances described above assist the polarization and separation of two aspects of the identity of the deceased: his idiosyncratic and his social personality.

The mimetic performances are *simultaneously* an attempt to revivify or retain memories of the person and to expunge those memories. The inept and ridiculous aspects of the women's imitations of the person may serve to turn people's attention to the more abstract and formal attributes of the ancestral persona. It is only when memories of the dead person's mannerisms and deficiencies are denied through repression or masking that the dead can exemplify, as an abstract category, the values and customs of the society. Unlike the physical and idiosyncratic aspects of the person, these "values and customs" have a more impersonal character; they belong to the perdurable domain of the social rather than to the mutable and perishable domain of the personal.

This theatrical "setting apart" of the dead person's idiosyncratic personality is paralleled by various customs, already referred to, which serve to drive away the dead person's spirit and dissociate the living from the dead. Thus, prolonged mourning is prohibited lest the spirit remain among and haunt the villagers as a malevolent ghost, the widows are quarantined, the grave is sealed with heavy logs and stones to prevent the spirit returning to the body, and sacrifices are offered to God and to the ancestors in order to speed the spirit to *lakira* and ensure its reception there.[16]

THE TAINT OF DEATH

I have already alluded to the interconnected processes of separating body from spirit, separating the idiosyncratic personality from the social personality, and separating the dead from the living. These are transformative processes, and until the separations are effected, a condition of impurity obtains.

AFTERMATH

The Kuranko term *bonke* ("dust," "dirt," "earth") or *fera bonke* (*fera* signifies the bush and, more generally, extrasocial space) refers to the physical body. God (*Ala*) makes each individual person from earth taken from one particular place. When a person dies, *Ala* is supposed to direct people to inter the body at that same place. The word *dugu* (or *duge*), which is used to refer to a particular place, location, or patch of ground, is also used in some contexts as a synonym for the human body. Sometimes, too, the metaphor of a seed within its husk is used to explain how the "life" is in the body. Just as the bush or wilderness surrounds the community, so the body surrounds the life. The complementary term *nie* may be translated as "life," "life force," or "spirit." Of a living person, one says *a ni' a ro* (literally, "he/she life is in"), and it is the *nie* which leaves the body at the moment of death and must be assisted, through human intervention, on its passage to *lakira*. Derived from the Arabic (*al-akhira*), *lakira* is where the ancestral spirits dwell, although some ancestors (particularly of ruling lineages) are often associated with certain landscape sites: a granite inselberg, a lake, a mountain, a river hole.

This vagueness about and indifference to the actual character of the afterlife is typical of the Kuranko. Funerals are seen as means of removing the dead person from the world of the living rather than transporting him to and installing him in the world of the dead. The dead person's spirit (*nie*) leaves the world of the living when two conditions have been met: the body is buried and sealed under the earth and the bereaved have ceased weeping and gone into isolation. But between the moment of death and the moment when the *nie* departs for good, the *nie* remains in the village as a clandestine and wandering ghost. This "pitiful yet dangerous" ghost (Hertz 1960:36–37) is likened, by the Kuranko, to a shadow (*ninne*; possible etymology, "life little"). The ghost (which is known as the *yiyei*) is unable to disentangle itself emotionally from kinsmen and friends and thus may be interpreted as a projection of subjective states—in this case, the mixture of "protest" and "searching" reactions on the part of the bereaved. Certainly the association of the *yiyei* with the "liminal" phase of a funeral is reflected in the anomalous characteristics attributed to it. Its footsteps or ghostly sobbing may be heard, yet it is as insubstantial as a shadow. It can haunt and afflict the living, yet it is intangible.

There is an important correlation between the emotional attachment between the dead person's spirit and the immediate bereaved and the condition of impurity or contagion that obtains while the attachment lasts. It can be argued that the "image" of impurity and contagion not only signifies a disordered social condition; it enables people to alter subjective states by manipulating external simulacra. Thus, physical separation is an outward expression of the emotional "forgetting" that is demanded. The deadpan faces of the *mamanianenu* are physically suggestive of the control and suppression of grief that is expected. It is as if the *mamanianenu* and the *sanaku* jokers were manipulated, or manipulated themselves, as objects in order to effect vicariously and magically a change in the subjective state of the bereaved. Their automatic and theatrical behavior stands in contrast to the spontaneous and genuinely emotional expressions of the immediate bereaved. By giving *public* prominence to the former it is perhaps hoped that the private condition of the latter will be eclipsed or transformed.

When we consider the kinds of situations which are polluting and the prescribed responses to these situations we can see how "pure" (emotionless) categories are used to transform "impure" (emotionally charged) situations. Order is created out of disorder, purity out of danger. Table 2 summarizes the main polluting circumstances and the appropriate ritual responses to them. It also indicates the extent to which the notion of taint or contagion is expressed through metaphors of improper sexual relations.

IMPURITY

The association of dirt and coitus and the association of death and sexuality have been discussed by many writers (notably Goody 1962:56–59; Buxton 1973:147–50; Beidelman 1966). Among the Kuranko it is not just that procreative sexuality and death are logically opposed (cf. Buxton on the Mandari, 1973:149); rather that sexuality has ambivalent connotations. Licit, conjugal, procreative sexuality creates social relations; it binds lineages together in reciprocal, life-giving compacts. Illicit, clandestine, adulterous, recreative sexuality sunders social ties; it engenders jealousy, uncertainty, and "darkness" among men.[17] This ambivalence of Kuranko attitudes toward sexuality may explain why sexuality is such a dominant symbol in the context of mortuary rites where conflicts between attachment and disengagement, binding and severing, creating and destroying are so ubiquitous.[18]

With reference to table 2, it can be seen that certain categories of persons are "pure" or "above contagion." They mediate, so to speak, between the community and the bereaved kin. The first category comprises women past menopause and, occasionally, sexually innocent (i.e., uninitiated) girls. Here, absence of sexual relations makes it possible for these women to touch the man's corpse with impunity. Wives and daughters must avoid contact with the corpse. They lead the keening.

The second category comprises the dead man's sisters' sons (singular, *berinne*; literally, "little maternal uncle"). A sister's son, usually a man both genealogically

TABLE 2.
Pollution and Response

Polluting Circumstance	Ritual Response
A man dying or gravely ill	Objects touched and used by the invalid or attendants must not leave the house; possible adulterers are avoided; sick man is attended by son and wife (if she is past menopause)
The grave, the corpse, and grave-digging tools; the burial party	Purification by washing
"Last rice" for the dead man	Prepared by virgin girls
Spontaneous and impetuous expressions of grief	"Social" control of affect
Adulterer participating in the sacrifice (i.e., a man who has had an affair with the deceased's wife)	Adulterer must avoid accepting or eating meat from the sacrificed animal lest he die
Widows, children, and property of the deceased	Quarantine; no direct communication with the widows is permitted; those who have never lost a kinsman should avoid seeing the widows; widows are purified by being dressed in white gowns and bathed by women past menopause
Mimetic performances in which the *mamane* or *mamusa* touches men in the crowd	Gifts given to "lay the ghost"

and emotionally close to his uncle, watches over and remains with the widows and property during the period of quarantine. All communications with the widows "go through" him, since for others the widows "still carry the death with them and are feared." It is explained that the sister's son prevents the dead man's ghost from making contact with the widows. Asked why a brother or sister of the deceased could not keep vigil, the Kuranko usually point out that a brother might be harboring a grudge and a sister would not have the courage. The sister's son "acts in the place of the dead man's sister." One man told me:

> We permit the sister's son to watch over the widows because if the dead man's *yiyei* approaches it will see the sister's son there on the porch of the house [where he sits by day and sleeps at night]; it will not go past him and frighten the women; it will immediately think of the sister's son as the sister [i.e., recollect the strict taboo against a man touching or offending his sister]; the sister will be inside the house to console the widows and prevent them from being frightened by their late husband's ghost.

The intervenient role of the sister's son is a reflection of the fact that he is simultaneously socially close (his mother is the deceased's sister and belonged to his lineage) and socially distant (he, like his father, belongs to another lineage).

A similar ambiguity obtains for the third and fourth categories: the *sanaku*-partners and the *mamanianenu*. I have discussed elsewhere the "status ambiguity" of the *sanakuiye* (Jackson 1974); here some further comments must be made on the role of the *mamanianenu*.

STAND-INS

A possible explanation for the fact that the principal actors in the mortuary ceremonies are not the immediate bereaved but rather persons ambiguously identified with the lineage of the deceased is that the powerful and impetuous emotions of the bereavement reaction could not generate or maintain a sequence and pattern of *social* events whose purposes go further than the mere psychological readjustment of individuals to the death of a loved one.

For the bereaved women, profound emotions determine their attitudes toward the deceased. By contrast, the association or identification of the *mamane* with her grandfather is founded upon an artifice of logic. But a woman may develop strong emotional attachment to her father's father or husband's grandfather simply because a formal principle in the social system—the identification of nonadjacent generations—makes such attachments possible and appropriate. Structurally speaking, the *mamane* is placed in an ambiguous position: closely identified with the grandfather yet also a stranger because of obvious age, sex, and status differences. As a real or fictive affine (a man jokingly calls his granddaughter "my wife") she is, as it were, halfway between strangerhood (*sundanye*) and kinship (*nakelinyorgoye*). Easily assuming her alternative or shadow role, she is well placed to act out on behalf of the bereaved wives and sons the emotional confusions and consternations of the bereavement reaction.[19] By "standing in" for the bereaved, the mimetic performers also "stand between" the bereaved and the malevolent ghost of the dead man. By "standing aloof" from the affective turmoil of the occasion, they are also in a position to assist the passage of the dead person's spirit from the world of the living (signified by close kinship attachments) to the world of the dead (where personal attachments and affections are transcended).

Another kind of significance possibly attaches to the derisive and derogatory elements in the mimetic performances. These performances are not only given by categories of persons who are at once identified with and dissociated from the dead person; they are indicative of the ambivalence which characterizes the attitude of the bereaved. The mixture of affection and animosity is conveyed by the gauche imitations which simultaneously celebrate and mock the memory of the deceased. On the intellectual plane, the derisive treatment of the idiosyncratic personality of the deceased is a crucial phase in the transformation of person into persona, of an individual into a category.

An example will indicate how the *mamanianenu* act out and reflect upon the anomalous position and possibly ambivalent emotions of a son at his father's funeral. As successor, a son is placed in an ambiguous position until the conclusion of the ritual period (forty days). His father is physically dead (buried), yet not socially dead (forgotten) until *chefare*. While the son assumes a formal and filial attitude, his daughters and junior wives ("joking wives" of the deceased) act in ways which make it manifestly clear that the son has become his father. They don their "husband's" cap and gown. Thus, while the son's piety and reserve seem to intimate the continued presence of the father, the actions of the *mamanianenu* signify the contrary and express openly the disguised status of the successor.

THEORETICAL AND COMPARATIVE CONSIDERATIONS

It is clear from the evidence adduced in the preceding account and analysis of Kuranko mortuary customs that a reductionist approach which seeks to explain a particular social configuration in terms of psychological or ethnological factors (i.e., in terms of linear causality) is inadequate. As information about the psychological or behavioral fragments is gained, so information about the total system is lost. The polysemic and multidimensional character of the ritual configuration can be respected and communicated only when we adopt an approach which integrates and synthesizes several available perspectives.

I have taken the view that the psychological processes and the behavior which characterize the bereavement reaction are phylogenetic adaptations. But this repertoire of affective states and behavior patterns is subject to social "control" and manipulation. The ways in which elements from this repertoire are arranged and the meanings ascribed to these elements vary significantly from one society to another and from one social context to another (Mead 1952:411–14; Volkart 1957: 286–301; Bastide 1972:158–60; Mandelbaum 1965:338–60; Huntingdon and Metcalf 1979). The actual configuration of these "given" elements is reflective of certain universal structuring principles, e.g., the principle of "dialectical negation." But the *purpose* of the ritual configuration, like its meaning, differs from society to society. This is undoubtedly because the problem of the bereaved is only one of many problems which mortuary rites are designed to solve. For example, among the LoDagaa the "main concern" of mortuary institutions is the reallocation of rights and duties of the dead man among the surviving members of the community, particularly property rights and sexual rights (Goody 1962:chap. 13). Jean Buxton (1973:153) has emphasized that both "personal emotional adjustments" and "social adjustments" have to be made through Mandari death rites. Among the Yoruba, Nuer, Lugbara, and many other African peoples, great emphasis is placed upon the transformation of the identity of the dead (Morton-Williams 1960; Evans-Pritchard 1956:chap. 6; Middleton 1971).

What remains typical in all these various cases is that the affective elements are managed, allocated, simulated, controlled, and interpreted in various ways depending upon the kinds of problems, both personal and social, to be solved. This means that identical *behavior* in two or more societies does not necessarily imply identical *affect* or *motivation*. Furthermore, the "social problems" to be solved are not necessarily mere secondary elaborations or extensions of the "psychological problems" of bereavement. To elucidate this point I want to consider briefly the manner in which the person is transformed into a category, i.e., an ancestor.

Freud noted that mourning "has a quite specific physical task to perform: its function is to detach the survivors' memories and hopes from the dead" (1965:65). More recent studies have shown how "selective forgetting" assists this detaching function and helps mitigate the pain of grieving (Parkes 1975; Kübler-Ross 1970). This psychological process is, however, acted out by persons other than the bereaved in order to perform a uniquely social task—a cognitive alteration in which the person is transformed into an ancestor by first suppressing awareness of his physical and idiosyncratic aspects. At the final funeral of a Kaguru man, the dead person is said to have been "forgotten" (Beidelman 1971:115). Among the Yoruba, before the second burial is held, an *engungun* masquerader simulates for the last time the "actual bodily appearance" of the deceased (Morton-Williams 1960:36). The Mandari, Tallensi, and Lugbara destroy possessions which represent aspects of the "social personality" of the deceased (i.e., with the individual); other "lineage property" is inherited (Buxton 1973:121; Fortes 1973:303; Middleton 1965:65–66).

The destruction of personal property, like the forgetting and expunging of the idiosyncratic personality of the dead, is of course a preliminary to creating the transcendent image of ancestor. For example, among the Tallensi a small strip of the deceased's clothing is referred to as the deceased's "dirt"; it "stands for the deceased" and "represents the dead during the interval between the mortuary and the final funeral ceremonies." Fortes notes that it

> is finally disposed of when a collection of his personal utensils, such as dishes for food and water, is ritually destroyed, to dispatch him finally to the ancestors. This clears the way for him to be brought back into his family and lineage in the character of an ancestor, that is not a human person, endowed with mystical and spiritual powers, and therefore with rights to worship and service. (1973:303)

This is comparable with the Nuer distinction between the individual (who should not survive) and the name (which should endure), or with the Lugbara notion that at death attributes of the physical body must be extinguished so that ideal attributes of the soul can survive (Evans-Pritchard 1956:162–63; Middleton 1971:194).

This process of "induced amnesia" is often said to take three generations, which is in fact approximately the time required for all those who knew a particular individual to die. Thereafter there is no direct knowledge or real memory of that individual (Iberall 1972:252). Thus, among the Mandari, three generations after death "a deceased person is merged in the ancestral collectivity and the dropping-out of the long dead reflects the working of actual memory in relation to passing time" (Buxton 1973:151). The Mende divide "ancestors" (*ndɔɔbla*) into *ndebla* ("the nameless and timeless dead") and *kɛkɛni* ("the fathers who are remembered"); this corresponds to a division between "ancient times when present patterns were established, and the past which is *in the memory of the oldest people in the town*" (Cosentino 1982:2, my emphasis). Bloch's superb study of the secondary funeral (*famadihana*) among the Merina of Madagascar indicates how the names and personalities of the dead are forgotten: a "ritually sacrilegious attitude" is forced upon the living, involving rough treatment of the corpse and obligations to handle the skeleton so that the close relatives will accept the irreversibility and finality of death (1971:158, 168–69). Among the Fang, reliquary figures represent "living persons in general" and not particular living persons (Fernandez 1973:204). One of Fernandez's informants explained why this should be so:

> The figure represents no ancestor. There are many skulls in the reliquary. Who should we choose to represent? And who would be satisfied with the choice if his own grandfather should be ignored? The figures were made to warn others that this was "the box of skulls" and they were made to represent all the ancestors within. (205)

The foregoing digression, which only touches upon a subject of immense interest and significance, does indicate that "psychological" factors and processes are often the raw material out of which consciously contrived ceremonial and metaphorical patterns are fashioned and elaborated. But these patterns should not be *reduced* to psychogenic factors, even though they frequently display a "vocabulary of affect." With reference to mortuary rites, there is a remarkable similarity between the psychological process of withdrawal or detachment prior to a new attachment being made, the socioeconomic process of withholding and then redistributing property and offices, and the intellectual process of suppressing or denying the idiosyncratic personality of the deceased in preparation for a new "ancestral" role.

But it would be incorrect, in my view, to regard any *one* of these processes as determinant. The psychological process of mourning, grieving, and the bereavement reaction constitute a repertoire of elements which are subject to manipulation, variant signification, rearrangement, and simulation for the purposes of resolving problems and effecting transformations which go beyond the domain of mere affect.

SIX

The Witch as a Category and as a Person

In February 1970 an epidemic of insect-borne encephalitis swept through the village of Kamadugu Sukurela in northern Sierra Leone. There were many deaths. The village was under a pall. In due course, the chief and elders summoned a male witch-hunting cult known as *Gbangbane* from Farandugu, four miles away. At night, as we huddled indoors, the "devil" moved among the houses. Its ominous, muffled voice, the shuffle of feet in the darkness, the staccato of wooden clappers—*gban gban, gban gban*—infected us all with deep disquiet.

My field assistant, Noah Marah, and I spent several days in the village, thinking we might be of some use, but there was little we could do, so we left. A couple of weeks later we returned and sought out a friend of Noah's, Morowa Marah, whom I'd met on our initial visit. We sat on the porch of Morowa's house. His wife served us a meal of rice and groundnut stew. I asked Morowa to tell us what had happened in our absence.

The witch-hunters had diagnosed the cause of one man's illness as witchcraft and promised to deal with the witch before returning to Farandugu. According to Morowa, *Gbangbane* had told the chief and elders that the offending witch would fall ill with chest, neck, and head pains and shit herself or himself before dying. The following day the sick man succumbed and died, as *Gbangbane* had predicted. Eight days later his sister fell gravely ill. In her pain and distress, she confessed she had killed her brother by witchcraft. "I was hunting him for a year," she said. "The first time I tried to kill him was when he went to brush his farm, but I missed him. The branch only knocked out some of his teeth [such an accident had occurred]. But this year we [her coven] lay in wait for him on the path to his palmwine trees. We beat him up and injured him. Then he fell ill." The woman also explained her motive for wanting to kill her brother: she had once asked him for some rice and he had refused her. But why she had used witchcraft against her brother rather than cursing him, as is a sister's right, was left unexplained. Then, as the woman lay ill inside her house, *Gbangbane* came again and ordered that she be buried at once. Men bound her hands and feet and dragged her to the outskirts of the village. There they dug a shallow grave and buried her alive. Banana leaves and stones were thrown in on top of her. During the entire episode, all the women of the village remained indoors.

When Morowa had finished his account I found it impossible not to accuse him of being accessory to a murder. My outrage astonished him, and he tried to help me understand.

"If it had been my choice," he said grimly, "I would have had her thrown into the bush without burial. But we buried her in the grassland beyond the Mabumbuli [stream] so that when the grass is dry we can set fire to it and turn her face into hell. A witch deserves no respect. A witch is not a person."

I knew Morowa and his wife had lost children as a result of witchcraft; I also knew what appalling tension the community was under. But the image of a woman being buried alive poisoned my feelings toward Morowa and, for a time, toward all Kuranko who shared his view. My only consolation came from Morowa's report that shortly after the murder (for I could not think of it otherwise), the witch's shade or *pulan* invaded the village and Morowa had been the first to be haunted.[1] As he slept, it settled on his head. He opened his eyes but could not cry out. He lay in terror as though an immense weight were pressing down on him. Other men in Kamadugu Sukurela were also afflicted. The *pulan* terrorized the village. Finally, the chief and elders summoned a *pulan*-catcher (*pulan brale*) from Bambunkura, a village twelve miles away. This man, Musa, bagged the *pulan* in the form of a lizard in the dead woman's house. However, her son, distressed by the awful circumstances of his mother's death, refused to accept that the lizard was his mother's shade. Piqued, Musa went back to Bambunkura. But the *pulan*-haunting continued, and the dead woman's son was now afflicted by it. Once more the *pulan*-catcher was summoned from Bambunkura, and the son was ordered by the chief and elders to pay the Le.8 fee as well as apologize to Musa for doubting his skills. Musa then caught the *pulan* (again in the form of a lizard) and killed it.

These events introduce the ethical and epistemological issues I want to address in this chapter. The most obvious question is whether the Kuranko word *suwage* corresponds to the English word "witch" and whether there is any justification for calling Morowa's haunting "guilt" or the killing of the woman "murder." This is not just a matter of semantics and "accurate translation"; we have to work out whether it is possible to gain access to ideas and experiences designated *suwa'ye* ("witchcraft") in Kuranko and understand them in terms of ideas and experiences familiar to us in our own culture. A critical issue here is elucidating the relationship between conventional notions of witchcraft and the experiences of women who actually confess to being witches—the relationship between episteme and experience, knowledge and event. But underlying all these questions, I shall argue, is a problem that affects Kuranko villagers as well as anthropologists: the way our discursive categories distort our perception of persons. Thus, the pathology of conventional Kuranko thought, which denies personhood to a woman who in extreme distress confesses herself a "witch," is uncannily like the pathology of much anthropological discourse which buries the experience of the individual subject in the categories of totalizing explanation.[2]

IMAGES OF THE WITCH

To understand what the Kuranko mean when they say a witch is not a person, it is necessary to clarify the indigenous concept of *morgoye* ("personhood"). *Morgoye* implies respect for and mindfulness of others, an abstract attitude in which personal purposes are consonant with collective goals. Ideally, a person is magnanimous, open, and straightforward in his or her dealings with others. A sociable person is "sweet" (*morgo di*), he or she likes the company of others. Or a person is "open" (*morgo gbe*; literally, person clear/white) and "straight" (*morgo telne*). An unsociable person is "bent" and "devious" (*morgo dugune*) like a crooked path. Or a person is "broken-down" (*kore*), on an analogy with a dilapidated house (*bon kore*), a broken calabash, worn-out clothes, an abandoned farm, and similar "useless" things. Sometimes an antisocial person is referred to as a "bush person" (*fira morgo*) or an "unwell person" (*morgo kende ma*), *kende* meaning physically "healthy" as well as socially or morally "proper." Anyone who sets himself or herself apart from others is quite simply "not a person" (*morgo ma*).

The stereotype of a witch includes all these notions of deviance, resentment, wildness, and sickness; essentially, it is a dialectical negation of the moral concept of *morgoye*. As the Kuranko word *suwage*[3] (literally, "night owner") suggests, a witch acts surreptitiously, under cover of darkness, using powers which are invisible to ordinary eyes: witch weapons, witch medicines, witch gowns, witch animals, even witch airplanes. These are the things the witch-hunting cults attempt to track down, for *Gbangbane* cannot directly destroy a witch, only disarm her. Witchcraft (*suwa'ye*) is not inherited; it is an inborn proclivity—which is why, though witches are criminals, a witch's kin are never tainted by or held accountable for her actions. Witches have "bad *yugi*," something that cannot be resisted or willed away.

A witch's "life" (*nie*) supposedly leaves her sleeping body at night and moves abroad, often in the body of an animal familiar. As her "life goes out" (*a nie ara ta*), her body may be shaken by convulsions and her breathing cease. In this state of suspended animation, the body is vulnerable; if it is turned around, then the witch's *nie* will not be able to reenter it and she will die.[4] A witch will also perish if the dawn finds her out of her body. The animals most commonly associated with witches sum up the traits of witchcraft: predatory (leopard), scavenging (hyena, vulture), underground (snakes), nocturnal (bats, owls); indeed, the owl (*gbingbinyaga*) is sometimes called the "witch bird" "because it is seldom seen and flies by night."

Witches are predatory and cannibalistic. But they do not attack a victim's "life" (*nie*) directly; they "consume" some vital organ (usually the liver, heart, or intestines) or drain away the victim's blood or break the victim's backbone by tapping him on the nape of the neck. It is said that witches work in covens and that the greatest threat of witchcraft attack lies within the extended family (*kebile*), i.e., "from those who share a common inheritance."[5] As one man put it, "Witchcraft is eating yourself" (meaning that a witch usually "eats" her own child, her co-wife's child, her grandchild, or her brother's child) but "sorcery is destroying others."[6]

Witchcraft operates through blackmail and indebtedness. A witch will somehow "open the door" of her own house by nullifying the protective medicines which the household head has placed over the lintel. Then a witch from her coven steals into the house and "eats" one of its occupants—usually a child, because children are less likely to be protected by personal medicines. The aggressor is obliged to discharge her debt at some later time by making it possible for her co-witch to claim a victim from her house. One informant told me that "only someone close to you could betray you to the witches by telling them where you sleep in the house and by opening the door to them." A Kuranko adage is often used in support of this reasoning: *sundan wa dugu koro worla bor duguranu de l sonti i ye* (if a stranger [guest] uncovers something hidden, someone living in that place [the host] must have told him where it was).

These popular stereotypes of witches and witchcraft are logically derived through a systematic inversion of what is regarded as ideal social behavior (cf. Beidelman 1986:chap. 9; Middleton 1971:238–50): day/night, open (*kenema*)/ underhanded (*duworon*), villagers/bush creatures, sociability/selfishness, generalized reciprocity/negative reciprocity.

So far I have summarized what Kuranko men told me about witchcraft when I broached the subject with them. But directed interviews and leading questions bring into relief only one dimension of the phenomenon. Consider, for instance, that many men were loath to discuss witchcraft with me in public lest their conversancy with the subject be taken as evidence that they themselves were witches. This immediately suggests that the definition of a witch as a nefarious and self-seeking woman does not exhaust the semantic range of the term *suwa'ye*. In fact the polysemic character of the term can be readily established. Thus, Kuranko acknowledge that the notoriously unstable and jealous relationship between nonuterine brothers (known as *fadenye*) is a potential source of witchcraft. It is also frequently pointed out that a farmer who produces a surplus above his subsistence needs, a man of wealth and position, and a child who excels at school or is well favored are all likely to be envied and resented—fertile grounds for witchcraft attack. The illicit use of destructive medicines, independent of a medicinemaster, to bring shame, adversity, or death to an enemy is also spoken of as witchcraft. So too is the use of poisons (*dabere*) such as *munke* ("gunpowder") and *gbenkan*,[7] which malevolent old women allegedly sprinkle in children's food or water.

Clearly, witches are not invariably women. Nor do they just use psychic powers, at the mercy of evil instincts. Nor is witchcraft unequivocally antisocial; *suwa'ye* is a common metaphor for extraordinary powers. Thus, white men may be likened to witches because of their technological wizardry and remarkable mobility (in ships and aircraft), and legendary figures such as Mande Sunjata and Yilkanani are sometimes said to have been witches because their powers were beyond ordinary comprehension. Even more significant is the fact that *Gbangbane* (or *Gbangbe*), the witch-hunter, is spoken of as a witch. This is how Saran Salia Sano of Firawa described *Gbangbe* to me:

It is like the other *sumafannu* ["secret things"]. When you are a boy, you try to imagine what it is. You are told it kills people. You are afraid. But you also feel it is something extraordinary, and want to see it. Then, when you are initiated, you see that it is a person—not an ordinary person, but a witch. Its witchcraft is greater than that of a host of people [*a suwa'ya morgo siyama n ko*]. *Gbangbe* is a *subingban* ["ruler of the night"]. He is immune to all evil, and has the power to rob men of their shape-shifting abilities. *Gbangbe* forces people to confess. He seizes their possessions. The person cries out, "He's taken my things!" and the kinsmen plead with *Gbangbe* not to destroy them lest the person die.

I asked Saran Salia to clarify what he meant by "seizure" of a witch's "posses-sions," since the word *miran* can denote both material things and psychological "self-possession." Were people "seized" by terror when *Gbangbe* was out, or did *Gbangbe* actually take their property and physically force them to confess? To the Western mind, always keen to discriminate between "psychic" and "physical" reali-ties, the question is crucial. To Saran Salia it seemed somewhat beside the point, but he gave me a specific example of what he meant.

The incident he described took place at Bandakarafaia six years earlier. It was night, and *Gbangbe* was abroad in the village. *Gbangbe* stopped outside a house:

It seized this woman's headtie, shirt, and shoes. Inside the house, the woman started struggling and shouting, "*Gbangbe* has got me! *Gbangbe* has got me!" [*m'bi Gbangbe bolo*, "I am Gbangbe's hand in"]. Her kinsmen gave *Gbangbe* Le.12, two mats, and ten kola nuts. *Gbangbe* said, "I have heard." He gave back the headtie and shirt, but not the shoes. The woman cried, "Give me the shoes." *Gbangbe* gave them to her. Then she shouted, "*Soburi* [hooray], I've got them!" She became normal again.

"But were the clothes real?" I asked.

"They were like real ones, but they were witch's clothes."

Seeing my perplexity, Saran Salia recounted another case. It was the first I'd ever heard in which a man confessed to witchcraft.

It happened in Firawa twelve years earlier. A man called Yimba Koroma be-came agitated and collapsed in his house one night while *Gbangbe* was out. On this occasion, *Gbangbe* seized the man in his witch's clothes and also seized his witch's things (*suwa'ya mirannu*).

The man's clothes tightened around his neck; he felt strangled. He cried out to *Gbangbe*, "Leave me alone, give me back my things!" He confessed to having eaten people's children. "I ate Yira, I ate Karifa and Yira. I ate them. Please give me back my things [*mirannu*]." *Gbangbe* told him to name his other victims. "No," he said, "I won't name anyone else." That is why he was not forgiven. He was a member of a night *kere*.

A *kere* is a labor cooperative (Jackson 1977b:8–11); it epitomizes the spirit of con-viviality and mutual aid in a community. Were witches in their night *kere* or coven bound by the same ties of reciprocity as bound men in a farming *kere*?

"Yes," Saran Salia said, "except witches join forces to take life, not make it."

In the company of women and children, men cultivate the fiction that

Gbangbane is a bush spirit, not a person. But *Gbangbane* is a person, as Saran Salia observes, though not an ordinary person; he is a witch. Underlying this view is the notion that the same wild powers that can destroy people can also protect them. In short, *suwa'ye* is not just semantically ambiguous; it denotes an indeterminate power or faculty. And though this power of *suwa'ye* is in essence "wild" or extrasocial, whether it becomes good or bad *depends entirely on how it is harnessed or used.*

This pragmatist emphasis on contexts of use brings me to a consideration of the analysis by Hallen and Sodipo of the Yoruba word *àjé*, commonly translated "witch." On the basis of detailed comparative research, they argue that it is impossible to define a universal category "witchcraft" that can cover without distortion all the phenomena commonly brought under this rubric (Hallen and Sodipo 1986:chap. 3; Prince 1970:915). Thus, while the Yoruba *àjé*, the Kuranko *suwage*, the Zande *mangu*, and the English *witch* all share some family resemblances, they also connote quite divergent phenomena and personality types. This point is vitally important. However, I do not go along with Hallen and Sodipo in construing this problem as basically semantic, a problem of accurate translation. True, the difference between Kuranko informants' stereotypes of witches and particular accounts (like those of Saran Salia) correspond to the distinction Quine makes between "standing sentences" and "observation sentences," the first being abstracted from immediate sensory experience, the second issuing from specific situations (Hallen and Sodipo 1986:17).[8] And it is imperative that we do not overlook the indeterminate relationship (the "empirical slack," the "evidential gap") between episteme and experience, knowledge and event (17, 41–42). But I do not see why we should want to overcome these discrepancies by defining our terms more precisely, trying to make words and world coalesce and correspond. My own interpretive preference is to consider not what words mean *in essence*, but what they are *made* to mean in the contexts of everyday life. It isn't words we want to compare when we try to understand the phenomenon we provisionally call "witchcraft," but the exigencies of life, the events and experiences which the words are brought to bear upon.

I now propose to shift my focus to the level of event—actual confessions to witchcraft—and explore the interplay of stereotypical ideas about witches and the experiences of Kuranko women who confess to witchcraft.

THE EVIDENCE OF CONFESSION

Within Africa, one can make a rough-and-ready distinction between accusation-oriented and confession-oriented societies, though in each society accusation and confession may be emphasized differently in different contexts (Douglas 1970b: xxxiv; Ruel 1970:333; Wyllie 1973:74–75).

Of the Azande, Evans-Pritchard reported: "I have never known a Zande admit his witchcraft" (1972:125) and "I have only received cases of confession from one Zande . . . perhaps the least reliable of my informants" (118). By contrast, other societies, most notably in West Africa, are characterized by a rarity or absence of direct accusation and the presence of confession: Effutu (Wyllie 1973), Banyang

(Ruel 1970), Ashanti (Ward 1956; Field 1960). Yet other African societies are not-able for the rarity of both direct accusation and confession: Dinka (Lienhardt 1951), Mbugwe (Gray 1969). And some, such as the Korongo, "have no witchcraft beliefs at all" (Nadel 1952).

Among the Kuranko, confession, not accusation, is the norm.[9] But the rare and elusive character of these confessions, coupled with the fact that women usu-ally confess during terminal illness or are killed on account of what they confess, makes it very difficult to gain direct knowledge of the experiences of the Kuranko women who own to being witches. The ethnographer is obliged to rely on hearsay accounts of events that have often been half-forgotten, if not actively suppressed. Particularly problematic are the manifest prejudices of Kuranko men when speaking of women witches. Witchcraft epitomizes the worst in women, and men make witches the scapegoats for their own anxieties about their vaunted autonomy and strength. Indeed, their stereotypes of women as weak-willed, impulsive, and in-clined toward hysteria are sadly similar to those still current in the discourse of many Western men.[10]

To understand the witch as a subject (pour-soi), to rehabilitate her as a person in a society which reduces her to a negative category, is not unlike the task contem-porary historians face writing about the consciousness of the colonized—their "cul-ture of silence" (Freire 1972). Nevertheless, as Ranajit Guha so brilliantly shows in his study of peasant insurgency in colonial India, it is possible to glean, from the distorted discourse of the oppressor, fragmentary clues "to the antonymies which speak for a rival consciousness" (1983:17). This is also our task.

Here, in summary form, are details of thirteen cases of witchcraft confession, giving first the relationship of the victim to the witch and then the background and confessed reason for the witchcraft:

1. No relationship. Man confessed to Gbangbe that he had "eaten" several chil-dren (all male). He died after confessing. (Case of Yimba Koroma of Firawa.) Infor-mant: Saran Salia Sano, elderly man, Firawa, 1979.

2. No victim. Woman "succumbed" to Gbangbe but did not confess to witch-craft. Her kinsmen "begged" and paid Gbangbe; the woman recovered her senses. (Case of woman from Bandakarafaia.) Informant: Saran Salia Sano, Firawa, 1979.

3. No relationship. A man, Fore Kande of Bandakarafaia, tested his witchcraft against Saran Salia. Dying, he confessed: "I went abroad as a witch; I went and saw his Kome; it killed me" (m'bora suwa'ye ro; n'tara a ma felen n'ya l Komeye; wo le m'faga); i.e., Saran Salia was immune to witchcraft attack, so the witchcraft was turned back on Fore, who died. He'd never before shown animosity toward Saran Salia. Informant: Saran Salia Sano, Firawa, 1979.

4. Brother's daughter's son. Informant's grandson died suddenly. A local woman was said to have confessed to killing him, but her kin hushed up her confes-sion. Informant: Bundo Mansaray, middle-aged man, Kamadugu Sukurela, 1972.

5. Brother. Eight days after her brother's sudden death, a woman fell ill and confessed she'd once asked her brother for rice and he'd refused her. After one unsuccessful attempt on his life, she and other witches beat him up and killed him.

She was buried alive. Informant: Morowa Marah, young man, Kamadugu Sukurela, 1970.

6. Husband. Woman fell ill with chest and head pains; on her deathbed she confessed that her husband had never liked her. Indeed, her husband blamed her for the awful tropical ulcers on his foot. A diviner had told him "evil people" (*morgo yugunu*) were getting at him; he formerly cursed the evil-doer who, he suspected, was his own wife. Her first husband had divorced her because of her "bad behavior" (*son yugi*). There were no children by the second marriage (four years). After she died, her *pulan* came out and had to be caught and dispatched. Informant: husband, Ali Koroma, middle-aged man, Kamadugu Sukurela, 1972.

7. Husband; brother's son's wife. A child died suddenly. A few days later the child's father's sister fell seriously ill and confessed that she was responsible for the child's death. She owed her coven a child, but being childless, gave them the life of her brother's grandson. She said she had "got her destiny through that child," i.e., her sickness was a punishment for having killed him. When she entered her brother's house to get the child, the house had been surrounded by fire from the antiwitchcraft fetish *sase;* she'd been badly burned when leaving. She also confessed that when, many years earlier, her husband had accompanied a white man into the Loma mountains to hunt elephants she had transformed herself into an elephant and tried to kill him. She'd also prevented him from becoming chief. Finally, she told how, when *Gbangbe* was abroad, she would assume the form of a vulture or fly by plane and sit near the moon to evade detection. She would take her co-witches with her in a back hamper, but one night *Gbangbe* came unexpectedly and "seized" her hamper. Her co-witches, left stranded, cried out to her: *"Mama Yeri, sole wara mintan de me tala minto?"* ("Grandmother Yeri, the hamper is burned, where are we going to go?") When her confession had been heard, she was taken from the house and left in the backyard to die. Informant: woman's brother's grandson, Noah Marah, young man, Kabala, 1970.

8. Husband. Woman confessed to feeling resentful when her husband gave more rice and meat from a sacrifice to her co-wives than to her. During terminal illness, she confessed to trying to kill him by witchcraft, but his protective fetishes turned the witchcraft back against her. After her death, her *pulan* came out, turning food and water bad. Informant: woman's co-wife's son, Steven Marah, schoolboy, Kabala, 1970.

9. Husband; co-wife's son. Woman confessed on her deathbed to killing her husband by witchcraft and eating her co-wife's son. My informant believed the confession to have been mistaken; the woman never showed animosity to anyone. Informant: woman's co-wife's son, town chief at Fasewoia, 1970.

10. Husband. During severe illness, a woman confessed that her husband had refused to have sex with her during her pregnancy. Humiliated, she hired a night *kere* to beat him up; when the coven failed to find him it fell on her instead. She delivered stillborn twins and died.

11. Not specified. A woman confessed on her deathbed that she was a witch and named four associates. *Gbangbane* brought the four women before the chief's court; they were ordered to demonstrate their powers and prove they were witches.

They asked that some pawpaws and a lizard be brought; they were then locked in a room. When they were let out of the room they told the elders to cut open the pawpaws; they were seedless. They told the elders to examine the lizard; it was dead. Each woman was fined a cow. Two of the cows were sacrificed and a curse was put on the livers; the women were then obliged to eat the livers together with raw rice flour (*dege*) from the sacrifice. Within a few weeks three of the women died; the fourth, it was said, wasn't a real witch: "she wasn't guilty of actually eating anyone; she was a witch but did not practice witchcraft." Informant: Keti Ferenke Koroma, Kondembaia, 1970.

12. Brother's son. When a small boy died suddenly, a diviner was consulted; witchcraft was diagnosed as the cause of death. The witch was cursed. Ten days later the boy's father's sister fell ill and confessed to having killed the child because her brother refused to give her rice. The woman was buried alive.

13. Co-wife's son's son. A woman quarreled with her co-wife's son's wife over the sharing of some locust-seed cakes. Shortly afterward, her co-wife's son's son became ill and died. When the woman also fell ill she confessed to having killed the child to get even with its mother. She died after confessing.

What is arresting about most of these cases is that there are so few allusions to the stereotypical imagery of witchcraft. Covens and cannibalism are mentioned in only four cases (witches usually "kill" or "beat up" their victims); animal familiars and out-of-body travel in only one (case 7). Clearly, general *beliefs* about witchcraft and the particular *experiences* of self-confessed witches are seldom congruent.[11] Like the Azande, the Kuranko "normally think of witchcraft quite impersonally and apart from any particular witch or witches" (Evans-Pritchard 1972:37).

The stereotype of the witch is, as I've already observed, a logical inversion of the stereotype of moral personhood. It encapsulates what Monica Wilson so aptly called "the standardized nightmares of the group." For the Kuranko, these collective anxieties center on self-containment and protection. However, the use of various objects or medicines, *kandan li fannu* ("enclosing/protecting things"), to magically seal off self, house, village, farm, and chiefdom reflects more than a history of actual invasions; it is an index of a quotidian problem: accommodating strangers who may also be enemies. To divine the thoughts of a stranger/guest (*sundan*) through the techniques of the *Due* cult or to disarm a visitor with gifts is thus a counterpart to the use of protective medicines (Jackson 1977b:57–60). But perhaps the central focus of men's fears is the figure of the in-marrying woman.

The notion of a witch as someone *within* the household yet in league with enemies without (her night *kere*) is grounded in the ambiguous social position of young married women, legally bound to their husbands yet emotionally attached to their natal families and "sisters." Something of this ambiguity is suggested by the phrases a man uses when giving his daughter in marriage to her husband's group: "Now we have come with your wife. She is your thief, your witch, your daughter, your all. We have brought her to you alive, but even in death she will remain your wife." It is also worth pointing out that the animals most commonly associated with witches—palmbirds, lizards, toads, snakes, cats, vultures, owls—are also structurally ambiguous: they are of the wild, yet often enter and live within the village.

WITCHCRAFT AND KINSHIP STRESS

To properly understand the sociogenesis of witchcraft confessions it is not enough to speak of women solely as wives. Here is how Keti Ferenke Koroma explained the sources of antagonism between men and women in everyday life:

> You know, if you see women showing treachery (*monkekoe*) toward men it is because, in this world, all men are in the hands of women. We say we are in the hands of women because women gave us birth. In the beginning it might have been a good idea had *Altala* declared that women lead and men follow. But women follow, because *Altala* gave the power of leadership to men. We had nothing to do with that. . . .
>
> Now, to know why we say women are not equals. It is because when a baby girl is born, it is a man who goes and pays bridewealth for her. She becomes his wife, subordinate to him. But when women think of how they gave birth to us and raised us, yet we pay bridewealth for them, they get angry. They use all manner of treachery to ruin us. For instance, if you have four wives and you call one to be with you for three days, the other three will spend all their time thinking of ways to get even. Women are treacherous because they want to control men. But this isn't possible because we pay bridewealth for them. And because they ate the forbidden fruit. (Jackson 1977b:88–89)

Apart from the light these remarks throw on Keti Ferenke's personal opinion of women, they bring into relief two distinct ways of explaining women's inferiority. The first is mythological; it invokes the disobedience of Mama Hawa (Eve), the first woman, to explain why women are *innately* weak-willed. The second is sociological and stresses the complementarity of a woman's role as wife and her roles as mother and sister. The key to understanding this complementarity is bridewealth. As a wife, a woman is subordinate to her husband and, if she is a junior wife, to his senior wife as well. Sinkari Yegbe, a middle-aged woman from Kamadugu Sukurela, summed up this situation of double disadvantage as follows:

> Men pay too much bridewealth for us. . . . It gives them control over us and the right to order us about. You cannot cook unless your husband gives you rice. You cannot go to market unless he tells you to go, and gives you money to spend. If you are a junior wife, whatever you get first goes to the senior wife. You cannot even wear clothes without them first going through her hands.

As a mother, however, a woman enjoys real control and influence because the fortunes of her children are entirely in her hands. "You are in your mother's hands" (*i i na le bolo*), goes a popular song. Proverbial wisdom points out that "A man has many children; a woman raises them; his children are in her hands" (*Ke l dan sia; muse don den; ke l den wo bolo*). More ominously: "If a child flourishes or if a child perishes, ask the mother the reason why." As a sister, a woman also enjoys some degree of control because her brother marries with bridewealth received from her marriage. In theory, this indebtedness entitles her to claim material and emotional support from her brother and curse him if he denies it.

Ordinarily, a woman's autonomy as sister or mother compensates her for her lack of autonomy as a wife, especially a junior wife. The resentments that nurture witchcraft stem from a loss of this balance, either through gross unfairness on the part of a husband or senior co-wife or neglect on the part of a brother. In four of the cases cited, unjust apportionment of food was the cause of resentment; in two cases, conjugal neglect. Understandably, the focus of witchcraft attack is either a husband (five cases) or brother (one case) or someone vulnerable and closely related to them: a co-wife's child (one case) or grandchild (one case) or a brother's child (one case) or grandchild (two cases).

But while witchcraft can be seen as a stratagem for regaining a sense of autonomy and control, it must also be seen as masochistic and suicidal. Why, one may ask, don't women explore less destructive ways of redressing injustices, appealing to a senior woman (the *dimusukuntigi*) with powers to represent cases of male injustices in the chief's court, enlisting the help of the women's cult, Segere, or, in the case of a brother's neglect, using the sister's power to curse? Or, if they feel hard done by, why don't women do as Sinkari Yegbe advocates: voice their grievances in stories that mock men, connive with their "sisters" to make trysts with other men, or refuse to work and slave for their husbands? (Jackson 1977b:102).

To answer these questions, an analysis of kinship stress and women's roles is not enough. Such factors condition women's experience but do not wholly explain it. It is therefore necessary to consider the psychology of witchcraft confession in more detail.

THE COMPULSION TO CONFESS

Kuranko people endure the tribulations of life with a fortitude that many Westerners, conditioned to expect medical science to guarantee them long lives without excessive suffering, might find unsettling. In the course of my fieldwork I helped sick people as much as my medical knowledge and supplies permitted. At first, however, it was usually I who sought people out, giving electrolyte solution to infants with dysentery and chloromycetin to people suffering from conjunctivitis, supervising courses of antibiotics. Even when distressed by the worsening condition of a child, parents showed no great interest in my medical resources. Afflicted by painful and debilitating diseases such as elephantiasis, encephalitis, malaria, and leprosy, men and women assented to my help rather than sought it. As for their attitude toward sick kinsmen or friends, it was often, to my mind, apathetic and perfunctory. *In toro*, you suffer, they would say in commiseration, then turn away.[12]

But what I saw as stoicism and fatalism is less a form of self-denial than self-mastery. And self-mastery is nowhere more deliberately cultivated than in the rites of initiation.

Initiation involves a whole battery of ordeals calculated to test the mettle of neophytes. To stay awake in a smoke-filled room, lashed with switches, upbraided and bullied by elders, to be tormented by tales of bush spirits and lethal medicines, to have one's genitals cut and not wince or cry out, to undergo traumatic separation from one's parents—all this to learn the sternest and most important lesson in life: to endure pain, show forbearance, be masterful in the face of every adversity. "To resist is hard ('not sweet')," the saying goes, "but freedom (from trouble) comes of it" (*in sa ro, a fo ma di, koni lafere hayi la*). Despite men's view that women control their feelings and withstand hardship less well than they do, this theme pervades both men's and women's initiations.

It is therefore understandable why Kuranko were indifferent to my medical intervention. To place themselves in my hands meant isolation from kin and from the tried and tested world of their own medicines, most of which, it must be remembered, have a *protective and insulating* function. It would entail forfeiting their autonomy. A Kuranko adage sums up the dilemma: *Morgo ben ta nyenne bolo komo ko* (Better to be in the hands of a *nyenne* than in the hands of *Kome*). Both *nyenne* and *Kome* are bush spirits, but *Kome* is especially awesome and capricious. Thus, the known is always preferable to the unknown, the familiar to the foreign—better the devil you know than the devil you don't.

It isn't only Kuranko who adopt this view. One encounters it often in our own society when a seriously ill individual prefers to decide his or her own treatment rather than submit to the impersonal and mystifying regimes of the medical system. Sometimes the risk of death is to be preferred to the sacrifice of one's autonomy and dignity.

The seemingly fatalistic attitude of Kuranko in the face of misfortune reflects not a blind acceptance of suffering but an active recognition that it is an inevitable part of life. Pain and sickness are not seen as aberrations from which one might be saved. The insane and sick are never sequestered. Death is not denied. Nor do people react to suffering with the outrage and impatience so familiar in our own society—the tormented sense that one has been hard done by, that one deserves better, that permanent health, unalloyed happiness, even immortality, might one day be guaranteed as a civil right. In my experience, Kuranko people show little interest in an afterlife where one might escape the tribulations of this world and yet retain one's mundane identity. To die alone, to be refused decent burial, to have one's lineage die out: such things are terrible, not one's own extinction.

The focus, then, is on the *field* of relationships of which one is a part, not one's self per se. Accordingly, illness is seen as a disturbance in the field of social relationships (which include ancestors, God, bush spirits, and witches), not a result of disease *entities* such as germs or viruses. Thus, if you behave badly or even harbor ill will toward another person *who is innocent or protected by medicines*, then the malice will react against you and make you ill. It will be said that the other person's *hake* has "got out" on you (*a hake ara bo*) or that his *hake* "goes against you" (*a hake si bo i ro*). To "set things straight" or "clear things up" (the Kuranko images are the same as ours), you will have to beg forgiveness (*ka madiyale ke*) of the person you have wronged or confess (*ka porondo*) your ill will.

So pervasive is this notion of agentless, retributive justice (*hake*) that diviners commonly advise confession as a way of making things well or "cool," of clearing or straightening the path between people. Indeed, it has the same redressive effect as offering a sacrifice to one's ancestors. And people often spontaneously confess animosity to neighbors and friends in everyday life, speaking of the "pain" (*koe dime*) oppressing them. Or women wishing to forestall possible punishment for adultery sometimes sit down with their husbands and unburden themselves with such words as "*M'buin, ma be Fore lon; i hake ka na n'to*" ("My husband, we and Fore are [having an affair]; may your *hake* not get out on me").

But why is the onus usually on women to confess? Why, when illness strikes and diviners are consulted, are women blamed? And why, when *Gbangbane* is abroad, do women fall prey to secret fears far more than men? The answer to these questions lies in the contrast between the confined life of women and the public life of men.

For the Kuranko it is a contrast between the house (*bon*) and backyard (*sundu kunye ma*), the domain of women, and the courtyard (*luiye*) which opens onto the village, the domain of men. Women, they say, are encompassed by men as a house is encompassed by *luiye* (Jackson 1986:130). As a consequence, men go out, women turn in upon themselves. While men seek the causes of discord in the world around them, women search for the causes within. Men apportion blame, women take the blame; men accuse, women confess.

But the pressures that bring a woman to find the cause of a child's death, a husband's bad luck, barrenness, or family discord *in her own thoughts and deeds* are not only social. Certainly the advice of a diviner, the carping of a husband or senior co-wife, kinship stress, village gossip, and the terrifying sound of *Gbangbane* moving about in the night all work to erode a woman's confidence (*miran*). But the precipitating cause of confession to witchcraft in over half the cases I collected was severe illness, illness seen as punishment for unconfided sins.

It is this existential crisis, in which both social and personal autonomy is momentarily lost, that I now want to consider.

"THE LAST FREEDOM"

It may appear that Kuranko women are so conditioned to bear responsibility for the misfortunes around them that they readily assent, when pressure is put upon them, to serve as men's scapegoats. The self-confessed witch would seem to embody this self-abnegation to an extreme degree: a victim of a world which denies her any legitimate outlet for her frustrations and grievances. But such a conclusion only recapitulates the prejudices of those Kuranko men who see women solely as a category—for "witch," "scapegoat," and "victim" are *all* category words, and negative ones at that.

For this reason it is important to recognize that witchcraft confession is also a desperate stratagem for reclaiming autonomy in a hopeless situation.[13] This is borne out by the allusions to witch-possessions (*suwa'ya mirannu*) in several cases (*miran* also means self-possession), and, in other cases (7, 11), by the defiant attitudes of the women in the face of death. But even when such defiance is not evident, witchcraft confession can still be seen as a powerful form of self-expression in which words and images substitute for acts (Reik 1966:194, 199). Confession to witchcraft exemplifies what Victor Frankl calls "the last freedom"—that which remains to us when external circumstances rob us of the power to act: the choice of determining how we will construe our plight, the freedom to live it as though it were our will. It is the freedom Genet discovered as a child (Sartre 1963). Accused of being a thief, he suddenly saw himself reduced to an object for others, a projection of their fears, a scapegoat for their anxieties. His escape was into neither suicide nor insanity; it was a decision to become his fate, to live it as though he himself had conceived it: "*J'ai décidé d'être ce que le crime à fait de moi—un voleur.*"

As our evidence shows, the self-confessed witch does more than passively submit to the succession of misfortunes that have overwhelmed her. Nor does she blindly recapitulate the stereotypes men promulgate; rather, she actively uses them to give voice to long-suppressed grievances and to cope with her suffering by declaring herself the author of it.[14] Thus, she determines how she will play out the role which circumstance has thrust upon her. She dies deciding her own identity, sealing her own fate.[15]

It is not enough for us to decide whether witchcraft is a social pathology or the individual witch a victim of some delusional psychosis, for our task is to throw light on the lived experience that lies behind the masks and facades of category words—even those used by the self-confessed witch herself. Such an approach demands to know not whether a witch's death is "suicide" or "murder" but how that death is lived. It seeks not to know whether *hake* is best translated as "guilt" or "shame" or whether *suwage* is semantically equivalent to "witch," but what experiences find expression in these words and how we might recover them. It is for this reason that I have no sympathy with those anthropologists and philosophers who debate endlessly over the rationality or irrationality of witchcraft beliefs. Beliefs have no reality apart from the people who make use of them, and to try to see how beliefs *correspond* to some allegedly "objective" reality or how they *cohere* as a so-called "system" seems to me far less edifying than trying to see what people do with beliefs in *coping* with the exigencies of life. At this level, the bizarre appearance of Kuranko witchcraft images is less significant than the realities of human distress that find expression through them—realities with which we can readily identify.[16]

SEVEN

The Man Who Could Turn into
an Elephant

From the very first months of my fieldwork among the Kuranko I was enthralled by anecdotes and reports of human beings who were able to transform themselves into animals. Such persons are known as *yelamafentiginu* ("change thing masters") and are regarded with awe and ambivalence because in the form of predatory or dangerous animals they can destroy the crops and kill the livestock of anyone they begrudge or dislike. Shape-shifting is a form of witchcraft. It suggests faculties outside the domain of secular activity and control. It conjures up images of the dark, trackless forests beyond human clearings and settlements—the domain of animality, the antithesis of social order. But while shape-shifting is sometimes likened to witchcraft, shape-shifters are not witches (*suwagenu*). Witches are usually women, the *yelamafentiginu* invariably men. While witches can transform themselves into animals associated with darkness and menace in order to pursue their nefarious ends, shape-shifters seem more often than not to transform themselves into the totemic animal of their clan: respected creatures and metaphorical kinsmen. And while witches are clandestine and abominated, shape-shifters sometimes vaunt their powers and draw grudging admiration from those who know of them.

For a long time my image of shape-shifters, like my image of witches, was conditioned by what Kuranko told me and by what I imagined, remembering nights alone in the dark forests of my native New Zealand when the inexplicable crack of a dead branch, the soughing of the wind, or an ominous shadow at the edge of a clearing would make my heart race and bring to mind childhood tales of hobgoblins and genies. The forests and grasslands of northern Sierra Leone exercised the same hold on my imagination, for was I not also an intruder there, prey to secret misgivings, and alone? I saw how easy it would be, startled by the glimpse of a solitary figure in the elephant grass or thornscrub in crepuscular light, to imagine one had seen someone in the process of changing from human to animal form. Steeped in ideas about shape-shifting from early childhood, one would be prone to interpret such ambiguous images in this way. The idea of shape-shifting was born and bolstered, I assumed, in such moments of panic and by such tricks of the light, much like UFOs in our own popular imagination. The problem was, however, that this conjecture left unexplained the absence of any skeptical attitude toward shape-shifting among the Kuranko with whom I discussed it. Furthermore, it became clear to me that beliefs about shape-shifting were not reducible to fugitive images and haphazard observations: they were conditioned by a complex of shared assumptions and ideas which required careful ethnographic elucidation.

Kuranko conventional wisdom on the subject of shape-shifting can be readily summarized. First, the ability to change from human to animal form is an inborn or God-given endowment. It is not a skill that can be learned or a gift that can be acquired. Second, shape-shifters can undergo metamorphosis only when alone in the bush. Third, serious perils are associated with shape-shifting. If one sees a man in the process of transformation one should not spread word of it around or even admit what one has seen. One must suppress or deny the evidence of one's own eyes—and the shape-shifter will implore a witness to do so—because public exposure brings precipitous or premature death to the *yelamafentigi*. Another danger comes from the possibility of being wounded or killed by a hunter while in animal form. If a shape-shifter in animal guise *is* mortally wounded, he will always return to a village or settlement in human form and die there.[1] Grave risks also attend a shape-shifter who boasts of his powers. In the event of animals marauding livestock or damaging crops, the self-confessed shape-shifter may be taken to court and accused of sorcery.

A skeptic might regard these beliefs as self-protective rationalizations. If a shape-shifter cannot change in the presence of others who are not themselves shape-shifters, then no independent evidence of the phenomenon can be adduced. If witnesses must forget or deny their accidental sightings lest they endanger the life of the shape-shifter, then little direct evidence of the phenomenon will be available. And if a mortally wounded shape-shifter cannot die half-man, half-animal, then no physical evidence of the process of transformation will ever be seen.

Rather than pursue the problem of how these beliefs may be justified from our point of view, I want to examine the grounds on which Kuranko accept them as true.

First, one is confirmed in the beliefs about shape-shifting because one's elders hold them to be true. The beliefs have the authority of custom (*namui*); they are a legacy of the ancestors, given in the words of the first people (*fol' morgon' kumenu*) and of the first people's making (*fol' morgonnu ko dane*). Second, shape-shifting occurs in myths concerning ancestral journeys and clan origins, and such myths, known as *bimba kumenu* ("ancestral words") or *kuma kore* ("venerable speech"), are held to be true.[2] Third, the Kuranko often cite hearsay evidence in support of the beliefs.

For example, in Firawa some years ago a man trapped a leopard which had been marauding his sheep and goats. One night, however, the leopard broke out of its cage and escaped, though not before wounding itself on the splintered bars. The following day the man's half-brother was seen to be badly lacerated on the face and arms. Since bad blood existed between the half-brothers (*fadennu*) it was assumed that the wounded man had been guilty of transforming himself into a leopard—the totemic animal of the clan—and killing the other man's livestock.

Another example of shape-shifting was given to me by a young Kuranko man, John Sisay, remembering an incident from his childhood when he had accompa-

nied an American missionary on a hunting trip near Yifin. The missionary and
the boy had been negotiating the banks of a river when the missionary's dog was
seized by a crocodile and dragged down into a deep hole. According to John, the
missionary then entered the water and disappeared beneath the surface, reappear-
ing two hours later some distance upstream. That same day the missionary went
to the Yifin chief who, it was rumored, could transform himself into a crocodile,
and told him he had seen a populous town beneath the river and had retrieved
his dog there. The missionary then told the chief that he intended shooting croco-
diles in the area and warned local shape-shifters that they risked their lives loitering
at the ford and attacking the livestock of traders crossing there. Although I argued
that John could have been confused by what he saw at the river and been con-
ned by the missionary who had simply been exploiting indigenous beliefs to as-
sert his authority over the local ruler, John dismissed any possibility of illusion
or lying. The beliefs did not rest upon his opinion or his particular experience;
they were common knowledge and others would just as readily attest to their
truth.

A fourth mode of indigenous evidence for shape-shifting is far from common
knowledge. It is derived from the apprenticeship of a *besetigi* or medicine-master,
a specialist in healing medicine as well as lethal medicine and its antidotes. Such
specialist skills and knowledge are not usually divulged, and it was not until my
third field trip, ten years after first beginning research among the Kuranko, that
the elderly medicine-master, my close friend Saran Salia Sano, agreed to impart
some of these skills and this knowledge to me.[3]

As an initiatory test during a three-year apprenticeship in Guinea as a young
man, Saran Salia had been taken to a remote stretch of a river by his teacher.
His teacher had gone ahead of him and transformed himself into a snake. The
snake had then swum back downstream and wrapped itself around Saran Salia's
leg, striking fear into his heart, a fear he had to master. Then the snake had
changed back into his teacher. Like John Sisay, Saran Salia was adamant that what
he had seen had not been a figment of his imagination.[4]

A fifth mode of evidence that the Kuranko adduce for shape-shifting is as rare
and privileged as the fourth: direct accounts by actual shape-shifters. For reasons
I have already given, shape-shifters seldom voice or confide their secrets, and it
was more a matter of luck than ethnographic diligence that gave me the insights
I now wish to review.

A SHAPE-SHIFTER'S STORY

It was my fourth field trip to Sierra Leone, in October 1979, and my encounter
with the self-styled shape-shifter took place ironically in the middle of Sierra
Leone's largest city and at a time when I was more interested in relaxing after the
rigors of the field than in pursuing ethnographic research.

I was staying with a Kuranko friend who was minister of energy and power.
Sewa had entered parliament two years before, in 1977, standing as an independent

candidate in Koinadugu South constituency and defeating the official All People's Congress candidate, who was minister of mines and a close friend of the nation's president.[5]

During his campaign, Sewa had attracted several devoted followers and acolytes, among them a luckless and restive diamond miner named Mohammed Fofona. Mohammed lived in Koidu in the Kono diamond district, but had come to Freetown to settle some kind of account with the tax department. Like me, he was enjoying the hospitality of Sewa's house during his stay in Freetown. He was fifty-four, thickset, stalwart, and amenable. People called him Fofona Bigbelly to his face, a nickname he took no exception to. He knew about me long before we actually met. A book of mine, *The Kuranko*, had been bought up in large quantities and used in the campaign to get Sewa elected into parliament; it was known as the *ferensola* book, *ferensola* being the catchword at that time for Kuranko identity. Mohammed regarded my anthropological research as significant and useful, and he was keen to figure in any further publications I might produce.

Mohammed and I spent a lot of time together. He gave me a detailed account of Sewa's political campaign, told me his own life-story, railed against corruption in national politics, and helped me cross-check details of ruling genealogies from his natal chiefdom of Mongo Bendugu. One day I happened to ask him what the totem of the Fofona clan was.[6]

"*Kamei*, the elephant," he said; "to eat elephant meat would make one's skin disfigured." Then he told me, "Some Fofona men can change into elephants," and added that he himself possessed that gift.

Given Mohammed's rather elephantine build, his claim amused as much as intrigued me. I asked him to tell me more. Would it be possible for me to accompany him to an isolated place in the bush and observe him undergo the change? When he changed, did he feel enlarged and powerful like an elephant, a change in the way he experienced his own body rather than an actual physical metamorphosis? His replies were disheartening. The change would not be possible in my presence, but yes he did actually undergo a physical metamorphosis. The power was something he had been born with; he had possessed it even as a child. It was, he said, an inborn gift, *i soron ta la i bole* ("you born it in your possession"), an inner faculty, *bu' ro koe* ("belly in thing"), a private matter, *morgo konta koe* ("person inner understanding"). It could only be discussed among and comprehended by others having the same bent.

Although I acknowledged the reality of Mohammed's experience of changing into an elephant, I could not accept his ontologizing of the experience. Sincerity or depth of experience are not proofs that the phenomenon experienced actually exists. I argued with Mohammed that his experiences were open to other interpretations, by which, on reflection, I guess I meant that they could be interpreted my way. Such skepticism has its place in academic discourse; among the Kuranko its social value is minimal. In effect, I was denying Mohammed's experience and casting doubt on the Kuranko belief in shape-shifting. Not surprisingly, Mohammed and I soon dropped the subject from our conversation, though not before he gave me a general account of shape-shifting which replicated nicely the Kuranko conventional wisdom with which I was already familiar.

I left Sierra Leone a few weeks later, notebooks filled with tantalizing notes and images, interpretive conjectures, but nothing conclusive. When I wrote about shape-shifting during the next couple of years it was imaginatively and poetically, not analytically.[7] Mindful that I had called Mohammed's experience and belief into question, my fictional and empathic accounts of changing from human to animal form perhaps constituted a kind of apology for the rude and subversive idioms of anthropological discourse. But poems and fictions did not resolve the interpretive issues that bothered me.

Then Foucault's work suggested a way out of the impasse. Rather than think about shape-shifting in terms of such antinomies as true/false, real/illusory, objective/subjective, rational/irrational, I began to explore the grounds for the possibility of the belief, the conditions under which the notion of shape-shifting could be entertained as reasonable and made intelligible and, most important, *realized*, as in Mohammed's case, *as a sensible truth*.

This entailed going beyond the justifications which the Kuranko themselves provided for the belief and examining aspects of Kuranko "subsidiary awareness" which lay outside the field of "focal awareness" already considered.[8] In particular, it meant examining Kuranko ontology and aspects of Mohammed's biography.

ONTOLOGY OF SHAPE-SHIFTING

In the Kuranko world view it is axiomatic that persons exist only in relation to one another.[9] The concept of *morgoye*, personhood, reflects the ontological priority of social relationships over individual identity. Although the word *morgo* denotes the living person, the empirical subject of speech, thought, will, and action that is recognized in all societies, the concept *morgoye* is at once more abstract and more far reaching. *Morgoye*, personhood, connotes ideal qualities of proper social relationships, and the word can be variously translated as mindfulness of others, generosity of spirit, magnanimity, and altruism. However, unlike the English word *personality*, *morgoye* does not suggest notions of personal identity, distinctive individual character, or autonomous moral being. *Morgoye* is a quality of being realized in social praxis rather than in personal style or appearance.

Another fundamental assumption in the Kuranko world view is that Being is not necessarily limited to human being. Thus, *morgoye*, though a quality of social being, is not necessarily or merely found in relationships between persons. Put another way, the field of social relationship may include ancestors, fetishes, bush spirits, a divine creator, and totemic animals *as well as persons*. *Morgoye*, the quality of moral being, may therefore be found in relations between people and ancestors, people and Allah, people and bush spirits, people and totemic animals, and so on. Indeed, in Kuranko clan myths it is the totemic animal's relationship with the clan ancestor which expresses in exemplary form the moral ideal of personhood.

Here are three such myths.[10]

Kuyate Clan—Monitor Lizard (*Kana* or *Kurumgbe*): We Kuyate do not eat the monitor lizard. Our ancestor went to a faraway place. There was no water there. He became thirsty and was near death. He found a huge tree. In the bole of the tree was some water left from the rains. The monitor lizard was also there. Our ancestor sat under the tree. Then the monitor lizard climbed into the tree bole and out again and shook its tail. The water splashed over our ancestor. He realized there was water there. He got up and drank. He said, "Ah, the monitor lizard has saved my life!" When he returned to town he told his clanspeople about the incident. He said, "You see me here now because of the monitor lizard." Since that time the monitor lizard has been our totem. If any Kuyate eats it his body will become marked and disfigured like the body of the lizard. His clan joking-partners (*sanakuie*) will have to find medicines to cure him.

Wulare Clan—Leopard (*Kuli*): As our ancestor was leaving Mande he had to cross a large river which was in flood. A leopard put our ancestor on his back and took him across the river. Our ancestor said, "Henceforth no Wulare should injure or eat the leopard."

Togole and Tegere Clans—Bushfowl (*Wolei*): The ancestors of the Togole and Tegere were warriors. During the wars, times were so bad that they both went into hiding to evade their enemies. One morning they were almost discovered and captured. They had left their hiding place because their enemies were approaching. Their enemies saw their footprints in the dewy grass. But just then a bushfowl came along the path. As the enemies approached the hidden warriors the bushfowl jumped out in front of them. The enemies said, "Heh, no one has passed this way; these are just bushfowl tracks." They went away. The two hidden warriors heard every word that had been spoken. They vowed never to eat bushfowl again and to instruct their descendants never to eat it. They placed a curse on the meat of the bushfowl. You will not die if you eat it but—because of that curse—your skin will become disfigured if you do so.

The qualities of moral personhood thus shift about within the Kuranko world, sometimes attributed to persons, sometimes to animals, bush spirits, plants, and even stones. Because personhood is distributed into the natural world and not fixed within the margins of the village, it is plausible that a grass fetish speaks with moral discernment, a bush spirit acts as an ally, a human being degenerates—as in the case of a witch—into mere animality, and an animal is regarded as an ancestor and kinsman. Such metamorphoses, familiar enough in the make-believe world of Kuranko folktales, assume special significance in the clan myths. Here the bond of kinship (*nakelinyorgoye*) said to exist between clansperson and clan totem becomes more than a metaphor, a rhetorical image; it implies a real moral and physical identification. If one eats the meat of one's totemic animal one's body takes on the superficial features of the animal. Eating one's totem is tantamount to "eating oneself." And, in the view of some Kuranko, the prohibition against killing or eating one's totem is prompted by the perennial possibility that the animal one eats may be an actual kinsman in animal form, i.e., a shape-shifter from one's own clan.

From an intellectualistic point of view we would say that the totem is a *symbol* of the clan, but if we are faithful to the more holistic reasoning of the Kuranko we would have to acknowledge that the totem *is* the clan. Mind and body are one. The *moral* bond between clansperson and clan totem is thus construed as an actual *physical* identification *and may be experienced as such.* [11]

So far we have seen how the belief in shape-shifting is grounded in Kuranko ontology and world view and does not derive its plausibility solely or directly from firsthand experience or hearsay accounts. Kuranko children grow up with folktales in which shape-shifting is common and accept as true clan myths in which meta-morphosis occurs. Such a grounding influences perception, makes hearsay reports of shape-shifting seem reasonable, and disposes a person to interpret certain altered states of consciousness in terms of shape-shifting.

Nevertheless, while all Kuranko share common ontological assumptions and are conditioned by the same conventional wisdom, we cannot conclude that indi-vidual experience is entirely explicable in such terms. Lived experience is irreduc-ible; no matter how fervently and uncritically Kuranko espouse their conventional beliefs in shape-shifting, it is evident that different individuals experience and con-strue the beliefs in different ways.

Let us then return to the case of Mohammed Fofona and ask why he, unlike others grounded in the same world view, came to actually *embody* the idea of shape-shifting and realize it as an immediate, personal, and sensible experience. At this point the sociology of knowledge exhausts its usefulness and we must turn to biogra-phy for our answers.

A SHAPE-SHIFTER'S STORY CONTINUED

Mohammed was born in 1925 in Tumania (Mongo Bendugu chiefdom, Koinadugu district) in northwest Sierra Leone. In 1942, when he was seventeen, he enlisted in the army and saw active service in the Middle East and Europe. In 1950 he was demobbed and returned to Tumania.

Like other Kuranko men of his generation, Mohammed regarded military ser-vice as a kind of initiatory ordeal, a way to manhood directly comparable to the traditional rites of initiation which were already on the wane. As he put it, "The army gave discipline, made you a man, made you a real force. In those days a soldier was like a white man in the villages; he commanded great respect." But like many other ex-soldiers, Mohammed found it hard to settle back into the routines of vil-lage life. Neither his wartime experience nor the respect he was momentarily ac-corded on account of it compensated for the tedium of Tumania. Lacking any tradi-tional position of authority and any status in the British adminstration, Mohammed drifted south into the diamond districts where the prospect of material wealth offered the possibility of power and renewed prestige.

From Lebanese diamond dealers in Kono, Mohammed hired the basic tools of the prospector—pick, shovel, and sieve—and tried his luck. In the years that followed he enjoyed sporadic success and built a mudbrick iron-roofed house in Koidu and married. But more often than not he found himself struggling against poverty and ill fortune, adversities not wholly attributable to his own failings or the disapproval of the ancestors. Observing the nepotism and corruption that governed the diamond business, Mohammed came to share the blighted view of many Kuranko men, that their lack of personal prosperity was a consequence of their political marginality. Even in 1979 Mohammed returned time and again in our conversations to the problem of corruption, of bribery and bias, exploitation and cronyism, and stressed the need in Sierra Leone for radical political change.

In 1977, when Sewa Bokari Marah bowed to popular Kuranko demand and stood for election in Koinadugu South,[12] Mohammed at once saw the possibility of an improvement in Kuranko political fortunes and in his own luck; he enlisted in Sewa's cause—the cause of *ferensola*—and actively campaigned for Sewa's election.

Sewa's electoral success came about through ironic and tragic circumstances. Criticisms of corruption had been leveled against the sitting member of parliament Kawusu Konteh for some time, but when he was implicated in the murder of several Kuranko villagers in Kurubonla and in the sacking of the village, the president was obliged to demand the withdrawal of his candidature and call an official inquiry. Sewa was elected unopposed. Two years later, Mohammed spoke to me of Kawusu Konteh with undisguised contempt, remembering how the minister had once tried to buy Mohammed's loyalty, kneeling before him, grasping his ankles, begging him to sell Sewa out with an offer of Le. 5,000. "The money," Mohammed said, "would have soiled me. I refused it."

Even this scant knowledge of Mohammed suggested to me in 1979 that there might be some connection between his boast of being able to transform himself into a powerful animal and his vaunted identification with a powerful political figure. Mohammed admitted that shape-shifting gave him a sense of clandestine power over others, and I could not resist relating this to his luckless, marginal situation in life. Had he called upon familiar Kuranko beliefs in metamorphosis to make sense of an unfamiliar and unpredictable world, to express an existential longing to regain control over his own destiny, to change his luck, to gain stature through associating with a successful and charismatic peer? As a young man he had found fulfillment in the army; did he now find the same vicarious satisfaction in the theatre of national politics?

Six years passed—years in which I lost contact with Mohammed yet continued to ponder these questions and plan further research. When I finally returned to Sierra Leone in October 1985 I made a trip to Koidu, where Mohammed was still living.

I passed the best part of a day, enervated by the heat, trying to find him. Each time I returned to the squalid quarter of mudbrick houses and rain-eroded laterite lanes where Mohammed lived, I would ask for him by name in Krio. "Oh dat fat pa, e don komot," I would be told, or someone would yell into the gloomy interior of a house and ask, "Fofona Bigbelly, e dae?" only to be told again that he had gone out. I left messages—could he be told I was looking for him?—and described the house across town where I was staying.

That evening he turned up. He was a changed man, taciturn, wary, and visibly older. He showed little enthusiasm for seeing me. Perhaps I too had changed, haunted by memories of Pauline and happier times, dispirited by news of the deaths of Kuranko friends, oppressed by the poverty around me, and suffering from a loss of faith in the authenticity of anthropological understanding. Yet I was determined to ask the questions that had weighed on my mind for so long.

I offered Mohammed a Coke and we sat opposite each other in the parlor, our faces shadowy in the penumbra of a hurricane lamp. At first we talked of the political and economic crisis in the country. A petrol tanker had delivered 420 gallons of petrol to Koidu that afternoon, and hundreds of people had mobbed the Mobil pumps fighting to get a share of petrol only to find that through bribes, obligations, and black-market deals most of the supply had been committed. Mohammed voiced a widespread pessimism: unless the president stepped down and elections were called the country would collapse into anarchy.

After a while I asked him if he remembered confiding in me six years earlier that he could change into an elephant. He seemed suspicious and slightly embarrassed, and disclaimed any such ability. I reminded him of our conversation about shape-shifting and asked why he had advertised a gift that other men would have kept secret. Grudgingly he accepted what he had once said, then added, "We know ourselves, we recognize only our own kind, we speak of these matters only among those of like mind." Shut out of experiences I had presumed to understand empathically, I suddenly realized my presumptuousness. Six years was a long time, and we were strangers.

In the event I pursued my questions anyway, and Mohammed answered them, guardedly and always in general terms, avoiding personal anecdote as if he had a canny grasp of the conventions of anthropological discourse.

Did he change by first conjuring up an image of an elephant in his mind? "No," he said, "that is not necessary. But you must have a purpose, such as destroying someone's crops. If someone offends you and you cannot take your revenge by any ordinary means you'll walk ahead of that person in the bush, change, then fall on him as he passes on his way back to his village."

"Do people change into animals to get a sense of power?" I asked.

"Yes."

"How long does the metamorphosis last?"

"That depends—but usually no more than twelve hours."

"Is it difficult to remain an elephant all that time?"

"No."

I then asked Mohammed if he retained full consciousness during metamorphosis. "Yes," he said, "because you must know to change back to human form." He reflected a moment. "But you must be alone in the bush to do it."

Our conversation petered out. I was tired. I felt I was encroaching on Mohammed's privacy, pressing him on matters he was reluctant to discuss but too polite to dismiss out of hand. I had wanted to take up his allusions to sorcery, to know whether his own shape-shifting was motivated by vengefulness, but it would have been churlish to do so. I went along with his decision to couch personal experiences in general terms, and in so doing was brought back to the impersonal idioms and generalizing conventions of anthropology. Mohammed had become, so to speak, like any average informant whose transitory, alienated relationship with the anthropologist can only generate pat answers and stereotypical views.

What had changed between October 1979 when Mohammed confided in me as an ally and October 1985 when he talked to me as a mildly bored stranger? The simple answer is that in 1979 Mohammed wished to impress me. Six years later, in quite another situation, he felt no such need. Nor was it only Mohammed who had changed. My weariness and remoteness must have influenced the course of our conversation as much as his sense of my strangeness and skepticism.

The manner in which understanding is constituted intersubjectively can be studied *ethnographically* by observing indigenous social interaction, but it can also be studied *reflexively* by focusing on the ethnographic encounter itself. In this context the limits of understanding are often set by the human limitations of the ethnographer and defined as much by his or her social relationships in the field or within the anthropological profession as by the methodology used and the theory espoused. Indigenous understanding is no less tied to context, and just as my personality and cultural bias and the exigencies of fieldwork ground my ethnographic knowledge, so too is Kuranko knowledge grounded in certain cultural assumptions and personal interests, as the case of Mohammed shows.

The variety of ways in which shared beliefs are used, experienced, and espoused makes it futile to try to elucidate their *essence* under the rubric of such antinomies as rational versus irrational, true versus false, good versus bad. Rather, we need to elucidate the place of beliefs in the context of actual *existence*—how they are experienced and employed, not what they may be said to register or represent. Such a pragmatist perspective demands that we consider Kuranko shapeshifting in critical, historical, psychological, and cross-cultural terms.

THE CRITICAL CONTEXT OF BELIEF

Under ordinary circumstances Kuranko appear to acquiesce in traditional stereotypes of shape-shifting, treating them matter-of-factly, espousing them without particular interest or fervor. Mohammed was an exception. In his case the beliefs were embraced actively and enthusiastically; they were realized as lived, bodily experience.

It is as though Kuranko beliefs in shape-shifting were ordinarily held in cold storage, a stock of what William James dubbed "extra truths"—ideas salted away in memory awaiting practical implementation during some crisis.[13] Mohammed gave vitality to beliefs which others held loosely, passively, and halfheartedly, realizing them with his whole being.

Such a shift from merely entertaining an idea to actually embodying it is usually precipitated by some social or personal crisis that disrupts normal habits and disconcerts normal awareness. Mohammed has suffered recurrent existential crises in his life, an erosion of his sense of self-mastery and social worth that he has tried to make good by calling upon beliefs in shape-shifting. As an elephant he is in his element, empowered by a sense of amplitude and control. But as with alcohol and drug use in our society, Mohammed's clandestine gains are at the cost of social integration. His vicarious mastery of the world entails ironically a separation from it, a marginality whose ambivalent images are those of solitude, sorcery, and the bush. Like a neophyte who does not return to his village after initiation in the bush, Mohammed's manhood fails to be realized socially. His power to shape-shift thus condemns him to the very marginality he struggles to escape.

The situation brings to mind the Kuranko women discussed in the previous chapter who confess to being witches during serious illness, calling upon the stereo-types of witchcraft to comprehend and cope with a crisis which erodes self-control and subverts identity. As in the case of shape-shifters, the confession is socially useful—it affirms the veracity of witchcraft beliefs—but self-defeating, for unless she dies of natural causes the self-confessed witch may be ritually killed.

THE HISTORICAL CONTEXT OF BELIEF

Let us reconsider a remark of Mohammed's concerning the purpose of shape-shifting: "If someone offends you and you cannot take your revenge by ordinary means you'll walk ahead of that person in the bush, change, then fall on him as he passes on his way to his village." Might not the sense of powerlessness and vengefulness that makes a man seek to augment his strength or regain self-mastery through shape-shifting arise from historical as well as personal crises?

In southern Sierra Leone between the 1860s and the early 1900s the govern-ment of the Colony of Sierra Leone endeavored through legislation to put an end to killings by so-called human leopard societies (Beatty 1915:1–14, Lindskog 1954:3, 6–7). The societies were secret, ritually focused on powerful medicines; members gave the illusion of being leopards, hacking a victim to death with an iron claw, leaving fake leopard prints on the ground, wearing leopard garb. But details of recruitment, how victims were selected, of the internal structure and practices of the societies, and their relationship to secular authority or "official" secret societies like Poro, are difficult to clarify (Lindskog 1954:43–46).

Thanks to the painstaking scholarship of Birger Lindskog we know that similar cults were widespread in Africa, though concentrated in the West African coastal area and northeast Congo (Lindskog 1954:5). Explanations of the cults have in-voked notions of savage mentality, cannibalistic appetites, totemic fixations, vengefulness and criminal conspiracy, and mindless obedience to cult leaders (59–87)—essentialistic notions that by reducing the cults to the status of savage other-ness deny the violent *situation* in which those who voice such opinions conspire, and deny the indigenous person recognition as a subject and maker of his own his-tory. Although colonial statutes and records insist that the leopard societies of Sierra Leone were "formed for the purpose of murder and cannibalism and existed simply to gratify the depraved tastes of [their] members" (60), it is, in my view, more edifying to see the cults as a response to sociopolitical deprivation, a form of defiance, negation, inversion, and revenge.[14] Although forms of ritualized rebellion such as sorcery, witchcraft, and cult activity were aspects of everyday life in traditional Sierra Leonean societies, the colonial encounter seems to have given these activities new impetus and purpose.

The sworn secrecy of leopard-men and the fact that our knowledge of human leopard societies comes from the records of administrators dedicated to the extirpation of the phenomenon make it difficult to grasp the indigenous point of view. But, as Ranajit Guha observes in his work on peasant insurgency in colonial India, "The difficulty is perhaps less insurmountable than it seems to be at first sight":

> It is of course true that the reports, despatches, minutes, judgements, laws, letters, etc. in which policemen, soldiers, bureaucrats, landlords, usurers and others hostile to insurgency register their sentiments, amount to a representation of their will. But these documents do not get their content from that will alone, for the latter is predicated on another will—that of the insurgent. It should be possible therefore to read the presence of a rebel consciousness as a necessary and pervasive element within that body of evidence. (1983:15)

This indeed proves to be the case with documents on counterinsurgency from Sierra Leone. In 1915, Tombo, a self-confessed member of a baboon society, on trial for murder, observed that the object of the society was "to be wealthy and influential."[15] A similar point was made by Gbanna ("The object of the Society is to be rich and to gain a big name and respect over every other person") while a third defendant, Lebbi, noted that "The object of the Society [was] to supply human flesh to the Chiefs and to increase their influence and continue the chieftaincy in their line" (Kalous 1974:93–94). In another case heard in 1908–9, Lamina told a court that he had joined the leopard society "in order to get riches." The medicine used by the cult would make a "man strong and successful" (104). Writing on "The Sierra Leone Cannibals" in 1912, Berry noted that the objects of the leopard society were "always material" and, according to native informants, a matter of getting "one word [unanimous support?] for the chief of the country," or getting "some blood to make the country cold, so that bad luck be taken away from the country, and they would all get plenty of money" (1912:51). The medicine of the society was thought to grant

> supremacy over the white man,[16] in the white man not being able to find out what was being done, and that the eating of human flesh would give power over the white man. For, say they, the white men have more power than the black men; but in this cannibalism you get some power so that when you do wrong you will not be found out by the white man. (51)

As Lindskog notes in summary, the medicine of the leopard society, *bofima*, was "the dominant factor in measures directed against neighboring chiefdoms and, in more modern times, even in securing allegiance to resistance, passive or otherwise, against the British government. Thus, the ritual sometimes served political and xenophobic purposes" (1954:61).

A more detailed account of the relationship between leopard societies and the sociopolitical situation in southern Sierra Leone in the late nineteenth century lends weight to the argument that the cults were forms of insurgency and rebellion. Earliest reports of leopard societies date from the period of the British annexation of the independent Sherbro country after a dubious treaty was signed with *some* local chiefs inducing cession of Sherbro to the British Crown (Fyfe 1962:308–12). At the time, Sherbro Island and its hinterland were already politically troubled areas. Tensions between the Sherbro and the dominant Mende, incursions of war refugees—many from the hut tax rebellions in Mende—and of immigrants from the interior seeking work, a high incidence of plundering and theft, recurrent wars between coastal and hinterland chiefs for control of new trading enterprises, and discontent among domestic slaves all contributed to this internal strife (Kalous 1974:1–2; Alldridge 1901:5–7; Fyfe 1962:440). Throughout the 1870s and 1880s there was increasing resistance to the arbitrary powers of chiefs involved in the slave trade, as well as resistance by chiefs to government laws banning slave trading.[17] Native resentment of mission meddling in their religious practices, of tax impositions, and of Creole traders whose land purchases and interference in local politics often had military backing further deepened the crisis (Beatty 1915:86–87; Kalous 1974:6–7; Fyfe 1962:298).

Given this anomic situation it is impossible not to interpret the phenomenon of human leopard societies in sociopolitical terms. A concatenation of personal grievances, political resentments, and economic frustrations found expression in peripheral cults and practices that were already part of the traditional culture: Poro, crocodile, and leopard miracle plays, shape-shifting, sorcery, and so on. Recruitment to the cults soon reflected social pressures and blackmail as much as individual interest (Kalous 1974). But while social and political forces underlay the growth of the cults, they were in the end socially and politically disastrous. The victims of the leopard-men were seldom the Creole traders, the whites, and the exploitative chiefs who oppressed the common people;[18] they were scapegoats from within the village world itself: children, young women, and members of the leopard-men's own families. The human leopards took out their grievances on their own social body. The power they exercised came from the magical manipulation of consciousness, not from any program of political action.[19] Vilified by traders and administrators as "bush people," the leopard-men sought control over their own situation by realizing the wildest imaginings and worst prejudices of their oppressors, but in the end they were victims of their own rituals and of their own involuted and clandestine strategies.

PSYCHOLOGICAL AND CROSS-CULTURAL CONTEXT OF BELIEF

A crisis or rupture in Mohammed's being-in-the-world throws him (like the Sherbro leopard-men of a hundred years ago) into a marginal situation. Calling upon images of liminal life from his own cultural background, he tries to make good his loss of mastery and control. He changes into an elephant, augmenting his flagging power and replenishing his strength. But as he realizes in his imagination an ancestral totemic bond, he falls back upon primordial attachments to the clan as family, as womb, and forfeits his social identifications *in the here and now*. The stratagem he uses to regain self-mastery is self-defeating. This is why the Kuranko regard shape-shifting so ambivalently. As a solitary and clandestine activity it calls the entire ontology of the group into question. It is, Kuranko say, a kind of witchcraft, a pathology. But insofar as an individual shape-shifter embodies and bears out many assumptions on which the Kuranko ethos is founded, he is a kind of hero. His very existence demonstrates the distributive theory of Being, proves the power of men to tap the powers of the wild, and affirms the moral bond between clanspeople and their totemic animals.

But all this rests on a blurring of the distinction we would tend to make between subjectivity and objectivity, a habit of interpreting interior states as signs of external events. Thus, while I was inclined to see Mohammed's shape-shifting as an altered state of consciousness, an intrapsychic event, Kuranko tend to ontologize the experience and see it as a change in objective reality.[20] They speak of it not as an inward change but as an exterior movement from town into the solitude of the bush. In other words, the idiomatic Kuranko distinction between village and bush corresponds, as it were, to our cultural distinction between ordinary and extraordinary frames of awareness. This tendency to exteriorize events which we would assign to interiority explains why the Kuranko interpret memory not as a mental trace of a past event but as a registration in the mind of an event happening *somewhere else* (Jackson 1986:6). It also explains why they interpret conscience (*hake*) as residing in social relationships, not in the individual psyche (Jackson 1982a:29–30) and regard the unconscious not as some profound level of the mind but as a kind of penumbra in social space, the shadowy domain beyond the perimeter of one's village. It may be because Kuranko so often interpret changes in experience as evidence of changes in the external world that many informants, Mohammed among them, were so dismissive of my questions as to whether shape-shifters *really* changed or only *thought* they did. Perhaps the Kuranko are more pragmatic than most anthropologists: if illusions have real and useful consequences then they are truths.[21]

The foregoing account of Kuranko animism might easily give the impression that Kuranko thought, in its concrete metamorphicality and pragmatism, is utterly foreign to our own. But metamorphosis is a part of our cultural tradition, too—a recurring metaphor from Ovid to Ionesco of radical moral transformation. It is, moreover, a metaphor which finds imaginative and bodily realization in the experiences of actual individuals. For instance, the split in Mohammed's life between social and "wild" identifications is echoed in Kafka's story of Gregor Samsa, who "woke up one morning from unsettling dreams" and "found himself changed in his bed into a monstrous vermin" (*ungeheueres Ungeziefer*).

Kafka deliberately chose to literalize the metaphor of Gregor as a bug,[22] to allow it to be lived as an immediate, bodily reality in order to make us experience the troubled relationship between Gregor's human consciousness and his buglike body, a relationship which suggests Kafka's own estrangement from his family, his struggle against the alienating effect of figurative language, his ambivalent feelings about intimate relations, and his precarious existence as a Jewish writer outside what he called "the house of life" (Corngold 1973). Adorno's *Notes on Kafka* could apply to Mohammed: the "individual and his social character are split. . . . The self lives solely through transformation into otherness. . . . The boundary between what is human and the world of things becomes blurred" (1967:255, 262).[23]

> It is as if
> Men turning into things, as comedy,
> Stood, dressed in antic symbols, to display
>
> The truth about themselves, having lost, as things,
> That power to conceal they had as men. . . .
> (Wallace Stevens, "An Ordinary Evening in New Haven")

Like Mohammed, Gregor's creative withdrawal has an awful social cost. In the end, reduced to the status of a thing, trapped inside his carapace and neglected by his family, Gregor dies and Mr. and Mrs. Samsa, putting their anomalous son from their minds, begin to look forward to their daughter's marriage—a *social* act, "the confirmation of their new dreams."

It is not, however, metamorphoses into animals that pervade the popular imagination of urban industrial societies but metamorphoses into machines, the most thinglike objects of all. Just as images of were-animals are conditioned by the ubiquitous dialectic of village and bush in preindustrial societies,[24] so images of bionic people, androids, and robots reflect the human/machine dialectic that shapes both mental and bodily consciousness in industrial societies. This connection between animal and machine images was borne home to me in 1979 in the course of a conversation with John Sisay, who, as a boy, had seen an American missionary change into a crocodile near Yifan.

At the time my response to John's story was skeptical. I told him that I knew of no Europeans who had the ability to shape-shift. His reply was categorical: "But Europeans can transform themselves into airplanes!"

I was suddenly reminded of an article by Bruno Bettelheim that appeared in *Scientific American* in 1959, an account of an autistic boy called Joey who converted himself into a machine. Trapped in this image of himself, he could not see himself or act except in terms of it; he functioned as if by remote control. Joey's machinelike behavior was so devastatingly convincing that even his therapists found it difficult to respond to him as a human being. Joey lived the mechanistic image as a literal and embodied truth:

> During Joey's first weeks with us we would watch absorbedly as this at once fragile-looking and imperious nine-year-old went about his mechanical existence. Entering the dining room, for example, he would string an imaginary wire from his "energy source"—an imaginary electric outlet—to the table. There he "insulated" himself with

paper napkins and finally plugged himself in. Only then could Joey eat, for he firmly believed that the "current" ran his ingestive apparatus. So skillful was the pantomime that one had to look twice to be sure there was neither wire nor outlet nor plug. Children and members of our staff spontaneously avoided stepping on the "wires" for fear of interrupting what seemed the source of his very life. (1959:117)

It might be argued that Mohammed, like Joey, escapes into a delusional world, shaped through *bricolage* "from bits and pieces of the world at hand" (117). In Joey's case it is a world of mechanical devices, in Mohammed's case of totemic identifications. But whether elephant or machine, these other selves, these borrowed bodies, these second skins, assist a sense of adequacy, amplitude, and solidity in a painfully unstable world. Mohammed speaks of the power he gains through shape-shifting. Joey too: "Machines are better than the body," he once told his teacher. "They don't break" (120).

There are, however, important differences between Mohammed, Gregor, and Joey which bear upon our interpretation of metamorphosis. First, the crises Joey suffered in early life were far more devastating than those Mohammed complained of. Bettelheim tells us that Joey was rejected by his parents even before he was born. "I never knew I was pregnant," his mother said. His birth "did not make any difference. . . . I did not want to see or nurse him. . . . I had no feeling of actual dislike—I simply didn't want to take care of him" (118).

In the second place, Joey's sense of himself as a machine was absolute and inescapable, unlike Mohammed's sense of himself as an elephant, which was occasional and controlled. While Mohammed cultivated and embodied the Kuranko idea of shape-shifting, it did not rule his life to the exclusion of everything else. As the contrast between my conversations with him in 1979 and 1985 makes clear, Mohammed was not stuck with his belief. He embraced it opportunistically. His attraction to shape-shifting was no more delusional than our desire for cars, yachts, and houses—material envelopes that compensate us for our human frailty and mutability in an intimidating world.

Finally, while Joey was clinically labeled "autistic" and "schizophrenic," signifying his complete alienation from social reality, Mohammed's shape-shifting was, in his society, grudgingly accepted. Although it is in the Kuranko view a form of witchcraft, it is also seen as a confirmation of basic moral assumptions, particularly those enshrined in clan myths.

For these reasons we cannot label Mohammed—or Gregor Samsa—as mad and deluded. Existentially, Mohammed remains, like most of us, more or less in control of his own life, even if, like the leopard-men of yore, his stratagems are socially limited and politically ineffectual. The different modalities of Kuranko shape-shifting reveal a search for autonomy, meaning, and control in a world that often appears unpredictable and ungraspable. It is a search we can readily identify with despite the seemingly bizarre idioms of the Kuranko dialectic. Like human beings everywhere, we often claim that what is true is that which corresponds to what is proven, given, or real, but in our quotidian lives we tend to act as pragmatists.

In crisis we make do with whatever is available in order to cope, and we judge the truth of whatever beliefs we take up in terms of where they get us. As William James put it:

> Any idea upon which we can ride . . . that will carry us prosperously from any part of our experience to any other part, linking things satisfactorily, working securely, simplifying, saving labor, is true for just so much, true in so far forth, true *instrumentally*. (1978:34)

EIGHT

Knowledge of the Body

There is always a risk in anthropology of treating the people we study as objects, mere means of advancing our intellectual goals. There is a similar discursive bias in our customary attitudes to our own bodies: the Cartesian division between subject and object also tends to assimilate the body to the same ontological category as the objects of physical science. Against this view, Merleau-Ponty (1962) argues that the human body is *itself* a subject, and this "subject" is necessarily, not just contingently, embodied. Moreover, if human beings differ from other organic and inorganic beings, this is due not to their having some distinctive, nonbodily features, but rather to the distinctive character of their bodies.[1]

Until I was in my mid-thirties, my awareness extended into my body only to the extent that I grew hungry, experienced lust, felt pain or weariness, and did not resemble the somatotype of popular advertising. My body passed into and out of my awareness like a stranger; whole areas of my physical being and potentiality were dead to me, like locked rooms.

When I took courses in hatha yoga (under Iyengar-trained teachers) it was like unpicking the locks of a cage. I began to live my body in full awareness for the first time, feeling the breath, under my conscious control, fill my lungs, experiencing through extensions and asanas the embodied character of my will and consciousness.

But this transformed awareness brought me up against the full force of habit, of set attitudes and ingrained dispositions. It quickly became clear to me that dystonic habits of body use cannot be changed by desiring to act in different ways. The mind is not separate from the body, and it is pure superstition to think that one can "straighten oneself out" by some kind of "psychical manipulation without reference to the distortions of sensation and perception which are due to bad bodily sets" (Dewey 1983:27). Habits cannot be changed at will because we *are* the habits; "in any intelligible sense of the word will, they *are* will" (25). To change a body of habits, physical or cultural, can never be a matter of wishful thinking and trying; it depends on learning and practicing new techniques. In the language of F. M. Alexander, whose work profoundly influenced John Dewey (Jones 1976:94–105), it is a matter of displacing "end-gaining" with new "means-whereby" (Alexander 1931).

The practice of hatha yoga prompted me to couch the dialectic of givenness and choice in terms of the relationship between bodily habits and intentions and to explore the interplay of habitual body sets, patterns of practical activity, and forms of consciousness—the field of what Mauss and Bourdieu call the *habitus*. However, my account here of creative "technologies of the self" (Foucault and Sennett 1982:10) will focus on culturally conditioned modes of consciousness and body use. Only incidental attention will be given to the therapeutic and mystical aspects of yogic and other techniques where ailments are treated by teaching the body musculature to function differently (Tinbergen 1974:21) and mental equanimity is induced through stability and suppleness of the body.[2]

CULTURE

If there is any one word which defines the common ground of the social sciences and humanities it is the word *culture*. But *culture* may be understood not only as an abstract noun but in a verbal sense as well. And it not only covers a domain of intellectual life; it also demarcates a field of practical activity.

In its original usage, *culture* (from the Latin *colo*) meant to inhabit a town or district, to cultivate, tend, or till the land, to keep and breed animals, and generally to look after one's livelihood "especially in its material aspects," such as clothing and adorning the body, caring for and attending to friends and family, minding the gods,[3] and upholding custom through the cultivation of correct moral and intellectual disciplines (*Oxford Latin Dictionary* 1969).

In tracing out the semantic history of *culture* we are, however, led further and further away from these grounded notions of bodily activity in a social and material environment. Throughout the late Middle Ages, *culture* was used increasingly to refer to moral perfection and intellectual or artistic accomplishment; and from the mid–eighteenth century, when German writers began to apply the term to human societies and history, *culture* almost invariably designated the refined mental and spiritual faculties which members of the European bourgeoisie imagined set them apart from the allegedly brutish worlds of manual workers, peasants, and savages.[4]

As Herbert Marcuse has shown, this kind of social demarcation inevitably gave rise to an epistemological division whereby the spiritual world was "lifted out of its social context, making culture a (false) collective noun" as in the idea of "Germanic culture" or "Greek classical culture" (Marcuse 1968:94–95). In this way, *culture* was made to denote a realm of authentic spiritual values, realized through "the idealist cult of inwardness" (129) and radically opposed to the world of social utility and material means. The individual soul was set off from and against the body, and sensuality was spiritualized in notions of romantic love and religious adoration. No longer pricked by conscience about the ways in which their enjoyment of so-called higher values depended upon the menial toil of the "lower orders," the bourgeoisie denied both the sensual body and the material conditions on which its privilege rested. Exclusion of the body from discourse went along with the exclusion of the masses from political life.[5]

In 1871 the English anthropologist Edward Tylor published his pioneering work, *Primitive Culture*, borrowing the term *culture* from the German tradition but defining it, after Gustav Klemm, in an apparently neutral way as "that complex whole which includes knowledge, belief, art, law, morals, custom, and any other capabilities and habits acquired by man as a member of society" (cited in Kroeber and Kluckhohn 1963:81). Although culture was held to be a distinctive attribute of *all* mankind, varying only in degree, the pejorative and historical connotations of the word *culture* remained in vogue, and Tylor, like Klemm and Herder before him, applied himself to the task of tracing out the progressive stages of social development in terms of the advance of scientific rationality and technological control over nature.

Taken up by American anthropologists as early as the 1880s, the term *culture* gradually lost its nineteenth-century glosses, and between 1920 and 1950 a new demarcation function was assigned to it: culture defined the emergent properties of mind and language which separated humans from animals. This view was already implied in Kroeber's seminal 1917 paper, "The Superorganic," and is echoed in Kroeber and Kluckhohn's 1952 review of the concept, where they define *culture* as "a set of attributes and products of human societies, and therewith of mankind, which are extrasomatic and transmissible by mechanisms other than biological heredity, and are as essentially lacking in sub-human species as they are characteristic of the human species as it is aggregated in its societies" (Kroeber and Kluckhohn 1963:284).

In recent years the paradigm has shifted again, partly through the impact of sociobiology, and although *culture* is still defined as exogenetic it is not regarded as exosomatic or considered apart from phylogeny. As John Tyler Bonner defines it in *The Evolution of Culture in Animals*, *culture* is "the transfer of information by behavioral means, most particularly by the process of teaching and learning" (1980:10). Culture is, in this sense, a property of *many* living organisms apart from humans, and while cultural evolution can be contrasted with genetic evolution, culture has a biogenetic base.[6] In the words of E. O. Wilson, "Aside from its involvement with language, which is truly unique, [culture] differs from animal tradition only in degree" (1975:168).

Now, whether we consider the idealist traditions of the eighteenth and nineteenth centuries which "etherealized"[7] the body or anthropological definitions of culture which play up the conceptual and linguistic characteristics of human social existence to the exclusion of somatic and biological processes, we find that science since the Enlightenment has always been pervaded by the popular bourgeois conception of culture as something "superorganic," a self-contained world of unique qualities and manners divorced from the world of materiality and biology.[8] Culture has thus served as a token to demarcate, separate, exclude, and deny,[9] and although at different epochs the excluded "natural" category shifts about among peasants, barbarians, workers, primitive people, women,[10] children, animals, and material artifacts,[11] a persistent theme is the denial of the somatic, a scotomacizing of the physical aspects of Being where our sense of separateness and distinction is most readily blurred.[12]

It is unfortunate that anthropology should have helped perpetuate the bourgeois myth of the superorganic; yet, when one considers that anthropology itself belongs to a privileged domain of activity—academe—and evolved as a by-product of European colonialism, it is not hard to see how the exclusion of the body from anthropological discourse is at the same time a defense against the unsettling knowledge that the very data on which that discourse depends are extracted from agrarian peoples for whom knowledge is nothing if not practical. To write prefaces to our monographs, acknowledging the generosity of informants or the support of a devoted spouse, is thus to gesture vacuously in the direction of a material truth which the work itself usually denies because of its abstract style, the disembodied view of culture it contains, and the privileged world to which it is addressed and in which it has value.

Thus, to bring back the body into discourse is inevitably related to questions about the use-value of anthropology, and the problem of finding some way of making our discourse consonant with the practices and interests of the peoples we study. Throughout the 1970s studies of body movement and body meaning appeared in increasing numbers, but analysis tended to be either overly symbolic and semantic or, in the case of ethological studies, heavily mechanistic.[13] Since the semantic model has dominated anthropological studies of the body, it is this mode of analysis which I will focus on here. My main contention will be that the "anthropology of the body" has been vitiated by a tendency to interpret embodied experience in terms of cognitive and linguistic models of meaning.

THE LANGUAGE OF REPRESENTATION

The first problem arises from the intellectualist tendency to regard body praxis as secondary to verbal praxis. For example, Mary Douglas, while critical of the "logocentric" bias in many studies of "non-verbal communication" whereby "speech has been over-emphasised as the privileged means of human communication, and the body neglected," still asserts that "normally the physical channel supports and agrees with the spoken one" (1978:85). This subjugation of the bodily to the semantic is empirically untenable. In the first place, from both phylogenetic and ontogenetic points of view, thinking and communicating through the body precede and to a great extent always remain beyond speech.[14] This may be recognized in the way our earliest memories are usually sensations or direct impressions rather than words or ideas, and refer to situated yet not spoken events.[15] It is, moreover, often the case that gestures and bodily habits belie what we put into words and give away our unconscious dispositions, betraying character traits which our verbal and conceptual habits keep us in ignorance of.[16] In therapies which focus on the embodied personality and the bodily unconscious, such as hypnotherapy and Reichian bioenergetic analysis, the "somatic mind" mediates understandings and changes in which verbal consciousness plays little part.[17] In the second place, as Ludwig Binswanger and Merleau-Ponty have argued, meaning should not be reduced to a sign which, as it were, lies on a separate plane outside the immediate domain of an act. For instance, when our familiar environment is suddenly disrupted we feel uprooted, we lose our footing, we are thrown, we collapse, we fall. But such falling, Binswanger says, is not "something metaphorical derived from physical falling," a mere manner of speaking; it is a shock and disorientation which occurs simultaneously in body and mind, and refers to a basic ontological structure of our being-in-the-world (Binswanger 1963:222–25; Reich 1949:435). In this sense, uprightness of posture may be said to define a psychophysical relationship with the world, so that to lose this position, this "standing," is simultaneously a bodily and intellectual loss of balance, a disturbance at the very center and ground of our Being.[18] Metaphors of falling and disequilibrium disclose this integral connection of the psychic and the physical; they do not express a concept *in terms of* a bodily image.

Another way of showing that the meaning of body praxis is not always reducible to cognitive and semantic operations is to note that body movements often make sense without being intentional in the linguistic sense: as communicating, codifying, symbolizing, signifying thoughts or things that lie outside or anterior to speech.[19] Thus, an understanding of a body movement does not invariably depend on an elucidation of what the movement "stands for." As David Best puts it, "Human movement does not symbolise reality, it *is* reality" (1978:137).[20] To treat body praxis as necessarily being an effect of semantic causes is to treat the body as a diminished version of itself.[21]

The second problem in the anthropology of the body is a corollary of the first. Insofar as the body tends to be defined as a medium of expression or communication,[22] it is not only reduced to the status of a sign; it is also made into an object of purely mental operations, a "thing" onto which social patterns are projected. Thus, Douglas speaks of the body as an "it"[23] and examines how "in its role as an image of society, the body's main scope is to express the relation of the individual to the group" (1978:87). As a result a Cartesian split is made which detaches the knowing and speaking subject from the unknowing inert body. At the same time, through a reification of the knowing subject, which is made synonymous with "society" or "the social body," *society* is made to assume the active role of governing, utilizing, and charging with significance the physical bodies of individuals.[24] In this view the human body is simply an object of understanding or an instrument of the rational mind, a kind of vehicle for the expression of a reified social rationality.[25] This view is fallacious on epistemological grounds; it also contradicts our experience of the lived body, wherein no sense of the mind as causally prior can be sustained and any notion of the body as an instrument of mind or of society is absurd. Dewey dismisses this kind of dualism by drawing attention to the "natural medium" in which bodies and minds exist equally:

> In ultimate analysis the mystery that mind should use a body, or that a body should have a mind, is like the mystery that a man cultivating plants should use the soil; or that the soil which grows plants at all should grow those adapted to its own physico-chemical properties. . . .
>
> Every "mind" that we are empirically acquainted with is found in connection with some organized body. Every such body exists in a natural medium to which it sustains some adaptive connection: plants to air, water, sun, and animals to these things and also to plants. Without such connections, animals die; the "purest" mind would not continue without them (1929:277–78).

A third problem arises from the dualistic and reified views on which I have commented above. In many anthropological studies of the body, the body is regarded as inert, passive, and static. Either the body is shown to be a neutral and ideographic means of embodying ideas or it is dismembered so that the symbolic value of its various parts in indigenous discourse can be enumerated. There seems to be a dearth of studies of what Merleau-Ponty called the "body subject," studies of interactions and exchanges occurring within the field of bodily existence rather than resulting from mechanical rules or innate preprogramming.

My aim in the following pages is to outline a phenomenological approach to body praxis. I hope to avoid naive subjectivism by showing how human experience is grounded in bodily movement within a social and material environment and by examining at the level of event the interplay of habitual patterns of body use and conventional ideas about the world.

INITIATIONS AND IMITATIONS

In the dry season of 1970 in northern Sierra Leone, not long after I had begun fieldwork in the Kuranko village of Firawa, I was lucky enough to see the public festivities associated with girls' initiation rites (*dimusu biriye*).[26] Each night from the veranda of the house where I was staying I would watch the girls performing the graceful and energetic *yatuiye* and *yamayili* dances which presaged the end of their childhood. With their hair specially braided and adorned with snail-shell toggles, and wearing brightly colored beaded headbands, groups of girls passed from house to house around the village, dancing, clapping, and singing that their girlhood days were almost over. The daylight hours too were crowded with activities. Visitors poured into the village, diviners were consulted to see what dangers might lie in store for the girls during the operations, sacrifices were made to avert such dangers, gifts were given to help defray expenses for those families whose daughters were being initiated that year, and all the while the neophytes continued to circulate around the village in the company of indefatigable drummers. Then, at dusk on the day before the operations, the girls were led down to the river by older women to be washed and dressed in long white gowns. That night they were sequestered in a special house and we did not see them. Nor in the morning, for they were ushered away into the bush at first light by the women to be made ready for the operations. They remained in the bush, lodged in a makeshift house, for three weeks, all the time receiving instruction from older women in domestic, sexual, and moral matters and waiting for the clitoridectomy scars to heal.

On the day the girls left the village, I sat about with the other men, talking and being entertained by groups of performers, mostly women and young girls, who came by the house just as the neophytes had done in the days before. These performers fascinated me. A young girl, her body daubed with red and white ochres and charcoal, stood before us with an immobile face. Another, wearing a man's hat and gown and carrying a cutlass hilt down, held a pad of cloth clamped over her mouth. When she and her companions moved on, another group took their place: small boys who pranced around in mimicry of a comical figure trussed in grass, a "chimpanzee" which fell to the ground from time to time to be "revived" by his friends' urgent drumming. Then women performers danced before us too. One was dressed in men's clothes with a wild fruit hung from a cord across her forehead. She imitated the maladroit dance movements of men, her face expressionless, while other women surrounded her, clapping, singing, and laughing. Other women had daubed their bodies with red and white clay and charcoal, and painted symmetrical black lines under their eyes. They too danced awkwardly with deadpan faces, some holding red flowers clenched between tight lips.

Three weeks passed and the girls returned to the village. More dancing took place, and the mimicry of men was a recurring motif. Several young women marched up and down shouldering old rifles, others had donned the coarse cloth leggings and tasseled caps of hunters, while others pretended to be the praise-singers of the hunters and plucked the imaginary strings of a piece of stick signifying a harp.

For as long as the festivities lasted I plied my field assistant with endless questions, always being given the same answers: that the performers were simply contributing to the enjoyment of the occasion, and doing what was customary during initiations. Although different performers had names such as *tatatie, komantere* ("scapegrace"), *kamban soiya* ("*kamban* soldiery"), *forubandi binye* (the name of the mossy grass in which the chimpanzee boy was trussed), and *sewulan* (*wulan*, red), the names yielded me no clues to the meaning of the performances. Similarly, the sung refrains which sometimes accompanied the dances were little more to me than banal and obvious commentaries on the events. In my notebooks, among detailed descriptions of what I saw, I listed searching questions which could not be phrased in Kuranko, let alone answered, and the following self-interrogations, culled from my field notes of that time, now remind me of the fervor with which I sought clues to hidden meanings:

> These mask-like expressions—are they a way in which these girls strive to sympathetically induce in their older sisters some measure of self-control? Is this impassivity a way in which they seek magically to countermand or neutralize the emotional turmoil in the hearts of the neophytes? These songs the women sing, assuaging fear and urging calm—are they ways in which the village tries to cool "the bush"? These girls in men's clothes—do they want to assimilate something of men's fortitude and fearlessness, or is this muddling of quotidian roles simply an expression of the confusion surrounding this moment of mid-passage? And the chimpanzee boy, falling to the ground and lying there utterly still before being roused by the drumming and resuming his dance—is this an image of death and rebirth?

Some years later when I published an account of the initiations I tried to answer these questions by making inordinate use of the slight exegesis which informants had given me, decoding the ritual activities as if they were symbolic representations of unconscious concerns. Determined, however, to be faithful to at least one aspect of the ritual form—its nonlineal mosaiclike character—I borrowed my interpretative model from the structural study of myth, claiming that the initiations could be seen as "a myth staged rather than spoken, acted out rather than voiced."

Noting that "ritual meanings are not often verbalised and perhaps cannot be because they surpass and confound language," I nevertheless applied a method of
analysis that reduces "acts to words and gives objects a specific vocabulary." And
while admitting that "ritual often makes language redundant" and makes questions
superfluous, I proceeded to paraphrase the ritual movements and translate its actions into words.[27]

With hindsight, I now realize the absurdity of this analytical procedure. As
Bourdieu observes:

> Rites, more than any other type of practice, serve to underline the mistake of enclosing
> in concepts a logic made to dispense with concepts; of treating movements of the body
> and practical manipulations as purely logical operations; of speaking of analogies and
> homologies (as one sometimes has to, in order to understand and to convey that under-
> standing) when all that is involved is the practical transference of incorporated, quasi-
> postural schemes. (1977:116)

In the first place I failed to take Kuranko comments at their face value and
accept that the performances I witnessed were "just for entertainment," or, as my
field assistant put it, "for no other reason but to have everyone take part." In the
second place I failed to accept that human beings do not necessarily act from opinions or employ epistemological criteria in finding meaning for their actions. In
Remarks on Frazer's Golden Bough, Wittgenstein argues that Frazer was not war-
ranted in assuming that primitive rituals are informed by erroneous conceptions
about the world, since "What makes the character of ritual action is not any view
or opinion, either right or wrong" (1979:7), though opinions and beliefs may of
course "belong to a rite."[28] Inasmuch as Kuranko ritual actions make sense to them
at the level of immediate experience and do not purport to be true in terms of
some systematic theory of knowledge, who are we to deny their emphasis on use-
value and ask impertinent questions about veracity? It is probably the separateness
of the observer from the ritual acts which makes him think that the acts refer to
or require justification in a domain beyond their actual compass.

For these reasons it is imperative to explore further what Wittgenstein called
"the environment of a way of acting" and accept that understanding may be gained
through seeing and drawing attention to connections or "intermediary links"
within such an environment, rather than by explaining acts in terms of preceding
events, projected aims, unconscious concerns, or precepts and rules.[29] After all,
I never thought to ask Kuranko farmers why they hoed the earth or broadcast grain;
neither did I interrogate women about the meaning of lighting a fire or the significance of cooking or raising children. In my approach to initiation I was clearly
applying a distinction which the Kuranko themselves do not recognize: between
pragmatic "work" and "ritual" activity. Or, rather, I regarded the ludic elements
in the ritual performances as exactly comparable to theatrical and stage performances in my own society where actions are scripted, deliberately directed, and
variously interpreted. My bourgeois conception of culture as something "superorganic," something separable from the quotidian world of bodily movements and
practical tasks, had led me to seek the script, the director, and the interpretation

in a rite which had none. This quest for semantic truths also explained my inability to participate in the spirit of the performances and why I spent my time asking people to tell me what was going on, what it all meant, as if the painted bodies and mimetic dances were only the insipid remnants of what had perhaps once been a symbolically coherent structure of myths and masks. Our longing for meaning frequently assumes the form of a nostalgia for the traditional.

But to hold that every act signifies something is an extravagant form of abstraction, so long as this implies that the action stands for something other than itself, beyond the here and now. In anthropology this "something other" is usually a reified category designated by such verbal tokens as "social solidarity," "functional equilibrium," "adaptive integration," or "unconscious structure."[30]

Many of these notions enter into the customary explanations which anthropologists have given for the kinds of imitative practices I saw during the Kuranko initiations. Max Gluckman's account of ritualized role reversals in the Zulu first fruits ceremony (*umkhosi wokweshwama*) and *Nomkhulbulwana* ("Heavenly princess") cult stresses how these "protests" and "rebellions" by normally subordinated women "gave expression, in a reversed form, to the normal rightness of a particular kind of social order" (1970:116; cf. 1963:118). Although Gluckman is wary of psychologistic explanations, it is suggested that the periodic catharsis afforded by the Zulu "rituals of rebellion" helps maintain social solidarity and functional equilibrium.[31] Edmund Leach emphasizes the relationship between role reversals and the ambiguous, liminal period during calendrical rites when, so to speak, time stands still and behavior is not constrained by any conventional structure (1961:132–36). Giving less emphasis to cathartic and saturnalian aspects of sex-role reversal, Peter Rigby has shown that among the Ugogo of Tanzania, such calamities as drought, barrenness in women, crop failure, and cattle disease are considered to be reversals in fortune which can be mitigated by the manipulation of gender categories. Thus, women dress as men, mimic male demeanor, and perform male tasks in order to induce a re-reversal in correlative domains of natural ecology (1968:172–73).

These studies convey invaluable insights, and in writing my original account of role reversals in Kuranko initiation I felt I had enough support from native exegesis to advance an interpretation along similar lines. But I have always had serious misgivings about the way this sort of interpretation tends to exclude—because of its focus on oblique aims, semantic meanings, and abstract functions—those very particularities of body use which are the most conspicuous elements of the rites, and refer not to a domain of discourse or belief but to an environment of practical activity. What I now propose to do is work from an account of *how* these mimetic performances arise toward an account of *what* they mean and *why* they occur, without any a priori references to precepts, rules, or symbols.

THE ENVIRONMENT OF A WAY OF ACTING

Let us first take up a problem posed by Franziska Boas in 1944: "What is the relationship between the movements characteristic of a given dance, and the typical gestures and postures in daily life of the very people who perform it?" (Boas 1944:55).[32]

In the case of the mimetic performances I have described, every bodily element can be seen in other fields of Kuranko social life as well. Thus, the women's uncanny imitations of male comportment are mingled with elements which are conspicuous "borrowings" from mortuary ritual, e.g., the miming, the deadpan faces, and the cutlass held hilt down. Still other elements refer us to the bush: the boy's imitation of the chimpanzee, the young men who pierce their cheeks with porcupine quills, the music of the praise-singer of the hunters (*serewayili*), the women's mimicry of hunters, the bush ochres daubed on the body, and the wild fruit worn by the *Sewulan*.[33] The following transpositions can therefore be recognized: from male domain to female domain; from mortuary rites to initiation rites; from bush to village.

The second crucial observation is that mimetic performers are women *not* immediately related to the neophytes. In this way they are like the women who, with flat and doleful faces, perform at a man's funeral and mimic the way he walked, danced, spoke, and moved. Often wives of the dead man's sons, these women simulate grief and repining *on behalf of* the immediate bereaved, who play no part at all in the public rites. We cannot, therefore, explain the mimetic performances at initiations or funerals in terms of individual interest or affect. Indeed, when I suggested to Kuranko women that acting as men might be a way of venting their resentment at men's power over them in everyday life, the women were bemused. "Was the 'mad *Kamban*' (*Kamban Yuwe*) really insane (*yuwe*) just because she behaved in a crazy way?" I was asked, in reference to another woman performer who, with distracted gestures, deadpan face, and male attire, joined the *Sewulan* in the final stages of the ritual.

The patterns of body use with which I am concerned are thus in a sense neutral and are transposable from one domain to another. Moreover, the regular or conventional character of these bodily practices is not necessarily the result of obedience to rules or conscious intentions but rather a consequence of ways peoples' bodies are informed by habits instilled within a shared environment and articulated as movements which are, to use Pierre Bourdieu's phrase, "collectively orchestrated without being the product of the orchestrating action of a conductor" (1977:72).

These "transposable dispositions" arise in an environment of everyday practical activities which Bourdieu calls the *habitus*. As Marcel Mauss and John Dewey have also stressed, habits are interactional and tied to an environment of objects and others.[34] Forms of body use ("*techniques du corps*") are conditioned by our relationships with others, such as the way bodily dispositions which we come to regard as "masculine" or "feminine" are encouraged and reinforced in us as mutually exclusive patterns by our parents and peers. Or, patterns of body use are ingrained through our interactions with objects, such as the way that working at a desk or with a machine imposes and reinforces postural sets which we come to regard as belonging to sedentary white-collar workers and factory workers, respectively. According to this view, collective representations such as those of gender and class are always correlated with patterns of body use generated within the *habitus*.[35]

Moreover, stereotypical ideas and bodily habits tend to reinforce each other in ways which remain "set" so long as the environment in which these attitudes are grounded itself remains stable.

Nevertheless, the habitual or "set" relations between ideas, experiences, and body practices may be broken. Thus, altered patterns of body use may induce new experiences and provoke new ideas, as when a regulation and steadying of the breath induces tranquillity of mind or a balanced pose bodies forth a sense of equanimity. Likewise, emotional and mental turmoil may induce corresponding changes in bodily attitude, as when depression registers in a slumped posture or grief is manifest in an absolute loss of muscle tonus. But it is the disruption of the environment which mainly concerns me here, and the way such disruption triggers changes in bodily and mental disposition.

Kuranko initiation is first and foremost a disruption in the *habitus*, and it is this, rather than any precept, rule, or stage management, that sets in train the social and personal alterations whose visible bodily aspect is role reversal. My argument is that this disruption in the *habitus*, wherein women enjoy a free run of the village and men must fend for themselves (even cooking their own meals) or stay indoors like cowered women (when the women's cult object is paraded through the village), lays people open to possibilities of behavior which they embody but ordinarily are not inclined to express. Furthermore, I believe that it is on the strength of these extraordinary possibilities that people control and recreate their world, their *habitus*. [36]

What then are these embodied yet latent possibilities which are realized during initiations? Some, such as the grieving behaviors, are phylogenetically given. Others, such as the entranced and dissociated rocking of the mimetic dancers, suggest a hypnotic element, the basis of which is a conditioned reflex whose origins are probably intrauterine. [37] As for the basis of the sexual mimeticism, it is important to point out that Kuranko children enjoy a free run of house and village space, unconfined by the conventional rules that strictly separate male and female domains. At the level of bodily knowledge, manifest in sexually amorphous modes of comportment, hair style and dress, prepubescent children are, as the Kuranko themselves say, sexually indeterminate and "dirty." The transformed *habitus* during initiation simply reactivates these modes of comportment and opposite sex patterns deeply instilled in the somatic unconscious.

Now to the question of why these particular possibilities are *socially* implemented and *publicly* played out. Let us first consider the transposition of bodily practices from domain to domain: male to female, funeral to initiation, bush to village. Here we find a parallel with those remarkable transpositions in nature whereby various organisms assume or mimic features of other organisms in the same habitat. [38] Just as this natural mimicry has survival value for a species, so it may be supposed that the survival of Kuranko society depends on the creation of responsible adults through initiatory ordeals every bit as much as it depends upon the physical birth of children. To create adults requires a concerted application of information from *throughout the environment*; it requires tapping the vital energies of the natural world, [39] "capturing" such "male" virtues as fortitude and bravery, and imitating the chimpanzee mother's alleged rejection of her offspring or the feigned indifference of public mourners at a funeral, both of which remind women of how they must endure their daughters' separation in order for the girls to become independent women themselves.[40] We can therefore postulate that initiation ritual maximizes the information available in the total environment in order to ensure the accomplishment of its vital task: creating adults and thereby recreating the social order. This process does not necessarily involve verbal or conceptual knowledge; rather, we might say that people are informed by and give form to a *habitus* which only an uninformed outside observer would take to be an object of knowledge.[41] Kuranko intentionality is thus less of a conceptual willing than a bodily in-tension, a stretching out, a habitual disposition toward the world.[42] Initiation rites involve a "practical mimesis"[43] in which are bodied forth and recombined elements from several domains, yet without script, sayings, promptings, conscious purposes, or even emotions. No notion of "copying" can explain the naturalness with which the mimetic features appear. Women performers do not, as it were, observe men's behavior in piecemeal fashion and then self-consciously put these observations together in an "act"; rather, this behavior is generated by an innate and embodied principle which only requires an altered environment to "catch on" and come into play. This innate principle is, of course, the mimetic faculty itself, though, as we have seen, it is always an environment of *cultural* practices which endows it with its specific expression.[44]

The way in which initiation opens up and allows the enactment of possibilities which would not normally be entertained has also to be seen from an existential viewpoint since, as Harvey Sarles notes, it is through attunement "and interaction with other bodies [that] one gains a sense of oneself and the external world" (1975:30). Although everybody is informed by common predispositions, it is the individual alone who bodies forth these predispositions as mimetic plays.[45] Insofar as they permit each individual to play an active part in a project which effectively recreates the world, initiation rites maximize participation as well as information, allowing each person to discover in his or her own personality a way of producing, out of the momentary chaos, something which will contribute to a renewal of the *social* order. In this process, each person makes the world himself or herself out of elements which ordinarily are not considered appropriate for him or her to use, e.g., women wearing the clothes and carrying the weapons of men. Yet, curiously enough, the principle of sexual complementarity in Kuranko society can be viable only if Kuranko men and women periodically re-cognize the other in themselves and see themselves in the other. Mimeticism, which is based upon a bodily awareness of the other in oneself, thus assists in bringing into relief a reciprocity of viewpoints.[46] As to why it is the same social order which is created over and over again, we must remember that the Kuranko *habitus* constrains behavior, and that when the bodily unconscious is addressed openly it answers with forms and features which reflect a closed social universe. Thus the creative freedom and interpretative license in mimetic play are always circumscribed by the *habitus* in which people have been raised. Freedom must therefore be seen as a matter of realizing and experiencing one's potential within this given universe, not above or beyond it.

Let us now turn to a second kind of transposition, in which patterns of body use engender mental images and instill moral qualities. Most of us are familiar with the way decontraction of muscular "sets" and the freeing of energies bound up in habitual deformations of posture or movement produce an altered sense of self, in particular a dissolution of those conceptual "sets" such as role, gender, and status which customarily define our social identity.[47] My argument is that the distinctive modes of body use during initiation tend to throw up images in the mind whose form is most immediately determined by the pattern of body use. This is not to say that all mental forms should be reduced to bodily practices; rather, that within the unitary field of body-mind-*habitus* it is possible to intervene and effect changes from any one of these points. By approaching cognition in this manner we are able to enter the domain of words and symbols by the back door, so to speak, and show that what the Kuranko themselves say about initiation can be correlated at every turn with what is done with the body.

Apart from the examples already mentioned in which facial impassivity is correlated with such moral qualities as the control of emotion and the acceptance of separation, other instances can be cited of bodily praxis inducing or suggesting ethical ideas. Thus, the value of moderation is inculcated through taboos on calling for food or referring to food while in the initiation lodge, the *fafei*. The interdiction on the neophytes' speaking out of turn, moving, or crying out during the operations is directly connected to the virtues of keeping secrets, promises, and oaths and of forbearance and circumspection.[48] Similarly, the importance placed on listening to elders during the period of sequestration in the bush is correlated with the virtue of respecting elders whose counsels guarantee social as well as physical life, a correlation pointed up by such adages as *sie tole l to* ("long life comes from attending") and *si ban tol sa* ("short life ear has not"). Again, the sleepless night (*kinyale*) which initiates must endure in a smoke-filled house on the eve of their return from the bush after initiation is a way of instilling in them the virtues of withstanding hardship and being alert, while the enforced confinement is connected to the value placed on self-restraint and self-containment. Other senses are developed too, so that keenness of smell is correlated with the quality of discrimination (newly initiated boys often quite literally "turn up their noses" at the sight of uninitiated kids, remarking their crude smell), and control of the eyes is connected with sexual proprieties, most notably mindfulness of those domains and secret objects associated with the other sex which one may not see except on pain of death. Finally, the donning of new clothes suggests in the initiate's mind the assumption of a new status, while the women's imitations of men are sometimes explained similarly as a way women take on "male" virtues of fortitude and bravery which they feel they sorely lack.[49]

These examples indicate how, in Kuranko initiation, what is done with the body is the ground of what is thought and said. From an existential point of view we could say that the bodily practices mediate a personal realization of social values, an immediate grasp of general precepts as sensible truths. Such a view is consistent with the African tendency to effect understanding through bodily techniques, to proceed through bodily awareness to verbal skills and ethical views.[50] Bodily self-mastery is thus everywhere the basis for social and intellectual mastery. The primacy given to embodied over verbal understanding is readily seen in a conversation I had with the Kuranko elder Saran Salia Sano about male initiation.

"Even when they are cutting the foreskin you must not flinch," Saran Salia said. "You have to stand stockstill. You must not make a sound from the mouth. Better to die than to wince or blink or cry out!"

"But what kind of instruction is given?" I asked.

"To respect your elders, not to be arrogant, that is all. Disrespectful boys are beaten. A pliable stick is flicked against the side of your face or ear if you begin to doze. In the *fafei* you get tamed properly."

It is not surprising to find such an emphasis on bodily praxis in a preliterate society where most practical learning is a matter of direct observation and "prestigious imitation."[51] This emphasis on embodied knowledge and "kinaesthetic learning"[52] may explain why failures to uphold ethical expectations are usually seen by the Kuranko in bodily terms: as leading to physical weakening, disease, or death. Furthermore, it is because bodily praxis in initiation imparts knowledge directly that the Kuranko do not need to formulate the meaning of the rite in terms of abstract verbal elaborations or moral concepts.[53] The fact is that knowledge is directly linked to the production of food and community and the relationship between thought, language, and activity is intrinsically closer in a preliterate subsistence society than in a modern literate society where knowledge is often abstracted and held aloof from the domains of bodily skills and material processes of production. It is noteworthy that when the Kuranko *do* supply verbal exegesis it tends to center on root metaphors which refer to bodily and practical activity in the *habitus*. Thus, initiation is said to be a process of taming (unruly emotions and bodies), of molding (clay), of making dry or cool (as in cooking, smoking, and curing), of ripening (as of grain and fruit), of strengthening (the heart), hardening or straightening (the body), of getting "new sense" (*hankili kura*).[54] These allusions to domestic and agricultural life are not mere figures of speech, for they disclose real connections between personal maturity and the ability to provide food for and give support to others. Bodily and moral domains are fused, and, as the Kuranko say, maturity is a matter of common sense, which is achieved when inner thoughts are consistent with spoken words and external actions.

Let us now take up the question why ritual action should accord such primacy to bodily techniques. In the first place, bodily movements can sometimes do more than words can say. In this sense techniques of the body may be compared with musical techniques, since both transport us from the quotidian world of verbal distinctions and categorical separations into a world where boundaries are blurred and experience transformed. Dance and music move us to participate in a world beyond our accustomed roles and to recognize ourselves as members of a community, a common body. This is not to say that music and bodily practices are never means of making social distinctions;[55] only that, within the context of communal rites, music and movement often take the form of oppositional practices which eclipse speech and nullify the divisions which dominate everyday life. The Kuranko say that music and dance are "sweet"; they loosen and lighten, by contrast with normal behavior which is contractual, binding, and constrained.[56] In this way, movement and music promote a sense of levity and openness in both body and mind and make possible an empathic understanding of others, a fellow-feeling, which verbal and cognitive forms ordinarily inhibit.[57] But such a reciprocity of viewpoints is often experienced bodily before it is apprehended in the mind, as in the case of mimetic practices in which one literally adopts the position or dons the clothing of another. Merleau-Ponty puts it this way:

> The communication or comprehension of gestures comes about through the reciprocity of my intentions and the gestures of others, of my gestures and intentions discernible in the conduct of other people. It is as if the other person's intention inhabited my body and mine his. . . . There is a mutual confirmation between myself and others. . . . The act by which I lend myself to the spectacle must be recognized as irreducible to anything else. I join it in a kind of blind recognition which precedes the intellectual working out and clarification of the meaning. (1962:185)

In Kuranko initiation, the women's imitations of men presumably promote a sense of what it is to be man. Yet, inasmuch as these body practices are not preceded by any verbal definition of intention, they are ambiguous. The imitations are therefore open to interpretation, and the meaning they may assume for either performer or observer is indeterminate. This indeterminacy is of the essence, and it is perfectly possible that the imitations will be experienced or seen variously as a way of "borrowing" male virtue, a kind of mockery of men, an inept copying that only goes to show that women could never really occupy the roles of men, a rebellious expropriation of male privileges, or even as a marker that men are temporarily "dead." This ambiguity, and the fact that the interpretations which do arise tend to confound everyday proprieties of gender and role, may account for Kuranko women's silence on the question of meaning: the imitations mean everything and nothing. By the same token, the anthropologist who seeks to reduce bodily praxis to the terms of verbal discourse runs the risk of falsifying both (cf. Bourdieu 1977:120, 223 note 40). Practical understanding can do without concepts, and as Bourdieu points out,

> the language of the body . . . is incomparably more ambiguous and overdetermined than the most overdetermined uses of ordinary language. . . . Words, however charged with connotation, limit the range of choices and render difficult or impossible, and in any case explicit and therefore "falsifiable," the relations which the language of the body suggests. (120)

It is because actions speak louder *and* more ambiguously than words that they are more likely to lead us to common truths; not semantic truths, established by others at other times, but experiential truths which seem to issue from within our own Being when we break the momentum of the discursive mind or throw ourselves into some collective activity in which we each find our own meaning yet at the same time sustain the impression of having a common cause and giving common consent.[58]

LIGHTING A FIRE

My main argument has been against undue abstraction in ethnographic analysis. Against the tendencies to explain human behavior in terms of linguistic models, patterns of social organization, institutions or roles, structures of the mind, or symbolic meaning, I have endeavored to advance a grounded view which begins with interactions and movements of people in an organized environment and considers in detail the patterns of body praxis which arise therein.

My focus on the embodied character of lived experience in the *habitus* also reflects a conviction that anthropological analysis should be consonant with indigenous understandings which, in preliterate societies, are frequently embedded in practices (doings) rather than spelled out in abstract ideas (sayings). Although such a consonance is, for me, a fundamental measure of adequacy in ethnographic interpretation, I do not think that interpretation necessarily consists in finding *agreement* between our verbal reactions to observed practices and the exegesis which may be provided by the practitioners. Inasmuch as bodily praxis cannot be reduced to semantics, bodily practices are always open to interpretation; they are not in themselves intepretations of anything.

If we construe anthropological understanding as principally a language game in which semiotic values are assigned to bodily practices, then we can be sure that in the measure that the people we study make nothing of their practices outside of a living, we will make anything of them within reason. But if we take anthropological understanding to be first and foremost a way of acquiring social and practical skills without any a priori assumptions about their significance or function, then a different kind of knowledge follows. By avoiding the solipsism and ethnocentricism that pervade much symbolic analysis, an *empathic* understanding may be bodied forth. Let me elaborate by considering the relationship between theoretical knowledge and fieldwork practices.

When I first lived in a Kuranko village I used to light my own fire to boil water for drinking or bathing. But I regarded such a mundane chore as having little bearing on my research work, and my way of building a fire was careless and wasteful of wood. It was a task to get done quickly so that I could get on with what I took to be more important things. Villagers joked about my fire-lighting but did not criticize or censure me, which was remarkable considering the scarcity of firewood and the time consumed in gathering it. Then one day, for no reason at all, I observed how Kuranko women kindled a fire and tended it, and I began to imitate their technique, which involved careful placement of the firestones, never using more than three lengths of split wood at one time, laying each piece carefully between the firestones, and gently pushing them into the fire as the ends burned away. When I took pains to make a fire in this way I found myself suddenly aware of the intelligence of the technique, which maximized the scarce firewood (which women have to split and tote from up to a mile and a half away), produced exactly the amount of heat required for cooking, and enabled instant control of the flame. This "practical mimesis" afforded me insight into how people economized both fuel and human energy; it made me see the close kinship between economy of effort and grace of movement; it made me realize the common sense which informs even the most elementary tasks in a Kuranko village.

Many of my most valued insights into Kuranko social life have followed from comparable cultivation and imitation of practical skills: hoeing on a farm, dancing (as one body), lighting a kerosene lantern properly, weaving a mat, consulting a diviner. To break the habit of using a linear communicational model for understanding bodily praxis, it is necessary to adopt a methodological strategy of joining in without ulterior motive and literally putting oneself in the place of other persons: inhabiting their world. Participation thus becomes an end in itself[59] rather than a means of gathering closely observed data which will be subject to interpretation elsewhere *after the event*.

George Devereux has shown that one's personality inevitably colors the character of one's observations and that the "royal road to an authentic, rather than fictitious, objectivity" is perforce the way of *informed* subjectivity (1967:xvi-xvii). In my view, subjective determinations are as much somatic as psychological in character. Thus, to stand aside from the action, take up a point of view, and ask endless questions as I did during the female initiations led only to a spurious understanding and *increased* the phenomenological problem of how I could know the experience of the other.[60] By contrast, to participate bodily in everyday practical tasks was a creative technique which often helped me grasp the *sense* of an activity by using my body as others did. This technique also helped me break my habit of seeking truth at the level of disembodied concepts and decontextualized sayings. To recognize the embodiedness of our being-in-the-world is to discover a common ground where self and other are one, for by using one's body in the same way as others in the same environment one finds oneself informed by an understanding which may then be interpreted according to one's own custom or bent, yet which remains grounded in a field of practical activity and thereby remains consonant with the experience of those among whom one has lived.

While words and concepts distinguish and divide, bodiliness unites and forms the grounds of an empathic, even a universal, understanding. That may be why the body so often takes the place of speech and eclipses thought in rituals, such as Kuranko initiation, whose point is the creation of community. The practical and embodied nature of Kuranko thought is thus to be seen as an ethical preference, not a mark of primitiveness or speculative failure.

SYMBOLS

Much of what I have said in this chapter implies a critique of the "intellectualist" approach to symbolism. A symbol was originally a token of identity, "a half coin carried away by each of the two parties to an agreement as a pledge of their good faith" (Boagey 1977:40).[61] To bring the two halves of the token back together, to make them "tally," confirmed a person's identity as part of a social relationship. The meaning of a symbol thus implied a presence and an absence; something always had to be brought from elsewhere to make the symbol complete, to round out its significance.

For Freud, the absent element was a past event or unresolved trauma. A symbol was essentially and by definition an effect of some hidden or repressed psychic cause (Needleman 1975:60–83). For many symbolic anthropologists, the same reductionist notion of a symbol obtains, except that the determining reality is social rather than psychic. In both cases, the meaning of a symbol is taken to reside in some predetermined essence rather than in the contexts and consequences of its use. Moreover, the complete understanding of the symbol does not reside in what the people who use it say or do; it depends on an expert's bringing meaning to it or revealing the meaning behind it.

My objection to this way of thinking about symbols is that it departs radically from the original sense of symbol, which implied contemporaneity and equivalence between an object or event and the idea associated with it. It ranks the idea over the event or object, while privileging the expert who deciphers the idea even though he or she may be quite unable to use the object or participate in the "symbolic" event. In short, I object to the notion that one aspect of a symbol is prior to or foundational to the other.

In particular, my argument is against speaking of bodily behavior as symbolizing ideas conceived independently of it. In my view, utterances and body movements betoken the continuity of body-mind, and it is misleading to see the body as simply a representation of a prior idea or implicit cultural pattern. Persons actively body forth the world; their bodies are not passively shaped by or made to fit the world's purposes. As Merleau-Ponty puts it, "Consciousness is in the first place not a matter of 'I think that' but of 'I can'" (1962:137).

NINE

Thinking through the Body

The subject of this chapter is a mode of thinking, speaking, and acting in which personal, social, and natural aspects of Being are made to correspond and coalesce.[1] This analogical mode of understanding is pervasive in all human societies, and it is my intention to use examples from both ethnography and poetry to explore one particular set of metaphorical correspondences which link personal, social, and natural *bodies.*

Let me first establish the domain of inquiry by adducing some specific examples of this kind of metaphorical correlation of person and world.

In the Hippocratic book on the number seven, there is a seven-part map which represents the earth as a human body: the Peloponnesus is its head, the Isthmus its spinal cord, and Ionia its diaphragm, "the navel of the world." The moral and intellectual qualities of the peoples inhabiting these regions were thought to be in some way dependent upon these localizations (Cassirer 1955:92). This image of the universe also finds expression in the Greek Stoic philosophers who argued that the world was an animate and rational being. Such a view led to detailed correspondences being traced out between Man and Nature, and the first-century Roman philosopher and statesman Seneca declared that Nature was like the body of Man, watercourses corresponding to veins, geological substances to flesh, earthquakes to convulsions, and so on.[2] This view, which persists throughout late antiquity and informs the hermetic tradition of Medieval and Renaissance Europe, has a corollary in the notion that correspondences exist between the human body and the state. This organic model of the body politic finds its way through Menenius and Plutarch into Shakespeare's plays[3] and continues to flourish as a root metaphor in positivist sociology (Brockbank 1976:38).

Traditional Chinese philosophy is similarly concerned with these symbolic correlations between the personal body and the body of the world. The conception of a world-organism, a resonant whole in which everything was mutually dependent, pervaded all branches of Chinese art and learning; it was also the basis of divinatory systems such as the *I Ching* (Needham 1978:164). As Philip Rawson notes, "the Chinese regard the inner and outer worlds of experience as having identical systems of physiology," and the aim of Chinese medicine and mysticism is to keep the two systems working in congruence, attuned one to the other (Rawson 1968:231). The close analogy drawn between the body of man and the body of the earth is perfectly illustrated in Chinese watercolor landscapes. Replete with sexual imagery, the paintings depict mountains as metaphors of yang, heaven, the bright, while the valleys with their effluent mists are images of yin, earth, the shadowy. From one to the other flow the fertilizing waters of heaven, in streams and waterfalls (256).

Comparable notions abound in Hindu scriptures. In the Chandogya Upanishad (V, xviii) the universal self is

> the brilliant [sky], its eye is [the sun] which possesses every form, its breath is [the wind] whose nature is to follow various paths, its body is broad [space], its bladder is the wealth [of water], its feet are the earth, its breast is the sacrificial altar, its hair is the sacrificial straw, its heart is the householder's fire, its mind is the southern sacrificial fire and its mouth is the eastern sacrificial fire. (Zaehner 1966).

In Vedic hymns all living things, including the sun, the moon, and the air, are created from parts of the body of purusha, a man offered up in sacrifice by the gods. And social groupings have the same bodily origin: "The Brahmin was his mouth, his arms were made the Rājanya [warrior], his two thighs the Vaiśya [trader and agriculturalist], from his feet the Śūdra [servile class] was born" (Thomas 1923:122). In Tantric philosophy too the macrocosm is thought to be contained within the microcosm of the human body, and the Tantric map of the universe employs sexual imagery to mediate the union of Shiva and Shakti (male and female principles), Self and World. Controlled movement of energy in the field of the body (through ritual intercourse, worship, pilgrimage, and prayer) becomes a means of resonating with and re-cognizing the ultimate ground of all Being (Bharavi 1965). As in all schools of yoga, the body is "the epitome of the universe," and biological and psychological life processes are seen as a microcosm of the world process (Dasgupta and Mukhopadhyay 1962:230).

Rather than multiply examples of this kind of synecdochism,[4] let us now consider in detail two specific cases of thinking through the body, one from poetry and one from ethnography, both of which focus on similar correspondences between particular bodily actions and particular landscape features.

These are the opening verses of Dylan Thomas's poem, "In the White Giant's Thigh" (1950):

> Through throats where many rivers meet, the curlews cry,
> Under the conceiving moon, on the high chalk hill,
> And there this night I walk in the white giant's thigh
> Where barren as boulders women lie longing still.
>
> To labour and love though they lay down long ago.
>
> Through throats where many rivers meet, the women pray,
> Pleading in the waded bay for the seed to flow
> Though the names on their weed grown stones are rained away,
>
> And alone in the night's eternal, curving act

They yearn with tongues of curlews for the unconceived
And immemorial sons of the cudgelling, hacked

Hill.

In these lines the human body is assimilated to the landscape, and the sexual and geomorphological images of the poem have exact parallels in the world views already referred to. The confluence of several rivers is likened to the throat or the cervix, a bay to the womb, a chalk hillside to the thigh, while fecundity and poetic fluency alike are linked to phases of the moon, tides in the bay, and seasonal rhythms of the weather and of animal life. Physiological, meteorological, geographical, and poetical processes are all condensed into unifying images whose ambiguity is expressed semantically by such key phrases as "conceiving moon" and "curving act."[5] As Thomas puts it later in the poem: "All birds and beasts of the linked night uproar and chime. . . ."

Let us now turn from this "most bodily universe" (Miles 1948:448) of Thomas's poem and consider an ethnographic analogue of it.

Two hundred miles north of San Francisco, the Redwood Highway enters a region of evergreen forest, sea fog, and mountain rain and, just before it reaches the Oregon border, crosses the estuary of the Klamath River, the traditional center of the Yurok Indian world. The Yurok conceived of their world as a great disk, divided by the Klamath River and surrounded by the sea. Yet they took no interest in whence the river came or in the ocean beyond the river's mouth. Their cultural and economic life was concentrated on the river itself and on the annual salmon run which supplied enough food for the entire year. The river was both the source of their livelihood and the focus of their cultural existence, and in the Yurok world view, ideas pertaining to the river and its environs, to the salmon and its biology, and to human physiology and anatomy were coalesced. Thus, the periodic affluence of the waterway had "a functional interrelation with the periodicity of vital juices in the body's nutritional, circulatory, and procreative systems," and the main concern of Yurok magical activity was to ensure "that vital channels be kept open and that antagonistic fluids be kept apart" (Erikson 1943:258).

This Yurok theory of correspondence is vividly illustrated by an anecdote told by Erik Erikson, who worked among the Yurok during the 1930s. When he first arrived on the Klamath, Erikson met an elderly female healer who treated somatic disorders and did psychotherapy with children. Erikson discovered that the principles of Yurok therapy were not unlike the principles of psychoanalysis, and he began to "exchange notes" with the old woman. But he noticed that, despite her willingness to talk, she seemed melancholy and withdrawn. It soon become apparent that her gloominess stemmed from an incident some days before when she had stepped out into her vegetable garden and, glancing down the hundred-foot slope to where the Klamath enters the Pacific, had seen a small whale enter the river's mouth, play about a little, and then disappear. Since the Creator (Wohpekumeu, "the widower across the ocean") had decreed that only salmon, sturgeon, and similar fish should cross the freshwater barrier, the episode portended that the world disk was slowly tilting from the horizontal, that saltwater was entering the river, and that a flood was approaching which might destroy all mankind. However, the old woman's anxieties went deeper than this and reflected the very nature of her profession as a healer.

A healer must have superb control over the oral-nutritional canal because he or she has to suck the "pains" from a patient's body and then, having swallowed two or three of these "pains," vomit them up. The "pains" are visualized as slimy, bloody stuff resembling tadpoles, and the healer is able to vomit them up without bringing up food as well. In preparing for such a healing session, a healer must abstain from drinking water because water and the bloody substances extracted from the patient's body are mutually antagonistic. The same reasoning explains why, after eating venison—a "bloody" meat—one should wipe one's hands clean and not wash them in water. The underlying principle is that contrasted fluids such as blood and water, semen and water, or urine and water should never meet in the same aperture or channel. Thus, salmon, which are water-born, must be kept away from the house of a menstruating woman; money, which originates in another "stream," must not be brought into association with sexual intercourse; a person must never urinate in the river; and oral sex is banned because cunnilingus prevents money flowing and interferes with the salmon run in the Klamath. All such inappropriate conjunctions are thought to lead to impoverishment and weakening of both people and the natural environment.

We can now understand how the saltwater whale entering the freshwater stream signals a more general disturbance of the geographical-anatomical environment. Something alien and inedible enters the mouth of the river, which only edible things like salmon and sturgeon should enter. This suggests an inversion of the oral scheme of things in which control of the mouth is fundamental to social and ethical integration. It is because the Yurok healer is preeminently a master of oral-nutritional processes—sucking, vomiting, avoiding the use of "dirty" words —that such an inversion affects the healer more deeply than others and requires his or her skills to redress the ecological imbalance. This may explain why, when the old woman saw the whale in the mouth of the river, her first reaction was to keep quiet about it, possibly hoping that by so controlling her mouth she might induce some change in the external world.

In both Yurok cosmogony and the poem by Dylan Thomas the world of things is merged with the world of Being, and as a consequence "things" like stones, hillsides, and whales assume the status of "signs" whose decipherment mediates understanding and action in the human world. This corporeal and sensible way of "reading" what the world means presupposes a continuity between language, knowledge, and bodily praxis, a view which is characteristic of preliterate societies where knowledge and speech cannot be readily abstracted from contexts of practical activity.[6] It is because, in such societies, knowledge is articulated in skills, formulae, and routines upon which physical livelihood directly depends that it is "logical" for preliterate peoples to emphasize the embodied character of knowledge and speech, as when the Dogon equate word and seed or speak of the ripe millet being "pregnant" (Calame-Griaule 1965:28).[7] Metaphor here is situated. It discloses the functional relations between proper knowledge, productive activity, correct speech, and sociophysical well-being. Metaphor is not merely a figure of speech, drawing an analogy or playing on a resemblance for the sake of verbal effect.

Dylan Thomas also took the view that body, world, and idea must be equated, and he saw the poet's task as one of registering and rendering these equations as succinctly and truthfully as possible.[8] From this view arises the notion that the world of physical things is continuous with the animate and articulate world of Mind. Thus, Thomas speaks of the rain wringing "out its tongues on the faded yard" much as the old Yurok healer speaks of the social repercussions of the whale which enters the mouth of the Klamath River. The Dogon too scrutinize the natural world for auguries that bear upon the human condition so that, for example, should a tree be found which fruits without first flowering, this may be said to be a sign that a woman could well conceive a child without having resumed menstruating after the birth of a previous child. The metaphor is founded on the correspondence which the Dogon say exists between flowering and fruiting in the vegetable world and menstruating and giving birth in the human world (Calame-Griaule 1965:28).

To fathom the significance of these anthropomorphic images we must first emphasize that they are socially constructed and not idiosyncratic. Although one becomes a healer among the Yurok through a mixture of parental persuasion and childhood dreams that suggest a latent ability for shamanistic healing, the system of therapeutic ideas and practices is constituted culturally and not personally. Even when a Yurok healer interprets an illness by applying personal knowledge of the patient's personality and family background, the diagnosis always conforms to social stereotypes such as that adulterous liaisons and malevolent thoughts about other people cause one to become ill. The same interplay of a unique biography and a conventional repertoire of ideas is shown in Thomas's poetry. Thus, although "In the White Giant's Thigh" is highly individual in style and reflects a private preoccupation with links between physical and verbal potency, its elegiac form and sprung rhythm recall traditional techniques, while its fund of images is culled from a common cultural heritage: the fertility-engendering giant cut on a chalk hill, the fertility-giving river flood, the double-understanding of conception, and, toward the close of the poem, the biblical allusions and the reference to Guy Fawkes' fires. Creativity, then, is a license exercised within a socially constituted frame of reference, which is why the Yurok healer's individual gifts are a boon for the whole community and why Thomas's poem can speak to and for us all.

METAPHOR AND EMBODIMENT

I now want to consider the social and psychophysical aspects of metaphor in everyday language. Here one finds abundant evidence that the world of the body and the body of the world have something in common. We readily speak of an angry sky, of stars looking down, of the wind blowing, of a brooding landscape, of social ills, and of economic depression and recovery as if these natural or social phenomena were themselves possessed of consciousness and will. Reciprocally, we speak of the shoulder or brow of a hill and the foot of a mountain, of being petrified with fright, of having roots, of being turned on, switched off, and burnt out, of a person reacting automatically or behaving mechanically as if the body of the earth and the actions of a machine were somehow connected to the world of the human body.

In analyzing these metaphors it is not enough to say that they arise because subjectivity can identify itself only through external objects,[9] or that they arise because "the human body and its functions are the primary frame of reference in naming objects of the perceived world" (Thass-Thienemann 1968:38–39), or that anthropomorphic metaphors simply reflect the fact that, ontogenetically, the first "language" of life is gestural, postural, and bodily (Diamond 1959; ThassThienemann 1968:38–39). For to emphasize the psychophysical or social aspects of metaphor construction and use is unhelpful as long as it implies a dualistic conception of human behavior and a linear form of reasoning which, in the case of metaphor, makes one aspect of the trope prior or primary. Such a lopsided view is immediately suggested whenever metaphor is defined as a way of saying something "in terms of" or "by way of" something else.[10] My argument is that metaphor must be apprehended nondualistically and that the idea or sensation and its bodily complements (social, mechanical, physiological, geographical) betoken, not an arbitrary or rhetorical synthesis of two terms—subject and object,[11] tenor and vehicle—which can be defined more realistically apart from each other, but a true interdependency of mind and body, Self and World. In my view, metaphor reveals unities; it is not a figurative way of denying dualities. Metaphor reveals, not the "thisness of a that" but rather that "this is that." Thus, in the famous Upanishadic parable of the fig tree, the indivisibility of the world is revealed through a seed which, when taken from the fig and then further divided, appears to be nothing at all, yet from this very essence the tree grows. The teacher tells the adept: "This finest essence,—the whole universe has it as its Self: That is the Real: That is the Self: That you are Śvetaketu!" (Chandogya Upanishad VI, xii).

R. H. Blythe expresses a poet's understanding of metaphor when he writes of it as "a consummation of identity," noting that in poetry "we often say more than we mean" and "speak more truly than we know" because we disclose the identity of that which the intellect separates (1942:154, 166). Haiku, Blythe says, are the purest expression of metaphor because they are this "thou art it" (tat tvam asi). "When a man becomes a bamboo grove swaying in the windy rain, a cicada crying itself and its life away, then he is 'it'" (1947:4–5).

If this identity of Self and World which metaphor discloses is real, then our awareness of it is decidedly impermanent and occasional, and it is necessary to consider in some detail the variability of metaphorical value.

QUIESCENT AND ACTIVE METAPHOR

The etymology of even the most abstract words often refers us to the body. Our word time is from the Latin tempus, originally denoting a "stretch," and cognate with *tempora*, "temples of the head"—perhaps because the skin stretches and corrugates here as one grows older.[12] The Chinese character meaning duration, *chiu*, was explained by the Han lexicographers as derived from the character *jen*, man; *chiu* was a man stretching his legs and walking "a stretch," just as a roof stretches across a space and time stretches from one event to another (Needham 1965:1). A third example, which I shall elaborate upon later in this chapter, is the verb *to know* which in all Indo-European languages is cognate with words meaning "king," "kin," "kind," "generation," "knee," and "can." Indeed, the embodied intentionality of human Being seems to be inextricably tied up with our views about the world, and "I think" (*cogito*) is inseparable from "I can" (*practico*). As Merleau-Ponty puts it:

> Our body, to the extent that it moves itself about, that is, to the extent that it is inseparable from a view of the world and is that view itself brought into existence, is the condition of possibility, not only of the geometrical synthesis, but of all expressive operations and all acquired views which constitute the cultural world. (1962:388)

Thus, the physical ability to move out into the world is at the same time an expression of growing up socially and of being capable of supporting others, which may be why the knees and parts of the leg are, in many societies, metaphors for kinship categories.[13] And it is because human consciousness is intentional and embodied that such metaphors readily rediscover themselves in our thought, as when Dylan Thomas writes of walking in the white giant's thigh where barren women pray to be able to conceive, and thus hits upon an old Indo-European connection between the thigh, conception, and kinship.[14]

But in such examples, references to the body are implicit and usually below the threshold of our awareness. In everyday life, when we say a nuisance is a "pain in the neck," a "headache," or a "handful" or that someone is "stiff-necked" or "looks down on us," we are seldom mindful of the *actual* links between the mental or emotional attitude signified and the bodily praxis which does the signifying. If a nuisance actually does give us a headache or sore neck we are still unlikely to regard the relationship between the verbal form and the actual event as anything other than arbitrary. This is, I believe, the case in both literate and nonliterate societies. For instance, when in English we speak of the mouth of a river it is usually without any thought or visualization of a human mouth. Among the Kuranko of Sierra Leone the same suspension of disbelief applies in everyday speech. One enters a house through its "mouth" (i.e., door) or "cuts one's mouth off" from one's natal home (when building a house of one's own) or "cuts one's mouth off from another person" (when one takes umbrage) without *necessarily* being aware of the psychophysical side of the metaphors, e.g., that leaving home *is* like "cutting one's mouth off the breast" at weaning because, thereafter, one can no longer depend on the family granary for one's food.[15] In fact, we would consider it very odd if anyone consciously required or sought a *real* connection between word and thing as a precondition of meaningful speech, though this is often one of the defining characteristics of schizophrenic thought and is found occasionally in nonpathological cases as well. A. R. Luria, the Russian neuropsychologist, describes such a case, a mnemonist for whom words immediately conjured up a wealth of synesthetic associations which blurred the boundary between objects and sensations, imagination and reality, perception and feeling. The colors, tastes, textures, and images that surrounded every word the mnemonist read or heard would become obstacles to logical and abstract reasoning, for he could dismiss nothing from his mind and could not avoid the sensations and reveries which continually fused words and things. Genuinely abstract ideas, such as infinity, eternity, and nothingness, frightened him, because they summoned up no concrete images. As he put it, "I can only understand what I can visualize" (Luria 1969:130). Socially, the mnemonist appeared to be slow-witted and dull simply because he could not easily disconnect the words which mediate social relationships from the inward sensations and associations with which the words were imbued.

Quotidian life goes on without any special significance being attached to the anthropomorphic figures which abound in common speech. On certain occasions, however, these mundane metaphors are activated and realized in quite extraordinary ways. Thus, when Thomas wrote his poems, his experience was not unlike that of the mnemonist: "When I experience anything, I experience it as a thing and a word at the same time, both equally amazing" (cited by Reid 1954:20).

Again, among the Ojibwa there is an *implicit* category distinction in the language between animate and inanimate. Stones are grammatically animate and Ojibwa sometimes speak to stones as if they were persons, but this does not mean that the Ojibwa are animists "in the sense that they dogmatically attribute living souls to animate objects such as stones"; rather, they recognize "potentialities for animation in certain classes of objects under certain circumstances. The Ojibwa do not perceive stones, in general, as animate, any more than we do" (Hallowell 1958:65).

If we now reconsider the Yurok metaphors described earlier we can be more specific about the circumstances in which the activation of anthropomorphic metaphor occurs. According to Erik Erikson, the geographical-anatomical imagery of the Yurok only really comes into force in situations of crisis: "wherever mysterious food sources beyond the Yurok's territory, technology, and causal comprehension need to be influenced, or whenever vague human impulses and fears need to be alleviated" (1943:258). In crisis, the Yurok apply the oral model of childhood conditioning in an attempt to grasp and master "geographic space by projecting nearest environment, namely body feelings, onto it" (276). In other words, metaphors which are ordinarily quiescent (yet are the verbal correlatives of actual bodily dispositions) are activated on such critical occasions to mediate changes in people's bodies and experience and to alter their relationships with one another and the world.[16] An elementary example of this activation of metaphor is the agonistic imagery in everyday English (arguments get attacked, demolished, shot down, lost or won, and so forth), which may become *realized* in actual physical fighting when people lose their tempers in an argument (Lakoff and Johnson 1980:4).

Crisis is also the key to understanding the way poetry activates metaphors which are ordinarily quiescent. Although, in the case of poetry, the crisis is often self-induced rather than adventitious, the transformation which realizes connections between personal, social, and natural bodies requires as its precondition a disruption of normal psychophysical and social patterns.[17] But, however it is induced, the movement which carries a poet into this new awareness, imbuing words with more than ordinary power, is of the very nature of metaphor (literally, "to exchange and move"). It is in this sense that Ezra Pound speaks of great literature as "simply language charged with meaning to the utmost possible degree" (1954:23) and Wallace Stevens writes in *Notes toward a Supreme Fiction:*

> The poem refreshes life so that we share,
> For a moment, the first idea. . . .

> The poem, through candor, brings back a power again
> That gives a candid kind to everything.

Now, some would argue that these applications of anthropomorphic metaphor are merely rhetorical or magical; beautiful, but based on illusory attributions of will and consciousness to the external, nonhuman world. At most, it might be said, these metaphors are instances of some mythopoeic propensity of the primitive or unconscious mind, inferior in all but aesthetic properties to the logical and abstract reasoning of a civilized person.[18] It may be admitted that anthropomorphic thinking is often prompted by crisis, when the logical or social structure of the world breaks down, but such recourse to metaphor is usually dismissed as neurotic, regressive, or downright erroneous.[19]

I want to argue a different view: that metaphor is a part of all thought, that it is a correlate of patterns of bodily action and interaction, that the use of metaphor in poetry and ritual is efficacious in a very real sense, and that the elaborate analogies drawn between personal, social, and natural bodies cannot be written off as mere figures of speech or regarded as more definitive of preliterate than of literate thought.

METAPHOR, BODY USE, AND *HABITUS*

Let us first consider the contention that metaphor is a verbal correlate of patterns of body use and interaction. Here I will turn from metaphors of waterways and discuss pathways and movement along paths. My examples are drawn from African ethnography, but metaphors of pathways are well-nigh universal, and later I will refer to examples from English poetry.[20]

The Kuranko use the word *kile* ("path," "road") as a metaphor for social relationship. For instance, the adage *nyendan bin to kile a wa ta an segi* describes the way a particular species of grass (used for thatching) bends one way as you go along a path through it and then bends back the other way as you return along the path. This movement to and fro of grass along a pathway is used as a metaphor for the movement of people, goods, and services within a community; it is a metaphor for reciprocity. Thus, in Kuranko one often explains the reason for giving a gift, especially to an in-law, with the phrase *kile ka na faga,* "so that the path does not die." If relations between affines or neighbors are strained, however, it is often said that "the path is not good between them" (*kile nyuma san tema*), and if a person disappoints a friend then people may comment *a ma kile nyuma tama a bo ma* ("he did not walk on the good path with his friend").[21]

As soon as one enters a Kuranko village one realizes how natural this metaphor is, because a village comprises a number of open spaces called *luiye* around which are clustered circular thatched houses, and these open spaces are interconnected by a labyrinth of narrow lanes and dusty paths. But the metaphor is not just descriptive. The physical movement of people within the community is largely determined by social, economic, and moral imperatives, such as visiting and greeting, sharing food, cooperating in food production and in festivals, and giving gifts or services according to commitments of in-lawship, neighborliness, or kinship. Community, say the Kuranko, is a matter of "pulling well together" or of "moving together." In these ways a *habitus* is produced: a configuration of structures such as houses, courtyards, gardens, lanes, and cooking yards which impose a habitual pattern on the movement of people.[22] Thus, the Kuranko house is divided into male and female domains[23] which impose a pattern of sexual segregation on those who live in it. This sexual segregation can always be seen to ramify beyond the house, as a result of a chain of linked ideas which refer simultaneously to the body, to the house, to the conception of children, and to political and economic practices. Men are associated with the front and forecourt of the house, provide the seed from which a child grows, sow rice and harvest grain, and control jural and political life; women are associated with the back of the house, provide the container (womb) in which a fetus grows, tend rice and cook grain, and are politically and jurally marginal.[24] Everyday tasks and objects reinforce these distinctions, so that the way women lift and let fall a pestle when pounding grain in a mortar, the sway of the body needed in winnowing rice, and the suppleness required in tending a hearth or bending to an infant all become habitual dispositions, defining for the Kuranko a mode of comportment which is typically "feminine." On the other hand, the arduous work of the men in felling trees or hoeing steep hillsides fosters muscular strength and rigidity which, in turn, become metaphors for the "masculine" disposition and justifications for male politicojural control. By contrast, the supple and fluent movements of women as they bend to their daily tasks give rise to metaphors which make women out to be capricious and unreliable. In all these instances, therefore, patterns of body use are correlated with metaphors which in effect mediate between the world of material objects and the world of ideas or sentiments. But there is always a very real connection between the physical disposition of objects in the material environment and the social or temperamental disposition of people. The metaphor of paths both recognizes these connections between material, social, bodily, conceptual, and temperamental horizons *and* fuses these horizons into a single image.

But how exactly does the imagery of pathways relate to the human body? In many African societies the metaphor of pathways applies not only to social relationships but also to individual anatomy and physiology. Among the Songhay of Mali, for instance, movements of "blood," "heat," and "breath" take place along pathways in the body (*fondo*, "pathway," "road"). When these movements of blood, heat, or breath flow unimpeded in the right direction a person is healthy, but if the flow is reversed or obstructed illness occurs. Vital organs such as the heart, liver, lungs, and stomach are likened to crossroads where blood or heat is concentrated and then diffused. Illness signifies that blood, heat, or breath has become blocked, withdrawn, or forced to flow backward (Bisilliat 1976:555–78).

This view of health and disease is based on a kind of reciprocal anthropomorphism whereby extrapolations are made from the social and material *habitus* in order to describe and explain individual psychophysiology. But the analogies are more than descriptive, because there are in fact vital links between the well-being of individuals and the quality of social relationships. Patterns of economic cooperation and exchange within an African village *are* the material bases of individual life, as well as symbols of community.[25]

The Songhai view is characteristic of the African notion that the fate of the individual is linked to the quality of his or her social relationships, and beyond this to economic and political realities. Like the riverine metaphors of the Yurok, African metaphors of pathways coalesce social, economic, political, and anatomical elements into a single image which in effect expresses the essential interdependence of those elements. Such metaphors are thus the verbal correlates of patterns of social interaction and bodily disposition within the *habitus*. And this may explain why metaphors of self refer universally to such immediate elements of the *habitus* as house, animals, plants, and in modern societies, machines.[26]

It is largely because metaphors refer simultaneously to the self and the socioeconomic *habitus* that they are instrumental in mediating between ideology and economic infrastructure. Metaphor is the bridge we use when teaching children the skills upon which economic production depends and, reflexively, when we try to think our way out of an impasse and find a way of moving back into the world of social activity.[27] Let us explore some examples of metaphor as a mode of praxis.

As we have already seen, the Songhai regard the circulation of people, goods, and services along paths in the village as vitally connected to the circulation of blood, heat, and breath in the individual body. The metaphor of pathways mediates this link between socioeconomic practices and ideas about health and disease. Among the Kuranko, this link between the social and the psychophysical is emphasized in a slightly different way. When there is a breakdown or rupture (to use our metaphors) in social relationships, the Kuranko often speak of the paths between people being obstructed or darkened. Diviners may say that "the gates are closed." A gift can "open" the path, just as a sacrifice to the ancestors "clears" or "purifies" the path between members of a lineage and their forebears. And if a person confesses a grudge or ill will toward a neighbor, it is thought that the confession makes good the path again.

The metaphor of walking along paths is also central in many Kuranko oral narratives. Thus, a key metaphor for impeded social communication is lameness, and a reluctance or difficulty in walking is associated with two kinds of social situation: when an eldest son is loathe to grow up and succeed to his father's position and when a girl is loathe to marry and bear children. While the first failure leads to an interrupted succession which threatens the continuity of a lineage, the second implies a breakdown in the system of marriage-exchanges on which are built the alliances among different clans in the village.[28] If we recall the etymological link which exists in Indo-European languages between *knee, knowledge,* and *generation* we gain an insight into the significance of the metaphor of lameness. An artificial prolonging of childhood involves in any society a sort of self-immobilization in which a person eschews knowledge of adulthood and refuses to generate either social relationships or children. Limping, like halting speech, is thus an expression of psychophysical ambivalence in which a deeply regressive urge inhibits the social imperative of growing up and "standing on one's own feet." In Kuranko narratives, the metaphor of lameness is a way of focusing attention on this social imperative, yet it refers to a mode of behavior in the real world—walking—which is one of the bases of all social praxis. It is not just linguistic convention that leads us to employ metaphors of walking and of paths but an inherent relation between these metaphors and patterns of practical activity. This is nicely shown by the Kabyle (Algeria) notion of the "measured pace" (neither lagging like a sluggard nor running ahead like a dancer) as an expression of a person's adjustment to the collective rhythms of work "which assign each act its particular moment in the space of the day, the year, or human life" (Bourdieu 1977:162).

It is the inseparability of conceptual and bodily activity which explains why metaphors often mediate the forms of human illness. Thus, a not untypical "conversion reaction" among neurotics who embody the contradictions of their familial environment is paralysis or pain in the legs and acute difficulty in walking.[29] Unconscious compliance in cultural metaphors about illness undoubtedly means that disease and theory of disease arise out of the same *habitus.*[30] And insofar as cognitive and physical aspects of our being-in-the-world are inseparable, it is impossible to accept the view that "illness is *not* a metaphor, and that the most truthful way of regarding illness—and the healthiest way of being ill—is one most purified of, most resistant to, metaphoric thinking."[31]

If metaphor mediates illness, it can also mediate cure. But before turning to consider the therapeutic value of metaphor we should note that metaphors mediate relationships between conceptual and physical domains of the *habitus* in a dialectical manner. For instance, Songhay metaphors of anatomical paths and Yurok metaphors of anatomical streams (like our "canals" and "ducts") emerge from a kind of reciprocal anthropomorphism whereby an element in the shared material *habitus* is internalized by individuals and becomes thereby a part of a collective ideology of self, a "common knowledge." But this internalization is an *active* appropriation of the *habitus,* not a passive or automatic process in which the social body, in some mysterious way, gets mirrored or projected on the static individual body where it serves as a kind of linguistic analogue of social structure. Moreover, this active realization of correlations between self and *habitus* presupposes an externalization which has already occurred, in which the self through bodily movement in concrete situations has discovered for itself an identity in relation to the immediate environment of cultural and natural objects: kinsmen, houses, animals, rivers, hills, and plants (both vegetable and industrial).[32] This extrapolation outward, in which more and more distance is tolerated between the body and the object

("knee" versus "knowledge") is the basis of abstraction, and when the world of objects is finally reassimilated through the process of reciprocal anthropomorphism
the person finds himself determined, not by subjective attitudes but by socially constructed ideas. In this dialectical movement, metaphors are crucial mediators or
synthesizers because they refer to the body on the one hand and to social and natural environments on the other. It is in this synthetic function that their power
as instruments of social learning lies. They can "make over" the person to the social world and reciprocally "imprint" the social world upon the person's body.
Thus, metaphors of cultivation, ripening, and harvest are used by the Kuranko
when initiating boys into manhood. Psychophysical maturity is thereby linked to
the growth of the rice, *but* the growth of rice depends reciprocally on a mature and
cooperative attitude among men. As the Kuranko put it, they must "move well
together."

METAPHORICAL INSTRUMENTALITY
AND THERAPY

Earlier in this chapter I drew a distinction between quiescent and active metaphor
and pointed out that the instrumental possibilities of metaphor are usually realized
in a crisis. It is now necessary to expand and illustrate this view that metaphors
are means of doing things and not merely ways of saying things.[33]

For the sake of argument let us define a crisis as any situation in which there
occurs an unbearable conflict between two or more ideas ("being in two minds"),
between two or more practical possibilities ("being pulled or tugged in two directions"), or between conceptual and practical alternatives ("wanting or knowing
what to do but not how to do it"). In all these "double-bind" situations an impasse
is reached which may be manifest mentally or verbally as a "dilemma" or "contradiction" or physically and energetically as a "bind," "knot," "spasm," "tearing,"
or "splitting." In short, the unity of being-in-the-world is broken.

Since metaphors coalesce social, personal, and natural aspects of Being, as well
as unifying ideas and practices, it is only to be expected that metaphors should
often be called upon in resolving these double binds and in making people whole
again. It is because anthropomorphic metaphors unite these various domains in
the one image that they facilitate movement from one domain to another. In particular, a movement is facilitated from the domain where the double bind is manifest
and where, therefore, anxiety is most intense to another domain which is relatively
free from anxiety and accordingly still open to control and manipulation. Metaphor
thus mediates a transference from the area of greatest stress to a neutral area which
is held to correspond with it.[34] In this process, metaphors which are usually quiescent and taken for granted are activated and given literal value.

For example, Aristotle recommended walking or running as a way of dealing
with mental depression. The key metaphor here makes fluency of body movement
analogous to fluency in thought: activating the body will alleviate the tendency
toward immobilization and depression in the mind. Among the Kuranko, diviners
are consulted when a person falls ill. By addressing river pebbles (neutral objects)

lain out on a mat, the diviner is able to "see" the cause of the illness. Bodily sickness is often attributed to a social event, such as a wife's infidelity, a grievance nursed toward a neighbor, or a failure to make sacrifices to one's ancestors. Appropriate social actions—a wife's confession, an apology to one's neighbor, a sacrifice to one's ancestors—have a correspondingly beneficial effect on the body and mind of the ailing individual. And a Yurok shaman responds to a geographical crisis, such as a whale entering the mouth of a salmon river, by asserting control over a corresponding zone of his or her anatomy: the oral-nutritional canal.

In the first case the domain of mind is manipulated by bodily activity; in the second case the domain of body-mind is manipulated by social activity; in the third case the domain of geography is manipulated by bodily activity. At first sight the choice of neutral domain seems to be arbitrary, and in most societies there is a certain amount of opportunism and experimentation in discovering a domain where action proves effective in dealing with the domain where the stress is manifest. Among the Kuranko, for example, the failure of an herbal remedy may lead a sick person to consult a diviner, who may prescribe a form of social therapy (gift-giving or sacrifice or confession); if this therapy fails, the person may well end up consulting a Western-trained doctor.[35] The same sort of medical pluralism occurs in modern societies when a failure of psychoanalysis (a talking cure) leads a person to try group therapy (a social cure) or some kind of physiotherapy (bioenergetics, hatha yoga, or gardening). In all these cases, however, it is not just a matter of discovering a neutral domain where action is possible but of discovering a neutral domain which is most *immediately* connected to the domain where stress is manifest according to an inherent patterning of causes involving *specific* elements of each domain of Being.[36] For example, in the case of hay fever ("caused" by hypersensitivity of the mucous membranes to foreign proteins such as pollen grains), the "original" cause is often found to be *social* anxiety connected with infantile sexual curiosity which was repressed by a sexually inhibited mother, rather than some *natural* factor such as genetic proneness or amount of pollen in the atmosphere (Black 1969:101). Nevertheless, these genetic and environmental factors remain causal, though distantly, and in seeking to alleviate the physical symptoms of hay fever a sufferer may well find that the proximate and therapeutically effective "cause" lies in his dealing with the guilt that led him into the habit of exploring the world by smell instead of touch, yet in such an ambivalent way as to lead to the self-punitive and self-immobilizing hay fever syndrome.

One of the drawbacks of much modern medicine is its reluctance to range over *all* the domains of Being—personal, social, natural—in diagnostic and therapeutic work. A kind of absolutism prevails in which specific symptoms are assigned determinate causes,[37] and doctors pour scorn on the opportunistic character of "alternative" or "primitive" medicine. Such doctrinal inflexibility undoubtedly reflects the fact that metaphor is no longer a key instrumentality in modern medical practice.[38] Yet, as we have seen, it is by facilitating movement within the total field of Being that metaphor is a crucial means of locating areas where we can act upon those areas where we have lost the power to act. Insofar as modern medicine makes the doctor the sole actor in diagnostic and therapeutic practice, the devalorization of metaphor may also be seen as a way of taking away from the patient the means of participating in his or her own diagnosis and treatment. Unlike specialist jargons, metaphors are part of a common fund, a common knowledge. And because this fund is equally accessible to both doctors and patients it tends to democratize medicine and prevent the establishment of social divisions based on different degrees of know-how.

It would be a mistake to disparage metaphorical instrumentality as a primitive mode of thought, a magical or primary-process activity. In my view, differences in modes of thought across cultures are idiomatic rather than formal, and if we take care to relate thought to context of use when we make cross-cultural comparisons this becomes quite obvious. If crisis be considered one such context, we find that metaphorical instrumentality is just as typical of modern societies as pre-industrial ones. For instance, Erik Erikson observes that the phenomenon of transference is as clearly understood and utilized by Yurok healers as by modern psychotherapists.[39] In both cases a shift is effected from a domain of anxiety to a comparatively neutral domain (from focus on parent to focus on parent-surrogate, i.e., therapist), the second domain, however, corresponding to the first. Again, recourse to jargon and to "experience-distant" concepts in the human sciences indicates how anxieties which arise in the course of research are alleviated through a shift to a neutral zone of abstract language or of number, which, nevertheless, is held to correspond to the domain of human events. And modern consumer societies afford us insight into how the manipulation of "things" such as cars, clothes, cosmetics, foodstuffs, and houses assists a displacement of affect away from the domain of social relationships, where anxiety and helplessness so commonly prevail.

As for the world of scientific theory, one has only to consider the mechanistic imagery of eighteenth-century philosophy (Turbayne 1962), the arboreal metaphor in nineteenth-century paleography, the topographical and archaeological imagery in psychoanalysis and in structuralism, the organic analogies in functionalist sociology (Leach 1961:6), and the metaphors of the mirror, the fountain, and the lamp in literary theory (Abrams 1958) to agree with Jorge Luis Borges that the history of ideas may be nothing more than the history of a handful of metaphors. Furthermore, if, as Stephen Pepper argues,[40] world theories are so often generated by drawing analogies from the immediate sensible world, might not adequacy in explanation be seen as a matter of choosing the right metaphor rather than a question of epistemological correctness? For, by revealing actual correspondences between the world of ideas and the world of things, a well-chosen metaphor may reveal an underlying link which makes *common* sense and so avoids the fallacy of misplaced concreteness. An excellent example of this kind of theory-building is given by Gregory Bateson, who, in trying to visualize and understand processes of social control among the Iatmul of Papua New Guinea, compared Western and Iatmul societies in terms of a contrast between radically symmetrical animals (such as jellyfish and sea anemones) and animals with transverse segmentation (such as earthworms, lobsters, and people) (Bateson 1973:50–51). The biological analogy got Bateson's thought moving in a new direction and revealed possible connections between the form of social and natural worlds.

IMMOBILIZED METAPHOR

In what circumstances can anthropomorphic metaphors be said to be ill chosen, irrational, or pathological? My argument has been that metaphorical instrumentality is not magical or irrational per se; on the contrary, it can be a way of healing, of making whole. But when metaphor becomes an end in itself and loses its instrumental value as a means of moving us among various domains of Being and of integrating these domains, then it can become pathological. In these circumstances, metaphor becomes fetishized; a person gets stuck on the metaphorical vehicle itself and, as in schizophrenia, plays endlessly with the associational possibilities of language but always in a narrowly denotative and idiosyncratic way as though words *were* things. As Silvano Arieti notes, the schizophrenic takes metaphors literally.[41] Metaphor thereby loses its value as a means of integrating many domains and, as such, ceases to be metaphor.

But contrary to the view of Arieti and others who speak of "primitive" peoples and schizophrenics alike as trapped in a world of concrete thinking, confounding words and things,[42] I hold that no a priori distinction between "them" and "us" is tenable on these grounds. Using metaphors as if they were real, as in the case of Yurok healers or in Dylan Thomas's poem, is a recognition of cosmic wholeness, not a sign that the person is stuck in one domain of the world, possessed by it and unable to move. Unlike the holistic and outgoing character of metaphorical thought, pathological thought is aholistic and autistic.[43] Indeed, if we define madness in terms of a kind of existential immobility, in which a person can no longer move out into the world and where intelligibility has no real connection with sensibility and sociability, then the following fragment from the autobiography of a schizophrenic girl could well describe much scientific writing and philosophy wherein metaphor is eschewed on the grounds that it is too concrete, too elaborate, or confuses that which should be distinguished.[44]

> This was it; this was madness, the Enlightenment was the perception of Unreality.[45] Madness was finding oneself permanently in an all-embracing unreality. I called it the "Land of Light" because of the brilliant illumination, dazzling, astral, cold, and the state of extreme tension in which everything was, including myself. . . .
> In the endless silence and the strained immobility, I had the impression that some dreadful thing about to occur would break the quiet, something horrible, overwhelming. I waited, holding my breath, suffused with inquietude; but nothing happened. The immobility became more immobile, the silence more silent, things and people, their gestures and their noises, more artificial, detached one from the other, unreal, without life. (Sechehaye 1951:24, 25)

POETRY AS THERAPY

It is now possible to return to the role of anthropomorphic metaphor in poetry and consider it in the light of what I have argued so far mainly by way of ethnographic examples.

In Thomas's "In the White Giant's Thigh," two transformations take place.

The first is an objectification whereby a shift is effected from the domain of individual anatomy to the comparatively neutral domain of landscape: the "waded bay" at the mouth of the river Towy and a cemetery on the side of a chalk hill. The second transformation, a corollary of the first, is a scale reduction in which the individual body and the body of the earth are made to assume the same proportions. These transformations make the world of subjectivity thinkable and graspable. Landscape supplies an "objective correlative" of personal and social concerns, the natural world being amenable because it appears to be on the same scale as the human world and viable because it is in reality linked to events in the poet's life. In this way, a poem made with well-chosen metaphors can move us toward a recognition of a unity which for a time had seemed lost.

A remarkable instance of this therapeutic power of poetry is recorded by John Stuart Mill in his *Autobiography*. When he was fifteen, Mill read Bentham for the first time and at once decided to devote his life to reforming the world. But five years later, in the autumn of 1826, he began to suffer serious misgivings about this project, and he put a question to himself, the answer to which plunged him into a deep crisis:

> "Suppose that all your objects in life were realized; that all the changes in institutions and opinions which you are looking forward to, could be completely effected at this very instant: would this be a great joy and happiness to you?" And an irrepressible self-consciousness distinctly answered, "No!" At this my heart sank within me: the whole foundation on which my life was constructed fell down. All my happiness was to have been found in the continual pursuit of this end. The end had ceased to charm, and how could there ever again be any interest in the means? I seemed to have nothing left to live for. (Mill 1981:139)

Mill's crisis was in part a realization that his education under his father's hand had given him the means of attaining happiness, yet these means were not in themselves strong enough to "resist the dissolving influence of analysis" and actually make him happy (145).[46]

> For I now saw, or thought I saw, what I had already before received with incredulity— that the habit of analysis has a tendency to wear away the feelings: as indeed it has when no other mental habit is cultivated, and the analysing spirit remains without its natural complements and correctives. (141)

He saw that his intellectual upbringing had made "precocious and premature analysis the inveterate habit of [his] mind," "undermining" and "weakening," as he put it, a feeling for nature and for the "pleasure of sympathy with human beings."

This profound disconnectedness of personal, social, and natural aspects of his Being immobilized him for more than two years, and he describes himself as living in a state of "dry, heavy dejection," performing his intellectual tasks "mechanically." But gradually his malady lifted, first through a resolve not to make happiness a direct goal or necessary precondition of his existence, and second through cultivating what he calls "passive susceptibilities." In this endeavor, Wordsworth's poetry, which he first read in the autumn of 1828, was a revelation, reawakening

a lost love of "rural objects and natural scenery" and helping him recover that disposition of mind which Keats called "negative capability." He describes Wordsworth's poems as "a medicine":

> They seemed to be the very culture of the feelings, which I was in quest of. . . . I
> needed to be made to feel that there was real, permanent happiness in tranquil contem-
> plation. Wordsworth taught me this, not only without turning away from, but with
> a greatly increased interest in, the common feelings and common destiny of human
> beings. (151, 153)

Through the poetry of Wordsworth, Mill recovered his wholeness of Being: the
natural world of natural contemplation was the way he found his way back into
social and personal completeness.

    Almost a hundred years later, Robert Graves, traumatized mentally and physi-
cally by his experiences in World War I, discovered the same healing powers of
poetry and came to regard poetry as "a form of psychotherapy," a mode of homeopathic healing (Stade 1967:12). In his critical essays, Graves emphasizes the bodily
aspect of metaphor, stressing how poetic rhythms can induce trance and so move
a poet into those unconscious areas of Being where healing occurs of itself. It is
interesting in this respect that Graves is one of the few writers on prosody who
relate poetic meter to human activity and movement within the *habitus*. He plays
up the practical role of the Nordic *scop* in both shaping charms for the protection
of king and realm and performing such mundane tasks as "persuading a ship's crew
to pull rhythmically and uncomplainingly on their oars against the rough waves
of the North Sea, by singing them ballads in time to the beat" (Graves 1955:72).
Thus, the slap of oars, the rattle of rowlocks, the ring of hammers on an anvil
in a forge, the beat of feet around altar or tomb, or the ploughman turning at the
end of each furrow (from *versus* to verse) all indicate the practical environment
of speech, sound, and movement in which poetry originated. Because he gives such
accent to the pragmatic and therapeutic power of poetry, it is not surprising that
Graves's early poems frequently refer to walking, the relaxed momentum of which
is, as we have already seen, often made a metaphor for social mobility and adequacy.[47]

    In forging links between personal, social, and natural worlds and in reforging
these links when we break them, poetry fosters wholeness of Being. But poetic metaphor also accomplishes this act through a scale reduction in which social, natural,
and personal worlds correspond *evenly*, so allowing us to feel equal to the wider
world. In this sense, poetry may be likened to the art of miniature painting. Here,
as Lévi-Strauss observes, "the intrinsic value of a small-scale model is that it compensates for the renunciation of sensible dimensions by the acquisition of intelligible dimensions" (1966a:24). Reduction in scale and objectification extend our
power over a homologue of a thing, so allowing it to be grasped, assessed, and apprehended at a glance. "A child's doll is no longer an enemy, a rival or even an
interlocutor. In it and through it a person is a made into a subject" (23).

    For many Westerners, the romantic appeal of traditional societies and Eastern
religions is possibly the scale compatibility that appears to obtain in them between
the individual and the cosmos. In an ashram or a village, a person can, it is sup-

posed, comprehend the universe as a whole, orienting himself within it by extrapolating from self to world, near to far. In the modern world, however, such easy synecdochism breaks down. As Devereux points out, there ceases to be any overall pattern one can grasp. Complexity, diversity, and change disorient the individual, and extrapolation from his own back yard to the wider world does not work. The whole symptomatology of schizophrenia, Devereux argues, is an attempt to overcome this scale incompatibility between the individual and the world, to "neutralize the dysphoria resulting from disorientation" by withdrawing into make-believe backyards (Devereux 1980:202–3). The same search for scale compatibility may explain why increasing numbers of Kuranko people have embraced Islam during the past decade (Jackson 1986). Baffled by sociopolitical changes that impinge upon their lives, yet unable to grasp or decide these changes, Kuranko villagers experiment with the seemingly straightforward practices of Islam as a way of magically regaining a sense of control—for Islam, like modernity, belongs to the world beyond their horizons, yet, in its elementary demands, lies well within their grasp.

Synecdochism has both a temporal and a spatial dimension. To make "here" seem continuous with "there" has similar existential implications to collapsing the present into the past through an abolition of duration, of history (Eliade 1959:35). Contriving to make the present continuous with the ancestral past, like making the individual appear to be continuous with the cosmos, brings the wider world within a person's grasp *in the here and now.* In effect, remote and thus "abstract" realms like the past are concretized. Tallensi ancestors become embodied in shrines of clay or stick; in Australia, Aboriginal dreaming-tracks and song-lines are visible, tangible forms in the contemporary landscape—a true geomythology; in Northern Luzon, the Illongot map mythological events onto the landscape rather than the calendar (Rosaldo 1980:48); among the Nuer, "the tree under which mankind came into being was still standing . . . a few years ago" (Evans-Pritchard 1940:108); and among French alpine peasants, anecdotes about the past often have the force of events recently experienced: "Once I was walking in the mountains with a friend of seventy," John Berger relates. "As we walked along the foot of a high cliff, he told me how a young girl had fallen to her death there, whilst haymaking on the *alpage* above." "Was that before the war?" I asked. "In 1833," he said (Berger 1979:8).

This kind of immediatization and concretization of space-time brings the world back home. Moreover, working with a *common* fund of accessible images—trees, paths, houses, the human body—and making personal, social, and natural domains coextensive, a seamless, unified whole, places self and world on the same scale. Not only does this make the universe coherent and comprehensible; it enables people to act upon themselves in the conviction that such action will have repercussions in social and even extrasocial realms. Conversely, this view enables people to manipulate external objects and words—as in divinatory, healing, and cursing rites—in the conviction that such actions will have repercussions on themselves or on others. Thus mastery of the external world is linked reciprocally to mastery of self, and people act as if the universe were extensions of themselves and they of it.

TEN

The Migration of a Name

Alexander in Africa

In 1970 my wife and I were living in Kabala, a small town in northern Sierra Leone. We had come to live there partly because of its intriguing name, and even though Kabala proved to have no etymological connection with the Hebrew *qabbalah* and its esoteric traditions of cosmic union and interpretation (it means, simply, "Kabba's place") its fascination for us was not diminished. Kabala had been a watering-place on one of the great caravan routes from Upper Guinea to the Atlantic Coast. During the colonial epoch it became an administrative headquarters for the Northern Province, and today it is a crossroads where people from five ethnic groups and three religious traditions mix, market, and sometimes intermarry.

Installed in our house on the outskirts of Kabala we would sit out on the veranda in the evening and watch the sun melt into the shoulder of the huge granite inselberg that overshadowed the town, a labyrinth of dirt lanes, a vista of battered, rusty iron roofs, mango and cotton trees, half lost in a haze of dust and smoke. At dusk we would hear the muezzin's call to prayer, then the contradictory pattern of pagan drums, and perhaps an ailing vehicle spluttering along a potholed road, before night fell with the sounds of frogs and cicadas.

We had also chosen Kabala as a place to live because it was on the edge of Kuranko country, where I had decided to do anthropological fieldwork. From Kabala I began making regular treks with my Kuranko field assistant, Noah Marah, to Noah's natal village of Firawa (literally, "place in the bush"), the main town of Barawa chiefdom in the heart of Kuranko. There were no roads to Firawa, and it was a good day's journey to get there, filing along tortuous paths across laterite plateaus covered with savanna and scrub, crossing turbid streams and swamps, passing through hamlets whose houses had conical thatched roofs and were arrayed around circular courtyards. But marking the way to Firawa, there was always the great tor of Senekonke, "golden mountain," in the east, where the Barawa rulers once offered sacrifices for the protection and well-being of the land.

Beyond Firawa, the path wound on into the dense forested foothills of the northwest Guinea Highlands, just visible from Firawa in the dry season as a blue smudge on the horizon. It is in that direction, still within Kuranko country, that the river Niger has its source.

During those first few months in Firawa, everything was strange and had to be interpreted for me.[1] I was like a child who could take nothing for granted, and completely dependent on Noah for my bearings. "What is the word for water?" "Why do men weave and women spin?" "What is the meaning of that scrap of white cloth and small brass bell hanging from the lintel of our neighbor's house?" "When do the rituals of initiation begin?" Luckily, Noah's patience was not tried too much by my incessant questioning. Living in Kabala on the edge of Kuranko country, with his wives hailing from other ethnic groups, his children speaking Krio, and his living earned by teaching English in a primary school, Noah was in some ways also an outsider, struggling to reconcile the disparate traditions of Europe and Africa.

Noah belonged to the ruling house of Barawa, a chiefdom founded in the early seventeenth century by a clan calling itself Marah (after the verb *ka mara,* to subjugate, conquer, place under one's command). Its members were staunch pagans and renowned warriors who may have migrated from the plains of the Upper Niger to escape Islamic jihads.

The Barawa succession includes twenty-one rulers from the time of settlement,[2] but the praise-singers and genealogists trace the lineage of the Marah chiefs back to rulers of Mande, the medieval kingdom of the West Sudan from whence numerous peoples of Guinea, Liberia, Mali, and Ivory Coast still confidently trace their origins. The greatest ancestor of the Marah was said to be a warlord called Yilkanani, whom the praise-singers described as "the first father," "the first ancestor," and as Wasiru Mansa Yilkanani "because in his chieftaincy he was proud without being arrogant."

The name *Yilkanani* captured my imagination just as *Kabala* had, and I was intrigued to know more about this legendary figure who had formidable gifts, fabulous wealth, numberless progeny, and outstanding virtue. I would ask old men to tell me what they knew about Yilkanani, hoping to augment the piecemeal knowledge I had gathered listening to praise-singers or overhearing anecdotes about a heroic ancestor who lived in Mande, ruled from where the wind rises to where the wind dies down, and had horns on his head of coins and gold. But all these informants insisted that only the praise-singers and genealogists would be able to tell me what I wanted to know.

Unfortunately, these masters of traditions are elusive and difficult men. In the first place, *jelibas* and *finabas* are the sole custodians of oral history. They are the memory of rulers, proud and jealous of their vast knowledge and well aware that chiefs depend on this knowledge to confirm their legitimacy. *Jelibas* and *finabas* are amply paid for their services in cattle, coin, kola, salt, and rice and will sometimes flatter a man of a ruling house simply to cajole a gift from him.[3] In the second place, these bards and orators have great rhetorical skill. They will demean their own forefathers, calling them "mere slaves," and exaggerate the illustriousness of a past ruler as ways of inspiring a chief to worthy deeds. Accompanying their flatteries with the stirring music of xylophones, they encourage chiefs to heroic acts when wiser counsels should prevail, and chiefs frequently lament that all the reckless deeds in the past, the failure of campaigns and the ruin of countries, can be blamed on passions aroused in rulers by cunning praise-singers. The power of praise-singers thus sits uneasily between knowledge which bolsters the status of a ruler and interpretive license which serves self-interest, and it is often hard to read the direction in which a *jeliba's* flattery is going. The ambivalence felt by rulers toward their praise-singers springs from the ambiguous social position of these bards, who form an inferior hereditary group whom members of a ruling clan may not marry yet possess the knowledge on which chieftaincy depends, who intercede between a chief and his ancestors as well as between a chief and his subjects. As with the classical myth of Hermes, the problem of the messenger is always one of discerning the difference between dutiful transmission and interested translation.[4]

It wasn't until my second period of fieldwork in 1972 that I was able to find a genealogist who would agree to talk to me about Yilkanani without first demanding an exorbitant fee. Faraba Demba was the genealogist of Noah's elder brother, Sewa. Sewa had been a member of parliament in the first post-independence government of Sierra Leone, and it was through my friendship with him that I was able to persuade Faraba Demba to give me a taped interview. But even after agreement had been reached, it took me several weeks to run Faraba Demba to earth. I would catch sight of him near the Kabala market—a tall man in a stone-blue djellaba and skullcap, a leather sachet containing suras from the Quran dangling around his neck, his white heelless Arabian shoes scuffing the red dust in the main street as he vanished, like the white rabbit, down a narrow lane. When I did accost him he demanded more time and a gift, and when we finally did sit down together, with Noah interpreting, on the shabby porch of his Kabala house, I suspected that Faraba Demba's consent might have been merely to rid himself of a nuisance.

These are sections of the narrative I recorded:

Allah gave Lord Yilkanani immeasurable wealth. So wealthy did Lord Yilkanani become that Wali Ibrahim Braima said to him: "Lord Yilkanani, your wealth is too great." Lord Yilkanani replied: "Then I will go and bathe in the Lake of Poverty so that my wealth will be reduced." But when he went to the Lake of Poverty and threw water across his right shoulder, a horn of gold appeared on his head, and when he threw water across his left shoulder, a horn of coins appeared on his head. He turned to Wali Ibrahim Braima and swore him to silence, saying, "If you tell anyone about this I will cut off your head." On that day a black headband appeared on Lord Yilkanani's forehead.

After they had returned to the town, Wali Ibrahim Braima found his secret unbearable, and his belly began to swell. When Lord Yilkanani sent for Wali Ibrahim Braima, the messenger came back and said that Wali Ibrahim Braima's belly was swollen and he could not come. Then Lord Yilkanani said, "Go and tell Wali Ibrahim Braima to put his mouth to the ground and confess what is in his belly." When Wali Ibrahim Braima put his mouth to the ground and confessed he had seen horns of gold and coin appear on Lord Yilkanani's head when he bathed in the Lake of Poverty, the ground split open.

Wherever in the world today you find the earth rent by chasms, it is because of Wali Ibrahim Braima's confession. . . .

It then happened that Allah spoke to his messenger, Muhammad, saying, "Muham-

mad, *namu.*"[5] Muhammad replied, *"Namu."* Allah told Muhammad that he should find
a mentor,[6] but Muhammad answered, "Oh, Allah, thou hast created the seven levels
of the earth and the seven heavens; why should I place my trust in anyone but thee?"
But Allah said, "You must find a mentor among men." So Muhammad declared, "I
will make Yilkanani my mentor.". . .
    Allah withheld nothing from Yilkanani; the riches and powers he did not possess
are not to be found in this world. . . .
    Second to Yilkanani in power and wealth was Muluku Sulaiman. His power was
in the wind. If he sat in one place and thought of another place, then the wind would
instantly spirit him there. But Yilkanani and Muluku Sulaiman did not rule at the
same time. Nor is our epoch continuous with the epoch of their rule. In their epoch
there were no clans. The clans began in Mande, and it is the Marah who are the descendants of Yilkanani to whom Allah gave chieftaincy and wealth, and whom Muhammad made his mentor.

After Faraba Demba, there were other informants who told me about Yilkanani, but their narratives often referred to quite different periods and places,
and the identity of the central figure was never quite the same. For example, from
an itinerant trader from Upper Guinea I learned that the Mandingo there claim
a certain Djurukaraneni as an ancestor.

    Djurukaraneni's father was a wealthy trader in Kankan, called Alpha Kabbane, who
married a student of a renowned Quranic scholar and teacher, known as Mariama-the-
Pure, at Mariama's behest. When Mariama died, Alpha Kabbane inherited her property and students. When Alpha Kabbane died, his son Djurukaraneni went to Sigasso
in Segu to seek the advice of Fili, a warlord, on whether he should share his father's
inheritance among the slaves, students, and others who claimed a part for having
helped create the fortune in the first place. Fili advised Djurukaraneni to leave off his
studies and become a warrior. Djurukaraneni took Fili's advice and seven years later
returned to Kankan where he refused to share the inheritance among the claimants.
A war immediately broke out, which Djurukaraneni won with the help of warriors from
Fili's army, and refugees fled Kankan as far as what is today northern Sierra Leone
where they became Kuranko. The following year, Fili demanded the return of his warriors, but Djurukaraneni refused to let them go. In the ensuing battle against Fili outside
Kankan, Djurukaraneni was the loser, and when he surrendered to Fili he declared
he had been wrong to wage war against his master. Fili accepted this apology; he divided his army and gave a moiety to Djurukaraneni, proclaiming him thenceforth Lord
Djurukaraneni of Kankan.

In 1972, with the coming of the rains, when roads in northern Sierra Leone
become impassable and the demands of farm work leave villagers no time for talking to an anthropologist, I returned to England. In Cambridge I found further references to Djurukaraneni in published oral traditions from the West Sudan. In a book
which appeared in 1929, the French colonial administrator Charles Monteil men-
tions Djurukaraneni as a chief of Ouagadou between 1200 and 1218 (1929:80),[7]
and in an essay published two years earlier, an Englishman in Sierra Leone, E.
F. Sayers, refers to an ancestor of the Marah called Yurukhernani who inherited

vast wealth and had "innumerable progeny." His son, Saramba, "came down" from Mande and occupied the westerly regions of the Guinea Highlands, apportioning fiefdoms among his fifteen sons (1927:80).[8]

What struck me in these accounts as well as in the oral traditions I had collected were recurring references to wealth and pride. Yet these motifs were glossed differently in different chronicles. For instance, a renowned *jeliba* from Firawa told me that Yilkanani's nickname, Wasiru Mansa Yilkanani, signified that Yilkanani was neither arrogant nor tyrannical; in this respect he epitomized the Kuranko ideal of a ruler. Yet, according to the Kuranko informant whom Sayers interviewed in the mid-1920s, it was Yurukhernani's "overweening pride" that brought about his downfall and left him destitute, though not before Allah had warned him by sending down an angel who posed the cabalistic question "Daraman?" to which Yurukhernani gave no answer. When Allah sent another angel with the message "Maraman," signifying that Yurukhernani would lose his wealth if he remained arrogant, Yurukhernani took no notice and thus lost everything he owned (Sayers 1927:80–81).

Concerning Yilkanani's fabulous wealth, there was slightly more agreement among traditions. In both Faraba Demba's narrative and in the Mandingo tradition summarized above, Yilkanani is loath to lose, reveal, or share his great riches. This motif is possibly an improvisation by bards and praise-singers who, by impugning the generosity of one ruler, hope to encourage favors from another or, by recalling the magnanimity of an ancestral figure, oblige a contemporary chief to give in the same measure.[9] Another possibility is that the motif encapsulates a collective memory of epochs when rulers exacted tithes from subject people but gave back little by way of protection or sustenance. Anecdotes about exploitative rulers often find their way into Kuranko folk traditions, and in this regard it is ironic that Kankan, where, according to one narrative, Djurukaraneni was overlord, is also the Kuranko word for theft.[10] My aim in this chapter, however, is not exegetical but hermeneutical, and rather than digress further into contextual analysis I will resume the story of my own search for Yilkanani.

The next stage in this search was a discovery that a more astute scholar would have made much earlier: that the names Yilkanani, Yurukhernani, and Djurukaraneni are Mande deformations of the Arabic Dhul-Quarnein, meaning "the two-horned" (Niane 1965:90; Sayers 1927:80; Budge 1933:xxvii),[11] who is referred to in the cave sura in the Quran (18.83–112) as a mighty ruler and prophet who built a rampart against Gog and Magog, enemies of the divine kingdom.

Dhul-Quarnein is Alexander the Great,[12] and the allusion to the two horns takes us back to 332 B.C. when Alexander journeyed into the Libyan desert and consulted the famous oracle of Ammon, the ram-headed god whose principal shrine was at Siwa oasis. This Libyan oracle apparently spoke for the Greek god Zeus, to whom Alexander, like Perseus and Heracles, referred his origins. Although Alexander never revealed the questions he put to the Siwa oracle, what he heard (according to Arrian, writing in the mid-second century) "was agreeable to his wishes"; thereafter he was publicly acknowledged to be a begotten son of Zeus, and he took Zeus Ammon to heart for the rest of his life.[13] When he died in 323

B.C. Alexander passed into legend, adorned with the curling ram's horns of Ammon.

In the Book of Daniel Alexander appears as a he-goat who attacks and breaks the horn of a ram, presumably signifying Darius.[14] In the Quran he is the two-horned prophet sent by Allah to punish the impure. In Roman times, emperors represented themselves as successors of Alexander, adopting his titles and promoting him as an exemplar. In Persia he becomes Sikander Dhulkarnein, whose miraculous feats are celebrated in epic poems and whose name is adopted by a sixteenth-century shah (Clarke 1881). In Arabian romances he is an ally of Muhammad, and in Indian legend he makes a pilgrimage to the holy sites of India and is a friend of the Buddha. In China he fights alongside Chinese heroes against monstrous beasts and discourses with Chinese sages under the Tree of Wisdom. In medieval European romances he is a pious and chivalrous Christian, a soldier of God. In Badakshan, Marco Polo meets a king who claims descent from Alexander, and even today, in Hunza, an isolated valley beyond the Himalayas noted for the health and longevity of its people, there rules a raja who traces his descent to Alexander (Sykes 1969:239).

That Alexander still lives is attested by the fact that the fishermen of Lesbos in the Aegean still shout to the wild sea with the question "Where is Alexander the Great?" and answer with the cry "Alexander the Great lives and is King," so that the sea will become calm (Fox 1973:26). And only ninety years ago, on the coast of Makran, an English telegraph official was murdered by Karwan tribesmen because they had heard that fellow Muslims, the Turks, had defeated the Greek nation of Iskander Zulkarnein, a nation to which all European countries were thought to be attached (Sykes 1969:240).

At this point we come full circle: the Macedonian world-conqueror who referred his origins to a North African god figures centuries later as an ancestor of a ruling lineage in a remote West African society. Ironically, this transmigration of Alexander's name has taken place as a result of Islam,[15] a faith which the Marah rulers steadfastly repudiated for centuries,[16] and a faith which did not even exist in Alexander's time.

Where then is the real Alexander, amid all these versions in which ancient events have become metamorphosed according to the preoccupations of different societies and different epochs?[17]

The quest for the historical Alexander has been compared to the quest for the historical Jesus, and many scholars would assent to the view of C. B. Welles, that "There have been many Alexanders. Probably there will never be a definitive Alexander" (1974:9).[18] Not only have different societies assimilated Alexander to their own concerns and values, but the very personality of the historian inevitably plays its part in the shaping and reshaping of the image.[19] In the end, there seems no metamorphosis, base or noble, which we cannot reasonably entertain. As Hamlet observed to Horatio (act 5, scene 1):

To what base uses we may return, Horatio! Why may not imagination trace the noble dust of Alexander till 'a find it stopping a bung-hole?

Horatio: Twere to consider too curiously to consider so.

Hamlet: No faith, not a jot; but to follow him thither with modesty enough, and likelihood to lead it, as thus: Alexander died, Alexander was buried, Alexander returneth
into dust; the dust is earth; of earth we make loam; and why of that loam whereto
he was converted might they not stop a beer-barrel?

These conversions of which Hamlet speaks involve historical, cultural, and
biographical imperatives, each of which helps shape the versions of a myth which
are, accordingly, only moments in an eternal narrative.

Here is one version, one moment: a poem I wrote in 1974 called "Yilkanani"
(Jackson 1976:10).

> Yilkanani, whom we approve,
> sacked a country
> and burned a stranger's camp;
> when told that one of his victims
> was his sister, drank a gourd
> of palm wine and drowned himself
> in the Black River
> from where he sings now
> with the voice of palmbirds.

When I wrote this poem it was one of those rare occasions when words make
themselves heard, as it were, through negative capability, the poem finding its way
onto the page fully formed without having perceptibly passed through the conscious
mind. The poem was, therefore, as much an object of curiosity to me as any of
the other romances of Alexander—Kuranko, Persian, or Ethiopian—which I knew.
Yet, deciphering this particular version of the greater narrative led me into biography as well as history and necessitated reflections not only on my African researches
but on my own personality.

What I now want to do is use my poem as an occasion for talking about interpretation. In particular I want to demonstrate what Sartre calls the progressive-
regressive method in which interpretation involves both a creative forward movement by which one grasps and articulates one's *possibilities* of being and a reflexive
analytical movement, which takes one back on a journey of exploration among
the objects, people, places, and events which make up the *grounds* of one's being
(Sartre 1968:chap. 3). The human "project" is thus a bringing into being which
discloses and conserves the prior conditions of our individual lives, yet at the same
time realizes and surpasses these conditions by addressing them as a field of instrumental possibilities. It is within this irreducible domain of lived experience (*le
vécu*)—embracing unconscious, conscious, and embodied aspects of our individual
being—that this dialectic must be traced out, though, as Sartre notes, lived experience may be "comprehended" but never entirely "known" by the person who exists
it.[20] In other words, the part can never know the whole without distortion so long
as it is a part. Interpretation is, in my view, therefore not a matter of trying to do
away with this distortion but rather of trying to disclose it and use it creatively.

With this proviso let me hazard an interpretation of my poem. It begins with a motif which is found in countless Alexander romances: the hero is a world-conqueror whose conquests gain him immense material wealth and great renown, yet also bring him to the verge of moral ruin. The poem develops this motif in an unusual way. While sacking a stranger's camp, the great warlord inadvertently slays his sister. We may presume she had been given in marriage to a man of the ruling lineage in this other country and that her brother had forgotten about the erstwhile alliance. Upon hearing of what he had done, Yilkanani suffers terrible remorse and drinks himself into near-oblivion before drowning himself in the Black River. Today we hear his voice in the twittering of palmbirds—voices of banality, void of sense.

My initial interpretation of the poem proceeded like the interpretation of a dream. First there were residues and allusions of an ethnographic and personal kind: a reminder of the great respect which Kuranko men pay their sisters, and of the sister's power and right to curse a brother if he denies her this respect; a reference to the Rivière Noire in the bas-Congo (Zaire) where, in 1964, I used to picnic with Swiss friends who, like myself, worked for the United Nations; and an image from a Kuranko narrative about an adulterer whose lover was the wife of a jealous chief. The chief slew, dismembered, and burned the adulterer and had his ashes thrown into the river. For years the disconsolate lover wandered along the river, singing for the dead man, until at last the spirits of the stream, the fish, and the palmbirds decided to answer her song and give the dead man voice. They miraculously reassembled the man, who was reunited with his lover and returned with her to their village, where he killed the chief and took his place (Jackson 1982a:203–8).

Then, deeper preoccupations began to come to light. After reading Ernest Becker I saw that the hero might be understood as a "reflex of the terror of death," an image of our search for immortality, for a triumph of the spirit over the flesh, of will over matter, of words over the flux of events (Becker 1973). My own field-work among the Kuranko had reflected a profound dilemma. On one hand I found myself striving for a wealth of data which I could convert into a book, a durable object which might make my name. But on the other hand I felt my ego threatened by a world of opaque languages, bizarre customs, and oppressive living conditions. Running counter to this will to amass knowledge was a profound desire to give up and let go, to allow my consciousness to be flooded by the African ambiance. In the poem, this regressive undercurrent becomes visible in images of drinking, drowning, and infantile babbling.

The killing of the sister is one expression of this ambivalence, and brings together ethnographic and personal themes. I am the second-born in a family of five children. Most of us are overachievers, and my elder sister is a successful academic who for many years I sought to emulate and outshine. The willful striving after knowledge which drove me to accomplish an ambitious research task in Sierra Leone in 1969–70 must have been associated in my mind with this sibling rivalry.[21] But while my striving became expressed obliquely as a desire to usurp my sister's position, the countermanding desire to relinquish this striving found expression

in an unconscious fantasy of killing my sister—the model, for me, of academic ambition. The poem finally registers atonement for this "act" in a forfeiture of the
position and properties gained as a result of it. As for the desire to regress beyond
all ego-striving, the hero fulfills this desire but at the cost of speech and intelligibility.

The figure of Yilkanani thus precipitated in me a kind of inadvertent self-
disclosure. The Kuranko hero served me as an objective correlative of my subjective
prepossessions, enabling me to voice them, albeit in the dark and distorting mirror
of a poem, and later study them as they distanced themselves in this poem, which
seemed only partly to be of my own making.

But what this study brings to the surface is not mere biography but also cultural
and historical processes embedded in biography. The imagery of the poem is not
free-floating but bound. I want to consider this binding in two ways, first by taking
up Shelley's idea (circa 1824) that all the poems ever written or that ever will be
written are but episodes of a single infinite poem whose complete form always
eludes us, and second by showing how every poem expresses historical and cultural
preoccupations of which the individual poet is seldom aware.

Leaving aside the biographical reasons already outlined, the question arises
why Yilkanani should have a sister in my poem and thus depart radically from the
Kuranko legends? An answer may be hazarded in a brief reference to a Greek folktale in which Alexander the Great has a sister. According to this tale, Alexander's
sister spilled the water of immortality, which her brother had asked her to safeguard. Stricken with remorse, the girl threw herself into the sea and became transformed into a Gorgon. Until this day she searches the seas, asking boatmen if her
brother is still alive. If the captain wisely answers, "He is alive, and rules, and
is master of the world," she is appeased and calm weather prevails. But if the captain answers thoughtlessly that her brother died long ago, the Gorgon becomes
frenzied and raises a storm to sink his boat (Yalouris 1980:20).

Not only does this tale bear an uncanny resemblance to the Kuranko story
in which a disconsolate woman searches up and down a river for years, hoping
to be reunited with her dead lover; it also presents in inverted form the principal
elements of my poem. Whereas in the poem the brother wrongs his sister and
drowns himself in a river, his voice becoming the voice of ineffectual palmbirds,
in the Greek tale the sister offends her brother and drowns herself in the sea, her
voice becoming the minatory voice of storms.

Every poem, like every myth, may therefore be seen as a variation of a finite
set of universal elements, and, as Lévi-Strauss has shown, structural analysis simply
reveals the interminable combinations and permutations of these elements, which
go on in the minds of men and women without their being aware of it (see the
Overture and Finale of *Mythologiques* 1970, 1981).

As to the second question, concerning the cultural and historical forms whose
shadows fall across the poem, let us consider the darkest of these: colonialism. The
anthropologist who spends time in another society, extracting raw data to bring
home and process for intellectual profit, is working within the determination of
a particular social formation whose more insidious expressions are political domina-

tion and economic exploitation. Nevertheless, his conditioned reflex to subjugate the world through the exercise of willful rationality[22] is often mellowed by a critical awareness of another mode of consciousness in which conviviality and communication figure more prominently than self-aggrandisement and competitiveness.[23] Since these other values are usually those emphasized by the people among whom anthropologists do their fieldwork, they find themselves split between two projects, one of which will absorb them further into the community, the other of which will estrange them. In my own case, I would, for example, excuse myself from joining in a Kuranko communal dance because I wanted to be free to take notes from the sidelines, and I would give priority to recording a narrative through an interpreter rather than take time to learn the language properly so that I myself could enter into a direct social relationship with the narrator. In my view, the two movements—becoming a part of another community and gaining repute in the academic world—are, in practice, though not necessarily in theory, mutually exclusive.

The opposition between these two sets of values, sociability and profitability,[24] is as much an aspect of my particular biography as it is a part of our cultural heritage. But this opposition is also problematic for Kuranko, and it is at this point that my own biographical concerns rejoin the ethnographic context of Kuranko social life.

Many Kuranko oral narratives are centered upon the problem of the hero (Jackson 1982a:chap. 6). Somewhat as the anthropologist ventures into the unknown in quest of knowledge, the protagonist in numerous Kuranko narratives risks his life in a journey out of his community into the wilderness in quest of some magical object—an initiation drum, a xylophone, a fetish—which gives power over life and death to its owner. Like the data gleaned by the ethnographer when he journeys into a remote corner of the world, the things gained by the Kuranko hero during his wanderings in the wilderness are ethically ambiguous: they can be used for private advantage or made to serve the commonweal. In Kuranko narratives this problem of reconciling self-interest and social duty is often dramatized as a struggle between a good and a bad ruler. According to the Kuranko ideal, the respect accorded a ruler deserves to be reciprocated by the protection a ruler gives his subjects. The privilege of power can only be justified by responsibility and magnanimity in its use. It is a paternalistic notion of authority. A bad ruler, like a bad father, uses his position of power to take advantage of those dependent on him, even descending to theft of food, alienation of property, and criminal neglect.[25] Kuranko anecdotes about Yilkanani reveal this ethical ambiguity of authority: the subtle differences between dignity and vanity, pride and arrogance, and moral and material wealth.

It is fascinating to find this same ambiguity in the European Alexander romances. Although the ancients were often divided over whether Alexander's liberality was a form of cunning and vanity or a benign and noble quality,[26] from Seneca and Cicero right through into the medieval romances, as well as in the poems of Chaucer, Lydgate, Gower, and, later, Dryden, the same themes recur: of a world-conqueror conquered by his own emotional weakness, of reason corrupted by passion, of learning ruined by moral ignorance. And time and time again, it is Alexander's visit to the oracle of Ammon and his subsequent elevation to the status of a god which is referred to as the point at which the hero's moral deterioration begins (Cary 1956:110–16).

This hubris assumes its more modern form in a story by Rudyard Kipling, "The Man Who Would Be King" (1888), in which two English adventurers, Daniel Dravot and Peachey Carnehan, stumble into a remote valley in northeast Afghanistan (Kafiristan) where a priesthood keeps alive the memory of Alexander the Great. Through bluff and cunning Dravot has himself accepted as the son of Alexander and enthroned as king, but, contrary to the wishes of the priests, he decides to take to wife a village girl, declaring that "A God can do anything." His arrogance finally costs him his crown and his life, and Peachey struggles back to India, where he recounts the tragedy to Kipling. This allegory of imperialism, in which Dravot is a kind of Cecil Rhodes,[27] reminds us that the themes of corrupt power and colonialism are inextricably linked and that Alexander the world-conqueror is still an embodiment of these themes. Shortly before he came to power in Ghana as leader of the first postcolonial nation of modern Africa, Kwame Nkrumah wrote that the blight of European expansionism had its precedent in "the idea of Alexander the Great and his Graeco-Asiatic Empire" (Nkrumah 1962:1). Ironically, only a few years passed before Nkrumah himself was deposed for corruption and self-aggrandizement.

What I have hoped to show in these diverse refractions of a historical figure is that certain abiding moral dilemmas find expression in a narrative which knows no cultural boundaries and recognizes no individual author. My poem participates in this narrative, as does this chapter. One is reminded of Borges's claim that the dream which drove a thirteenth-century Mongolian emperor to build "a stately pleasure dome" in Xanadu and the dream which inspired an English poet on a summer's day in 1797 were one and the same dream (Borges 1964:16).[28]

I do not wish to make Borges's conjecture serve as an aesthetic justification for a particular style of interpretation, however, for my intention here is to show that interpretation has to be justified *practically*, as a form of disclosure which works back through autobiography to discover the points at which individuality loses itself in the trans-subjective processes of history, culture, and ultimately nature. But this recognition of one's historicity should not entail a reductionist explanation, for, whether we admit it or not, every act of cool analysis is also a creative act initiated within our particular personality and explicable in terms of our biography. In my view, true objectivity in interpretation does not consist in repressing, masking, or setting aside this biographical field of choice and intention but in revealing it clearly as it interacts with history, producing new syntheses in the shape of a poem, an essay, or even a revolutionary act.[29] This therapeutic aspect of the hermeneutic process is shown by my discovery that a poem I seemed to write unconsciously was in fact a logjam of images to keep me from reading the real preoccupations of my unconscious: an unresolved moral dilemma over the exercise of power, the value of ambition, and the profitability of knowledge. If the poem was written in bad faith—fetishized as an object which I did not have a hand in making—then the interpretive "reading" of the poem is a kind of redemption. The so-called object is brought back into subjectivity only to be made over again to the world of objectivity, but this time as something which expresses rather than represses the author's effective history.

In this dialectic, self-reflection and scholarly study, creativity and interpretation, arise together and are united. For me, this process of reuniting aspects of our being which are habitually fragmented is a form of making whole, of healing.[30] And I have sought a form of writing which unites the poet and the ethnographer in one script, which merges the poetic and ethnographic in a single style, and which follows the hermeneutical example of Gadamer: "to see through the dogmatism of asserting an opposition and separation between the ongoing natural 'tradition' and the reflective appropriation of it" (1976:28). It is in this sense that my quest for Yilkanani, which began in a town in northern Sierra Leone in 1969, was eclipsed by a wider search for Alexander and became finally a journey into that region where history and biography converge.

An anthropology which so forthrightly reflects upon the interplay of biography and tradition and makes the personality of the anthropologist a primary datum entails a different notion of truth than that to which a scientistic anthropology aspires. It is a notion of truth based less upon epistemological certainties than upon moral, aesthetic, and political values.[31] It is, indeed, a pragmatist notion of truth in which, rather than reduce experience to abstract categories by a process of systematic totalization, we seek to disclose the complex and open-ended character of experience and the role interpretation plays in the process of self-making.[32] It is a conception of the anthropological project which leads us directly to a concern with the way we say things, for we become less interested in announcing definitive explanations than in opening up new possibilities for thinking about experience. Richard Rorty uses the term *edification* for this process "of finding new, better, more interesting, more fruitful ways of speaking" (1979:360). While edification "may consist in the hermeneutic activity of making connections between our own culture and some exotic culture or historical period, or between our own discipline and another discipline," Rorty notes that "it may instead consist in the 'poetic' activity of thinking up such new aims, new words, or new disciplines, followed by, so to speak, the inverse of hermeneutics: the attempt to reinterpret our familiar surroundings in the unfamiliar terms of our new inventions." Edifying discourse is "*supposed* to be abnormal, to take us out of our old selves by the power of strangeness, to aid us in becoming new beings" (360).

For more than a decade now it has been clear that cultural anthropology is developing as much through the innovation of new styles of discourse as through continuing empirical research. We are nowadays more confident about speaking of anthropology as a kind of philosophizing or writing and no longer need the trappings of the natural sciences to bestow legitimacy on what we do. Unlike many other social scientists, anthropologists are fortunate in having to hand a wealth of exotic images, world views, and metaphors. Rather than assimilating these elements to our own familiar metaphors (where kinship is a "web" or "network" and groups undergo "fission" and "fusion"), it is often proving more edifying to use and extend indigenous metaphors in novel ways, participating in rather than subverting the discursive idioms to which our researches introduce us.

Moreover, we are now more keenly aware that the texts generated by the discursive practices of cultural anthropology are embedded in a wider cultural and historical milieu and that our essays in explanation are in this sense on a par with the ritual and mythological "texts" we collect in the field. We no longer assume that *our* texts have some kind of intrinsic epistemological superiority over *theirs*. All are, in the final consideration, metaphors, more or less masked, for an existential quest for meaning, and anthropology, like philosophy, is, in Nietzsche's famous phrase, "a species of involuntary and unconscious autobiography" (1973:10).

This Nietzschean perspective also pervades the work of Michel Foucault, who regards all discourses as available perspectives: "if one has more value than another that is not because of its intrinsic properties as 'truth,' or because we call it 'science,' but because of an extra-epistemological ground, *the role the discourse plays in constituting practices*" (Poster 1984:85, my emphasis).

Not only do I find this view congenial on temperamental grounds; it commends itself as coming very close to articulating the Kuranko view that the practical, social, and moral consequences of discourse define its truth-value, not abstract epistemological rules.[33] Perhaps this pragmatist point can best be made by considering the character of Kuranko narrative.

Although the anecdotes and legends about Yilkanani belong to a "true" tradition of discourse which the Kuranko call *kuma kore*, "ancestral words," there is another genre of Kuranko narrative which falls halfway between truth and make-believe. These narratives, which we might call folktales, are told on moonlit nights in the villages by skilled performers before a random audience of men, women, and children. Many of these narratives pose a moral dilemma which everyone present will try to solve, and these intervals of casuistry are half the fun of a storytelling session.

What impressed me about Kuranko storytelling was the way in which old and young alike participated actively in a search for moral meaning. Seldom were these meanings self-evident, for the art of Kuranko narrative is to mask or nullify the orthodox rules which people use in forming moral judgements. Accordingly, each individual must arrive at his or her own solution to the quandary and refer to his or her own experience in doing so. Although the unanimity reached by the end of an evening belies the variability of opinions brought forward, the most important point is that consensus is reached through participation rather than imposed by convention. In other words, the truth finally agreed upon reflects less an interest in making truth accord with individual experience than in making it a vehicle for communal action. The therapeutic character of Kuranko storytelling does not, therefore, stem from the self-reflection which narratives may inspire but from the convivial occasion they create. For the Kuranko, interpretive activity is a tool for conviviality (Illich 1973)—a means of communication—and as such it is not evaluated primarily in terms of literal or logical standards.[34]

In this chapter I have not eschewed these standards, but I have tried to show that ethical, aesthetic, and practical standards are of no less importance in interpretation. And I hope also to have told a story, a story whose unfolding reflects fortuitous encounters and happy coincidences, yet is still only half-told and open to further possibilities of interpretation and invention.

ELEVEN

On Ethnographic Truth

Kurt Vonnegut majored in anthropology at the University of Chicago just after the end of World War II. Twenty-three years later, in *Slaughterhouse 5*, he recalled the relativistic spirit of the courses he took there: "At that time, they were teaching that there was absolutely no difference between anybody. . . . Another thing they taught was nobody was ridiculous or bad or disgusting."

This humanistic attitude did not, however, help Vonnegut when he submitted his master's thesis, "Fluctuations between Good and Evil in Simple Tales," for examination in the Department of Anthropology. It was unanimously rejected. Vonnegut dropped out of anthropology, worked for a while as a public relations official for General Electric in Schenectady, then as a free-lance writer. Then, twenty-five years after failing to gain his master's degree in anthropology at Chicago, Vonnegut was awarded an honorary degree by the same university for his contributions to the field of anthropology. These contributions were, however, not ethnographic monographs or empirical findings, but novels, in particular a satirical science fiction called *Cat's Cradle* (1963), which returns to the theme of his failed dissertation—the ambiguity of good and evil—through an account of a make-believe West Indian religion called Bokononism. Bokonon is amused by the problem of truth. He tells his followers not to believe a word he says. The first sentence of *The Books of Bokonon* reads: "All of the true things I am about to tell you are shameless lies." Vonnegut adds: "My Bokonist warning is this: Anyone unable to understand how a useful religion can be founded on lies will not understand this book either" (1963:16). Elsewhere he writes, "Nothing in this book is true," and confesses: "I just have trouble understanding how truth, all by itself, could be enough for a person."

I first read *Cat's Cradle* in Melbourne in 1963. A Jamaican friend, Patrick Johnson, loaned me his copy to read. Sometime between then and now I am sure I read a Caribbean ethnography which gave details of a religious cult centered on a prophet called Bokonon. However, all the critical works on Vonnegut that I have consulted refer to Bokonon as a fictional figure and Bokononism as an invented religion. I have searched for that Caribbean ethnography in vain, cursed myself for not having made a note of the one detail which might now prove the critics wrong and Vonnegut slyly right, which would make *Cat's Cradle*—as the title itself suggests—a kind of ethnographic science fiction. At the moment, however, writing this, I do not know what to believe, what the facts are, who is telling the truth.

We have here a series of ironies: a prestigious North American university confers a degree in anthropology on a writer of fiction; the novel which is accepted as his dissertation, *Cat's Cradle,* is about a West Indian prophet who claims that truths are lies and lies are truths; Bokononism, which is generally regarded as Vonnegut's creation, may in fact exist. These ironies define the subject of this chapter: the vexed issue of whether cultural anthropology is a hard science or more akin to literature; whether it is built on the solid ground of impartial observations and empirically tested views or the shifting sands of rhetoric, history, and subjectivity; whether, in a nutshell, its modes of understanding human social life are true or false.

These questions also bring us back to the beginning of this book, where I discussed the different emphases of humanist and empiricist anthropology. My approach to these seemingly opposed traditions—the first which seeks what is existentially common to all human beings, the second which researches what is ethnographically particular—follows the example of Michel Foucault. Rather than attempt to resolve the dilemma over whether anthropology is in essence literature or science—whether its truths are invented or found, fictional or factual—I propose to explore the conditions under which these antinomies make their appearance and gain currency, to account for why they are presently of such pressing concern to us and what produces the deep disquiet and bruising debate among us over the identity of our discourse.

Such an approach implies that merely classifying discursive styles in terms of essential differences is a rather futile and unedifying thing to do. My aim, therefore, will be to disclose the dialectical interplay of this disjunctive mode of reasoning, which orders the world in terms of linked pairs of polar opposites (true/false, fact/fiction, science/art), and a conjunctive mode of reasoning characterized by a quest for similitudes, resemblances, and unity.

ANALOGY

If there is any mode of thought common to all people, in all societies, at all periods of history, it is analogy.[1] Analogy, as Keynes observed, encompasses both "positive" and "negative" comparison, the identification of similarities *and* differences between the things compared (1921). The ubiquity and scope of reasoning by analogy make it a useful point of departure in our attempt to account for the perceived similarities and differences not only between anthropological science and anthropological literature, or modern and primitive thought, but between the thought of anthropologists and the thought of the people they study.

In *Les mots et les choses* (1966), Foucault discusses at length a hiatus in European thought in the early seventeenth century. In the sixteenth century, and for a long time before, knowledge was principally a matter of discovering similitudes in the order of things. "To search for a meaning is to bring to light a resemblance. To search for the law governing signs is to discover the things that are alike. . . . The nature of things, their coexistence, the way in which they are linked together and communicate is nothing other than their resemblance" (1970:29). Within this tangled "semantic web" of resemblances which constituted knowledge in Western culture, Foucault identifies four main forms of similitude. First, *convenientia*, in which things are supposed to be alike because they occur together or occupy the same space. Here are two examples, the first from Porta's *Magie naturelle* (1650), the second from my own Kuranko ethnography:

> As with respect to its vegetation the plant stands convenient to the brute beast, so through feeling does the brutish animal to man, who is conformable to the rest of the stars by his intelligence; these links proceed so strictly that they appear *as a rope stretched from the first cause as far as the lowest and smallest of things*, by a reciprocal and continuous connection; in such wise that the superior virtue, spreading its beams, reaches so far that *if we touch one extremity of that cord it will make it tremble and move all the rest.* (Cited by Foucault 1970:19, my emphasis)

> The interdependence of members of the community or of a family may be expressed in terms of the network of ropes which are tied over the rice farms when the crop is nearing maturity. One end of the rope is always tied to the foot of the bird-scaring platform where the children sit with slingshots and keep birds from scavenging the rice. When this main rope is tugged, all the tributary ropes shake. This scares away the birds. It is sometimes said that "one's birth is like the bird-scaring rope" (*soron i le ko yagbayile*), or "one's birth is like a chain" (*soron i la ko yolke*) because one's fate is always inextricably tied to the fate of others. (Jackson 1982a:16–17)

Foucault's second mode of similitude is *aemulatio*, the relation of emulation whereby things mirror or "imitate one another from one end of the universe to the other without connection or proximity" (1970:19). Paracelsus likened this relation to the relation between identical twins; one could never be said to be the original and the other merely a duplicate or reflection. An ethnographic example of *aemulatio* is immediately suggested by this image of twinship.

> The Nuer assert "that twins are one person and that they are birds" . . . because twins and birds, though for different reasons, are both associated with Spirit and this makes twins, like birds, "people of the above" and "children of God," and hence a bird a suitable symbol in which to express the special relationship in which a twin stands to God." . . . "In respect to God twins and birds have a similar character." (Evans-Pritchard 1956:128, 131–32)

A third mode of similitude is *analogy*, whereby the microcosm is shown to correspond in every detail to the macrocosm. "Man's body is always the possible half of a universal atlas," his flesh is glebe, his bones are rocks, his veins great rivers, his bladder the sea, and his seven principal organs the metals hidden in the shafts of mines (Foucault 1970:22, referring to Crollius's *Traité des signatures*). The Dogon of Mali provide a contemporary ethnographic example of this painstaking elucidation of correspondence between the human body and the body of the world. According to Geneviève Calame-Griaule, the Dogon conceive the world in its totality as a gigantic human organism, and parts of the Dogon world reproduce this image on a greater or lesser scale (1965:27). Thus the village is conceptualized as a person, lying north-south, the smithy at his head, shrines at his feet, and the Dogon

house is an anthropomorphic representation of a man lying on his side and procre-
ating (Griaule 1954:95–98). Moreover, a regular geology of the human body is recognized by the Dogon, for whom different kinds of minerals correspond to different
bodily organs, various earths being organs "within the belly," rocks being assimilated to the "bones" of the skeleton, and a family of red clays made to represent
the blood. Different rocks and stones stand for different parts of the body, so that
one rock balanced on another is the "chest" and small white river pebbles are
"toes." The Dogon also maintain that each of these phenomenal correspondences
"speaks" to man, auguring or signifying something which must be deciphered if man
is to flourish. Thus, words are likened to grain, speech to germination, and divination to winnowing. And body parts have analogues in parts of the grain (heart
= cotyledon, nose = germ, and so on) as well as in intonations of the voice
(Calame-Griaule 1965:27–57).

Foucault's fourth mode of similitude, *sympathy*, is really a corollary of the other
modes, as is suggested by the Dogon view that things which are analogous *also influence one another*. Foucault takes an example from Porta's *Magie naturelle*, where it
is observed that mourning roses which have been used at obsequies can, simply
from their former adjacency with death, render all persons who smell them "sad
and moribund" (Foucault 1970:23). Sympathy, which transforms things "in the direction of identity," is, however, complemented by its twin, antipathy, which
"maintains the isolation of things" (24). Anthropologists are familiar with these
notions in the form of sympathetic magic and pollution beliefs. Among the
Kuranko, pregnant women sometimes bind a strip of antelope skin around their
wrists so that the children they bear will be imbued with the antelope's litheness
and grace. Among the Fang of Gabon, squirrels are prohibited for pregnant women
because squirrels shelter in holes of trees and a future mother who ate their flesh
would run the risk of the fetus imitating the squirrel and refusing to leave the
uterus. As Tessmann notes: "The worst danger threatening pregnant women is from
animals who live or are caught in any sort of hole (in the ground, in trees). One
can positively speak of a *horror vacui*. If a pregnant woman eats an animal of this
kind, the child might also want to stay in its hole, 'in the belly,' and a difficult
birth is to be expected" (quoted in Lévi-Strauss 1966a:61).

The sixteenth-century episteme was characterized by what Foucault calls a
"teeming abundance of resemblances" (1970:26)—limitless, plethoric, and indiscriminate. This preoccupation with similitudes, analogies, and correspondences
had two important consequences.

In the first place, our contrasted notions of "magic" and "science" had little
currency in the sixteenth century. Observations and discoveries that we would recognize as "scientific" *were* made, to be sure, but they were often accidental or incidental to the overriding passion for divining the internal harmonies of the world.
Consider this observation from Belon's *Histoire de la nature des oiseaux* (1555),
which likens the wing of a bird to the human hand: "the pinion called the appendix
which is in proportion to the wing and in the same place as the thumb on the
hand; the extremity of the pinion which is like the fingers in us . . . " (quoted

in Foucault 1970:22). It so happens that these correspondences between the wing of a bird and the upper limb of a human being provide an excellent example of what biologists call homology, an organic or structural connection which derives from a similar phylogenetic prototype, that is, a connection which reveals common descent (Gould 1987). But Belon's comparative anatomy was neither "scientific" nor "magical." It was just one of the innumerable correspondences which the world revealed to the fascinated human mind, no more or less significant than the connection assumed, say, between apoplexy and storms (Foucault 1970:22–23).

One is reminded strongly of Taoist thinkers whose mystical desire to see into the unity of nature led, almost inadvertently, to alchemical experimentation, a healthy skepticism toward preconceived theories, disinterested observations of the natural world, a search for hidden causes, and what we would now call an attitude of "scientific naturalism" which brought the Taoists "intuitively to the roots of science" (Ronan 1978:95). Joseph Needham draws an analogy between the Taoists and Paracelsus (1493–1541):

> Standard-bearer of alchemy applied to medicine, proponent, against all opposition, of mineral drugs, first observer of the occupational diseases of miners, he was an experimentalist and a theoretician. . . . Paracelsus had much in common with the Taoists. Indeed it can be shown that his alchemical medicine derived ultimately from the elixir concept of China mediated through Arabic and Byzantine culture. (Ronan 1978:104)

It is because the thought which we sometimes disparage as "mystical" or "magical" usually goes hand in hand with experimentation and exhaustive observations of the natural world that Lévi-Strauss argues that it must be regarded as a different but parallel mode of scientific thought. This "science of the concrete," through its meticulous and methodical classification of things on the basis of similitudes and sensible properties (hard/soft, sweet/sour, long/short, and so on) makes possible, albeit inadvertently, discoveries of a practical and theoretical kind:

> Not all poisonous juices are burning or bitter nor is everything which is burning and bitter poisonous. Nevertheless, nature is so constituted that it is more advantageous if thought and action proceed as though this aesthetically satisfying equivalence also corresponded to objective reality. It seems probable . . . that species possessing some remarkable characteristics, say, of shape, colour or smell give the observer what might be called a "right pending disproof" to postulate that these visible characteristics are the sign of equally singular, but concealed, properties. To treat the relation between the two as itself sensible (regarding a seed in the form of a tooth as a safeguard against snake bites, yellow juices as a cure for bilious troubles, etc.) is of more value provisionally than indifference to any connection. (Lévi-Strauss 1966a: 15–16)

A second important consequence of the sixteenth-century preoccupation with resemblances was a fervor for divining and deciphering the system of signatures which were their visible form. As in hermetic philosophy, where the natural world was spoken of as the "book of God" (Needleman 1975:6), the sixteenth-century episteme saw the world as bristling with signs, blazons, omens, and figures, that is to say, *as a text*. Erudition was a matter of making the signs speak, of elucidating

their cryptic meanings, of revealing the laws which governed the connections between them. Renaissance knowledge was, in a word, interpretive —a palimpsest
of hermeneutical and semiological styles (Foucault 1970:25–30).

MEASUREMENT AND DIFFERENCE

In the early seventeenth century, the quest for synthetic resemblances began to
give way to analytical methods for establishing identity and difference. In Galileo's
work intelligibility is sought through deductive reasoning—an abstract mathemati-
zation of the world (*mathesis universalis*)—rather than through the confusing testi-
mony of the senses. Descartes attacked the indiscriminate habit of seeing resemblances everywhere and losing sight of essential differences. The "proper order of
things" could only be worked out through rational means, such as mathematics
and geometry:

> Those long chains of reasoning, simple and easy as they are, of which geometricians
> make use in order to arrive at the most difficult demonstrations, had caused me to
> imagine that all those things which fall under the cognizance of man might very likely
> to be related in the same fashion. (1931:92, originally published 1637)

As reason is separated from the senses, so man, the rational subject, becomes
split from nature. The external world of nature and the inner world of instincts
and passions are now to be mastered, subdued, and ordered by the rational will.
The "central concern must be to keep the emotions from biasing judgements"
(Horkheimer 1947:107). Nature is a resistance to be overcome, something to be
dominated with mind rather than enjoyed with the senses (Marcuse 1969:96–97).

It is because Enlightenment thinkers regarded nature as an object that man
examines and dominates *from a distance* that they sought to abolish mythical and
magical modes of thought. Such modes of thought, with their emphasis on similitudes, affinities, and sympathies between man and nature, were anathema to the
new scientists such as Francis Bacon, partly because they were often still deeply
influenced by magical, alchemical, and hermetic traditions.[2]

The efforts of the new scientists to expunge anthropomorphism from their discourse[3] had repercussions for the ways in which they regarded primitive peoples.
The separation of reason from affect, man from nature, entailed a greater emphasis
on the *differences* between educated Europeans and people thought to exist in a
state of nature. Writing in the 1570s, Montaigne spoke in relativistic terms about
the South American Indians he had met:

> I do not believe, from what I have been told about this people, that there is anything
> barbarous or savage about them, except that we all call barbarous anything that is con-
> trary to our own habits. Indeed we seem to have no other criterion of truth and reason
> than the type and kind of opinions and customs current in the land where we live.
> . . . We are justified . . . in calling these people barbarians by reference to the laws
> of reason, but not in comparison with ourselves, who surpass them in every kind of
> barbarity. (*On Cannibals*)

Ninety years later, in his *Essays on the Law of Nature*, John Locke admitted only absolute differences between civilized and primitive men:

> anyone who consults the histories both of the old world and new world, or the itineraries of travellers, will easily observe how far apart from virtue the morals of these people are, what strangers they are to any humane feelings, since nowhere else is there such doubtful honesty, so much treachery, such frightful cruelty in that they sacrifice to the gods and also to their tutelary spirit by killing people and offering kindred blood. And no one will believe that the law of nature is best known and observed among these primitive and untutored tribes, since among most of them there appears not the slightest trace or track of piety, merciful feeling, fidelity, chastity, and the rest of the virtues; but rather they spend their life wretchedly among robberies, thefts, debaucheries, and murders. (1954:141)

HISTORY AND CRITIQUE

The very possibility of drawing contrasts, as Foucault does, between Renaissance and Enlightenment thought reflects a mode of discourse whose notion of order is based neither upon the perception of similitudes between microcosm and macrocosm nor upon the privileged status of the rational subject. Its foundation is history, a sense that human conceptions of both order *and* reason, and even the appearance and disappearance of the human subject, are determined historically and grounded in the circumstances of social life. It is the episteme of the nineteenth century, of Hegel, Marx, Darwin, and Nietzsche—a unifying motif despite arguments over whether history is a structured whole or open-ended, or whether or not truth is inevitably relative to time and circumstance. It is also the episteme of the social sciences and anthropology, despite the ahistorical tenor of functionalism and the refusal of structuralism to address history except as "mere contingency." It is the episteme in which we are still caught up, despite ourselves, and for that reason comprehend with difficulty (Foucault 1970:221).

Reviewing the historical mutability of discourse, I am also mindful that no one episteme ever completely supersedes another. The historical matrix in which our present discourse is embedded contains other discursive styles and strategies, and makes use of them. Despite Foucault's persuasive arguments for great discontinuities at the beginning of the seventeenth century and in the last years of the eighteenth century, there is abundant evidence of epistemic pluralism and ample room for reference to the individual subjects who negotiated the no-man's land between the different styles. As Foucault himself notes elsewhere, "the episteme is not a motionless figure that appeared one day with a mission of effacing all that preceded it" (1972:192); it implied, as Cassirer insists, a shift in "the ideal center of gravity of all philosophy"—new trends that coexist with rather than supplant the old (1951:33). In the work of Bodin and Montaigne, as we have seen, the importance attached to reason in the individual life anticipates the Enlightenment, while in the seventeenth century scientists such as Bacon and Newton often fall back upon magical thought while, at the same time, seeking to reconcile natural philosophy with divine authority.[4] Clearly, science does not of necessity bring about the demise of religion. Alchemical and physiological imagery abounds in rational economic discourse to this day (markets "crash," "hemorrhage," "hurt," are "volatile" or "nervous" and suffer "wounds"). Nor does reason foreshadow the end of poetry. And despite attempts by the *philosophes* to expunge mythical thought from their well-reasoned treatises, anthropomorphism and magic continue to pervade the European consciousness. Rather than erase the hermeneutical and semiological modes of thinking characteristic of the Renaissance, the Enlightenment eclipses them. There is, so to speak, a shift in the balance of power among discursive formations which brings one to the fore by occluding others, often displacing or relegating them to an alien category. In this way, the Enlightenment made reason not only its privileged episteme but a defining characteristic of the *social* elite to which its thinkers belonged or to which they aspired; anthropomorphism, the passions and instincts, as well as the bodily life in general, were systematically displaced onto peasants, savages, and women.[5] "Truth" was thus a function of power.

The polarization of science and art, reason and myth, fact and fiction, which arises in the seventeenth century and persists to this day, is both historically *and* dialectically inevitable. Just as Bacon celebrated science through a condemnation of magic and alchemy and Descartes extolled reason by denouncing the indiscriminate search for magical analogies, so many scholars nowadays are troubled by the interpenetration of what they see as antithetical discourses. But the deep disquiet felt by many scientists over the invasion of their domain by fictional and interpretive styles is, like the traditionally defensive attitude of artists toward science, good evidence that these discourses can never really isolate themselves from each other. Though they vie for dominance, perhaps, like quarreling lovers, the truth is that they cannot exist without each other.

THE FIELD OF ANTHROPOLOGY

The disquiet I have alluded to—and the epistemic pluralism from which it arises—pervades contemporary anthropology and lies behind the recent so-called Freeman-Mead controversy. The cavalier dismissal of Derek Freeman's Samoan research findings (Freeman 1983) by so many anthropologists and the distorted views of his work as "sociobiology" and "scientism" (Clifford 1986a:102) undoubtedly reflect the current vogue for exploring ethnography as a literary genre and even declaring ethnographies to *be* fictions (Clifford 1986a:6; Leach 1987:17). Replacing "reason" with the notion of "meaning," anthropologists such as Geertz invoke hermeneutics and rhetoric to blur the distinctions between science and art, a move which, in anthropology, risks encouraging the production of bad science and bad art. Others hypostatize science on the one hand, and literary-cum-interpretive styles of discourse on the other, adopting a tone of intolerance and derogation when speaking of the category with which they do not identify. Consider, for example, these excerpts from two books published in 1986, the first unrelentingly hermeneutical, the second rigidly analytical:

Evocation—that is to say, "ethnography"—is the discourse of the post-modern world, for the world that made science, and that science made, has disappeared, and scientific thought is now an archaic mode of consciousness surviving for a while yet in degraded form without the ethnographical context that created and sustained it. (Tyler 1986:123)

Hence anthropology was exhorted to renege on its scientific delusions and to adopt instead the wishy-washy style of hermeneutic interpretation which was to become the hallmark of humanistic explanation. It was left to Malinowski to lead an obscurantist crusade against a nascent scientific social anthropology. (De Meur 1986:viii)

I have already expressed the opinion that it is futile to try to decide what anthropology *in essence* is or should be. Anthropology is *in history*, and history is in it. It is for this reason that any attempt to understand the contending viewpoints over the status of anthropological knowledge must begin with the ways this discourse is grounded in history and social circumstance.

First, let us remember that anthropology is part of the Enlightenment tradition. As Horkheimer and Adorno observe (1972), however, the Enlightenment quest to dominate nature through the exercise of scientific rationality *necessarily* entails hierarchy, repression, and coercion.[6] Reason is opposed to irrationality, objectivity to subjectivity, science to art, and nature—together with those categories of humanity identified with nature—becomes an object of colonization, subjugation, and exploitation. Here is Lévi-Strauss's merciless description of the relationship between anthropology and colonialism:

Anthropology is not a dispassionate science like astronomy, which springs from the contemplation of things at a distance. It is the outcome of an historical process which has made the larger part of mankind subservient to the other, and during which millions of innocent human beings have had their resources plundered and their institutions and beliefs destroyed, whilst they themselves were ruthlessly killed, thrown into bondage, and contaminated by diseases they were unable to resist. Anthropology is the daughter to this era of violence. *Its capacity to assess more objectively the facts pertaining to the human condition reflects, on the epistemological level, a stage of affairs in which one part of mankind treats the other as an object.* (1966b:126, emphasis added)

The *tristesse* that pervades this passage leads us at once to the second major theme in anthropological discourse, one which stresses the other not as estranged from us through a lack of reason or a closer identification with nature but as our coeval—our sister, our brother, ourselves. This romantic notion, which can be traced back to the Italian Renaissance, finds expression in von Humboldt, Diderot, Goethe, Rousseau, and Marx. In its emphasis on *communitas* over hierarchy, the creative individual over the technicist, it implies a utopian vision of human association and unity transcending difference and division (Lukes 1973:67–72).

In Lévi-Strauss this romantic ideal is contrasted with the instrumental rationality that accompanies all forms of social domination. *Tristes tropiques* is, as Derrida notes, a kind of supplement to Diderot and Rousseau, "an episode of what may be called the anthropological war, the essential confrontation that *opens communi-*

cation between peoples and cultures, even when that communication is not practised under the banner of colonial or missionary oppression" (1976:107, emphasis added). As Lévi-Strauss observes toward the end of *Tristes tropiques,* however, it is the "maligned" and "misunderstood" Rousseau, not Diderot, who is his exemplar. The psychic unity of humankind is best demonstrated through empirical observations of others, a procedure which will help build *not* a utopian society but a perfect *model* of society (1973:390–91). In this sense, romantic and rationalist ideals are reconciled in Lévi-Strauss, which may account for why so many admire him for his humanism even when they abhor the formalism of his structural analysis.

The second point to be made about the historically constituted character of anthropology brings us back to Foucault. As we have seen, anthropologists are, often without realizing it, heir to a plethora of discursive styles and paradigms. Following Foucault, and for the sake of argument, I have reduced them to three and characterized them in terms of their emphases on similitude, difference, and history. The first episteme, prevalent in the sixteenth century, focused on sensible and sympathetic resemblances. Its anthropomorphic emphasis contrasts dramatically with the seventeenth-century scientific bias toward rational measurement, identity, and difference. Historicity defines a third episteme, one which makes possible the emergence of the human sciences in the nineteenth century and enables us to trace out a dialectic in which the other epistemes are counterpointed, producing in anthropology a tension between analytical methods and models comparable to those of the natural sciences *and* hermeneutical or semiological modes of knowledge often reminiscent of magic and poetics.[7]

Before endeavoring to explain the epistemic shifts which grant differential truth values, powers, and privileges to different modes of knowledge at different times, I want to examine in more detail the way anthropology reveals in its ways of making comparisons these different discursive traditions.

First, let us consider the exciting laboratory studies made in the late 1960s and early 1970s on the acquisition and use of "sign languages" among nonhuman primates (Gardner and Gardner 1969; Premack 1971). The emotions and hopes which researchers invested in their chimpanzees and gorillas (they often raised them from early infancy) may account for the tendency of some to see humanlike intentions and conceptual skills which, in the view of other scientists, could not, for neurophysiological reasons, be present in apes (Sebeok and Sebeok 1980). In other words, the close *mutual* bonds formed between researchers and apes may have led some anthropologists into the pathetic fallacy of projecting human motivations and sentiments onto their experimental animals. Whether or not apes can manipulate signs to spontaneously create new meanings and enjoy conversations with humans is thus an open question. Clearly, there is a discursive tension here between notions of similitude and difference, sympathy and detachment, with regard to both language use and cognition.[8]

Second, I want to reflect a little on the sign language of anthropology itself, especially the way we use analogy. That analogy is fundamental to our discourse goes without saying. But are the analogies we draw between society and an organism (functionalism), a language (structuralism), or a text (poststructuralism) founded upon fact or fiction? Does our discourse correspond to objective reality or is it, like the mythopoeic discourse which Bacon wanted to purge from science, pervaded by fortuitous and "merely apparent" analogies, "curious resemblances, such as the writers on natural magic . . . are everywhere parading" and replete with "similitudes and sympathies that have no reality" (Bacon 1905:334–335)? Consider the following passage from Radcliffe-Brown, who defined anthropology in positivist terms as a branch of comparative sociology, the aim of which was to arrive at "acceptable generalisations" through the systematic "observation, description, comparison and classification" of "the process of social life" (1952:1–3):

> The concept of organic function is one that is used to refer to the connection between the structure of an organism and the life process of that organism. The processes that go on within a human body while it is living are dependent on the organic structure. It is the function of the heart to pump blood through the body. . . . if the heart ceases to perform its function the life process comes to an end and the structure as a living structure also comes to an end. . . .
>
> In reference to social systems and their theoretical understanding one way of using the concept of function is the same as its *scientific use* in physiology. It can be used to refer to the interconnection between the social structure and the process of social life. It is this use of the word function that seems to me to make it a useful term in comparative sociology. (12, emphasis added)

This kind of analogy between the human body and the social body can be traced back to the Presocratics (Lloyd 1966:232–71) and is directly comparable to the vitalist and anthropomorphic notions of primitive people. It is certainly not typical of the scientific rationality of the seventeenth century, when the organic metaphor was superseded by physical imagery and nature and society were seen not as organisms but as automata and machines (Brown 1977:139).

Let us now turn to the work of an anthropologist directly influenced by Radcliffe-Brown: Meyer Fortes.[9] In *The Web of Kinship among the Tallensi* (1949), as the title itself suggests, Fortes sustains an image of Tale social life as a "fabric" with a warp and a woof. There are "networks" of "ramifying ties," ties "interwoven to form an elaborate mesh," "filaments of cognatic kinship," while, through marriage, "new threads of kinship are spun," groups "knit together," and extraclan kinship ties "woven into the lineage fabric." This elaborate analogy between a society and woven cloth is not, however, drawn by the Tallensi themselves, for whom kinship is "the power of procreation"—dɔyam—a word derived from the verb dɔy, "to bear or beget a child." "If people say 'we are dɔyam,' the basic analogy they have in mind is that of siblings" (1949:16–19).

Why does Fortes avoid the use of organic imagery in his study of Tale kinship, especially when this imagery is central to structural-functionalist discourse *as well as to the Tale way of conceiving kinship relationships in their own society*? Fortes does use organic imagery in his account of Tale clanship, speaking of a "morphology of the social body," of "intestinal dissensions," "segmentation," social units "like cells" (1945:232) and describing the lineage system as "the skeleton of their social structure, the bony framework which shapes their body politic" (1945:30). Yet here again the anthropologist's trope does not tally with native discourse, where a lineage is spoken of as the "house" (*yir*) or the "children" (*biis*) of its founding ancestor, and a lineage "segment" as a "room" (*dug*) within the "house" (1949:10–11).

Despite Fortes's observation that "metaphors are proverbially treacherous" (1945:231), it is possible to see a consistent principle governing his choice of tropes: an avoidance of any overlap or fusion between Tallensi discourse and his own. It is as if the would-be scientist feels he must simultaneously maintain a social and epistemological distance from those he studies, distinguishing *their* hermeneutic, with its surfeit of animistic correspondences, from *his* rational, disinterested analysis. Moreover, a "scientific" account must, in Radcliffe-Brown's view, move from the ideographic to the nomothetic, that is, it has to transcend the immediate, phenomenal level of social life in order to arrive at "acceptable general proposition" (Radcliffe-Brown 1952:1).

The very real difficulty of proving that Newtonian or Einsteinian laws exist in the social world has not, of course, prevented anthropologists from interpreting social life in terms of laws. The question is, do we really need to believe that the regularities and systems we come up with correspond to how the world actually *is*, in the way our image in a mirror corresponds to who we really are? Do we have to believe that our representations of the world "are not merely ours but its own, as it looks to itself, as it would describe itself if it could" (Rorty 1982:194)? And, if we abandon the belief that our scientific integrity is only guaranteed while we remain faithful to the goal of describing objective reality, are we then thrown into intellectual anarchy, where data get fudged, empirical rigor is despised, fictions masquerade as facts, and any harebrained interpretive idea is given as much value as any other?

These questions all bear upon the anxiety that troubles many anthropologists who want to ditch the positivist notion of value-neutral social science, yet cannot accept the relativistic, solipsistic kind of anthropology they imagine will follow in its wake. It is an anxiety common to all human beings faced with the aleatory character of existence and the provisionality of their understanding. In the sense that magic and science both protect and console us against the uncertainty of life, they are very much on a par. As Dewey observed, speaking of the troubling contrast between the seen and the unseen:

> We may term the way in which our ancestors dealt with the contrast superstitions, but the contrast is no superstition. It is a primary *datum* in any experience. . . . Our magical safeguard against the uncertain character of the world is to deny the existence of chance, to mumble universal and necessary law, the ubiquity of cause and effect the uniformity of nature, universal progress, and the inherent rationality of the universe. (1929:44)

But the anxiety felt by many contemporary anthropologists is not just existential. It reflects a particular cast of mind, as well as a recent shift in the power base of anthropology itself.

Construing anthropology as *either* science *or* art, fact *or* fiction, true *or* false, knowledge *or* opinion implies an absurd antinomy between objectivity and subjectivity, and the idea that we must somehow choose between one or the other. As we have seen, however, the discourse of anthropology is a curious blend of both sorcery and science. The jargon of positivism—borrowed from allegedly more dis-passionate sciences such as mathematics, mechanics, biology, and linguistics—often seems to be *depicting* reality when in fact it is *playing games* with it.[10] When Fortes or Radcliffe-Brown draws analogies between organic and social systems, the name of the game is not exact science but sympathetic magic. The tropes are not what they pretend to be, neutral means for expressing facts; they constitute the facts in certain ways and imply hidden assumptions and aims. As in magical thought, language is confused with the reality it depicts. By playing with the "cold," "inhuman," "mathematical" language of science, positivist anthropology in-duces in us a sense of concreteness, rationality, and method (Rorty 1982:194). It achieves, however, only the aura, not the authority, of science. This is not to say that ridding anthropology of the jargon of science will necessarily make it any more capable of depicting things as they really are, any more than filling anthropology with the jargon of poetics will necessarily make it more authentic. Just as imper-sonal idioms create little more than an illusion of objectivity, so too the adoption of a reflexive, first-person, confessional idiom—what Adorno called a "jargon of authenticity"—creates little more than an illusion of sincerity.

Let us then accept that there is no ahistorical, absolute, nonfinite reality *either outside or within us* that we can reach by adopting a particular discursive style. The *world* is out there, to be sure, and deep within us too, *but not the truth* (Rorty 1986:3). This view leads us at once to another way of understanding anthropolo-gists' anxiety about the status of anthropological knowledge.

TRUTH AND POWER

As I noted earlier, since the 1970s there has been an epistemic shift within anthro-pology away from an analytical, positivist conception of knowledge to a hermeneu-tical one which, to adapt Weber's phrase, sees both the anthropologist and the people he or she studies as suspended in webs of significance they themselves have spun.[11] This "interpretive turn," as Rabinow and Sullivan call it, does not, as some anthropologists fear, signify a lapse into romanticist subjectism, but in its insistence that "understanding any action is analogous to textual interpretation" (Rabinow and Sullivan 1979:12) the new hermeneutic anthropology is reminiscent of the sixteenth-century episteme, characterized by a search for hidden meanings through the reading, divination, and deciphering of visible signatures and signs. I will have more to say later about this textualist view of anthropology. For the moment, let us try to account for the vogue it presently enjoys.

In the first place, the interpretive turn is one consequence of a widespread disenchantment with the mechanistic, reductionist, and formalistic character of positivist anthropology (cf. Habermas 1983:252). This disenchantment is so great that many anthropologists no longer care to distinguish between science and scien-tism.

Second, the 1970s saw a gradual decline in the prestige of structuralism.

Throughout the 1960s, structural anthropology captured the imaginations of historians, literary theorists, natural scientists, and journalists alike. Susan Sontag, writing of Lévi-Strauss in 1967, spoke of "the anthropologist as hero" (69–81). Now, however, the heroes are literary theorists such as Geoffrey Hartmann and Edward Said, historians such as Hayden White, and "poststructuralist" thinkers such as Jacques Derrida and Michel Foucault—thinkers whom Richard Rorty calls "textualists" (1982:139). In a sense, anthropology has lost its glamor and gone into the wings, from where it tries to retrieve power vicariously through conjuring with the texts and names which are at center stage.

But, to my mind, the most critical event that bears upon the transformations in contemporary anthropology is the loss of our empirical field, a loss which is inextricably tied up with decolonization and the loss of empire. But the loss of our traditional laboratories, or the difficulty we experience persuading postcolonial governments to grant us access to those that remain, cannot alone account for why anthropologists have turned more and more to exploring their own archive of ethnographic texts and contemplating the history and field of their own discourse. Decolonization gave rise to intense debate about the relationship between knowledge and power, and searching critiques—particularly during the Vietnam War—of the ways anthropological knowledge is linked to imperialism and oppression (Asad 1973; Condominas 1977; Hymes 1969).[12] But while many anthropologists were galvanized into political action as a result of these critiques, others looked back nostalgically to a pristine world or indulged a kind of remorse over the link between the instrumental rationality that underpinned both anthropology and the structure of social domination. This mood of melancholy pervades Lévi-Strauss's *Tristes tropiques:*

> The first thing we see as we travel round the world is our own filth, thrown in the face of mankind. . . .
> The anthropologist is the less able to ignore his own civilisation and to dissociate himself from its faults in that his very existence is incomprehensible except as an attempt at redemption; he is the symbol of atonement. (1973:38, 389)

It is my view that this need for redemption is one reason for the epistemic shift toward reflexive and interpretive anthropology. It is one aspect of our attempt to "reinvent" anthropology, adapting it to survive in the postcolonial world (Hymes 1969). But in bemoaning the scientific rationalism that accompanies colonialism and in seeking to identify with the oppressed by placing their knowledge on a par with our own, we may be doing nothing but salving our consciences through a form of sympathetic magic and using science as the scapegrace for our sins.

Just as seventeenth-century science did not become truer by derogating magic and alchemy, interpretive anthropology gains little more than a semblance of truth by pointing out the poverty of positivism. Behind the current polarization of analytical and interpretive modes of anthropological knowledge lies a struggle for intellectual and moral authority in which scholars promise to save us from false gods only to end up trying to sell us their own idols. In its antagonism to natural science and its privileging of literary criticism, textualism claims too much, just as positivistic social science does. By fetishizing texts, it divides—as the advent of literacy itself did—readers from authors, and separates both from the world. The idea that "there is nothing outside the text" may be congenial to someone whose life is confined to academe, but it sounds absurd in the village worlds where anthropologists carry out their work, where people negotiate meaning in face-to-face interactions, not as individual minds but as embodied social beings. In other words, textualism tends to ignore the flux of human interrelationships, the ways meanings are created intersubjectively as well as "intertextually," embodied in gestures as well as in words, and connected to political, moral, and aesthetic interests. Quite simply, people cannot be reduced to texts any more than they can be reduced to objects.

My own hope is for the kind of pragmatist approach exemplified by Gregory Bateson. Such an approach avoids crude either/or antinomies, uses different epistemes strategically, clarifies the relation between our thought and our own personal or social situation, and always treats our understanding as provisional. Bateson's epistemological openness means using the methods of both natural science and interpretive anthropology.

As a natural scientist Bateson considers it imperative to understand through painstaking empirical work how it is neurophysiologically possible for us to receive impressions of the world in which we live, that is, how our eyes and brains work. But this approach to vision requires a complementary understanding of how we create, out of the showers of impulses brought to the brain by the optic nerve, meaningful pictures of the world. The grounds for the possibility of being human are both neurophysiological and cultural, innate and learned. We can neither discover the world as it is "out there" nor just "make it up":

> I have the use of the information that that which I see, the images, or that which I feel as pain, the prick of a pin, or the ache of a tired muscle—for these, too, are images created in their respective modes—that all this is neither objective truth or is it all hallucination. There is a combining or marriage between an objectivity that is *passive* to the outside world and a creative subjectivity, neither pure solipsism nor its opposite. (Bateson 1977:245)

In elucidating this interplay between the world we find and the worlds we make up, Bateson notes the importance of analogy, for analogy is the visible expression of the way we are continually comparing the novel with the known in what J. Z. Young calls a dialectic of doubt and certainty (1951).

Bateson also discusses the vital role of analogy in his own thought by recounting the way he formulated a model of Iatmul social organization. Iatmul society, unlike our own, lacks any form of chieftaincy. Control of the individual is through "lateral" sanctions rather than "sanctions from above." In pondering this contrast, Bateson hit upon the notion that it was "like the difference between the radially symmetrical animals (jellyfish, sea anemones, etc.) and the animals which have transverse segmentation (earthworms, lobsters, man, etc.)" (1973:50).

Extending this analogy, Bateson argues that Iatmul clan organization resembles the morphology of the sea anemone—near-identical segments arranged around a center, like the sectors of a circle. Iatmul clans tend to imitate and borrow from one another, rather than differentiating themselves serially like the segments in our own society or the legs of a lobster.

> I followed up the analogy in another direction. Impressed by the phenomena of meta-meric differentiation, I made the point that in our society with its hierarchical systems (comparable to the earthworm or the lobster), when a group secedes from the parent society, it is usual to find that the line of fission, the division between the new group and the old, marks a differentiation of mores. The Pilgrim Fathers wander off in order to be *different*. But among the Iatmul, when two groups in a village quarrel, and one half goes off and founds a new community, the mores of the two groups remain identical. In our society, fission tends to be heretical (a following after other doctrines or mores), but in Iatmul, fission is rather schismatic (a following after other leaders without change of dogma). (1973:51)

Bateson admits that this organic analogy can be pushed too far, but as a "vague" or "wild" hunch it proved useful in helping him see his data in a novel and edifying way.[13] Unlike Radcliffe-Brown and Fortes, Bateson uses an organic analogy without apology, as a way of loosening his thinking and using his imagination. Though his knowledge of natural science is greater than most anthropologists', there is no pretense of a "strict" inductive method whereby generalizations and patterns emerge directly from the data. Referring to the strategic use of both loose and strict thinking, Bateson observes:

> We ought to accept and enjoy this dual nature of scientific thought and be willing to value the way in which the two processes work together to give us advances in understanding of the world. We ought not to frown too much on either process, or at least *to frown equally on either process when it is unsupplemented by the other.* (1973:60, emphasis added)

Although comparing the difference between Iatmul society and our own in terms of the difference between sea anemones and lobsters may be *essentially* absurd,[14] there is always the possibility that artificial or magical analogies may have practical or scientific value. Thus, although much non-Western medicine is magical and homeopathic, not allopathic, it is estimated that 25 to 50 percent of its pharmacopoeia is empirically effective. Indeed, a large number of modern drugs are derived from non-Western "magical" medicines: rauwolfia, digitalis, opium, cinchona, podophyllin, quassia, acacia, sarsparilla, kousso, copaiba, guaiac, jalap, coca, and more (Hughes 1978:154). That things are used on the basis of magical similitudes does not preclude their having intellectual and therapeutic value. Indeed, as Joseph Needham observes with respect to the Taoists, "they realised that, in the light of experience, the technologist will often manage to do the right thing in a given situation, even if sometimes he does it for the wrong theoretical reasons" (Ronan 1978:103).

This epistemic pluralism suggests an opportunistic, improvisatory attitude to ethnographic inquiry. Truth is seen pragmatically, not as an essence but as an aspect of existence, not as some abstraction such as Science, Rationality, Beauty, or God, to be respected whatever the circumstances, but as a means of coping with life. Such a view brings us back to Bokonon's notion that it is often useful to think of truth as a lie and to think of lies as useful truths. It is a notion that would also be congenial to Keti Ferenke Koroma, the Kuranko storyteller I knew, who was always insisting that the value of fiction lies in its consequences.

The Kuranko make a distinction between two genres of oral narratives: *kuma kore* ("ancestral words"), which are true, and *tilei* ("folktales"), which Keti Ferenke had a genius for creating and telling and which are admittedly make-believe. But the difference between these genres is not simply a difference between truth and falsity, history and fantasy. Although *tilei* are bracketed apart from the quotidian world—told at night, set in far-off places and distant times, with animal characters to mask their link to the human world—they reveal and help resolve ambiguities and tensions in the conventional order of things. By suspending disbelief, scorning rigid codifications, and unsettling orthodox beliefs, the *tilei* inspire each person to reconstruct and reinvent the world. *Tilei* are thus concerned with existential truth, not dogma. Although the devices used to annul the normal order of things are fictional, the result of listening to the tales and discussing the dilemmas posed by them is that each person comes to decide the world for himself or herself rather than passively accepting it as a fait accompli.

While *tilei* represent a pragmatist notion of truth, *kuma kore* represent an essentialist notion of truth, since epics and clan myths, like ethnographic realist writing, allegedly correspond to some "objective" reality. The point is, though, that *tilei* and *kuma kore* are mutually necessary. Each engenders the other. Each is a moment in the dialectic of Kuranko social life in which norms are defined as much through negating and confounding them as through slavish imitation and formal respect (Jackson 1982a).

In my own writing I have also felt the force of this dialectic, simply because my experience overflows the confines of orthodox discursive styles, refusing to recognize any *essential* division between ethnographic experience and other modes of experience, personal, ethical, or political.[15] This spirit of what William James called "radical empiricism" has sometimes led me to depart from analogies which are true (in the sense that they purport to reveal real connections in the objective world) and use analogies which have no such pretensions. It is like the difference between comparing one's thoughts and feelings to a winged creature and speaking of the *functional* connections between the wings of birds and of bats (a true analogy) or the *phylogenetic* connections between the wings of birds, the front flippers of seals, and our own upper limbs (a relation of homology) (Gould 1987).

But this is not to celebrate with Nietzsche that "the lie—and *not* the truth—is divine!"—only to stress that the domains of experience which we conventionally call fact and fiction, science and art, are mutually necessary as well as intimately connected. The value and place of different discursive styles have to be decided by the situation we find ourselves in and the problems we address. It is a question of existential strategies, not strict rules. Rather than pretend there is no difference between science and art or argue that one can be epistemologically privileged over the other, we have to learn to play them both off against the other. This is what

Bateson means by epistemological openness and what Rorty means when he advocates an "ironic attitude towards 'truth'"—using literature as a dialectical foil for
science *and vice versa,* but not losing sight of their mutual dependency. Just as anthropology needs to be rescued from its positivist proclivities, so the poet sometimes needs to be saved from his friends (Rorty 1982:137).

CAT'S CRADLE

Truth is on the margins. It is lost when it is claimed. It makes its appearance fleet-
ingly, when systems collapse and dogmas are exploded. And untruth, as Nietzsche
observed, is "a condition of life" (1973:17).

Mendacity, make-believe, and gainsaying are constitutive of our very humanity. The linguistic and mental ability to recognize "the thing which is not" (Steiner
1973:223), to create counterworlds—the skill of what George Steiner calls
"alternity"—is what makes us subjects and agents of our own existence:

> whatever their bio-sociological origin, the uses of language for "alternity," for mis-
> construction, for illusion and play, are the greatest of man's tools by far. With this
> stick he has reached out of the cage of instinct to touch the boundaries of the universe
> and of time.
>
> At first the instrument probably had a banal survival value. It still carried with it
> the impulse of instinctual mantling. Fiction was disguise: from those seeking out the
> same water-hole, the same sparse quarry, or meagre sexual chance. To misinform, to
> utter less than the truth was to gain a vital edge of space or subsistence. Natural selec-
> tion would favor the contriver. Folk tales and mythology retain a blurred memory of
> the evolutionary advantage of mask and misdirection. Loki, Odysseus are very late,
> literary concentrates of the widely diffused motif of the liar, of the dissembler elusive
> as flame and water, who survives.[16] (1973:224–25)

This reference to the trickster brings us back to Bokonon, back to the connection between storytelling and selfhood, and back to cat's cradles. The Maori trickster Maui was the inventor of the cat's cradle (variously called *he whai, huhi,* and
maui). Like the Kuranko folktale and our own ethnographic discourse, the cat's
cradle is stretched, tensed, and held between the poles of reality and make-believe.
With a single endless loop of string, the Polynesians could illustrate stories, depict
mythological scenes and persons, or suggest the forms of houses, weapons, articles
of clothing, canoe and adze lashings, landmarks, flora and fauna (Jayne 1906:3;
Handy 1925:3–7). Can our discourse be likened to these string figures, a game we
play with words, the thread of an argument whose connection with reality is always
oblique and tenuous,[17] which crosses to and fro, interlacing description with interpretation, instruction with entertainment, but always ambiguously placed between
practical and antinomian ends? If so, truth is not binding. It is in the interstices
as much as it is in the structure, in fiction as much as in fact.

Notes

PREFACE

1. Several chapters in this book are revised or rewritten versions of previously published essays: chapter 4 (1978b), chapter 5 (1978a), chapter 7 (1975), chapter 8 (1983a), chapter 9 (1983b), chapter 10 (1987a), chapter 11 (1987b).

ONE. INTRODUCTION

1. In his early writings, Lévi-Strauss often comes very close to the view of Merleau-Ponty, that "the process of joining objective analysis to lived experience is perhaps the most proper task of anthropology, the one which distinguishes it from other social sciences" (Merleau-Ponty 1964:119). Thus, in his introduction to the works of Marcel Mauss (1950), he observes:

> la preuve du social, elle, ne peut être que mentale; autrement dit, nous ne pouvons jamais être sûrs d'avoir atteint le sens et la fonction d'une institution, si nous ne sommes pas en mesure de revivre son incidence sur une conscience individuelle. Comme cette incidence est une partie intégrante de l'institution, toute interpretation valable doit faire coincider l'objectivité de l'analyse historique ou comparative avec le subjectivité de l'expérience vécue. (Lévi-Strauss 1950:xxvi)

In his later writings, too, Lévi-Strauss often notes, albeit grudgingly, that "Recognition of the fact that consciousness is not everything, nor even the most important thing, is not a reason for abandoning it. . . ." (1981:629). "The subject, while remaining deliberately at the background so as to allow free play to this anonymous deployment of discourse, does not renounce consciousness of it, or rather does not prevent it achieving consciousness of itself through him" (629).

Similarly, Foucault, who took such umbrage at Sartre's reliance on a centered subject as a source of meaning and, in his projects of the 1970s, ruled out individual self-consciousness as an object of knowledge, turns to study the centered subject in *The History of Sexuality* and applauds Sartre's views on creativity and praxis (Poster 1984:26–28, 140–41).

2. Adorno used the term *identity-thinking* for our habit of regarding concepts and the objects they pertain to as related in some determinate, mirrorlike way. Non-identity-thinking, or negative dialectic, recognizes the problematic, indeterminate, illusory connections between concepts and the things they represent. It counters the reification which is always implied by identity-thinking, the spurious belief that a concept really covers or mirrors its object or is congruent and isomorphic with the experience it purports to denote. "The name of dialectics says no more, to begin with, than that objects do not go into their concepts without leaving a remainder, that they come to contradict the traditional norm of adequacy. Contradiction . . . indicates the untruth of identity, the fact that the concept does not exhaust the thing conceived" (Adorno 1973:5).

Sartre's dialectic also allows that lived experience contradicts or overflows the cognitive limits which we sometimes imagine we can set upon it. "Lived experience," he writes, "is perpetually susceptible of comprehension, but never of knowledge. Taking it as a point of departure, one can know certain psychic phenomena by concepts, but not this experience itself" (Sartre 1969:49).

3. Adorno captures this point of view nicely:

Traditional philosophy thinks of itself as possessing an infinite object, and in that belief it becomes a finite, conclusive philosophy. A changed philosophy would have to cancel that claim, to cease persuading others and itself that it has the infinite at its disposal. Instead, if it were delicately understood, the changed philosophy itself would be infinite in the sense of scorning solidification in a body of enumerable theorems. Its substance would lie in the diversity of objects that impinge upon it and of the objects it seeks, a diversity not wrought by any schema; to those objects, philosophy would truly give itself rather than use them as a mirror in which to reread itself, mistaking its own image for concretion. (1973:13)

The concluding image reminds one of the argument Richard Rorty advances in *Philosophy and the Mirror of Nature* (1979) against the Cartesian and Kantian notions that knowledge can be an accurate representation, or mirroring, of the world, a reproduction of its own intrinsic vocabulary and grammar.

4. James's pragmatism and Husserl's phenomenology make their appearance on either side of the Atlantic at about the same time. Both philosophers sought

> to "dissolve" traditional metaphysical problems by *a return to experience.* At the same time, James and Husserl (and Bergson) are distinguished from the logical positivists and from traditional empiricists (particularly the British empiricists) by a conception of experience as something much more complex . . . much more existential than that allowed by the purely "cognitive" (and "sensationalist") accounts of experience accepted by earlier empiricists. Further, James and Husserl conceived philosophy to be primarily concerned with the realm of *meaning.* . . . This necessarily led them to place *man-the-experiencer* at the center of their philosophical preoccupations, to replace metaphysics, so to speak, with "philosophical anthropology." (Edie 1965:114–15)

5. Consider, for instance, Malinowski's functionalist views in the light of his own personal turmoil in the Trobriands. By making Trobriand society hold together, was he perhaps struggling magically, vicariously, to rescue his own self from disintegration? James Clifford would appear to agree: "One of the ways Malinowski pulled himself together was by writing ethnography. Here the fashioned wholeness of a self and of a culture seem to be mutually reinforcing allegories of identity" (Clifford 1986a:152).

6. Victor Turner's elucidation of the polysemic term *experience* is worth quoting at length:

> Scholars trace the word right back to the hypothetical Indo-European base *per,* "to attempt, venture," whence the Greek, *peira,* πεῖρα, "experience," whence we also derive "empirical," and the Old English, *faer,* "danger," from which we derive our modern word "fear." More directly, "experience" derives, via Middle English and Old French, from the Latin *experientia,* denoting "trial, proof, experiment," and is itself generated from *experiens,* the present participle of *experiri,* "to try, test," from *ex-* "out" + base *per* as in *peritus,* "experienced," which is, of course, related to *periculum,* "danger" or "peril." Etymologists like Skeat relate the Greek *peirao,* πειράω, "I try" to *perao,* περάω, "I pass through." If culture is really to be regarded as the crystallized secretion of once living human experience (which is still capable of liquefaction back into similar if not identical lived-through experience under favorable conditions, like the reputed miracle of Saint Januarius' dried blood), then we may perhaps see the term "experience" in its connotational penumbra at least, as preconsciously, if not unconsciously, linked with *rites de passage,* with danger, with "faring" or travel and "ferrying," its Anglo-Saxon form, and with "fear" and "experiment," which is, of course, "test, trial, the action of trying anything, or putting it to the proof" (Oxford English Dictionary). Thus, experience is a journey, a test (of self, of suppositions about others), a ritual passage, an exposure to peril, and an exposure to fear. Does this not sum up to something akin to fieldwork, even to pilgrimage, which is, again etymologically, a journey "through fields" (*per agros*), a peregrination? Anthropological fieldwork surely deserves its very own kind of *experiential theory,* its own edifice of practical, yet poetical, knowledge. (Turner 1985:226)

7. It should be noted, however, that the equation of thought and vision—the image of the mind's eye—was established well before Locke's time. Summarizing Bruno Snell's

study of classical Greek verbs for seeing, James Edie shows how sight became reified as our primary and unitary metaphor for knowing:

> Even the later and more technical term for sight, the one adopted by Plato and Aristotle for philosophical contemplation, *theorein* (θεωρεῖν), was not originally a verb but a noun, *theoros* (θεωρός), meaning "to be a spectator," from which it derived its later meaning of "looking at," ultimately "to contemplate." Here, clearly, the same word was used to designate in a confused way both seeing (the optical phenomenon) and intellectual comprehension, and this is even more clear with the term *noein* (νοεῖν), which in early Greek "stands for a type of seeing which involves not merely visual activity but the mental act that goes with the vision." It was probably through the use of this word, *noein* (νοεῖν, νόος), that the Greeks were first enabled to distinguish clearly the experience of "thinking" as such. Then, through the process of analogy so important in the evolution of language, the classical word for sight, *idein*, also came to designate (especially in the form *eidenai*, εἰδεναι˙) the process of thinking, since the word for thought, *noein*, also meant, in its primary sense, "to see." Professor Snell has shown that in early Greek the eye served as the "model for the absorption of experiences," and we can add that the earliest epistemological vocabulary is therefore a vocabulary of *seeing*. (Edie 1976:173)

8. Cf. Rorty 1979:12:

> It is pictures rather than propositions, metaphors rather than statements, which determine most of our philosophical convictions. The picture which holds traditional philosophy captive is that of the mind as a great mirror, containing various representations—some accurate, some not—and capable of being studied by pure, nonempirical methods. Without the notion of the mind as mirror, the notion of knowledge as accuracy of representation would not have suggested itself. Without this latter notion, the strategy common to Descartes and Kant—getting more accurate representations by inspecting, repairing, and polishing the mirror, so to speak—would not have made sense. Without this strategy in mind, recent claims that philosophy could consist of "conceptual analysis" or "phenomenological analysis" or "explication of meanings" or examination of "the logic of our language" or of "the structure of the constituting activity of consciousness" would not have made sense.

9. Edie notes that

> the family of words related to the Greek *gignoskein* (γιγνώσκειν), such as *cognoscere* in Latin, *connaitre* in French, *recognize* in English, originally signified "to be with" and then "to recognize" in the sense of "seeing or meeting the same person again." It designated the ability to identify other persons—as one recognizes one's friends, acquaintances, one's comrades in battle, etc. (1976:238)

10. During my first period of fieldwork I used simple perspective drawings to test Kuranko villagers' perceptions of objects depicted on a plane surface in conformity with the way they are seen from a fixed point of view. Villagers invariably perceived objects as small or large according to their relative size in the drawing rather than according to their relative distance from the observation point in the foreground.

11. In *Birth of the Clinic* (1973), Foucault traces the emergence of modern medicine in the closing years of the eighteenth century to a particular application of clinical gaze, and in *Discipline and Punish* (1979) he discusses at length how Bentham's *Panopticon* may be seen as a compelling "architectural figure" of the late eighteenth century preoccupation with control through centralized structures of surveillance. This supervisory perspective thus privileges and empowers not only the eye as a means of knowing but also the observer as a social and political being to whom others must submit as objects of his gaze. Paul Stoller has written brilliantly on the "recurrent 'monarch-of-all-I-survey' convention" in anthropological monographs, travel literature, and fiction (1984:101).

12. Even professional genealogists and bards (*finabas*) often differ in the ways they relate lines of chiefly succession and fail to discriminate between filial and fraternal links.

13. For examples of the equation of lineage and dwelling, see Goody 1967:65–68 (LoWiili); Karp 1978 (Iteso); Fernandez 1982:75 (Fang); Little 1951:96–97 (Mende); Paulme 1954:79 (Kissi); Mayer 1949:4–5 (Gusii); Southall 1952:25 (Luo). For examples of the equation of lineage and begetting, see Rattray 1923:76–78 (Ashanti); Ardener 1959:118 (Ibo); Jackson 1977b:67 (Kuranko). The Zulu example is worth quoting: "A lineage (*umndeni* or, much more commonly in Nyuswa, *uzalo*, from *zala*, to bear, hence 'of common birth') is composed of people who can trace descent to a common agnatic ancestor" (Ngubane 1977:13). Our word *nation* comes much closer than *lineage* to this African sense of social identity as deriving from "birth" or "being born" (see Vico 1968:xx–xxi).

14. Consider the time it took for anthropologists to seriously question the analytical usefulness of Africanist lineage theory in understanding social organization in the New Guinea Highlands (Barnes 1962; Lederman 1986:40–61) and then the time it took for Africanists to question the excessive systematization of lineage theory in African studies (Karp 1978).

15. This viewpoint is nicely summarized by Nikos Kazantzakis in his novel *Zorba the Greek:* "To say 'yes' to necessity and change the inevitable into something done of their own free will? That is perhaps the only human way to deliverance. It is a pitiable way, but there is no other" (1961:274).

16. Some ambiguity arose in translating the English word *giant*. The nearest equivalent in Kuranko is *ke yan* ("long man"), which designates a tall bush spirit that sometimes allies itself with hunters. I was told that if this bush spirit appears in a dream it wishes to help the dreamer.

17. For detailed accounts of Adorno's indebtedness to Schönberg, see Buck-Morss 1977:13–17 and Jameson 1971:11–59. The following passages, the first from his Overture to *The Raw and the Cooked*, the second from the Finale of *The Naked Man*, encapsulate Lévi-Strauss's view of the relationship between mythical and musical form. After speaking of "his reverence, from childhood on, for 'that God, Richard Wagner,'" Lévi-Strauss notes:

> If Wagner is accepted as the undeniable originator of the structural analysis of myths (and even of folk tales, as in *Die Meistersinger*), it is a profoundly significant fact that the analysis was made, in the first instance, *in music*. Therefore, when I suggested that the analysis of myths was comparable with that of a major musical score, I was only drawing the logical conclusion from Wagner's discovery that the structure of myths can be revealed through a musical score. (1970:15)

> . . . music, in its own way, has a function comparable to that of mythology. The musical work, which is a myth coded in sounds instead of words, offers an interpretative grid, a matrix of relationships which filters and organizes lived experience, acts as a substitute for it and provides the comforting illusion that contradictions can be overcome and difficulties resolved. (1981:659)

TWO. TWO LIVES

1. Senegalese fire finches (*tintinburuwe*) nest in the eaves of houses and fly about in the cooking yards—a reason, one supposes, why the Kuranko say the birds harbor the spirits of infants who have died before weaning and been buried, as is customary, in the area of the rubbish heap or hearth (*sundu kunye ma*).

2. As in the adage *Baranen dama na keli ma, koni katar' la min bi birindi kela ma* ("Bananas [on a single comb] are kin, but those on a hand are especially close"), i.e., the oneness of kinship (*nakelinyorgoye*, lit. "mother-one-partners") is like the oneness of a hand of bananas.

3. The unavoidability of initiation connotes the inevitability of one's separation from one's parents and one's movement from the nurturance and shelter of one's natal home into the world. Hence the Kamban song that often accompanies preparations for initiation:

Hali i fa ya a ya wulan la bor ma si ke bo i ro, yenyen, dannu, yenyen. . . .
Hali i na ya a ya wulan la bor ma si ke bo i ro, yenyen, dannu, yenyen. . . .

("Even if your father's eye is red we will take you away from him, *yenyen*, children, *yenyen*.
. . .

Even if your mother's eye is red we will take you away from her, *yenyen*, children, *yenyen*. . . .")

The red eye (*ya wulan*) signifies covetousness, longing, and annoyance.

4. Such moments of reversal and turmoil may be biographical and adventitious or socially implemented and ritualized, as in initiations and myths. The contrast may be spoken of as one between "rituals of affliction" and "rituals of rebellion."

5. "*Man muss diese versteinerten Verhältnisse dadurch zum Tanzen zwingen, dass man ihnen ihre eigene Melodie vorsingt!*" (Marx 1953:311). I have paraphrased the translation by Erich Fromm (1973:83).

6. Kuranko often use images of networks or chains to describe the way one's fate is inextricably tied to the fate of others: "one's birth is like the network of ropes tied over the rice farm to keep birds away" (*soron i le ko yagbayile*); "one's birth is like a chain" (*soron i le ko yolke*).

7. Poisons (*dabere*) constitute a separate category in the Kuranko pharmacopoeia, associated with women not men.

8. It is instructive, by contrast, to consider the following case of hubris which involved a *Kometigi* from Kamadugu Sukurela and a *besetigi* renowned throughout Kuranko for his skills in sorcery:

> The *Kometigi*, a man in his mid-twenties, ran away with another man's wife. The woman's father and husband took the matter to court and the chief of the *Kometigi*'s own village ordered him to allow the woman to return to her husband. When he refused, people felt that his scorn and arrogance came from his sense of power and invincibility as *Kometigi*. He put himself above the law. Unable to get justice by normal secular means, the woman's father secured the services of a renowned *besetigi* who placed a curse on the young man. Soon after the man succumbed to encephalitis—allegedly because of the curse—and died.

9. The stock phrases are "that is how it happened" (*maiya ta ra nya na*), "that is how our ancestors let it happen" (*ma bimban' ya ta nya na*), and "that is what we encountered" (*maiya min ta ra*).

10. Keti Ferenke speaks of his "grandfathers/forebears/ancestors" (*bimbannu*), but I have translated this as great-grandfather or great-great-grandfather whenever genealogically appropriate. The bracketed indications of whether the relationship is matrilateral or patrilateral are also mine.

11. Kuranko say the elder child "calls" the next-born. I have translated the expression by the phrase "came before."

12. Keti Ferenke's paternal and maternal great-grandfathers married women from Sambaia Bendugu; both women were Fula (or Fule).

13. In other words, Keti Ferenke was not born yet.

14. Keti Ferenke is speaking here on behalf of his sibling group, his generation.

15. *Sinkari ma kono* (lit., "Saturday wait for me").

16. *Sinkari or Sunkeri*—Ramadan (lit., "Saturday," the day on which Kuranko calendrical rites always begin).

17. The implication is that witchcraft and sorcery were suspected as the causes of both his parents' deaths.

18. Kuranko refer to Freetown as Saralon (Sierra Leone), an indication of how remote it is felt to be.

19. "Kola four," a sympathy gift to the bereaved.

20. The answer to both riddles is "two." There are two people in the world, man and woman, and a person takes two steps in the course of a day, one with the right foot and one with the left.

21. Of the forty-one Keti Ferenke stories I recorded, seven had as their main theme

women as seducers and deceivers of men (see, for example, N.33 and N.34 in Jackson 1982a).

22. This emphasis on the structure of the commonsense world of everyday life (*Lebenswelt*), rather than theoretical thought and ideological knowledge (*Weltanschauungen*), derives from the work of Alfred Schutz (see Berger and Luckmann 1966:26–28).

THREE. AJALA'S HEADS

1. Existence is from the Latin *ex-sistere*, "to stand out, to emerge." Existentialism thus emphasizes the human being "not as a collection of static substances or mechanisms or patterns but rather as emerging and becoming" (May 1958:12). "World is never something static, something merely given which the person then 'accepts' or 'adjusts to' or 'fights.' It is rather a dynamic pattern which, so long as I possess self-consciousness, I am in the process of forming and designing" (60).

2. Cf. Lévi-Strauss: "Every effort to understand destroys the object studied in favour of another object of a different nature" (1973:411). Niels Bohr referred to this as the *Abtötungsprinzip:* one can kill off the experimental subject by too deep a material probing of its behavior. Devereux notes that extreme reductionist models of behavior have the same fatal consequences (1967:288).

3. For accounts of the leg as a symbol of power and generative potency, see Jackson 1979:122–25; Onians 1973; Bunker and Lewin 1965; Bradley 1970.

4. The word *intention* aptly conveys the nondualistic character of the African world view. Intention is a "set" of the body as well as a "purpose" in the mind. The Latin stem *intendere* suggests "stretching" and "tension" so that intention is a "stretching towards something" (May 1972:228).

5. This conflict assumes different forms in different West African societies. Among the Kalabari the key contrast is between competitiveness and noncompetitiveness (Horton 1961:114, 1983:72). Among the Tallensi the key opposition is between the father's Destiny and the Destiny of his first-born son (Fortes 1983:22). Among many Mande-speaking peoples there is a forceful contrast between the rivalry among sons of the same father but different mothers (*fadenya*) and the amicability among sons of the same mother (*badenya, nadenye*) (Bird and Kendall 1980:14–15).

6. Among the Ufipa people of Tanzania, the hands signify praxis, the active measures man takes to make his world. As Fipa see it, "it is through such action that he constitutes himself as a person. The significance Fipa symbolism and medicine attach to the human hands (*amakasa*) reflects a perception that these organs are the means by which consciously mediated intentions are realised in a transformation of the natural environment. Through their social praxis, mediated through the hands, human beings transform nature and in so doing create their society and culture" (Willis 1977:283).

7. During his fieldwork among the Jelgobe Fulani, Paul Riesman noted that feelings of hurt or pain were rarely indulged or expressed to solicit sympathy. "It was the same with all pain, physical and mental: people talked about it freely and objectively, so to speak, but they did not *express* it by that language of intonation and gesture which is familiar to us" (1977:147). According to Riesman this equanimity was the result of neither repression nor stoicism but of control. "To name pain and suffering in a neutral tone is to master them, *because the words do not escape thoughtlessly but are spoken consciously*. . . . (148, my emphasis).

8. Unlike the Tallensi, Akan, Igbo, and Edo peoples mentioned earlier, the Kuranko imply that one's destiny is decided not prenatally but at the time of one's second "symbolic" birth during initiation (see Jackson 1977b:chap. 11).

9. Of all the powers acquired through initiation none is more important than *hankilimaiye*, moral understanding, common sense, gumption. It is acquired by listening to

elders, and Kuranko say that both social well-being and personal longevity depend on it: *sie tole l to* ("long life is in the listening," i.e., heed your elders and you will live long and prosperously); *si' ban to l sa* ("short life ear has not," i.e., if you do not heed your elders you will not live long). Social intelligence is associated with the head (*kunye*) so that a fool (*yuwe*, "crazy" or "socially stupid") is someone "without salt in his head" (*kor' sa kunye ma*) or "without brains" (*kun' por' sa*), while a responsible person has "good thoughts in his head" (*miria nyima a kunye ro*); his "head is full."

10. Elsewhere (Jackson 1982a) I have discussed in detail the Kuranko concept of *kenteye*, which means both physical well-being and social propriety. A breakdown in health is thus often related to a breach of a social rule or the breaking of trust.

11. In Kuranko narratives these extremes are represented by the cunning hare (the youngster) and the stupid hyena (the elder). The struggles between them allegorize the interplay of natural and social fields of being (Jackson 1982a).

12. Among the Dogon, diviners mark out sand diagrams at dusk on the edge of the village, hoping for the night imprint of Yourougou, the pale fox, who represents extravagance and disorder as well as oracular truth (Calame-Griaule 1965). The Dogon contrast Yourougou with Nommo, who represents reason and the social order. Among the neighboring Bambara, a similar contrast exists between Nyalé, who was created first and signifies "swarming life," uncontrolled power and exuberance, and Faro and Ndomadyiri, who were created next and signify equilibrium and restraint. With the advent of human society a dialectic appeared in which Nyalé and Ndomadyiri form "antithetical impulses." According to Bambara thought, the harmonizing of extrasocial energies and social order depends on every person acquiring moral understanding and taking an active part in communal life (Zahan 1974:15). The existential tenor of these ideas is stressed by Zahan: the person "sees himself as the synthesis of the universe . . . neither a toy nor a straw between the hands of the forces which would escape him. He is the arbiter of his own game with these forces; he is above them" (1979:156).

13. See for examples Ortigues and Ortigues 1966 and Parin, Morgenthaler, and Parin-Matthey 1980.

14. In fact it was Leibniz in 1704 who first proposed a theory of the unconscious supported by purely psychological arguments (Ellenberger 1970:312).

15. Yet Freud often wrote as if the unconscious could be located, and this topographical conception of the unconscious underlies Freud's choice of spatial imagery to compare the unconscious to a large anteroom adjoining "a second, smaller apartment, a sort of reception-room, in which consciousness resides" (1922:249). Freud compared the unconscious censor to a doorkeeper who stands on the threshold between the two rooms. However, this account, which in its concreteness and embodiedness resembles the African model, is dismissed by Freud as "crude" and "fantastic" and "*not at all permissible in a scientific presentation*" (my emphasis).

16. The metaphor of unmasking belongs to African and European discourse alike. As Ellenberger notes, psychoanalysis "belongs to that 'unmasking' trend, that search for hidden unconscious motivations characteristic of the 1880s and 1890s." For both Freud and Nietzsche "the unconscious is the realm of the wild, brutish instincts that cannot find permissible outlets, derive from earlier stages of the individual and of mankind, and find expression in passion, dreams, and mental illness. Even the term 'id' (*das Es*) originates with Nietzsche" (1970:277).

17. This point is also made by Roy Willis, writing on the Ufipa of Tanzania. Fipa liken the "public" and "private" spheres of the self to the outside and inside of a hut. "In the close-packed huts of the typical Fipa village, spatially interrelated by no overt principle of social organization, and each with its dark and private interior, there is a physical analogue of the Fipa concept of the self and its relation to human society. . . . This concept of the self as a duality in which the light, public aspect constantly seeks to extend its organizing

power into the realm of the dark and unknown aspect is structurally homologous with the Fipa concept of the universe, in which a collective human rationality endeavours to understand and control the world of wild nature" (1974:90).

18. Kuranko often explain madness, visionary dreams, and sexual hallucinations in terms of possession by a bush spirit (*nyenne*) (Jackson 1977b:37).

19. For a critique of the epistemological claims and logical foundations of Freud's model of the unconscious, see MacIntyre 1958.

20. Consider, for example, Lévi-Strauss's distrust of "native models." For him, structural analysis is the elucidation of unconscious models. True meanings are thus always beyond our immediate awareness (1963:19–24, 281–82), and "conscious data are always erroneous or illusory" (1972:76; see also Lévi-Strauss 1963:281). The goal of the anthropologist "is to grasp, beyond the conscious and always shifting images which men hold, the complete range of unconscious possibilities. . . . " The understanding of man "goes from the study of conscious content to that of unconscious forms . . . seeking to attain, through the conscious . . . more and more of the unconscious" (1963:23, 24).

21. Fernandez cites Tessmann's work on the Fang as an example of how anthropologists sometimes invoke the notion of the unconscious in order to invest native consciousness with their own a priori ideas:

> Tessmann's "informants could not always give him the kind of commentary that would suit [his] interests. He had to interpolate. This led him to complain that 'the earliest ideas survive unrealized in the Fang and only through incidental, unconscious expressions can their coherence be grasped.' He treated with impatience explanations that did not meet his needs. Often he was forced to draw his own conclusions, for 'the Fang will not split their heads over such matters.'" (Fernandez 1982:245)

22. Cf. Sartre's critique of Freud's hypothesis of the unconscious. Sartre argues for the unity of consciousness—the way the "unconscious" is constituted through conscious acts and choices as much as it is reciprocally constitutive of us. To invoke the "unconscious" in explaining our actions and choices is to displace responsibility onto an alien source—a form of "bad faith" (Sartre 1957). Many of Sartre's criticisms were presaged by Politzer (see Lapointe 1971:15–16).

23. The first part of this quotation is from Ortigues and Ortigues (1966), on whom Riesman relies for his psychoanalytic interpretations. See Wober (1975:167–68) for a considered review of African studies in which the same invidious comparison is made between "externalized" African and "internalized" European superegos.

24. *Nkrabea* (lit., "manner of taking leave") is the Akan term for "destiny" (Minkus 1984:132).

25. Cf. Danquah, who notes that among the Akan the *e-su* (*phusis*, or "fundamental biophysical nature of man") is complementary to *n'kara*, or "chosen soul" (*nous*, or "intelligence"). But destiny, for the Akan, is not "wooden or cast-iron, but something lively, full of feeling, desired and rational" (1944:205).

26. Although Sartre is committed to an identification with the oppressed (1983), the ponderous and cabalistic structures of his philosophical work often constitute a form of oppression (Poster 1984:24–25). Sartre's identification with the oppressed thus comes perilously close to an identification *on his terms*, with no two-way traffic between the subject who discourses and the object of that discourse.

27. This struggle between subjectivity and objectivity is the subject of a brilliant discussion by Nagel (1986).

28. Even epistemologically false models can have "true" therapeutic or practical efficacy. Moreover, as Rorty notes,

> The utility of the 'existentialist' view is that, by proclaiming that we have no essence, it permits us to see the descriptions of ourselves we find in one of (or in the unity of) the *Natur-*

wissenschaften as on a par with the various alternative descriptions offered by poets, novelists, depth psychologists, sculptors, anthropologists, and mystics. The former are not privileged representations in virtue of the fact that (at the moment) there is more consensus in the sciences than in the arts. (1979:362)

29. While existential models are hardly "scientific," they cannot be defined as "folk" models, which makes it difficult to accommodate Wiredu's prescription that we compare Western and non-Western folk models rather than Western scientific models and traditional folk models (1980). The problem with using the scientific/folk dichotomy is further brought home when one considers that Freud's allegedly "scientific" model of the unconscious had its roots in "folk" models (the ergodynamic-hydraulic concepts in his early writings) and took root in popular consciousness to the extent that people became conditioned to experience life crises in "Freudian" terms (Devereux 1969b:20).

FOUR. HOW TO DO THINGS WITH STONES

1. Richard Rorty has argued eloquently against the neo-Kantian and positivist image of "mind" or "language" *mirroring* nature:

The notion that our chief task is to mirror accurately, in our own Glassy Essence, the universe around us is the complement of the notion, common to Democritus and Descartes, that the universe is made up of very simple, clearly and distinctly knowable things, knowledge of whose essences provides the master-vocabulary which permits commensuration of all discourses. (1979:357)

2. See, for example, Einstein's letter to Max Born, where he writes: "Quantum mechanics is very impressive, but I am convinced that God does not play dice" (Einstein 1971:91).

3. On the aleatory character of human existence and the role of magic and science in protecting us against uncertainty, Dewey writes:

The visible is set in the invisible; and in the end what is unseen decides what happens in the seen; the tangible rests precariously upon the untouched and ungrasped. The contrast and the potential maladjustment of the immediate, the conspicuous and focal phase of things, with those indirect and hidden factors which determine the origin and career of what is present, are indestructible features of any and every experience. We may term the way in which our ancestors dealt with the contrast superstitions but the contrast is no superstition. It is a primary *datum* in any experience. . . . *Our* magical safeguard against the uncertain character of the world is to deny the existence of chance, to mumble universal and necessary law, the ubiquity of cause and effect, the uniformity of nature, universal progress, and the inherent rationality of the universe. (1929:44, my emphasis)

4. Among the Mende of southeast Sierra Leone the term for a diviner is *toto-gbe-moi*, i.e., the man who sets in motion intensive seeing; *toto* is an intensive form of *to*, to look at, see, as a result of a search, i.e., to find (Harris and Sawyerr 1968:136).

5. The traditional mode of divination among the Temne, *an-bere*, derives its name from the Mande word *bere*, pebble (Shaw 1985) and the ancestral diviner's name among the Temne, Konkomusa, could well be a Mande derivation (*Konke*, large stone; mountain).

6. Kuranko diviners are never women, but women diviners are common in many African societies: Gusii (Levine and Levine 1966:58–59); Nguni (Hammond-Tooke 1959:348); Lugbara (Middleton 1969:224).

7. A detailed account of a Kuranko man's initiation into the arts of divination is given in Jackson 1986.

8. That Lai confided details of consultations to me indicates the anomalous character of the anthropological interview and the way aberrant behavior patterns may arise from the peculiar nature of our mode of acquiring knowledge.

9. Of the three major categories of the divine, only the bush spirits (*nyennenu*) and God are alluded to in this context. Ancestors are never held to be the source of divinatory messages or considered to be the mystical tutors in divinatory skills as they are among the Yoruba (Bascom 1969), the Fon, the Ewe (Nukunya 1973), and in Dahomey (Herskovits 1967). In Kuranko thought the ancestors do not intervene actively or directly in human affairs. This may explain why individuals are never inspired or possessed by ancestral spirits. Nevertheless, diviners often attribute misfortunes to the ancestors' withdrawal of blessings; propitiatory sacrifices are then directed in order to return things to a state of blessedness (*baraka*).

10. Sometimes diviners speak of *hearing* the stones speak rather than *seeing* a message in them.

11. Such sympathetic responses are even more in evidence in the case of dream interpretation recorded in Jackson 1978b:120–21.

12. As James puts it:

> The true thought is useful . . . because the [thing] which is its object is useful. The practical value of true ideas is thus primarily derived from the practical importance of their objects to us. Their objects are, indeed, not important at all times. . . . Yet since almost any object may some day become temporarily important, the advantage of having a general stock of *extra* truths, *of ideas that shall be true of merely possible situations*, is obvious. We store such extra truths away in our memories. . . . *Whenever such an extra truth becomes practically relevant to one of our emergencies, it passes from cold-storage to do work in the world, and our belief in it grows active.* (1978:98, my emphasis)

13. Among the Azande, for example, some men

> are less credulous than others and more critical in their acceptance of statements made by witch-doctors. These differences of opinion depend largely upon modes of upbringing, range of social contacts, variations of individual experience, and personality. (Evans-Pritchard 1972:183)

FIVE. THE IDENTITY OF THE DEAD

1. The faculty of similitude is also a biogenetic given, and George Steiner's eloquent comments on the "dialectic of 'alternity,' the genius of language for planned counter-factuality" are apposite here:

> Uniquely, one conjectures, among animal species, we cultivate inside us, we conceptualize and prefigure the enigmatic terror of our own personal extinction. . . . It is unlikely that man, as we know him, would have survived without the fictive, counter-factual, anti-determinist means of language, without the semantic capacity, generated and stored in the "superfluous" zones of the cortex, to conceive of, to articulate possibilities beyond the treadmill of organic decay and death. (1973:227)

2. Simulation implies, of course, both genuine and feigned sympathy. Mourning is not only the reaction to the loss of a loved person; it occurs with "the loss of some abstraction which has taken the place of one, such as fatherland, liberty, an ideal, and so on" (Freud 1957:153).

3. As when death, grief, and bereavement supply the root metaphors in initiation ritual (see Jackson 1977b:181–217).

4. Evolutionary biology recognizes the "power to delay or withhold the instinctive responses as an essential precondition for the emergence of adaptive variability from within the rigidity of instinct-systems" (Stenhouse 1974:80).

5. I employ Bowlby's terminology here. Kübler-Ross, in her account of how people cope with imminent death, distinguishes five stages: denial/isolation, anger, bargaining, depres-

sion, acceptance. But her pattern is directly comparable with the one elucidated by Bowlby and others in research on separation trauma and bereavement reaction (see Kübler-Ross 1970).

6. Certain localities, known as *morgo faga funema,* "person, kill, grassed area," were once used for the slaying of captive enemies; it was forbidden for anyone but warriors to go there.

7. The senior *jeliba* passes the gift to his own sister's son, who then passes it on to the deceased's brothers. The intermediary position of the sister's son will be discussed later.

8. For full details see Jackson 1977a.

9. The term *quarantine* comes from *quarantina,* the Italian for "forty," which was the number of days of sequestration expected of the widow (Parkes 1975:188).

10. A "sense of the continued presence of the deceased" is characteristic of the bereavement reaction of widows (Parkes 1975:79). Among the Kuranko, this may be sharpened by self-reproach and self-blaming, introspective reactions which are often characteristic of Kuranko women in crisis (see chapter 6). During *labinane,* unfaithful wives are liable to suffer from insomnia (Kamara 1932:98).

11. The significance of the *sundu kunye ma* is discussed in greater detail in Jackson 1977b.

12. Buxton (Mandari) 1973:145; Morton-Williams (Yoruba) 1960:34. Among the LoDagaa, however, "the loss of a child should be felt more intensely than that of a parent" (Goody 1962:92) and it is clear that *manifestations* of grief (as contrasted with actual *emotions* of grief) vary from society to society, depending upon concepts of the person, status, role, relationship, etc.

13. The Kuranko associate salt with tears; it signifies sympathy and attachment to the deceased. Sayers (1925:27) records that salt is thrown in the bonfire, together with old clothes of the deceased, as "a sacrifice which is to cleanse the soul of the departed from the guilt of the sins he committed during his lifetime." As a gift from visiting allies, salt may have had the significance attached to it in Arabic cultures—to sanctify friendships and alliances—but it certainly was a form of wealth, exported to Kuranko from the coast and from the Guinea plains for gold (Kup 1975:32, 37, 41). Salt and cattle had similar "value in exchange" and would have been appropriate gifts from political allies.

14. *Kole,* or *Koli,* was a cult association, one of its main purposes being to admonish indolent boys who were lax in their duties of frightening birds from the rice farms. The brass masks and costume of pelts which Sayers (1925:26) describes are unknown today; the *Kole* dancer wears a cloth "mask" with cowries sewn across it.

15. A *sanaku* link implies nullified or at least anomalous status differentiation between clans. The symbols of the hearth—ash, faggots, cinders—may suggest the essential ambiguity of the situation in which the "superiority" of the *sanaku* joker over the dead person (just by being alive) must be countermanded by equally exaggerated status abasement.

16. Goody (1962:107, 123–24) has referred to the psychological value of "reversed emotions" in distracting the bereaved from the gravity of the situation. He has also noted the ambivalence of the mimetic performances among the LoDagaa: they simultaneously serve an obituary or celebrative/ commemorative function and a mocking or eliminating function.

17. The relationship between Kuranko notions of sexuality and the instability of affinal ties is more fully explored in Jackson 1977b.

18. Joking relationships between grandparents and grandchildren "play up" an idiom of sexual abuse. Among *sanaku* partners, the prevailing idiom is one of status abuse. In both cases the (sexual or status) identifications are ambiguous: possibly real, probably fictitious or figurative.

19. This is reminiscent of what Turner calls the "structural invisibility" of liminal personae. In this context the *mamane* assumes the guise of the woman with whom she is nominally identified: her grandmother (*mama*). In this way the grandmother's identity and grief are disguised. Cf. Goody (1962:89, 127) on "mourning disguises" among the LoDagaa.

SIX. THE WITCH AS A CATEGORY AND AS A PERSON

1. When a confessed witch dies, his or her shade is known as *pulan.* The *pulan* haunts, oppresses, and terrorizes people, especially small children. It is often said that the *pulan* resembles a lizard or assumes the form of a lizard, and a *pulan*-catcher may show people a lizard wriggling inside the bag with which he has allegedly caught a witch's shade. A *pulan*'s power enables it to lift country-pots or oppress people in their sleep. So terrified do some people become that they are physically immobilized and have to be straightened out in the morning. Theoretically, a *pulan* will not enter a house that has white cotton over the doorway. If it does enter an unprotected house it counts off people in pairs, declaring "this and this are all right, this and this are all right" until it comes to a single and therefore vulnerable person when it says, "this and myself are all right" and proceeds to oppress him or her. Since *pulan* cannot attack two people at once, one may take precautions against *pulan*-haunting by sleeping in pairs.

2. Niels Bohr referred to this "principle of destruction" as the *Abtötungsprinzip.* Explanations, when pushed too far, destroy ("explain away") the phenomenon one seeks to understand (Devereux 1978a:9–13).

3. Cf. Mandinka (Gambia) *suubaga* ("night person") (Innes 1974:313).

4. If anyone disturbs the sleeping body of a suspected witch or is witness to such an event he will not make this publicly known lest the kinsmen of the alleged witch accuse him of murder. The Kuranko point out that in such cases there is no real evidence of witchcraft. Furthermore, to accuse a person of witchcraft is a serious matter. Of all cases heard in the Native Court in Sengbe chiefdom between 1946 and 1967 only two cases of witchcraft accusation are recorded (the defendants were fined and ordered to "beg," i.e., apologize to, the plaintiffs). The sole case of witchcraft accusation which came to my attention during fieldwork occurred in Kamadugu Sukurela in 1966. Two women, weeding a farm, quarreled. One said, "Now look, you are a witch!" The other rejoined, "Yes, I used to sit on your house." The case came before the chief's court and the accuser was ordered to withdraw her accusation and apologize; the women were not related. In another case (also from Kamadugu Sukurela) a woman was rumored to have confessed killing her brother's daughter's son by witchcraft, but the confession was made within her family, and her husband was a "big man"; no one dared accuse her publicly of witchcraft. Even *Gbangbane* does not make direct or specific accusations; the cult masters, like ordinary diviners, simply ascertain whether or not witchcraft is the cause of a person's illness or death. When I asked one informant to give me evidence that witchcraft really did exist he said that his knowledge came from three sources: "it has a name and we have heard of it"; "we have seen people die because of witches"; "witches confess."

5. Cf. LoDagaa (J. Goody 1969:71). The Kuranko admit that the father's sister could be a witch but the mother's brother never; "he belongs to another *kebile.*"

6. Although "sorcery" (the use of powerful magical medicines, *besekoli*) may be distinguished from witchcraft in terms of externally controlled and internally controlled powers (Douglas 1970b:119; Leach 1961:22–25), in practice the distinction is not always clear. According to Saran Salia Sano, a medicine-master (*besetigi*) usually specializes in one of three branches of medicine: curative and prophylactic (deals with afflictions "caused by God," *altala kiraiye,* and with antidotes for afflictions "caused by persons," *morgo kiraiye*); destructive (involving the use of harmful medicines); and destructive (involving the use of curses, *gborle*). Many Kuranko adopt a fatalistic attitude to diseases "caused by Allah" but take active steps to prevent and cure afflictions caused by human agency, i.e., witchcraft and sorcery.

As Saran Salia observed on a number of occasions, witchcraft and the use of magical medicines were quite different things; he himself knew nothing of witchcraft. He could only protect people from witches—and in fact young boys often stayed in his house when their parents felt they were vulnerable to witchcraft attack. The second and third categories of medicine might be labeled "sorcery," but a *besetigi* usually works on behalf of a client and is not culpable for what happens to the victim of his medicines. If a person has a legitimate grievance against someone else and all other avenues of legal redress are closed, then he may enlist the services of a *besetigi*. Checks against the abuse of harmful medicines and curses do, however, exist. If a grievance is entirely a matter of personal malice, then the medicines will be ineffective against the victim and they will return to harm the person on whose behalf they are being "sent out." Before a *besetigi* will curse a man, his client must also take an oath, declaring "If I am unjust/wrong in my accusation against X then may I suffer; if I am just/right in my accusation against X then may he suffer." However, a person can sometimes circumvent these checks by purchasing powerful medicines from a foreign sorcerer or from a *mori* (Muslim medicine-master) and then using them independently. The curse, on the other hand, can never be purchased; it must always be uttered by a *besetigi*. Moreover, the curse must always be made public. Not only is it an extension of secular legal controls; its efficacy depends upon the victim knowing he has been cursed. The curse is only lifted when the offender confesses or, if he dies, when representatives of his family pay the *besetigi* to do so. The curse (*gborle*) used by medicine-masters is, of course, quite different from the curse (*danka*) associated with certain kinship roles (sister, mother, father).

7. *Gbenkan* is said to be pounded in a mortar at midnight by a person standing on his or her head and using his or her feet to grasp the pestle; the pestle makes the sound *gbenkan gbenkan*.

8. Cf. Marwick: "Informants may . . . make very different statements about the same phenomenon when they are speaking generally and when they are referring to a series of specific instances" (1970:284).

9. Accusation and confession *under duress* are reported from other areas of Sierra Leone: Limba (Finnegan 1965), Mende (Harris and Sawyerr 1968), Temne (Littlejohn 1967), Kono (Parsons 1964:51–52).

10. Consider, for example, the views of Freud on the "psychology of women":

> It must be admitted that women have but little sense of justice, and this is no doubt connected with the preponderance of envy in their mental life; for the demands of justice are a modification of envy; they lay down the conditions under which one is willing to part with it. We also say of women that their social interests are weaker than those of men, and that their capacity for the sublimation of their instincts is less. (Freud 1932:183)

Thomas Szasz cites this as just one example of "scapegoating in the phenomena called witchcraft, hysteria, and mental illness" (1972:197).

11. This discrepancy has been noted by other Africanists: Gray (1969:171), Levine (1969:239), Ruel (1970:338). Ruel's hypothesis that "introspective" witchcraft and rigid stereotypes tend to be mutually incompatible is confirmed by the Kuranko data (Ruel 1970:334–35).

12. During his fieldwork among the Jelgobe Fulani, Paul Riesman noted that feelings of hurt or pain were rarely indulged or expressed to solicit sympathy. "It was the same with all pain, physical and mental: people talked about it freely and objectively, so to speak, but they did not *express* it by that language of intonation and gesture which is familiar to us" (Riesman 1977:147). According to Riesman this equanimity was the result of neither repression nor stoicism, but of control. "To name pain and suffering in a neutral tone is to master them, *because the words do not escape thoughtlessly but are spoken consciously.* . . ." (148, my emphasis).

13. See Kluckholn (1967:83–84) and Brain (1970:170) on witchcraft confession as an "attention-seeking device" among "deprived" individuals. Keith Thomas (1973) advances a similar argument in his work on European witchcraft: the role of witch offered downtrodden and outcast women a means, albeit illusory, of protest and vengeance.

14. In his study of Mohave suicide, Devereux observes that witches often persuade them-

selves "by a retroactive self-deception of the 'opportune confabulation' type" that they actually bewitched someone who just happened to die at a time when they were experiencing strong suicidal impulses (1969b:387). Witchcraft confession is thus a kind of "vicarious suicide," an impulse, Devereux notes, that "is a human, rather than a specifically Mohave impulse."

15. Cf. Oliver Sacks (1986:4): "it must be said at the outset that a disease is *never a mere loss or excess*—that there is always a reaction, on the part of the affected organism or individual, to restore, to replace, to compensate for and to preserve its identity, however strange the means may be" (emphasis added).

16. Some Kuranko men can identify with the situation of self-confessed witches as a result of their experiences as migrant workers in the diamond districts of Kono. It seems that one reason why Kuranko men are so readily hired for positions of trust in the Security Police Force is that they are honest to a fault, often confessing to crimes they have not committed simply to "clear the air." Kuranko men like to vaunt their openness and integrity, but does their marginality and powerlessness make them "like women" and therefore predisposed to assume responsibility for some of the resentments and tensions that pervade the diamond fields?

SEVEN. THE MAN WHO COULD TURN INTO AN ELEPHANT

1. Diviners always dream bush spirit allies in *human* form, and in Kuranko oral narratives (*tilei*) wild animals tend to assume human form when they enter a village. Thus, the domain of culture "tames" or transforms animality, just as the bush makes human beings susceptible to transformation into animals.

2. See Jackson 1982b:167. Although shape-shifting is a common motif in Kuranko *tilei*, which are admittedly make-believe, the fictional character of the tales does not imply that shape-shifting is phantasmagoric (see Jackson 1982a:291 for examples).

3. See Jackson 1986:chaps. 26–28 for details.

4. A fuller account of Saran Salia's apprenticeship is given in Jackson 1986:chap. 27.

5. The sitting member's candidature was withdrawn and Sewa was elected unopposed.

6. My previous research on Kuranko totemism had given me to understand that the totems of the Fofona clan were the same as those of the Koroma clan: horned vipers, the bronze mannikin bird, and eagle (Jackson 1974:403).

7. See Jackson 1986:185–87.

8. The terms are borrowed from Polanyi (1958:55–56).

9. A fuller account of this subject is given in Jackson 1982a:15–30 and Jackson 1982b:174–75.

10. Excerpted from Jackson 1982b:160–61, 179.

11. For a critique of the intellectualistic approach to symbols, see Dewey 1929:82, 126–29; Bourdieu 1977; Merleau-Ponty 1962; and chapter 8 of this book.

12. Sewa had been an M.P. in the first postindependence government of Sierra Leone but withdrew from political life in 1967.

13. See James 1978:98; also see Devereux 1961a:378–79 and 1969:123 for very similar views.

14. Other contemporary commentators suggested that leopard societies came into existence as "counter-measures to slave-trading activities" and formed to protect people "from the arbitrariness of their chieftains and kings" (Lindskog 1954:84). Thus, Barret in 1888 saw the phenomenon of *hommes-pantheres* as "an outlet for the pent-up resentment of the slaves for their captors; it was the means of relieving the hunger for vengeance of the oppressed" (cited by Lindskog, 68). In this context it is interesting to note the reasons for the spread of the Ngbe (leopard) cult among the Banyang of the Upper Cross river circa 1940:

One of the main reasons given by Upper Banyang for the spread of Ngbe is the loss of status suffered by men from their area when during the early period of administration they visited the Lower area (where the administrative headquarters were and where Ngbe was already established) and were obliged to drink their palm-wine standing. . . . (Ruel 1969:217)

The same theme of redressing injustices runs through Buxton's account of were-men among the Mandari:

The appearance of beast-men is not random; they are deliberately summoned by those who feel themselves denied justice through customary channels, and are a recognized, if rarely used, ritual sanction. An informant first raised the subject of them with me in this context, comparing them with acts like deliberate "rain-spoiling." All are legitimate but dangerous ways of drawing attention to wrongs, because the user, who confesses in the hope of regaining redress, runs a calculated risk if widespread harm is thought to have resulted. (Buxton 1973:262)

15. Another of the accused, Bokari, noted in the same trial that the baboon society in his chiefdom was the same as the leopard society elsewhere (Kalous 1974:94).

16. It is important to note that Creole traders were often known as "white men." The term designated political status rather than physical appearance (Fyfe 1962:298).

17. It is impossible to ascertain the social background and status of all leopard-men, but many were slaves (Kalous 1974:51).

18. Though whites and traders *were* attacked (Fyfe 1962:310; Kalous 1974:51).

19. It is tempting to relate certain contentious features of the cults to this theme of power: the notion that donning the skin of a leopard gave "super-human strength" (Kalous 1974:65), the notion that eating one's victim "reinvigorated" or "rejuvenated" men past their primes (Griffith 1915:vii-viii), the notion that chiefs profited from leopard killings because they could seize goods from the village nearest the place of murder and fine those found guilty of it (Fyfe 1962:442).

20. Melchert uses Kant's argument concerning the "parlogisms of pure reason" to refute a common ontological claim of mystics to have undergone complete ego loss:

The rational psychologist, taking for granted that this "I think" is a universal and necessary condition for any experience whatsoever, believes that he can show by a priori reasoning alone that the "I" (or the *soul*) is a substance, that it is simple, and that it can exist separate and distinct from matter. What Kant brilliantly shows is that this cannot be done; from the consideration of the (supposedly) necessary and universal structure of experience, *nothing whatsoever can be known about the nature of the being having the experience.*

Though the argument for each of the four properties of the soul is distinctive, in each case a similar mistake is made. A move is made from a necessary feature of our *representation of the I* to a conclusion about the *real nature of the I.* To put it another way, the move is from a statement true by virtue of the analysis of concepts to a synthetic claim about the nature of some existing being. (1976–77:452, italics in original)

21. This is how some Kuranko informants see their oral narratives (*tilei*). Though make-believe, they serve as vehicles for the articulation of social and moral truths (Jackson 1982a:51).

22. *Ungeziefer:* a low and contemptible person, a "louse"; lit., "the unclean animal not suitable for sacrifice."

23. In his letters and diaries, Kafka "frequently represents himself as a thing and as an animal" (Corngold 1973:52). One could also remark here the dehumanizing effects of mechanistic, objectivist language in the social and psychological sciences. R. D. Laing observes that schizophrenics often experience themselves as automata, robots, bits of machinery, or animals.

Such persons are rightly regarded as crazy. Yet why do we not regard a theory that seeks to transmute persons into automata or animals as equally crazy? . . . Treating people as things is just as false as treating things as persons. We disparage the latter as animist thinking and wrong, but elevate the former to objectivity and science (1966:23, 24).

24. See Jackson 1982a:290–91; Ignatieff 1984:40, 50–51.

EIGHT. KNOWLEDGE OF THE BODY

1. I am indebted to Russell Keat for helping me clarify Merleau-Ponty's ideas. My opening sentences paraphrase sections of Keat's paper "Merleau-Ponty and the Phenomenology of the Body," presented as a seminar at the Humanities Research Centre, The Australian National University, 1982.

2. Patanjali's classical definition of yoga, which introduces the Sutras, is *citta vrtti nirodha*, "withholding the mind from all discursive objects, or a total resorption of the cognitive, conative, and volitional functions of the mind" or "the blockage of the object-directed tendency of the mind" (Bharati 1976:96, 92). The mind becomes, not a blank, but is "ideally devoid of discursive ideas and concepts" (92). The importance of physical techniques in yoga practice is summarized by Eliade:

> The important thing is that *āsana* gives the body a stable rigidity, at the same time reducing physical effort to a minimum. Thus, one avoids the irritating feeling of fatigue, of enervation in certain parts of the body, one regulates the physical processes, and so allows the attention to devote itself solely to the fluid part of consciousness. (1979:53)

Foucault's "political technology of the body" (1979:26) is also relevant to my field of study but is not explored in depth in the present work.

3. Many of the religious figures in Roman life were firmly grounded in agricultural practices (Flora, Pomona [fruit], Consus ["the storer"], Robigus [blight], Ceres [growth, cf. *creare*] etc.), and ancient lists of invocations demonstrate how the gods were generally thought of in terms of pragmatic functions (the "springiness of Neptune" as in the gushing of a fountain; the "growing power of Vulcan"; the "strength of Mars"; the cult of Mercury associated with business transactions, etc.). The gods were not looked upon to make people *morally* better but to control the natural forces upon which the *material* bases of prosperity and happiness directly depended; practical and religious activity were one (Ogilvie 1969:10–21).

4. In this account of the meaning of *culture* I have focused on German antecedents to the anthropological use of the term; French and English intellectual traditions bestow slightly different values on the concepts of culture and nature (see Lovejoy 1948:69–71).

5. Cf. Dewey, who notes how the classical distinction

> between vegetative, animal and rational souls was, when applied to men, a formulation and justification of class divisions in Greek society. Slaves and mechanical artisans living on the nutritional, appetitive level were for practical purposes symbolized by the body—an obstruction to ideal ends and as solicitations to acts contrary to reason. . . . Scientific inquirers and philosophers alone exemplified pure reason . . . *nous*, pure immaterial mind. (1929:251)

6. There is an echo here of Dobzhansky's arguments, based on biogenetic considerations, against the culturological assumptions of Leslie A. White, who claims that culture can "be considered as a self-contained, self-determined process; one that can be explained only in terms of itself" (Dobzhansky 1962:73–75).

7. I have borrowed this term from Russell Keat, who argues that the body has been excluded from social scientific discourse through a twofold process of "etherealization" and "materialization." While the first gives the body to the humanities, the second assigns it to the biological sciences (Keat, personal communication, 1982).

8. Such a view can be traced back even further to the Aristotelian metaphysical doctrine that nature is an ordered series from lower to higher potentialities and actualizations in

which the organic body was "the highest term in a physical series and the lowest term in a psychical series" (Dewey 1929:250).

9. Cf. Norman O. Brown's thesis that "Culture originates in the denial of life and the body" and "the recovery of life in the body is the hidden aim of history" (1959:297).

10. Here one should note the male bias in anthropology toward adopting uncritically the male emphasis in many preliterate world views, defining women as subservient, passive, and low in status and assuming that women are logically if not biologically closer to nature than men are (McCormack 1980:1–21; Etienne and Leacock 1980:3). It is interesting that feminism has played a significant role in bringing the body back into discourse by making issues such as rape and abortion crucial to an understanding of social inequality.

11. Studies of "material culture" have come to occupy an increasingly marginal place in anthropology, artifacts being defined as insignificant unless, like masks, they can be assimilated into the field of cognitive and symbolic analysis.

12. It is really only since the 1960s that studies of bodily movement and dance have begun to assume a significant place in anthropological inquiry. Hitherto, Morgan's dismissive nineteenth-century view of music and dance seemed to prevail: "These amusements of our primitive inhabitants are not, in themselves, devoid of interest, although they indicate a tendency of mind unbefitting rational men" (cited in Royce 1977:190).

13. For an excellent critique of such ethological approaches to "non-verbal communication" and the problem of objective meaning, see Poole 1975:74–106.

14. According to Thass-Thienemann:

> Whereas the conscious ego speaks through the rational verbal language, the observable behavior of the body speaks an expressive language of its own. It may even say "no" when the verbal language asserts "yes." We understand this language of facial expression, posture, gesture, or involuntary bodily changes first and best. The small child understands the facial expression of his mother long before he understands the verbal language. (1968:38–39)

On the phylogenetic and ontogenetic primacy of nonlinguistic thinking, see Vygotsky 1962:42–44; Hewes 1973:5–12; Reich 1949:361, 381; Blacking 1977:21.

15. Cf. Bachelard's notion of the "housed" unconscious, and of the way memories are housed. He suggests that the systematic exploration of the "sites of our intimate lives" would be a topoanalysis rather than a psychoanalysis (1964:8).

16. Cf. Reich: "The living body not only functions before and beyond word language; more than that, it has *its own specific forms of expression which cannot be put into words at all . . . the biopathy, with its disturbed expression of life, is outside the realm of language and concepts*" (1949:361, 363, emphasis in original).

17. Cf. Black on the background to hypnotherapy: "There is thus a 'somatic mind' which is unconscious and presumably without any means of verbalisation of experience—and a 'cerebral mind' which is conscious. But since the brain and nervous system are also part of the body . . . the dividing line between the two is not always clearly defined" (1969:133). On the background to activity therapies, including ritual, see d'Aquili, Laughlin, and McManus 1979:143; Lowen 1971:xii; Reich 1949; Ferenczi 1955.

18. Being is "standing presence," says Heidegger. The root *sta* is found in terms for physical, conceptual, *and* social Being: standing, estate, understanding, status, institution, constitution, statute, etc. (Straus 1966:143; cf. Jantsch 1975:28–32).

19. Best 1978:139–45. In a similar vein, referring to dance studies that relate dance to language categories such as syntax and grammar, Anya Royce notes: "It may be, in fact, that we are distorting the phenomenon of dance by forcing it into a taxonomic system designed for a qualitatively different kind of phenomenon. This type of comparison may ultimately tell us that we have to deal with dance on its own terms" (1977:201).

20. Speaking of an angry or threatening gesture, Merleau-Ponty makes a similar point: "The gesture *does not make me think* of anger, it is anger itself. . . . The sense of the gestures

is not given, but understood, that is, seized upon by an act on the spectator's part. The whole difficulty is to conceive this act clearly without confusing it with a cognitive operation" (1962:184–85, emphasis in original).

21. This view is elaborated on by Wittgenstein in his *Philosophical Investigations* (1953).

22. This is at once evident in the titles of books and essays which have proliferated such phrases as "body language," "body symbolism," "body syntax," "body semiotics."

23. See, for instance, the second part of the introductory paragraph of chapter 5 ("The Two Bodies") of *Natural Symbols* 1970a:93.

24. "It was thus not the body that imposed its law on the mind. It was society that, through the intermediacy of language, took the commands of the mind and imposed its law on the body" (Starobinski 1982:29). Cf. Polhemus's comment on the dual preoccupation of the anthropology of the body with problems of communication and with a Durkheimian model of society "as a holistic beast" (1975:30).

25. Insofar as Western notions of culture have alienated us from the body, the reduction of the body to mere instrumentality is an expression of a long-standing historical bias (see May 1972:239).

26. The ethnographic data to which this account refers are published elsewhere (Jackson 1977b), and detailed description here is kept to a minimum.

27. All quotations in this paragraph are from Jackson 1977b:181–82.

28. Cf. "A religious symbol does not rest on any *opinion*. And error belongs only with opinion" (Wittgenstein 1979:3). Also Maurice Leenhardt's comment on Canaque myth (New Caledonia, Loyalty Island): "What is lived cannot be disputed" (1979:19).

29. Cf. Michael Oakeshott's arguments against the notion that activity springs from "premeditated propositions about the activity" such as the grammar of a language, rules of research, canons of good workmanship, etc. (1962:91). His example of the cookery book succinctly summarizes his view: "The cookery book is not an independently generated beginning from which cookery can spring; it is nothing more than an abstract of somebody's knowledge of how to cook; it is the stepchild, not the parent of the activity" and already presupposes a knowledge of cooking and a capable cook (119).

30. See Elster 1979:28–35 for a critique of such theories of meaning.

31. See Rigby 1968:166–74 and Ngubane 1977:151–55 for critiques.

32. Alfred Gell also observes: "I have been much impressed by the many continuities which seem to exist between the physical style of Umedas moving in non-dance contexts, and the movements they produce while dancing" (1979:29).

33. For exact descriptions, see Jackson 1977b:188–95.

34. Mauss 1973:73; Dewey 1929:277–78. Frank Pierce Jones has pointed out that Dewey's account of habit draws closely on F. M. Alexander's theory and practice of "use" (Jones 1976:100–103), and I also acknowledge an indebtedness to Alexander's work, especially *The Use of Self* (1931).

35. See Bourdieu 1979. Blacking makes a fascinating observation about the relationship between material artifacts and patterns of body use:

> careful analyses of the body movements related to the manufacture or uses of an object may contribute to our understanding of the social and mental processes of different cultures. Even when only the artefacts are available and they may not have been retrieved from the places where they were made, it should be possible to derive from them some idea of the sequences of *total* body movement involved in their manufacture. (1976:12)

36. See my *Allegories of the Wilderness* (1982a), where I argue that oral narratives similarly provoke in people a realization of possibilities which are regarded as being extrasocial and belonging to the "bush" yet are vitally essential to the recreation and continuity of the social order.

37. Hypnotic induction depends on rhythmic stimulation and some kind of constriction.

Swaddling of infants may condition hypnotic responsiveness, but Stephen Black argues that the intrauterine environment is probably the basis for the hypnotic patterning (1969:161–63).

38. Black 1969:280–81 discusses specific examples.

39. As when men draw their strength from stones and from mountains in the *Konke* ("stone mountain") cult or from bush spirits in other cults (e.g., *Kome*).

40. As I have shown in chapter 5, control of emotions at funerals is considered essential to the separation of the deceased's shade from the living community.

41. Cf. May: "in the process of knowing, we are *in-formed* by the thing understood, and in the same act, our intellect simultaneously *gives form* to the thing we understand" (1972:225, emphasis in original).

42. This notion of "embodied will" is conveyed in the etymology of the word *intentionality*. The Latin stem *intendere* consists of *in* plus *tendere, tensum*, the latter meaning "to stretch." "This tells us immediately that intention is a 'stretching' toward something" (May 1972:228; also see 240–42).

43. Cf. Bourdieu on the difference between "practical mimesis" and verbal analogy or metaphor (1977:116).

44. For an account of the anatomical bases of mimetic behavior and the mimetic faculty, see Goss (1959) and Sarles (1975:25–26).

45. This means that imitative practices have both a passive and an active aspect; the performer both discovers in himself things already there *and* makes those things happen or come alive, as well as charging them with meaning. This ambiguous sense of the concept of "imitation" is clearly present in Aristotle's account of mimesis in the *Poetics* (see Else 1957:321).

46. Body praxis thus reinforces emotional *and* cognitive attitudes (ethos *and* eidos). Cf. Bateson's arguments concerning the periodic offsetting of complementary schismogenetic tendencies with ritualized forms of symmetrical schismogenesis (1958:289–90).

47. Cf. Reich (1949) on the relation between character and specific patterns of muscular spasm and "armoring."

48. For a complete account of these moral precepts and the keeping of secrets, see Jackson 1982a:chap. 1.

49. A comparable explanation has been offered for female imitations of male behavior in the Zulu *nomkhulbulwana* rites. When Zulu girls dress in their lovers' clothes they say it is a way of inducing thoughts of and exerting influence over their lovers who are often living away in the mines: "the ones we are thinking of when we do this thing are the men who love us. We wish to think of them. . . . If we wear the dress of our lovers then *Nomkhulbulwana* sees that we want her to assist us in marrying them. . . . " (Berglund 1976:68).

50. Zahan notes:

> One thing becomes remarkably clear as soon as we begin to look at initiation. This is that, first and foremost, initiation constitutes a progressive course of instruction designed to familiarize the person with the significations of his own body and with the meaning he gives to the environment. Moreover, each of these is in a sense a function of the other: the human body and the world constitute two inseparable entities conceived in relation to each other. (Zahan 1979:56)

51. The phrase is used by Mauss to designate a person's imitation of actions which he has seen successfully performed "by people in whom he has confidence and who have authority over him" (1973:73).

52. An excellent account of this mode of learning is Bateson and Mead's account of Balinese learning: "The Balinese learn virtually nothing from verbal instruction" (1942:15).

53. Cf. "Words must be captured and repeated to have meaning for action, but there is no need at all to translate action into words (Bateson and Mead 1942:15).

54. The Kuranko word for intelligence, *hankilimaiye*, designates common sense and savoir faire, a mode of being in-formed, of having social *and* practical skills. As one informant defined it, "intelligence is the way you do things."

55. As Blacking has pointed out, musicality and musical production in European societies have increasingly come to define distinctions at the levels of ability, taste, and class and to generate the illusion that musicality is not a universal faculty. Comparing the European with the African situation, where musicality is a common property and musicians choose musical forms that enable participation, Blacking asks: "Must the majority be made 'unmusical' [in European societies] so that the few may become more 'musical'?" (1973:4).

56. See Jackson 1982a for a detailed discussion in the context of oral narratives.

57. I share Blacking's view, that his "concern for an anthropology of the body rests on a conviction that feelings, and particularly fellow-feeling, expressed as movements of bodies in space and time and *often without verbal connotations*, are the basis of mental life (1977:21, my emphasis). A brilliant ethnographic example of the intimate relationship between patterns of body use and states of mind is Gell's study of swinging, dancing, and ecstatic consciousness (1980).

58. Cf. Marcel Marceau: "Everything can be expressed through the art of mime, which shuns the deceitful words that raise barriers of misunderstanding between men" (cited in Royce 1977:160).

59. F. M. Alexander speaks of a "means-whereby" to contrast such patterns of "use" with "end-gaining" (1931).

60. Cf. Bourdieu:

> Objectivism constitutes the social world as a spectacle presented to an observer who takes up a "point of view" on the action, who stands back so as to observe it and, transferring into the object the principles of his relation to the object, conceives of it as a totality intended for cognition alone, in which all interactions are reduced to symbolic exchanges. (1977:96)

61. I am indebted to Chris Gregory for providing me with information concerning the classical notion of the symbol as a token or tally.

NINE. THINKING THROUGH THE BODY

1. That this theme has long been part of both religious *and* scientific traditions is established by the following quotations:

> You never Enjoy the World aright, till the Sea it self floweth in your veins, till you are Clothed with the Heavens, and Crowned with the stars; and perceiv your self to be the Sole Heir of the whole World; and more then so, becaus Men are in it who are evry one Sole Heirs, as well as you. (Thomas Traherne, *Centuries of Meditation* 1, 29)

> But when you separate mind from the structure in which it is immanent, such as human relationship, the human society, or the ecosystem, you thereby embark, I believe, on fundamental error, which in the end will surely hurt you. (George Bateson, *Pathologies of Epistemology*)

2. Needham 1978:169. Aristotle was the first writer to use the word *microcosm*; Needham notes that in the *Physics* Aristotle asked: if something "can happen in the living being, what hinders it from happening also in the All? For if it happens in the little world [microcosm], [it happens] also in the great." Contrary to the impersonal view of the body fostered by modern medicine, ancient notions of medical science favored this correspondence theory. Thus, the Islamic philosopher al-Ghazali (1058–1111) wrote: "Man has been truly termed a 'microcosm,' or little world in himself, and the structure of his body should be studied not only by those who wish to become doctors, but by those who wish to attain to a more intimate knowledge of God." And the Belgian physician Andreas Vesalius, in the Preface to his disquisition *On the Fabric of the Human Body*, published in the same year

as Copernicus's revolutionary work *On the Revolution of Celestial Orbs* (1543), wrote: "For this [human body] in many particulars exhibits a marvellous correspondence with the universe, and for that reason was by them of old not inappropriately styled 'a little universe.'" (Al-Ghazali and Vesalius cited by Needleman 1975:38, 39.)

3. See esp. *Coriolanus*, act 1, scene 1, where Menenius's celebrated parable of the belly is beautifully exploited.

4. In ethnography, synecdochism is the "belief or practice in which a part of an object or person is taken as equivalent to the whole, so that anything done to, or by means of, the part is held to take effect upon, or have the effect of, the whole" (*Oxford English Dictionary*).

5. Poetry may in fact be defined as "the most concentrated form of verbal expression"; *dichten* (= *condensare*) is the German verb corresponding to the noun *Dichtung*, poetry. Thus poetry = to condense (Pound 1961:36).

6. This may be partly explained by the way practical learning in preliterate societies is usually a matter of direct imitation and not mediated by books or abstract verbal descriptions. The Navaho view of language as embodied is not untypical: "in the beginning were the word *and the thing*, the symbol *and the object*" (Witherspoon 1977:46, my emphasis). This inseparability of knowledge and physical being is brought home by the Maori view that improper divulgence of knowledge can lead to *physical* wasting and death; cases are often cited of this happening in historical times (Tawhai 1981).

7. Cf. the Malinké, whose speech (*kúmá*) is associated with various parts of the body (Camara 1976:237–49), and the Kuranko, whose word *kole* (seed or bone) is used metaphorically of words and things, e.g., *saan kole* ("the deep sky"), *dugu kole* ("the bare ground"), *kuma kole* ("germane speech," i.e., the words and know-how of the elders upon which everyone's livelihood depends).

8. As Moynihan writes:

> In his correspondence, Thomas stressed that all ideas and actions began in the body. As a result, he insisted, the best way to render a thought or action, however abstract, was to express it in as physical a way as possible. Every thought, for him, could find an equivalent in blood, flesh, or gland. He saw it as his particular task to find and express all the equations between body and world, between body and idea. (Moynihan 1966:48)

9. See, for instance, James Fernandez, who defines metaphor as "the predication of a sign-image upon an inchoate subject" (1974:120). "In the growth of human identity, the inchoate pronouns of social life—the 'I,' 'you,' 'he,' 'it'—gain identity by predicating some sign-image, some metaphor upon themselves. These pronouns must, in Mead's (1934) terms, become objects to themselves, by taking the point of view of 'the other,' before they can become subjects to themselves" (122).

10. E.g., "Metaphor is a device for seeing something in terms of something else. It brings out the thisness of a that, or the thatness of a this" (Burke 1945:503). In making his distinction between tenor and vehicle, I. A. Richards speaks of the tenor as "the underlying idea or principal subject which the vehicle or figure means" (1936:97). More recently, Lakoff and Johnson observed that "the essence of metaphor is understanding and experiencing one kind of thing in terms of another" (1980:5).

11. Fernandez, for example, defines the study of metaphor as "the study of the way . . . subjects take objects unto themselves or are assigned them" (1974:133).

12. Thass-Thienemann (1968:370–71) offers a more involved explanation.

13. As Meinhard notes:

> Limits in the recognition of cognatic kin by reference to "joints," "little knees," etc., are already recorded in the folk-laws (*Leges Barbarorum*) of the post-migration period (fifth to early ninth century). Thus the Salian Franks reckon "usque ad sextum genuculum," the Riparian Franks, "usque quinto genuclo," the Thuringians, "usque ad quintam generationem," the Lombards, Visigoths, and Baiuvarians, "usque in septimum geniculum." The differences are usually explained

by variations in the mode of reckoning, e.g., including Ego as the point of departure so that the sibling represents the second geniculum, or beginning with the nearest collateral as the first geniculum. (1975:3)

Degrees of kinship are also expressed in terms of body joints among the Fang (Fernandez 1982:88–89).

14. See Thass-Thienemann 1968:283 and, for the significance of "curving act," 277.

15. The Kuranko word for household or family is *dembaiye* (from *demba*, a mother breast-feeding a child) and the same root *de*, meaning "mouth," occurs in the word for the door of a house, *bundon de*; lit., "granary mouth."

16. Such thinking is *not* characteristic of everyday life in either nonliterate or literate societies, and Devereux has criticized Lévy-Bruhl and Freud for their failure to recognize that crisis and stress are the universal preconditions for this kind of "prelogical" thinking (1939:332–33). Fernandez makes a similar point: "Even in supposedly sophisticated societies, men in *situations of ambiguity or conflict* return to likening each other and themselves to hawks, doves, or owls, dogs or their offspring, donkeys" (1974:122, my emphasis).

17. For instance, through alcohol and drug abuse, illness, domestic turmoil, exile, antisocial behavior, etc., which may explain why some poets are social misfits and negligent of their health and why mystical experience is sometimes precipitated by illness or crisis.

18. Preliterate thought has been variously called animistic (Tylor, Piaget), paleological (Arieti), mythopoeic (Cassirer), prelogical (Lévy-Bruhl), archaic (Eliade), and primary process (Freud), often with pejorative implications.

19. In his sociological theory of schizophrenia (1939), Devereux notes that schizoid mechanisms may be seen as attempts to adapt to the disorienting magnitude and complexity of modern societies where there is no real-scale compatibility between the individual person and the social and technological worlds which lie beyond his complete knowledge and control. Anthropomorphic thinking is evidence of an endeavor to extrapolate from the familiar to the unfamiliar, a way of making the external world seem responsive and thereby manageable. Such thinking is often a central feature of schizoid thought, which strives to control panic about the traumatic unresponsiveness of matter by interpreting physical processes animistically, i.e., on a par with the self (1967:18–19, 32–33). While I am greatly indebted to Devereux's insights, I do not accept that anthropomorphic thinking is *necessarily* erroneous.

20. See Keesing (1988) on metaphors of paths in Austronesian languages; Brunton (1981:361–62) on the significance of "exchange roads" on Tanna (Melanesia); Willis (1977:279, 1978:143) on metaphors of pathways among the Fipa (Tanzania); and Janzen (1978:169–71) on the Kongo (Zaire) correspondences between body and village.

21. Kuranko diviners sometimes refer to "gates," open or closed, which signify the status of relationships between a person and extrasocial agencies such as bush spirits or ancestors.

22. I have borrowed the term *habitus* from Mauss (1973:73) and Bourdieu (1977:72).

23. Respectively *ke dugu* and *musu dugu* ("male ground/area" and "female ground/area"). That *dugu* suggests the embodied nature of this conceptual distinction is shown by the fact that the word means, in various contexts, "earth," "ground," "place," and "body."

24. Seven days after a child is born it is brought out the front door of the house if it is a boy or the back door if it is a girl. Among the neighboring Malinké, gender distinctions are affirmed in a slightly different way, yet still based on the material *habitus*: at the birth ceremony a paternal uncle enters the house of the newborn child and comes out with the mother and the child, which has a bow around its neck if it is a boy or holds a kitchen utensil if it is a girl (Camara 1976:51).

25. See Levine (1976:121–31) on this African pattern of characterizing social relationships in terms of types of material transactions. It should also be noted that the Songhai use the metaphor of pathways *only* when treating the illnesses they describe as "village diseases." "Bush diseases" involve a different *habitus* and so require different metaphors and elements in the therapeutic process (Bisilliat 1976:579).

26. House (Bachelard 1964:4; Bourdieu 1977:89–95; Zahan 1979:69–71); animals (Fernandez 1974:121–22); plants (Leenhardt 1979:16–20); machines (Laing 1966:22; Bettelheim 1959).

27. Fernandez refers to the behaviorist contention that "metaphor is the device men possess for leaping beyond the essential privacy of the experiential process" (1974:119) and cites Boas, who observed that metaphors are often taken literally in rituals and made the basis of the rite, i.e., metaphors are not only rhetorical devices for persuasion but performative devices as well (125).

28. See Jackson 1979 for more detailed discussion.

29. See Miller 1967:134–35 for clinical examples. Fisher (1970:537–38) suggests that women are more prone to leg anxiety than men; men are accustomed to moving out aggressively into the world while women are expected to stay put in the domestic domain.

30. See Devereux's superb account (1969:489–90) of Mohave patterns of psychosomatic illness.

31. Sontag 1977:3. For a healthier view see Guirdham 1957.

32. Cf. Devereux on the social construction of the idea of "spirit roads" and "transferable souls" among the Sedang Moi (1978a:271).

33. Cf. J. L. Austin's definition of performative utterances: "the issuing of the utterance is the performing of an action—it is not normally thought of as just saying something" (1962:6–7).

34. As Devereux has shown, such transference also occurs in science. The Copernican revolution paradoxically offered a way out of emotional dilemmas: "By transferring anxiety-arousing internal and interpersonal conflicts to the vaults of heaven, man was able to take his distance from the problems besetting him and to speculate about them with some measure of objectivity" (1967:4).

35. See Horton 1967:167–72 on "secondary elaboration" in African divination where various explanations and therapies are tried serially. By contrast, Janzen has shown (1978:200–201) another kind of pluralism among the BaKongo where people seek several different diagnoses and employ several different therapies simultaneously.

36. The diagnostic model suggested here closely resembles the Taoist model, which does not rank causes in a hierarchy or chain but explores the "side-by-side" patterning of causes and the "induction effect" which interrelates them within a unitary field, rather like the "endocrine orchestra" of modern biology (Needham 1978:163–68).

37. Cf. Cassirer: "Whereas empirical thinking is essentially directed toward establishing an unequivocal relation between *specific* 'causes' and *specific* 'effects,' mythical thinking . . . has a free selection of causes at its disposal. Anything can *come from* anything, because anything can stand in temporal or spatial contact with anything" (1955:46).

38. One notable exception is the Simontons' use of visualization and metaphorization in cancer therapy (Simonton and Simonton 1980).

39. Erikson notes that if a child is ill a grandmother is often summoned to sing the ailment away. "American Indians in general seem to have a fine understanding of ambivalence, which dictates that in certain crises near-relatives are of no educational or therapeutic use" (1943:261).

40. Pepper on "root metaphors" (1957:87, 91).

41. This "restriction to concreteness . . . prevents the patient from giving a metaphorical meaning to proverbs; they are interpreted literally or very concretely" (Arieti 1967:279).

42. Arieti 1967:280. Cf. Cassirer, who claims that in "mythical consciousness" "the 'image' does not represent the 'thing'; it *is* the thing; it does not merely stand for the object, but has the same actuality, so that it replaces the thing's immediate presence" (1955:38). My objection to this way of characterizing preliterate thought is that it implies that preliterate peoples are somehow trapped by a propensity to confuse words and things. Anyone who has actually lived among preliterate peoples knows very well that this is nonsense and that the concreteness and fusions in preliterate world views reflect an ethical preference for a

philosophy that is conducive to community rather than individualism; it is an index of positive commitment, not of inadequacy or intellectual impoverishment.

43. See Arieti 1967:286 for the notion of aholism (inability to perceive wholes; the disintegration of wholes) and Bettelheim (1959) for a remarkable account of an autistic child who was stuck with a view of himself as a machine. "Not every child who possesses a fantasy world is possessed by it. Normal children may retreat into realms of imaginary glory or magic powers, but they are easily recalled from these excursions. Disturbed children are not always able to make the return trip; they remain withdrawn, prisoners of the inner world of delusion and fantasy" (Bettelheim 1959:117).

44. Laing writes that people who regard themselves as automata, robots, bits of machinery, or animals are crazy, "yet, why do we not regard a theory that seeks to transmute persons into automata or animals as equally crazy?" (1966:22). One philosopher who accepts that metaphor has a place in philosophical discourse is Max Black, who argues that metaphor is "constitutive of meaning" and not merely an embellishment which can best be replaced by "plain language" (1962:46).

45. The reference to the "Enlightenment" puts one in mind of the view of Horkheimer and Adorno (1972:3–42) that the dominance of scientific rationalism during the Enlightenment could only be achieved through a denial of the anthropomorphic view that man's body was linked to social and natural bodies. The associated splitting of the thinking subject—his personality and historicality—from discourse was also accompanied by a splitting of the physical body from Mind (Poole 1972:107–9).

46. That Mill was struggling with unresolved Oedipal conflicts is suggested by the fact that the only "small ray of light" that broke in upon his gloom during this period was a direct result of his reading Marmontel's *Memoirs:* "I . . . came to the passage which relates his father's death, the distressed position of the family, and the sudden inspiration by which he, then a mere boy, felt and made them feel that he would be everything to them—would supply the place of all that they had lost. A vivid conception of the scene and its feelings came over me, and I was moved to tears. From this moment my burthen grew lighter" (Mill 1981:145).

47. Paul Valéry regularly used the rhythms of walking to bring him a "quickened flow of ideas" (Welsh 1978:12), and John Bowlby has pointed out, in his discussion of the soothing effects of rocking a baby, that the most effective rocking rhythm is sixty cycles a minute or above, i.e., "the rate at which an adult walks" (1971:353).

TEN. THE MIGRATION OF A NAME

1. This sense of estrangement which fieldwork involves means that anthropologists might be especially attracted to hermeneutics, which calls attention to the fact that "the lack of immediate understandability of texts handed down to us historically or their proneness to be misunderstood is really only a special case of what is to be met in all human orientation to the world as the *atopon* (the strange), that which does not 'fit' into the customary order of our expectations based on experience" (Gadamer 1976:24).

2. As Yves Person has noted, "A fairly general rule, which holds good for oral tradition as a whole, is that memory is only as good as far back as the last migration and begins with the settlement of a group in their present territory" (1973:211). Thus, different oral sources of Barawa tradition vary and conflict beyond the time of Marin Tamba,' whose two sons, Morowa and Balansama, established two ruling houses within the one Marah ruling lineage.

3. Person notes that the farther south one goes from northern Mali, the more the archival role of *griots* degenerates and they become flatterers of chiefs, official praise-singers, and public entertainers (1973:206).

4. See Norman O. Brown (1969) on the role of Hermes as bard, herald, intercessory, and controller of strangers. I have discussed the ambiguity of messengers elsewhere (Jackson

1979, 1982a), and the corruption of messages is a central motif in African myths explaining the origins of death (Abrahamsson 1951).

5. *Namu* is from the Arabic *na'am*, an interjection to signify that one has heard and understood what someone is saying, particularly a chief.

6. In Kuranko *yigi* means "hope" or "trust," and a person can place his trust in another person (i.e., a mentor) by saying *"ne n'yigi sigi bi ma na sina,"* "let me my trust/hope place in you, not for today but for tomorrow." In brief, a mentor is a helpmate outside the kinship circle whom one can call upon in times of need.

7. Wagadu is the Mandingo name for the land of old Ghana, ruled over by the Tounkara-Cissé. Ghana was eclipsed by the advent of the Mande empire in the early thirteenth century.

8. According to oral traditions I have collected in northern Sierra Leone, the various Kuranko "countries" were not occupied by Saramba's sons but were allocated by Saramba to subsequent arrivals belonging to other clans, notably Kargbo and Koroma.

9. Sayers notes: "If no other praise has succeeded in extracting a present from a miserly chief, the Yeli will play his trump card, that of comparing his patron to the great Yurukhernani, and this rarely fails to loosen the purse strings" (1927:80). In medieval Europe, troubadors and jongleurs did likewise, making their home "in that court where they were best rewarded" and combining "praise of their liberal lord with as gratifying a disparagement of his close-fisted rivals" (Cary 1956:214).

10. No less ironic is the fact that the classical figure of Hermes, the patron of interpreters, is associated with theft and trickery (Brown 1969:6–10).

11. Sayers gives a Mandingo folk etymology based on *kere* (horn) plus *nani* (four). Dulcarnon is also a name for the forty-seventh proposition of the first book of Euclid (the *syllogismum cornutum*).

12. Actually, Niane says that Dhul-Quarnein was another name of Sunjata, who ruled in Mande between about 1230 and 1255 (1965:90), and Sayers says that Yurukhernani was "probably a Mali king under another name" (1927:80). Certainly the Ghana kings, whom Sunjata eclipsed, traced their descent to Alexander, and Sunjata clearly imitated and emulated Alexander in his campaigns and in his life (Tronson 1982).

13. The sources and reasons for Alexander's journey to Siwa are confusing. Robin Lane Fox has clarified matters considerably, especially the historical background to how the Greeks came to acknowledge Ammon (the Egyptian Amun; cf. Greek *ammos*, sand) as a form of their Olympian Zeus (Fox 1973:200–218).

14. According to St. Jerome the ram's two horns represent Darius's two kingdoms of Media and Persia (Cary 1956:120).

15. The Islamic empire of the Almoravids conquered Ghana in 1076, and the Mande empire, which reached its zenith between the early thirteenth and late fourteenth centuries, retained close trading links with the Arab world (see Oliver and Fage 1962:77–91).

16. The Marah call themselves *sunike*, which may mean "ruler" or "non-Muslim," a fact which corroborates oral traditions that the Marah have always kept themselves aloof from Islam (the *moriye*). Nevertheless, Islamic heroes (Moses, Muhammad, Noah, Solomon) often figure in Kuranko tradition, without any awareness of their actual origins. In the case of Yilkanani, who is associated with Muhammad in Faraba Demba's narrative (because Faraba Demba is a Muslim), it is usually the case that praise-singers do *not* associate this hero with Islam, since the Marah are non-Muslim.

17. Most of the Alexander romances can be traced back to some time after A.D. 200, when an anonymous Alexandrian wrote a fabulous account of Alexander which was falsely attributed to Callisthenes, Alexander's companion and historian. This work was translated from the Greek into Latin by Julius Valerius, an African and freedman, about A.D. 320–30, but both Latin and Greek versions were disseminated widely through Europe and the East, and it was not until the Renaissance that the histories of Arrian, Plutarch, Diodorus, and Quintus Curtius were referred to as means of establishing the truth about Alexander's

conquests (Fox 1973:26–27; Budge 1933:xv-xvii; Cary 1956:9–10; Boyle 1974:217, 1977:13–16). It is fascinating that the pseudo-Callisthenes text, from which Alexander's metamorphosis began, came to light during the same century which saw the disappearance of Alexander's body from the golden casket where it had lain in state since his death, and that the appearance of the fabulous story and the disappearance of the body should have occurred in the same place.

18. Cf. Fox (1973:27): "Alexander is the subject for a search, not a story, for such was the style and content of his first written histories that any confident narrative can only be disreputable."

19. Cf. Borza (1974:5):

No amount of rational method in historical study has ever quite been able to displace certain personal idiosyncracies in the investigators themselves. Thus the modern image of Alexander, while heavily dependent on the use of the technique of rational inquiry, still often reflects the personality of the historian.

20. In Sartre's words:

Ce que j'appelle le vécu, c'est précisément l'ensemble du processus dialectique de la vie psychique, un processus qui reste nécessairement opaque à lui-même car il est une constante totalisation, et une totalisation qui ne peut être consciente de ce qu'elle est. Ou peut être conscient, en effet, d'une totalisation exterieure, mais non d'une totalisation qui totalise également la conscience. *En ce sens, le vécu est toujours susceptible de compréhension, jamais de connaissance.* (1972:111, my emphasis; cf. Sartre 1969:49)

21. In fact, as part of my research on the impact of literacy among the Kuranko I enlisted my sister's help in finding and using psychological tests, though I was temperamentally unsuited to this kind of methodology. It was as if I was striving to produce data which were sound by her (positivist) standards.

22. As Marcuse (1969:96–97) and Horkheimer and Adorno (1972) have pointed out, this aggressive and domineering form of rationality emerges with the Enlightenment; yet, in its twofold obsession to control nature and coerce other human beings, it epitomizes the modern ethos, ramifying into science, politics, art, and technology. This technicist attitude tends, moreover, to exclude the thinker from the domain of thought, creating thereby a fatuous objectivity in which self-critical and self-reflective activity are almost nonexistent (Poole 1972:107–9).

23. Conviviality designates "the opposite of industrial activity" and refers to "autonomous and creative intercourse among persons, and the intercourse of persons with their environment; and this in contrast with the conditioned response of persons to the demands made upon them by others, and by a man-made environment" (Illich 1973:11).

24. These terms can readily be assimilated into those used by Marx: use-value versus exchange-value.

25. Max Gluckman (1970) speaks of "the frailty in authority" and I have discussed this theme at length in my study of Kuranko oral narratives (Jackson 1982a).

26. The ambiguity of the word *magnanimity* throughout the medieval period should be noted: "It means a quality of greatness that may consist in nobility of mind, in the narrower meaning of determined and ambitious bravery, or even in ferocious and fool-hardy self-confidence; its exact interpretation must differ in every writer" (Cary 1956:200).

27. In the 1890s Kipling would spend part of the year in South Africa to escape the English winters. In Cape Town he met Rhodes and fell under his spell. "Daniel Dravot is a kind of Rhodes, long before Kipling had any thought of meeting him" (Mason 1975:145–46).

28. Borges also observes that "In comparison with this symmetry, which operates on the souls of sleeping men and spans continents and centuries, the levitations, resurrections, and

apparitions in the sacred books are not so extraordinary" (1964:14). A comparable development of this idea is to be found in Lévi-Strauss's essay on the structural study of myth. After noting that myth consists of "all its versions," he urges that Freud's use of the Oedipus myth be placed alongside the version of Sophocles, since both "versions" address the same problem: how one can be born from two (Lévi-Strauss 1963:216–17). The Ulysses story in all its versions, from Homer to Tennyson to Joyce, can be cited as another example of such a myth (see Stanford 1969).

29. The antireductionist view is nicely expressed by Sartre, speaking of Flaubert: "It is the work or the act of the individual which reveals to us the secret of his conditioning. Flaubert by his choice of writing discloses to us the meaning of his childish fear of death— not the reverse" (1968:152). In an imaginative essay called "If Alexander the Great Had Lived On," Arnold Toynbee argues in a similar vein, that although we can detect patterns in the past we cannot extrapolate from them the exact course of the future: "I believe that these patterns are authentic, but I also believe that they were not inevitable, and, *a fortiori*, I believe that they are not bound to recur in a future that is at least partly determinable by present and future human acts of will" (1974:164). The significance of the nonreductionist view in hermeneutics is brought home by Paul Ricoeur:

> The only radical way to justify hermeneutics is to seek in the very nature of reflective thought the principle of a *logic of double meaning*, a logic that is complex but not arbitrary, rigorous in its articulations but irreducible to the linearity of symbolic logic. This logic is no longer a formal logic, but a transcendental logic established on the level of the conditions of possibility; not the conditions of objectivity of nature, but the conditions of our appropriation of our desire to be. (1970:48)

30. This process of making whole may be understood in neurophysiological terms as a balancing or harmonizing of the right and left sides of the brain. Gregory Bateson writes: "Mere purposive rationality unaided by such phenomena as art, religion, dream, and the like, is necessarily pathogenic and destructive of life" (quoted in May 1981:222).

31. Richard Rorty has brilliantly elucidated the importance of Heidegger, Gadamer, and Sartre in showing how the search for objective knowledge is only one among many ways of describing ourselves in the world (1979:360–61). The choice of an objectivist mode of theoretical knowledge reflects temperamental and cultural interests as much as does the choice of subjectivist or praxeological perspectives.

32. Both Dewey (1929) and Devereux (1967) have shown how the search for objective certainty and universal laws reflects a deep anxiety about the aleatory and capricious nature of human existence. While we are often bemused by "primitive" magic, Dewey points out that "Our magical safeguard against the uncertain character of the world is to deny the existence of chance, to mumble universal and necessary laws, the ubiquity of cause and effect, the uniformity of nature, universal progress, and the inherent rationality of the universe" (1929:44).

33. In the pragmatist view, "ideas (which themselves are but parts of our experience) become true just in so far as they help us get into satisfactory relation with other parts of our experience" (James 1978:34), a view that allows that fictions create truths and regards "untruth as a condition of life" (Nietzsche 1973:9).

34. Innes makes the same observation about the recitation of the Sunjata epic in the Gambia: "the story is true for the Mandinka at a deeper level than that of literal historical fact. The Sunjata epic is true in all its versions in that *it is true to the facts of the moral and social life of the Mandinka*" (1974:30). He makes the same point in another study of variability in the telling of the Sunjata epic: "griots commonly hear other griots relating versions of the Sunjata legend substantially different from their own version, but this does not seem to worry them, nor their audiences. The question of which version is 'correct' or 'true' just does not arise; in some sense, they are all regarded as 'true'" (1973:107).

ELEVEN. ON ETHNOGRAPHIC TRUTH

1. See Lloyd 1966:172–75 for an excellent review of the importance of analogy in the thought of Bacon, Hume, Mill, and Keynes.

2. For a fuller account of Bacon's ambivalent attitude toward magic and alchemy, see Farrington 1966:51–55. As for Newton:

> Significantly, he had read Henry More, the Cambridge Platonist, and was therefore introduced to another intellectual world, the magical Hermetic tradition, which sought to explain natural phenomena in terms of alchemical and magical concepts. The two traditions of natural philosophy, the mechanical and the Hermetic, antithetical though they appear, continued to influence his thought and in their tension supplied the fundamental theme of his scientific career (*Encyclopaedia Britannica* 1987;13:17).

Keynes calls Newton "the last of the magicians," whose "deepest instincts were occult, esoteric, semantic" (1951:311).

3. The Enlightenment antipathy to anthropomorphism and myth is discussed at length in Horkheimer and Adorno's *Dialectic of Enlightenment* (1972). For a lucid summary of the argument, see Connerton 1980:66–67.

4. Bacon observed in *Novum Organum* that "natural philosophy is after the word of God at once the surest medicine against superstition, and the most approved nourishment for faith, and therefore she is rightly given to religion as her most faithful handmaid, since the one displays the will of God, the other his power" (1905:286).

5. Such a view can be traced back to the Aristotelian metaphysical doctrine that nature is an ordered series from lower to higher potentialities and actualizations in which the organic body was "the highest term in a physical series and the lowest term in a psychical series" (Dewey 1929:250). The classical distinction

> between vegetative, animal and rational souls was, when applied to men, a formulation and justification of class divisions in Greek society. Slaves and mechanical artisans living on the nutritional, appetitive level were for practical purposes symbolized by the body—an obstruction to ideal ends and as solicitations to acts contrary to reason. . . . Scientific inquirers and philosophers alone exemplified pure reason . . . *nous*, pure immaterial mind. (251)

6. "For the colonized person, objectivity is always directed against him" (Frantz Fanon, quoted in Wilden 1972:xxiii).

7. Susan Sontag writes: "Modern sensibility moves between two seemingly contradictory but actually related impulses: surrender to the exotic, the strange, the other; and the domestication of the exotic, chiefly through science" (1967:70).

8. The Sebeoks refer to Heidegger's distinction between two modes of training, *apprentissage* and *dressage*, to clarify the way in which the relationship between human researchers and experimental apes conditioned the explanations of data: "*apprentissage* entails a reduction of the animal-man nexus to as close to zero as may be feasible. *Dressage*, on the other hand, requires a maximum intensification of the ligature, with the richest possible emotional involvement" (Sebeok and Sebeok 1980:4). The Sebeoks argue that the tension between these modes of training interaction created varying degrees of objectivity, as well as different interpretive emphases on similitude (including anthropomorphism) and difference (21–25).

9. In the Foreword to his *Dynamics of Clanship among the Tallensi* (1945), Fortes writes:

> My debt to Professor A. R. Radcliffe-Brown is . . . great. The final draft of this book was written while I was working with him at Oxford and every significant problem in it was discussed with him. The results are obvious in every chapter. My approach to the study of social structure in primitive society is basically derived from him. (1945:xiv)

10. Richard Rorty observes that this contrast between treating language as a picture or a game corresponds roughly to the difference between the early and later Wittgenstein (1982:110).

11. Clifford Geertz has given Weber's phrase great currency among anthropologists (1973:5).

12. In many ways the traumatic impact of the Vietnam War on the consciousness of anthropologists is reminiscent of the profound influence of Nazism on the philosophers of the Frankfurt School.

13. Even Francis Bacon allowed that "fortuitous analogies" may have real value in discovering "Conformable Instances":

> although they are of little use for the discovery of forms, they nevertheless are very serviceable in revealing the fabric of the parts of the universe, and anatomizing its members; from which they often lead us along to sublime and noble axioms, especially those which relate to the configuration of the world rather than to simple forms and natures. (1905:333)

14. Perhaps the structures of lobsters, sea anemones, and different human societies *are* unified and alike in some marvelous way, but the problem is that when we search for finite unifying structures in nature and in culture we come up against the finite structures of our own thought. Even if life were a unity, we would have no way of getting outside our minds and knowing it.

15. Adorno captures this idea beautifully: "The name of dialectics says no more, to begin with, than that objects do not go into their concepts without leaving a remainder, that they come to contradict the traditional norm of adequacy" (Adorno 1973:5).

16. Eccles makes a similar point: "perhaps the most important moment in the emergence of human language was the moment when man was able to *tell a story*; to tell a story that was not true and thereby to invent the difference between truth and falsehood. For this distinction opened up the possibility both of imaginative invention and of critical discussion" (1974:106). Umberto Eco illuminates the existential implications of this idea by noting the ways in which literature subverts language. Language, he observes, "is structured so fatally that, slaves inside it, we cannot free ourselves outside it, because outside the given language there is nothing. . . . How can we escape what Barthes calls, Sartre-like, this *huis-clos*? By cheating. You can cheat with the given language. This dishonest and healthy and liberating trick is called literature" (1986:241–42).

17. It was only after completing this chapter that the mystery concerning Bokonon's "true" identity, posed at the beginning of it, was cleared up. Swedish friends Carl Von Rosen and Inger Andersson brought to my attention that Bokonon is a Western mishearing of Makonnen, the last part of the name of the Emperor Haile Selassie of Ethiopia: Ras Tafari Makonnen.

Bibliography

Abimbola, W. 1973. "The Yoruba Concept of Personality." In G. Dieterlen (ed.), *La notion de personne en Afrique noire*, pp. 72–89. Centre National de la Recherche Scientifique, Paris.

Abrahamsson, H. 1951. *The Origin of Death*. Studia Ethnographica Upsaliensia, no. 3, Uppsala.

Abrams, M. H. 1958. *The Mirror and the Lamp: Romantic Theory and the Critical Tradition*. Norton, New York.

Achebe, C. 1975. *Morning Yet on Creation Day: Essays*. Heinemann, London.

Adorno, T. W. 1967. "Notes on Kafka" (translated by S. and S. Weber). In *Prisms*. Spearman, London.

———. 1973. *Negative Dialectics* (translated by E. B. Ashton). Seabury Press, New York.

Alexander, F. M. 1931. *The Use of Self*. Methuen, London.

Alldridge, T. J. 1901. *The Sherbro and its Hinterland*. Macmillan, London.

Ardener, E. 1959. "Lineage and Locality among the Mba-Ise Ibo." *Africa* 29(2):1–13.

Arendt, H. 1968. "Introduction: Walter Benjamin 1892–1940." In Walter Benjamin, *Illuminations* (translated by H. Zohn). Harcourt, Brace and World, New York.

Arieti, S. 1967. *The Intrapsychic Self: Feeling, Cognition, and Creativity in Health and Mental Illness*. Basic Books, New York.

———. 1974. *Interpretation of Schizophrenia*, 2d ed. Basic Books, New York.

Asad, T. (ed.). 1973. *Anthropology and the Colonial Encounter*. Ithaca Press, London.

Austin, J. L. 1962. *How to Do Things with Words*. Clarendon, Oxford.

Bachelard, G. 1964. *The Poetics of Space* (translated by M. Jolas). Beacon Press, Boston.

Bacon, F. 1905. *The Philosophical Works of Francis Bacon* (edited with an introduction by J. M. Robertson). Routledge, London.

Barnes, J. 1962. "African Models in the New Guinea Highlands." *Man* 62:5–9.

Bascom, W. 1969. *Ifa Divination: Communication between Gods and Men in West Africa*. Indiana University Press, Bloomington.

Bastide, R. 1972. *The Sociology of Mental Disorder* (translated by J. McNeil). Routledge and Kegan Paul, London.

Bateson, G. 1958. *Naven*. Stanford University Press, Stanford.

———. 1973. *Steps to an Ecology of Mind*. Paladin, Frogmore.

———. 1977. "Afterword." In *About Bateson* (edited by J. Brockman). Dutton, New York.

———, and Mead, M. 1942. *Balinese Character: A Photographic Analysis*. Special Publications of the New York Academy of Sciences, vol. 2.

Beattie, J. 1964. "Divination in Bunyoro, Uganda." *Sociologus* 14:44–61.

Beatty, K. J. 1915. *Human Leopards*. Hugh Rees, London.

Becker, E. 1973. *The Denial of Death*. Free Press, New York.

Beidelman, T. O. 1966. "Utani: Some Kaguru Notions of Death, Sexuality and Affinity." *Southwestern Journal of Anthropology* 22(4):354–80.

———. 1971. *The Kaguru*. Holt, Rinehart and Winston, New York.

———. 1986. *Moral Imagination in Kaguru Modes of Thought*. Indiana University Press, Bloomington.

Benjamin, W. 1968. *Illuminations* (translated by H. Zohn; edited and with an introduction by H. Arendt). Harcourt, Brace and World, New York.

Berger, J. 1979. *Pig Earth*. Writers and Readers Publishing Cooperative, London.

Berger, P. L., and Luckmann, T. 1966. *The Social Construction of Reality: A Treatise in the Sociology of Knowledge*. Penguin Books, Harmondsworth.

Berglund, A-I. 1976. *Zulu Thought-Patterns and Symbolism*. C. Hurst, London.

Berry, R. G. 1912. "The Sierra Leone Cannibals, with Notes on Their History, Religion, and Customs." *Proceedings of the Royal Irish Academy* 30:15–69.

Best, D. 1978. *Philosophy and Human Movement*. George Allen and Unwin, London.

Bettelheim, B. 1959. "Joey: A 'Mechanical Boy.'" *Scientific American* 200(3):117–27.

Bharati, A. 1965. *The Tantric Tradition*. Rider, London.

———. 1976. "Techniques of Control in the Esoteric Traditions of India and Tibet." In *The Realm of the Extra-Human: Ideas and Actions* (edited by A. Bharati), pp. 89–99. Mouton, The Hague.

Binswanger, L. 1963. *Being-in-the-world: Selected Papers* (translated by J. Needleman). Basic Books, New York.

Bird, C. S., and Kendall, M. B. 1980. "The Mande Hero." In *Explorations in African Systems of Thought* (edited by I. Karp and C. S. Bird). Indiana University Press, Bloomington.

Bisilliat, J. 1976. "Village Diseases and Bush Diseases in Songhay: An Essay in Description with a View to a Typology" (translated by J. B. Loudon). In *Social Anthropology and Medicine* (edited by J. B. Loudon), A.S.A. Monograph 13, pp. 555–93. Academic Press, London.

Black, M. 1962. *Models and Metaphors: Studies in Language and Philosophy*. Cornell University Press, Ithaca.

Black, S. 1969. *Mind and Body*. William Kimber, London.

Blacking, J. 1973. *How Musical Is Man?* University of Washington Press, Seattle.

———. 1976. "Dance, Conceptual Thought and Production in the Archaeological Record." In *Problems in Economic and Social Archaeology* (edited by G. de G. Sieveking, J. H. H. Longworth, and K. E. Wilson), pp. 1–13. Duckworth, London.

———. 1977. "Towards an Anthropology of the Body." In *The Anthropology of the Body* (edited by J. Blacking), pp. 1–28. Academic Press, London.

Bloch, M. 1971. *Placing the Dead: Tombs, Ancestral Villages and Kinship Organization in Madagascar*. Seminar Press, London.

Blythe, R. H. 1942. *Zen in English Literature and Oriental Classics*. Hokuseido Press, Tokyo.

———. 1947. *Haiku*, vol. I. Hokuseido Press, Tokyo.

Boagey, E. 1977. *Poetry Workbook*. University Tutorial Press, London.

Boas, F. 1944. *The Function of Dance in Human Society*. Dance Horizons, New York.

Bohannan, L. 1970. "Political Aspects of Tiv Social Organization." In *Tribes without Rulers* (edited by J. Middleton and D. Tait), pp. 33–66. Routledge and Kegan Paul, London.

Bonner, J. T. 1980. *The Evolution of Culture in Animals*. Princeton University Press, Princeton.

Borges, J. L. 1964. *Other Inquisitions* (translated by R. L. C. Simms). University of Texas Press, Austin.

Borza, E. N. 1974. Introduction. In *The Impact of Alexander the Great* (edited by E. N. Borza). Dryden Press, Hinsdale.

Bourdieu, P. 1977. *Outline of a Theory of Practice* (translated by R. Nice). Cambridge University Press, Cambridge.

———. 1979. *La distinction: critique sociale du jugement*. Editions de Minuit, Paris.

Boyle, J. A. 1974. "The Alexander Legend in Central Asia." *Folklore* 85:217–28.

———. 1977. "The Alexander Romance in the East and the West." *Bulletin of the John Rylands University Library of Manchester* 60:13–27.

Bowlby, J. 1961. "Processes of Mourning." *International Journal of Psycho-Analysis* 44(3):317–40.

———. 1971. *Attachment and Loss*, 1: *Attachment*. Penguin Books, Harmondsworth.

———. 1975. *Attachment and Loss*, 2: *Separation: Anxiety and Anger*. Penguin Books, Harmondsworth.

Bradbury, R. E. 1973. *Lenin Studies* (edited by P. Morton-Williams). Oxford University Press, London.

Bradley, N. 1970. "The Knees as Fantasied Genitals." *Psychoanalytic Quarterly* 57:65–94.
Brain, R. 1970. "Child-Witches." In *Witchcraft Confessions and Accusations* (edited by M. Douglas), A.S.A. Monograph 9. Tavistock Press, London.
Brockbank, P. 1976. Introduction to *Coriolanus*. Arden Edition, pp. 1–89. Methuen, London.
Brown, N. O. 1959. *Life against Death: The Psychoanalytical Meaning of History*. Routledge and Kegan Paul, London.
———. 1969. *Hermes the Thief: The Evolution of a Myth*. Vintage Books, New York.
Brown, R. H. 1977. *A Poetic for Sociology*. Cambridge University Press, Cambridge.
Brunton, R. 1981. "The Origins of the John Frum Movement: A Sociological Explanation." In *Vanuatu: Politics, Economics and Ritual in Island Melanesia* (edited by M. Allen), pp. 357–77. Academic Press, Sydney.
Buck-Morss, S. 1977. *The Origin of Negative Dialectics: Theodore W. Adorno, Walter Benjamin, and the Frankfurt Institute*. Harvester Press, Hassocks, Sussex.
Budge, E. A. W. 1933. *The Alexander Book in Ethiopia*. Oxford University Press, London.
Bunker, H. A. and Lewin, B. D. 1965. "A Psychoanalytic Notation on the Root GN, KN, CN." In *Psychoanalysis and Culture* (edited by G. B. Wilbur and W. Muensterberger). International Universities Press, New York.
Burke, K. 1945. *A Grammar of Motives*. Prentice-Hall, New York.
Buxton, J. 1973. *Religion and Healing in Mandari*. Clarendon Press, Oxford.
Calame-Griaule, G. 1965. *Ethnologie et langage: la parole chez les Dogon*. Gallimard, Paris.
Camara, S. 1976. *Gens de la parole: essai sur la condition et le rôle des griots dans la société Malinké*. Mouton, Paris.
Cary, G. 1956. *The Medieval Alexander*. Cambridge University Press, Cambridge.
Cassirer, E. 1951. *The Philosophy of the Enlightenment* (translated by F. C. A. Koelln and J. P. Pettegrove). Princeton University Press, Princeton.
———. 1955. *The Philosophy of Symbolic Forms*, vol. 2: *Mythical Thought* (translated by R. Manheim). Yale University Press, New Haven.
Clarke, H. W. 1881. *The Sikander Nama, E Bara or Book of Alexander the Great*. W. H. Allen, London.
Clifford, J. 1986a. "On Ethnographic Self-Fashioning: Conrad and Malinowski." In *Reconstructing Individualism: Autonomy, Individuality, and the Self in Western Thought* (edited by T. C. Heller, M. Sosna, and D. E. Wellberg, with A. I. Davidson, A. Swidler, and I. Watt). Stanford University Press, Stanford.
———. 1986b. "Introduction: Partial Truths." In *Writing Culture* (edited by J. Clifford and G. E. Marcus), pp. 1–26. University of California Press, Berkeley.
Condominas, G. 1977. *We Have Eaten the Forest* (translated by A. Foulke). Hill and Wang, New York.
Connerton, P. 1980. *The Tragedy of Enlightenment: An Essay on the Frankfurt School*. Cambridge University Press, Cambridge.
Corngold, S. 1973. *The Commentator's Despair*. Kennikat Press, Port Washington, New York.
Cosentino, D. 1982. *Defiant Maids and Stubborn Farmers: Tradition and Invention in Mende Story Performance*. Cambridge University Press, Cambridge.
Danforth, L. M. 1982. *The Death Rituals of Rural Greece*. Princeton University Press, Princeton.
Danquah, J. B. 1944. *The Akan Doctrine of God: A Fragment of Gold Coast Ethics and Religion*. Lutterworth Press, London.
d'Aquili, E. G., Laughlin, C. D., and McManus, J. 1979. *The Spectrum of Ritual: A Biogenetic Structural Analysis*. Columbia University Press, New York.
Darwin, C. 1872. *The Expression of the Emotions in Man and Animals*. J. Murray, London.
Dasgupta, S., and Mukhopadhyay, F. K. L. 1962. *Obscure Religious Cults*. Calcutta.

De Meur, G. 1986. *New Trends in Mathematical Anthropology*. Routledge and Kegan Paul, London.

Derrida, J. 1976. *Of Grammatology* (translated by G. C. Spivak). Johns Hopkins University Press, Baltimore.

———. 1981. *Dissemination* (translated, with an introduction and additional notes by B. Johnson). Athlone Press, London.

Descartes, R. 1931. "Discourse on Method." In *The Philosophical Works of Descartes* (rendered into English by E. S. Haldane and G. R. T. Ross), vol. 1. Cambridge University Press, Cambridge.

Devereux, G. 1939. "A Sociological Theory of Schizophrenia." *Psychoanalytic Review* 26:315–42.

———. 1961a. "Art and Mythology, Part 1: A General Theory." In *Studying Personality Cross-Culturally* (edited by B. Kaplan). Harper and Row, New York.

———. 1961b. "Two Types of Modal Personality Models." In *Studying Personality Cross-Culturally* (edited by B. Kaplan). Harper and Row, New York.

———. 1967. *From Anxiety to Method in the Behavioural Sciences*. Mouton, The Hague.

———. 1969a. "Normal and Abnormal: The Key Concepts of Ethnopsychiatry." In *Man and His Culture: Psychoanalytic Anthropology after Totem and Taboo* (edited by W. Muensterberger), pp. 113–36. Taplinger, New York.

———. 1969b. *Mohave Ethnopsychiatry and Suicide: The Psychiatric Knowledge and the Psychic Disturbances of an Indian Tribe*. Smithsonian Institution Bureau of American Ethnology Bulletin 175, U.S. Government Printing Office, Washington.

———. 1978a. *Ethnopsychoanalysis: Psychoanalysis and Anthropology as Complementary Frames of Reference*. University of California Press, Berkeley.

———. 1978b. "The Works of George Devereux." In *The Making of Psychological Anthropology* (edited by G. D. Spindler), pp. 364–406. University of California Press, Berkeley.

———. 1980. *Basic Problems of Ethnopsychiatry* (translated by B. M. Gulati and G. Devereux). University of Chicago Press, Chicago.

Devisch, R. 1983. "Le corps sexué et social ou les modalités d'échange sensoriel chez les Yaka du Zaïre." *Psychopathologie Africaine* 19:5–31.

———. 1984. *Se recréer femme: manipulation sémantique d'une situation d'infecondité chez les Yaka*. Reimer Verlag, Berlin.

———. 1985a. "Symbol and Psychosomatic Symptom in Bodily Space-Time: The Case of the Yaka of Zaire." *International Journal of Psychology* 20(4–5):589–616.

———. 1985b. "Polluting and Healing among the Northern Yaka of Zaire." *Social Science and Medicine* 21(6):693–700.

de Waelhens, A. 1978. *Schizophrenia: A Philosophical Reflection on Lacan's Structuralist Interpretation* (translated by W. ver Eecke). Duquesne University Press, Pittsburgh.

Dewey, J. 1929. *Experience and Nature*. Allen and Unwin, London.

———. 1958. *Art as Experience*. Capricorn Books, New York.

———. 1960. "An Empirical Survey of Empiricisms." In *John Dewey on Experience, Nature, and Freedom: Representative Selections* (edited and with an introduction by R. J. Bernstein). Liberal Arts Press, New York.

———. 1980. *The Quest for Certainty: A Study of the Relation of Knowledge and Action*. Perigree Books, New York.

———. 1983. "Human Nature and Conduct." In *John Dewey: The Middle Works, 1899–1924*, vol. 14 (1922) Southern Illinois University Press, Carbondale.

Diamond, A. S. 1959. *The History and Origin of Language*. Methuen, London.

Dobzhansky, T. 1962. *Mankind Evolving*. Yale University Press, New Haven.

Dostoyevsky, F. 1961. *Notes from Underground* (translated by A. R. MacAndrew). New American Library, New York.

Douglas, M. 1970a. *Natural Symbols*. Barrie and Jenkins, London.

———. 1970b. Introduction to *Witchcraft Confessions and Accusations* (edited by M. Douglas), A.S.A. Monograph 9. Tavistock, London.

———. 1978. *Implicit Meanings: Essays in Anthropology*. Routledge and Kegan Paul, London.

Eccles, J. 1974. "Falsifiability and Freedom." In *Reflexive Water* (edited by F. Elders), pp. 71–131. Souvenir Press, London.

Eco, U. 1986. *Faith in Fakes* (translated by W. Weaver). Secker and Warburg, London.

Edie, J. 1963. "Expression and Metaphor." *Philosophy and Phenomenological Research* 23(4):538–561.

———. 1965. "Notes on the Philosophical Anthropology of William James." In *An Invitation to Phenomenology: Studies in the Philosophy of Experience* (edited with an introduction by J. Edie), pp. 110–32. Quadrangle Books, Chicago.

———. 1976. *Speaking and Meaning: The Phenomenology of Language*. Indiana University Press, Bloomington.

Einstein, A. 1971. *The Born-Einstein Letters*. Macmillan, London.

Eliade, M. 1959. *Cosmos and History*. Harper and Row, New York.

———. 1979. *Yoga: Immortality and Freedom* (translated by W. R. Trask). Princeton University Press, Princeton.

Ellenberger, H. F. 1970. *The Discovery of the Unconscious: The History and Evolution of Dynamic Psychiatry*. Allen Lane: Penguin Press, London.

Else, G. F. 1957. *Aristotle's Poetics: The Argument*. Harvard University Press, Cambridge.

Elster, J. 1979. *Ulysses and the Sirens: Studies in Rationality and Irrationality*. Cambridge University Press, Cambridge.

Erikson, E. 1943. "Observations on the Yurok: Childhood and World Image." *University of California Publications in American Archaeology and Ethnology* 35:257–301.

Etienne, M., and Leacock, E. 1980. Introduction to *Women and Colonization: Anthropological Perspectives* (edited by M. Etienne and E. Leacock). Praeger, New York.

Evans-Pritchard, E. E. 1940. *The Nuer*. Clarendon Press, Oxford.

———. 1956. *Nuer Religion*. Clarendon Press, Oxford.

———. 1972. *Witchcraft, Oracles and Magic among the Azande*. Clarendon Press, Oxford.

Ey, H. 1978. *Consciousness: A Phenomenological Study of Being Conscious and Becoming Conscious* (translated by J. H. Flodstrom). Indiana University Press, Bloomington.

Fabian, J. 1983. *Time and the Other: How Anthropology Makes Its Object*. Columbia University Press, New York.

Farrington, B. 1966. *The Philosophy of Francis Bacon*. Liverpool University Press, Liverpool.

Ferenczi, S. 1955. *Final Contributions to the Problems and Methods of Psychoanalysis*. Hogarth Press, London.

Fernandez, J. 1973. "The Exposition and Imposition of Order: Artistic Expression in Fang Culture." In *The Traditional Artist in African Societies* (edited by W. L. d'Azevedo). Indiana University Press, Bloomington.

———. 1974. "The Mission of Metaphor in Expressive Culture." *Current Anthropology* 15(2):119–145.

———. 1982. *Bwiti: An Ethnography of the Religious Imagination in Africa*. Princeton University Press, Princeton.

Field, M. J. 1960. *Search for Security*. Faber and Faber, London.

Finnegan, R. 1965. *Survey of the Limba People of Northern Sierra Leone*. Her Majesty's Stationery Office, London.

Firth, R. 1956. *Human Types*. Nelson, London.

Fisher, S. 1970. *Body Experience in Fantasy and Behavior*. Appleton-Century-Crofts, New York.

Fortes, M. 1945. *The Dynamics of Clanship among the Tallensi*. Oxford University Press, London.

———. 1949. *The Web of Kinship among the Tallensi*. Oxford University Press, London.

———. 1966. "Religious Premises and Logical Technique in Divinatory Ritual." *Philosophical Transactions of the Royal Society of London*, Series B, 251:409–22.

———. 1973. "On the Concept of the Person among the Tallensi." In *La notion de personne en Afrique Noire* (edited by G. Dieterlen). Centre National de la Recherche Scientifique, Paris.

———. 1983. *Oedipus and Job in West African Religion*. Cambridge University Press, Cambridge.

Foucault, M. 1970. *The Order of Things*. Tavistock, London.

———. 1972. *The Archaeology of Knowledge* (translated by A. M. Sheridan Smith). Tavistock, London.

———. 1973. *The Birth of the Clinic: An Archaeology of Medical Perception* (translated by A. M. Sheridan-Smith). Tavistock, London.

———. 1979. *Discipline and Punish: The Birth of the Prison* (translated by A. Sheridan). Penguin Books, Harmondsworth.

———, and Sennett, R. 1982. "Sexuality and Solitude." In *Humanities in Review* (general editor D. Rieff), vol. 1. Cambridge University Press, Cambridge.

Fox, R. L. 1973. *Alexander the Great*. Allen Lane, London.

Freeman, D. 1983. *Margaret Mead and Samoa: The Making and Unmaking of an Anthropological Myth*. Harvard University Press, Cambridge.

Freire, P. 1972. *Cultural Action for Freedom*. Penguin Books, Harmondsworth.

Freud, S. 1922. *Introductory Lectures on Psycho-Analysis* (translated by J. Riviere). Allen and Unwin, London.

———. 1932. *New Introductory Lectures on Psycho-Analysis*. Norton, New York.

———. 1950. "Mourning and Melancholia." In *Collected Papers*, vol. 4. Hogarth Press, London.

———. 1957. "The Unconscious." In *Standard Edition of the Complete Psychological Works of Sigmund Freud* (edited by J. Strachey). Hogarth Press, London.

———. 1965. *Totem and Taboo* (translated by J. Strachey). Routledge, London.

Fromm, E. 1973. *The Crisis in Psychoanalysis*. Penguin Books, Harmondsworth.

Fyfe, C. 1962. *A History of Sierra Leone*. Oxford University Press, London.

Gadamer, H-G. 1975. *Truth and Method*. Seabury Press, New York.

———. 1976. *Philosophical Hermeneutics* (translated and edited by D. Linge). University of California Press, Berkeley.

Gardner, R. A., and Gardner, B. T. 1969. "Teaching Sign Language to a Chimpanzee." *Science* 165:664–72.

Geertz, C. 1973. *The Interpretation of Cultures*. Basic Books, New York.

Gell, A. 1979. "On Dance Structures: A Reply to Williams." *Journal of Human Movement Studies* 5:18–31.

———. 1980. "The Gods at Play: Vertigo and Possession in Muria Religion." *Man* 15(2): 219–48.

Giedion, S. 1941. *Space, Time and Architecture: The Growth of a New Tradition*. Oxford University Press, London.

Gluckman, M. 1963. *Order and Rebellion in Tribal Africa*. Cohen and West, London.

———. 1970. *Custom and Conflict in Africa*. Basil Blackwell, Oxford.

Goldschmidt, W. 1979. "Freud, Durkheim, and Death among the Sebei." In *Death and Dying: Views from Many Cultures* (edited by R. A. Kalish), pp. 34–38. Baywood, Farmingdale, New York.

Goody, J. 1962. *Death, Property, and the Ancestors: A Study of the LoDagaa of West Africa*. Tavistock, London.

———. 1967. *The Social Organization of the Lo Wiili*. Oxford University Press, London.

———. 1969. *Comparative Studies in Kinship*. Routledge and Kegan Paul, London.

Goss, C. M. (ed.). 1959. *Gray's Anatomy of the Human Body*. Lea and Febiger, Philadelphia.

Gould, S. J. 1987. *Time's Arrow, Time's Cycle: Myth and Metaphor in the Discovery of Geological Time*. Harvard University Press, Cambridge, Mass.

Graves, R. 1955. *The Crowning Privilege*. Cassell, London.

Gray, R. F. 1969. "Some Structural Aspects of Mbugwe Witchcraft." In *Witchcraft and Sorcery in East Africa* (edited by J. Middleton and E. H. Winter). Routledge and Kegan Paul, London.

Griaule, M. 1954. "The Dogon of the French Sudan." In *African Worlds* (edited by D. Forde), pp. 83–110. Oxford University Press, London.

Griffith, W. B. 1915. Preface to K. J. Beatty, *Human Leopards*. Hugh Rees, London.

Guha, R. 1983. *Elementary Aspects of Peasant Insurgency in Colonial India*. Oxford University Press, Delhi.

Guirdham, A. 1957. *A Theory of Disease*. Spearman, London.

Habermas, J. 1983. "Interpretive Social Science Versus Hermeneuticism." In *Social Science as Moral Inquiry* (edited by N. Haan, R. N. Bellah, P. Rabinow, and W. M. Sullivan), pp. 251–268. Columbia University Press, New York.

Hallen, B. 1975. "A Philosopher's Approach to Traditional Culture." *Theoria to Theory* 9(4):259–72.

———. 1976. "Phenomenology and the Exposition of Traditional African Thought." *Second Order: An African Journal of Philosophy* 5(2):45–65.

———, and Sodipo, J. O. 1986. *Knowledge, Belief and Witchcraft: Analytic Experiments in African Philosophy*. Ethnographica, London.

Hallowell, A. I. 1958. "Ojibwa Metaphysics of Being and the Perception of Persons." In *Person Perception and Interpersonal Behavior* (edited by R. Taguiri and L. Petrullo), pp. 63–85. Stanford University Press, Stanford.

Hammond-Tooke, W. D. (ed.). 1959. *The Bantu-Speaking Peoples of Southern Africa*. Routledge and Kegan Paul, London.

Handy, W. C. 1925. "String Figures from the Marquesas and Society Islands." *Bernice P. Bishop Museum Bulletin* 18. Honolulu.

Harris, W. T., and Sawyerr, H. 1968. *The Springs of Mende Belief and Conduct*. Sierra Leone University Press, Freetown.

Heidegger, M. 1977. "Building Dwelling Thinking." In *Martin Heidegger, Basic Writings* (edited, with general introduction and introductions to each selection by D. K. Krell), pp. 320–39. Harper and Row, New York.

Heisenberg, W. 1958. *The Physicist's Conception of Nature* (translated by A. J. Pomerans). Hutchinson, London.

Helliwell, C. 1988. "Good Walls Make Bad Neighbours: Public and Private Space in a Dayak Longhouse." *Canberra Anthropology* 11(1).

Herskovits, M. 1967. *Dahomey: An Ancient West African Kingdom*, vol. 2. Northwestern University Press, Evanston.

Hertz, R. 1960. *Death and the Right Hand* (translated by R. and C. Needham, introduction by E. E. Evans-Pritchard). Cohen and West, London.

Herzfeld, M. 1985. *The Poetics of Manhood: Contest and Identity in a Cretan Mountain Village*. Princeton University Press, Princeton.

———. 1987. *Anthropology through the Looking-Glass: Critical Ethnography in the Margins of Europe*. Cambridge University Press, Cambridge.

Hewes, G. W. 1973. "Primate Communication and the Gestural Origin of Language." *Current Anthropology* 14:5–24.

Horkheimer, M. 1947. *Eclipse of Reason*. Oxford University Press, New York.

———, and Adorno, T. W. 1972. *Dialectic of Enlightenment* (translated by J. Cumming). Herder and Herder, New York.

Horton, R. 1961. "Destiny and the Unconscious in West Africa." *Africa* 31:110–16.

———. 1962. "The Kalabari World-View: An Outline and Interpretation." *Africa* 32:197–220.

———. 1967. "African Traditional Thought and Western Science." *Africa* 37:50–71, 155–187.

———. 1983. "Social Psychologies: African and Western." In M. Fortes, *Oedipus and Job in West African Religion*. Cambridge University Press, Cambridge.

Hughes, C. C. 1978. "Medical Care: Ethnomedicine." In *Health and the Human Condition* (edited by M. H. Logan and E. E. Hunt), pp. 150–58. Duxbury Press, North Scituate, Mass.

Huntingdon, R., and Metcalf, P. 1979. *Celebrations of Death: The Anthropology of Mortuary Ritual*. Cambridge University Press, Cambridge.

Hymes, D. 1969. "The Uses of Anthropology: Critical, Political, Personal." In *Reinventing Anthropology* (edited by D. Hymes), pp. 3–79. Pantheon, New York.

Iberall, A. S. 1972. *Towards a General Science of Viable Systems*. McGraw-Hill, New York.

Idowu, E. B. 1962. *Olodumare: God in Yoruba Belief*. Longmans, London.

Ignatieff, M. 1984. *The Needs of Strangers*. Chatto and Windus, London.

Illich, I. 1973. *Tools for Conviviality*. Caldar and Boyars, London.

Innes, G. 1973. "Stability and Change in Griot Narrations." *African Language Studies* 14:105–18.

———. 1974. *Sunjata, Three Mandinka Versions*. School of Oriental and African Studies, University of London, London.

Jackson, M. 1974. "The Structure and Significance of Kuranko Clanship." *Africa* 44(4):397–415.

———. 1975. "Structure and Event: Withcraft Confession among the Kuranko." *Man* 10(3):387–403.

———. 1976. *Latitudes of Exile*. McIndoe, Dunedin.

———. 1977a. "Sacrifice and Social Structure among the Kuranko." *Africa* 47(1 and 2):41–49, 123–39.

———. 1977b. *The Kuranko: Dimensions of Social Reality in a West African Society*. C. Hurst, London.

———. 1978a. "The Identity of the Dead: Aspects of Mortuary Ritual in a West African Society." *Cahiers d'Etudes Africaines* 66–67(2–3):271–97.

———. 1978b. "An Approach to Kuranko Divination." *Human Relations* 31:117–38.

———. 1979. "Prevented Successions: A Commentary upon a Kuranko Narrative." In *Fantasy and Symbol: Studies in Anthropological Interpretation* (edited by R. Hook). Academic Press, London.

———. 1982a. *Allegories of the Wilderness: Ethics and Ambiguity in Kuranko Narratives*. Indiana University Press, Bloomington.

———. 1982b. "Meaning and Moral Imagery in Kuranko Myth." *Research in African Literatures* 13(2):153–80.

———. 1983a. "Knowledge of the Body." *Man* 18:327–45.

———. 1983b. "Thinking through the Body: An Essay on Understanding Metaphor." *Social Analysis* 14:127–49.

———. 1986. *Barawa, and the Ways Birds Fly in the Sky*. Smithsonian Institution Press, Washington.

———. 1987a. "The Migration of a Name: Reflections on Alexander in Africa." *Journal of Cultural Anthropology* 2(2):235–54.

———. 1987b. "On Ethnographic Truth." *Canberra Anthropology*, 10(2):1–26.

James, W. 1976. *Essays in Radical Empiricism*. Harvard University Press, Cambridge.

———. 1978. *Pragmatism*. Harvard University Press, Cambridge.

Jameson, F. 1971. *Marxism and Form: Twentieth-Century Dialectical Theories of Literature*. Princeton University Press, Princeton.

———. 1972. *The Prison-House of Language*. Princeton University Press, Princeton.

Jantsch, E. 1975. *Design for Evolution: Self-Organization and Planning in the Life of Human Systems*. George Braziller, New York.

Janzen, J. M. 1978. *The Quest for Therapy in Lower Zaire.* University of California Press, Berkeley.

Jayne, C. F. 1906. *String Figures: A Study of Cat's-Cradle in Many Lands.* Scribners, New York.

Jones, F. P. 1976. *Body Awareness in Action: A Study of the Alexander Technique.* Schocken Books, New York.

Jung, C. G. 1968. Foreword to *The I Ching or Book of Changes* (translated by R. Wilhelm). Routledge and Kegan Paul, London.

Kalous, M. 1974. *Cannibals and Tongo Players of Sierra Leone.* Wright and Carman, Trentham, New Zealand.

Kamara, K. 1932. "Notes on Some Customs of the Kurankos." *Sierra Leone Studies* 17:94–100.

———. 1933. "Kuranko Funeral Customs." *Sierra Leone Studies* 19:153–57.

Karp, I. 1978. "New Guinea Models in the African Savannah." *Africa* 48(1):1–16.

Kazantzakis, N. 1961. *Zorba the Greek.* Faber and Faber, London.

Keats, J. 1958. *The Letters of John Keats 1814–1821* (edited by H. E. Rollins), vol. 1. Cambridge University Press, Cambridge.

Keesing, R. 1988. " 'Earth' and 'Path' as Complex Categories: Semantics and Symbolism in Kwaio Culture." Paper presented at Conference on the Representation of Complex Cultural Categories at Kings College, Cambridge, March 1988.

Keynes, J. M. 1921. *A Treatise on Probability.* Macmillan, London.

———. 1951. *Essays in Biography.* Rupert Hart-Davis, London.

Kluckholn, C. 1967. *Navaho Witchcraft.* Beacon Press, Boston.

Korzybski, A. 1941. *Science and Sanity.* Science Press, New York.

Kroeber, A. L. 1917. "The Superorganic." *American Anthropologist* 19:163–213.

———, and Kluckholn, C. 1963. *Culture: A Critical Review of Concepts and Definitions.* Vintage Books, New York.

Krupp, G. R. 1962. "The Bereavement Reaction." *Psychoanalytic Study of Society* 2:42–74.

Kübler-Ross, E. 1970. *On Death and Dying.* Tavistock, London.

Kup, A. P. 1975. *Sierra Leone: A Concise History.* Newton Abbot.

Laing, R. D. 1966. *The Divided Self.* Penguin Books, Harmondsworth.

———. 1976. *The Politics of the Family.* Penguin Books, Harmondsworth.

Lakoff, G., and Johnson, M. 1980. *Metaphors We Live By.* University of Chicago Press, Chicago.

Lapointe. F. H. 1971. "Phenomenology, Psychoanalysis and the Unconscious." *Journal of Phenomenological Psychology* 2:5–25.

Leach, E. R. 1961. *Rethinking Anthropology.* Athlone Press, London.

———. 1987. Remarks reported in *Anthropology Today* 3(3):17.

Lederman, R. 1986. *What Gifts Engender: Social Relations and Politics in Mendi, Highland Papua New Guinea.* Cambridge University Press, Cambridge.

Lee, D. 1970. "Lineal and Nonlineal Codifications of Reality." In *Explorations in Communication* (edited by E. Carpenter and M. McLuhan), pp. 136–54. Jonathan Cape, London.

Leenhardt, M. 1979. *Do Kamo: Person and Myth in the Melanesian World* (translated by B. Miller-Gulati). University of Chicago Press, Chicago.

Levine, R. A. 1969. "Witchcraft and Sorcery in a Gusii Community." In *Witchcraft and Sorcery in East Africa* (edited by J. Middleton and E. H. Winter). Routledge and Kegan Paul, London.

———. 1976. "Patterns of Personality in Africa." In *Responses to Change: Society, Culture, and Personality* (edited by G. A. deVos), pp. 112–36. Van Nostrand, New York.

———, and Levine, B. B. 1966. *Nyansongo: A Gusii Community in Kenya.* Wiley, New York.

Lévi-Strauss, C. 1950. "Introduction à l'oeuvre de Marcel Mauss." In *Marcel Mauss, Sociologie et Anthropologie*, pp. 9–52. Presses Universitaires de France, Paris.

————. 1963. *Structural Anthropology* (translated by C. Jacobson and B. G. Schoepf), vol. I. Basic Books, New York.

————. 1966a. *The Savage Mind (La pensée sauvage)*. Weidenfeld and Nicolson, London.

————. 1966b. "Anthropology: Its Achievement and Future." *Current Anthropology* 7:124–27.

————. 1969a. *The Elementary Structures of Kinship (Les structures élémentaires de la parenté)* (translated by J. R. von Sturmer and R. Needham). Eyre and Spottiswood, London.

————. 1969b. *Totemism* (translated by R. Needham). Penguin Books, Harmondsworth.

————. 1970. *The Raw and the Cooked: Introduction to a Science of Mythology* (translated by J. and D. Weightman). Jonathan Cape, London.

————. 1972. "A Conversation with Claude Lévi-Strauss." (by A. Akoun, F. Morin, and J. Mousseau). *Psychology Today* 5:37–39, 74–82.

————. 1973. *Tristes Tropiques* (translated by J. and D. Weightman). Jonathan Cape, London.

————. 1981. *The Naked Man* (translated by J. and D. Weightman). Harper and Row, New York.

Lienhardt, G. 1951. "Some Notions of Withcraft among the Dinka." *Africa* 21:303–18.

————. 1961. *Divinity and Experience: The Religion of the Dinka*. Clarendon Press, Oxford.

————. 1985. "Self: Public, Private. Some African Representations." In *The Category of the Person* (edited by M. Carrithers, S. Collins, and S. Lukes), pp. 141–55. Cambridge University Press, Cambridge.

Lindskog, B. 1954. *African Leopard Men*. Studia Ethnographica Upsaliensia 7. Almqvist and Wiksells, Uppsala.

Lindstrom, M. 1983. "Metaphors of Debate on Tanna." *Naika* 12:6–9.

Little, K. 1951. *The Mende of Sierra Leone*. Routledge and Kegan Paul, London.

Littlejohn, J. 1967. "The Temne House." In *Cosmos and History* (edited by J. Middleton). American Sourcebook in Anthropology. Natural History Press, New York.

Lloyd, G. E. R. 1966. *Polarity and Analogy*. Cambridge University Press, Cambridge.

Locke, J. 1954. *Essays on the Law of Nature* (edited by W. von Leyden). Clarendon Press, Oxford.

Lovejoy, A. O. 1948. *Essays in the History of Ideas*. Johns Hopkins Press, Baltimore.

Lowen, A. 1971. *The Language of the Body*. Collier-Macmillan, London.

Lukes, S. 1973. *Individualism*. Basil Blackwell, Oxford.

Luria, A. R. 1969. *The Mind of a Mnemonist* (translated by L. Solotaroff). Jonathan Cape, London.

McCormack, C. P. 1980. "Nature, Culture and Gender: A Critique." In *Nature, Culture and Gender* (edited by C. P. McCormack and M. Strathern), pp. 1–24. Cambridge University Press, Cambridge.

MacIntyre, A. C. 1958. *The Unconscious: A Conceptual Analysis*. Routledge and Kegan Paul, London.

McLuhan, M. 1962. *The Gutenberg Galaxy: The Making of Typographic Man*. Routledge and Kegan Paul, London.

————, and Fiore, Q. 1967. *The Medium is the Massage: An Inventory of Effects*. Penguin Books, Harmondsworth.

Mandelbaum, D. G. 1965. "Social Uses of Funeral Rites." In *Death and Identity* (edited by R. Fulton). Wiley, New York.

Marcuse, H. 1968. *Negations: Essays in Critical Theory*. Allen Lane, London.

————. 1969. *Eros and Civilization*. Sphere Books, London.

Marwick, M. 1965. "Witchcraft and Sorcery." In *African Systems of Thought* (edited by M. Fortes and G. Dieterlen). Oxford University Press, London.

———. 1970. "Witchcraft as a Social Strain-Gauge." In Witchcraft and Sorcery (edited by M. Marwick). Penguin Books, Harmondsworth.

Marx, K. 1953. Die Frühschriften (edited by S. Landshut). A. Kröner, Stuttgart.

Mason, P. 1975. Kipling: The Glass, the Shadow and the Fire. Jonathan Cape, London.

Mauss, M. 1973. "Techniques of the Body" (translated by B. Brewster). Economy and Society 2:70–88.

May, R. 1958. "The Origins and Significance of the Existential Movement in Psychology." In Existence: A New Dimension in Psychiatry (edited by R. May, E. Angel, and H. F. Ellenberger), pp. 3–6. Basic Books, New York.

———. 1972. Love and Will. Fontana, London.

———. 1981. Freedom and Destiny. Norton, New York.

Mayer, P. 1949. "The Lineage Principle in Gusii Society." International African Institute Memorandum 24. Oxford University Press, London.

Mead, M. 1952. "Some Relationships between Social Anthropology and Psychiatry." In Dynamic Psychiatry (edited by F. Alexander and H. Ross). University of Chicago Press, Chicago.

Meek, C. K. 1931a. Tribal Studies in Northern Nigeria. Kegan Paul, Trench, Trubner, London.

———. 1931b. A Sudanese Kingdom. Kegan Paul, Trench, Trubner, London.

Meinhard, H. H. 1975. "The Patrilineal Principle in Early Teutonic Kinship." In Studies in Anthropology (edited by J. H. M. Beattie and R. G. Lienhardt), pp. 1–29. Clarendon Press, Oxford.

Melchert, N. 1976–77. "Mystical Experience and Ontological Claims." Philosophy and Phenomenological Research 37:445–63.

Menkiti, I. A. 1984. "Person and Community in Traditional African Thought." In African Philosophy (edited by R. A. Wright). University Press of America, Lanham.

Merleau-Ponty, M. 1962. Phenomenology of Perception (translated by C. Smith). Routledge and Kegan Paul, London.

———. 1964. "From Mauss to Lévi-Strauss." In Signs (translated by R. C. McLeary), pp. 114–25. Northwestern University Press, Evanston.

———. 1965. The Structure of Behaviour (translated by A. L. Fisher). Methuen, London.

Middleton, J. 1969. "Spirit Possession among the Lugbara." In Spirit Mediumship and Society in Africa (edited by J. Beattie and J. Middleton). Routledge and Kegan Paul, London.

———. 1965. The Lugbara of Uganda. Holt, Rinehart and Winston, New York.

———. 1971. Lugbara Religion: Ritual and Authority among an East African People. Oxford University Press, London.

Miles, J. 1948. Continuity of Poetic Language. University of California Press, Berkeley.

Mill, J. S. 1981. Autobiography and Literary Essays (edited by J. M. Robson and J. Stillinger), vol. 1. University of Toronto Press, Toronto.

Miller, P. R. 1967. Sense and Symbol: A Textbook of Human Behavioral Science. Harper and Row, New York.

Minkus, H. K. 1984. "Causal Theory in Akwapim Akan Philosophy." In African Philosophy (edited by R. A. Wright). University of American Press, Lanham.

Montaigne, M. de. 1958. Essays (translated with an introduction by J. M. Cohen). Penguin Books, Harmondsworth.

Monteil, C. 1929. Les empires de Mali. G.-P. Maisonneuve et Larose, Paris.

Moore, O. K. 1957. "Divination: A New Perspective." American Anthropologist 59:69–74.

Morton-Williams, P. 1960. "Yoruba Responses to the Fear of Death." Africa 30(1):34–40.

Moynihan, W. T. 1966. The Craft and Art of Dylan Thomas. Cornell University Press, Ithaca.

Nadel, S. F. 1952. "Witchcraft in Four African Societies." American Anthropologist 54:18–29.

Nagel, T. 1986. The View from Afar. Oxford University Press, New York.

Needham, J. 1965. "Time and Eastern Man." *Royal Anthropological Institute Occasional Paper*, no. 21.

———. 1978. *The Shorter Science and Civilization in China* (abridged by C. Ronan), vol. 1. Cambridge University Press, Cambridge.

Needleman, J. 1975. *A Sense of the Cosmos: The Encounter of Modern Science and Ancient Truth.* Doubleday, New York.

Ngubane, H. 1977. *Body and Mind in Zulu Medicine.* Academic Press, London.

Niane, D. T. 1965. *Sundiata, an Epic of Old Mali* (translated by G. D. Pickett). Longmans, London.

Nietzsche, F. 1973. *Beyond Good and Evil: Prelude to a Philosophy of the Future* (translated with an introduction and commentary by R. J. Hollingdale). Penguin Books, Harmondsworth.

Nkrumah, K. 1962. *Towards Colonial Freedom.* Heinemann, London.

Nukunya, G. K. 1973. "Some Underlying Beliefs in Ancestor Worship and Mortuary Rites among the Ewe." In *La notion de personne en Afrique Noire* (edited by G. Dieterlen). Centre National de la Recherche Scientifique, Paris.

Oakeshott, M. 1962. *Rationalism in Politics and Other Essays.* Methuen, London.

Ogilvie, R. M. 1969. *The Romans and Their Gods.* Chatto and Windus, London.

Oliver, R., and Fage, J. D. 1962. *A Short History of Africa.* Penguin Books, Harmondsworth.

Olney, J. 1972. *Metaphors of Self: The Meaning of Autobiography.* Princeton University Press, Princeton.

Ong, W. J. 1982. *Orality and Literacy: The Technologizing of the Word.* Methuen, London.

Onians, R. B. 1973. *The Origins of European Thought.* Arno Press, New York.

Ortigues, M-C., and Ortigues, E. 1966. *Oedipe Africaine.* Plon, Paris.

Parin, P., Morgenthaler, F., and Parin-Matthey, G. 1980. *Fear Thy Neighbour as Thyself.* University of Chicago Press, Chicago.

Park, G. K. 1963. "Divination and Its Social Contexts." *Journal of the Royal Anthropological Institute* 93:195–209.

Parkes, C. M. 1975. *Bereavement: Studies of Grief in Adult Life.* Penguin Books, Harmondsworth.

Parsons, R. T. 1964. *Religion in an African Society.* E. J. Brill, Leiden.

Paulme, D. 1954. *Les gens du riz: Kissi de Haute-Guinée Française.* Plon, Paris.

Pepper, S. C. 1957. *World Hypotheses: A Study in Evidence.* University of California Press, Berkeley.

Person, Y. 1973. "Oral Tradition and Chronology." In *French Perspectives in African Studies* (edited by P. Alexandre). Oxford University Press, London.

Polanyi, M. 1958. *Personal Knowledge.* Routledge and Kegan Paul, London.

Polhemus, T. 1975. "Social Bodies." In *The Body as a Medium of Expression* (edited by J. Benthall and T. Polhemus), pp. 13–35. Allen Lane, London.

Pollock, G. H. 1974. "Mourning and Adaptation." In *Culture and Personality: Contemporary Readings* (edited by R. A. Levine). Aldine, Chicago.

Poole, R. 1972. *Towards Deep Subjectivity.* Allen Lane, London.

———. 1975. "Objective Sign and Subjective Meaning." In *The Body as a Medium of Expression* (edited by J. Benthall and T. Polhemus), pp. 74–106. Allen Lane, London.

Popper, K. R. 1969. *Conjectures and Refutations.* Routledge and Kegan Paul, London.

Poster, M. 1978. *Critical Theory of the Family.* Seabury Press, New York.

———. 1984. *Foucault, Marxism and History.* Polity Press, Cambridge.

Pound, E. 1954. "How to Read." In *Literary Essays of Ezra Pound* (edited by T. S. Eliot). Faber and Faber, London.

———. 1961. *The Art of Reading.* Faber and Faber, London.

Premack, D. 1971. "Language in Chimpanzee?" *Science* 172:808–22.

Prince, R. 1970. Review of *Witchcraft* (by L. Mair). *American Anthropologist* 72(4):915–17.

Rabinow, P., and Sullivan, W. M. 1979. *Interpretive Social Science: A Reader.* University of California Press, Berkeley.

Radcliffe-Brown, A. R. 1952. *Structure and Function in Primitive Society.* Cohen and West, London.

Rattray, R. S. 1923. *Ashanti.* Clarendon Press, Oxford.

Rawson, P. 1968. *Erotic Art of the East.* Weidenfeld and Nicolson, London.

Reich, W. 1949. *Character Analysis.* Noonday Press, New York.

Reid, A. 1954. "A First Word." *Yale Literary Magazine.* November.

Reik, T. 1966. *The Compulsion to Confess: On the Psychoanalysis of Crime and Punishment.* Wiley, New York.

Richards, I. A. 1936. *The Philosophy of Rhetoric.* Oxford University Press, New York.

Ricoeur, P. 1970. *Freud and Philosophy: An Essay on Interpretation* (translated by D. Savage). Yale University Press, New Haven.

Riesman, D. 1970. "The Oral and Written Traditions." In *Explorations in Communication* (edited by E. Carpenter and M. McLuhan), pp. 109–16. Jonathan Cape, London.

Riesman, P. 1977. *Freedom in Fulani Social Life.* University of Chicago Press, Chicago.

Rigby, P. 1968. "Some Gogo Rituals of 'Purification': An Essay on Social and Moral Categories." In *Dialectic in Practical Religion* (edited by E. R. Leach), pp. 153–78. Cambridge University Press, Cambridge.

Róheim, G. 1970. *Magic and Schizophrenia.* Indiana University Press, Bloomington.

Ronan, C. (ed.). 1978. *The Shorter Science and Civilization in China,* vol. 1 (an abridgement of Joseph Needham's original text). Cambridge University Press, Cambridge.

Rorty, R. 1979. *Philosophy and the Mirror of Nature.* Princeton University Press, Princeton.

————. 1982. *Consequences of Pragmatism.* University of Minnesota Press, Minneapolis.

————. 1986. "The Contingency of Language." *London Review of Books,* 17 April, 3–6.

Rosaldo, M. 1980. *Knowledge and Passion: Illongot Notions of Self and Social Life.* Cambridge University Press, Cambridge.

Rosaldo, R. I. 1980. *Illongot Headhunting, 1883–1974: A Study in Society and History.* Stanford University Press, Stanford.

————. 1984. "Grief and a Headhunter's Rage: On the Cultural Force of the Emotions." In *Text, Play, and Story: The Construction and Reconstruction of Self and Society* (edited by E. M. Bruner), pp. 178–95. Proceedings of the American Ethnological Society, Washington.

Rossi, I. 1974. "Intellectual Antecedents of Lévi-Strauss's Notion of the Unconscious." In *The Unconscious in Culture* (edited by I. Rossi), pp. 7–30. Dutton, New York.

Royce, A. P. 1977. *The Anthropology of Dance.* Indiana University Press, Bloomington.

Ruel, M. 1969. *Leopards and Leaders.* Tavistock, London.

————. 1970. "Were-Animals and the Introverted Witch." In *Witchcraft Confessions and Accusations* (edited by M. Douglas). A.S.A. Monograph 9. Tavistock, London.

Sacks, O. 1986. *The Man Who Mistook His Wife for a Hat.* Pan, London.

Said, E. 1978. *Orientalism.* Basic Books, New York.

Sarles, H. B. 1975. "A Human Ethological Approach to Communication: Ideas in Transit around the Cartesian Impasse." In *Organization of Behavior in Face-to-Face Interaction* (edited by A. Kendon, R. M. Harris, and M. Ritchie), pp. 19–45. Mouton, The Hague.

Sartre, J-P. 1957. *Being and Nothingness* (translated by H. Barnes). Methuen, London.

————. 1963. *Saint-Genet* (translated by B. Frechtman). George Braziller, New York.

————. 1968. *Search for a Method* (translated by H. Barnes). Vintage Books, New York.

————. 1969. "Itinerary of a Thought." *New Left Review* 58:43–66.

————. 1972. *Situations.* Gallimard, Paris.

————. 1973. *Existentialism and Humanism* (translated by P. Mairet). Methuen, London.

————. 1982. *Critique of Dialectical Reason* (translated by A. Sheridan-Smith). Verso, London.

————. 1983. *Between Existentialism and Marxism* (translated by J. Matthews). Verso, London.

Sayers, E. F. 1925. "The Funeral of a Koranko Chief." *Sierra Leone Studies* 7:19–29.

————. 1927. "Notes on the Clan or Family Names Common in the Area Inhabited by Temne-Speaking People." *Sierra Leone Studies* 12:14–108.

Schrag, C. O. 1969. *Experience and Being: Prolegomena to a Future Ontology*. Northwestern University Press, Evanston.

Sebeok, T. A., and Sebeok, J. U. 1980. "Introduction: Questioning Apes." In *Speaking of Apes: A Critical Anthology of Two-Way Communication with Man* (edited by T. A. and J. U. Sebeok), pp. 1–59. Plenum Press, New York.

Sechehaye, M. 1951. *Autobiography of a Schizophrenic Girl* (translated by G. Rubin-Rabson). Grune and Stratton, New York.

Seeger, A. 1981. *Nature and Society in Central Brazil: The Suya Indians of Mato Grosso*. Harvard University Press, Cambridge.

Shaw, R. 1985. "Gender and the Structuring of Reality in Temne Divination: An Interactive Study." *Africa* 55(3):286–303.

Simonton, O. C., and Simonton, S. 1980. *Getting Well Again*. Bantam Books, New York.

Sontag, S. 1967. *Against Interpretation and Other Essays*. Eyre and Spottiswoode, London.

————. 1977. *Illness as Metaphor*. Farrar, Straus and Giroux, New York.

Southall, A. 1952. "Lineage Formation among the Luo." *International African Institute Memorandum*, no. 26. Oxford University Press, London.

Spiro, M. 1961. "Social Systems, Personality, and Functional Analysis." In *Studying Personality Cross-Culturally* (edited by B. Kaplan), pp. 93–127. Row, Peterson, Evanston.

Stade, G. 1967. *Robert Graves*. Columbia University Press, New York.

Stanford, W. B. 1969. *The Ulysses Theme: A Study in the Adaptability of a Traditional Hero*. Basil Blackwell, Oxford.

Starobinski, J. 1982. "A Short History of Body Consciousness." In *Humanities in Review* (edited by D. Rieff), vol. 1. Cambridge University Press, Cambridge.

Steiner, G. 1973. *After Babel*. Oxford University Press, London.

————. 1978. *Heidegger*. Fontana/Collins, Glasgow.

Stenhouse, D. 1974. *The Evolution of Intelligence: A General Theory and Some of Its Implications*. Allen and Unwin, London.

Stoller, P. 1984. "Eye, Mind and Word in Anthropology." *L'Homme* 24(3–4):91–114.

————. 1987. *In Sorcery's Shadow: A Memoir of Apprenticeship among the Songhai of Niger*. University of Chicago Press, Chicago.

————, and Olkes, C. 1986. "Bad Sauce, Good Ethnography." *Cultural Anthropology* 1(3):336–52.

Straus, E. W. 1966. *Phenomenological Psychology*. Basic Books, New York.

Sykes, P. 1969. *A History of Persia*, vol. 1. Routledge and Kegan Paul, London.

Szasz, T. 1972. *The Myth of Mental Illness*. Paladin, St. Albans.

Thass-Thienemann, T. 1968. *Symbolic Behavior*. Washington Square Press, New York.

Thomas, E. J. 1923. *Vedic Hymns*. John Murray, London.

Thomas, K. 1973. *Religion and the Decline of Magic*. Penguin Books, Harmondsworth.

Tinbergen, N. 1974. "Ethology and Stress Diseases." *Science* 185:20–27.

Toynbee, A. 1974. "If Alexander the Great Had Lived On." In *The Impact of Alexander the Great* (edited by E. N. Borza). Dryden Press, Hinsdale.

Tronson, A. 1982. "The 'Life of Alexander' and West Africa." *History Today* 32:38–41.

Turbayne, C. M. 1962. *The Myth of Metaphor*. Yale University Press, New Haven.

Turner, V. 1970. *The Forest of Symbols*. Cornell University Press, Ithaca.

————. 1972. *The Drums of Affliction*. Clarendon Press, Oxford.

————. 1975. *Revelation and Divination in Ndembu Ritual*. Cornell University Press, Ithaca.

————. 1978. "Encounter with Freud: The Making of a Comparative Symbologist." In *The*

Making of Psychological Anthropology (edited by G. D. Spindler), pp. 558–83. University of California Press, Berkeley.

———. 1985. *On the Edge of the Bush: Anthropology as Experience* (edited by E. L. B. Turner). University of Arizona Press, Tucson.

Tyler, S. 1986. "Post-Modern Ethnography: From Document of the Occult to Occult Document." In *Writing Culture* (edited by J. Clifford and G. E. Marcus), pp. 122–40. University of California Press, Berkeley.

Uchendu, V. 1965. *The Igbo of Southeast Nigeria*. Holt, Rinehart and Winston, New York.

Vico, G. 1968. *The New Science of Giambattista Vico* (revised translation of the 3d edition [1744] by T. G. Bergin and M. H. Fisch). Cornell University Press, Ithaca.

Volkart, E. H., in collaboration with Michael, S. T. 1957. "Bereavement and Mental Health." In *Explorations in Social Psychiatry* (edited by A. H. Leighton, J. A. Clausen and R. N. Wilson). Tavistock, London.

Vonnegut, K. 1971. *Cat's Cradle*. Gollancz, London.

———. 1979. *Slaughterhouse 5*. Triad Grafton, London.

Vygotsky, L. S. 1962. *Thought and Language* (edited and translated E. Hanfmann and G. Vakar). Wiley, New York.

Ward, B. 1956. "Some Observations on Religious Cults in Ashanti." *Africa* 26:47–61.

Welles, C. B. 1974. "There Have Been Many Alexanders." In *The Impact of Alexander the Great* (edited by E. N. Borza). Dryden Press, Hinsdale.

Welsh, A. 1978. *Roots of Lyric*. Princeton University Press, Princeton.

Whitehead, A. N. 1947. *Adventures of Ideas*. Cambridge University Press, Cambridge.

Wilden, A. 1972. *System and Structure: Essays in Communication and Exchange*. Tavistock, London.

Willis, R. 1974. *Man and Beast*. Hart-Davis, MacGibbon, London.

———. 1977. "Pollution and Paradigms." In *Culture, Disease, and Healing: Studies in Medical Anthropology* (edited by D. Landy), pp. 278–85. Macmillan, New York.

———. 1978. "Magic and 'Medicine' in Ufipa." In *Culture and Curing: Anthropological Perspectives on Traditional Medical Beliefs and Practices* (edited by P. Morley and R. Wallis), pp. 139–51. Peter Owen, London.

Wilson, E. O. 1975. *Sociobiology: The New Synthesis*. Belknap Press of Harvard University Press, Cambridge.

Wiredu, K. 1980. *Philosophy and an African Culture*. Cambridge University Press, Cambridge.

Witherspoon, G. 1977. *Language and Art in the Navajo Universe*. University of Michigan Press, Ann Arbor.

Wittgenstein, L. 1953. *Philosophical Investigations* (translated by G. E. M. Anscombe). Basil Blackwell, Oxford.

———. 1979. *Remarks on Frazer's Golden Bough* (translated by A. C. Miles; edited and revised by R. Rhees). Humanities Press, Atlantic Highlands, N.J.

Wober, M. 1975. *Psychology in Africa*. International African Institute, London.

Wolf, E. 1964. *Anthropology*. Prentice-Hall, Englewood Cliffs, N.J.

Wyllie, R. W. 1973. "Introspective Witchcraft among the Effutu of Southern Ghana." *Man* 8:74–79.

Yalouris, N. 1980. "Alexander and His Heritage." In *The Search for Alexander*. New York Graphic Society, Boston.

Young, J. Z. 1951. *Doubt and Certainty in Science: A Biologist's Reflections on the Brain*. Clarendon, Oxford.

Zaehner, R. C. 1966. *Hindu Scriptures* (selected, edited and translated by R. C. Zaehner). Dent, London.

Zahan, D. 1974. *The Bambara*. E. J. Brill, Leiden.

———. 1979. *The Religion, Spirituality, and Thought of Traditional Africa* (translated by K. E. Martin and L. M. Martin). University of Chicago Press, Chicago.

Index